UWorld | ACC

STUDY GUIDE

Part 2: Strategic Financial Management

CMA Exam Review

UWorld
9111 Cypress Waters Blvd
Suite 300
Dallas, TX 75019

Printed in English, in the United States of America.

Contents

About the Exam

CMA Exam Procedures and Registration

Becoming a Certified Management Accountant requires time and effort—but the opportunities for career advancement are worth it.

Meet These Requirements

Maintain membership in IMA. If you aren't a member, join IMA now at www.imanet.org/membership.

- Hold a bachelor's degree from an accredited college/university or a related professional certification. Please refer to the IMA's CMA Requirements section at www.imanet.org/cma-certifcation/getting-started
- Have at least two continuous years of professional experience in management accounting or financial management.
- Enter into the CMA program. Visit www.cmacertifcation.org for more information.
- Complete and pass Parts 1 and 2 of the CMA Exam.
- Abide by the IMA's Statement of Ethical Professional Practice, found at www.imanet.org/insights-and-trends/business-leadership-and-ethics/ima-statement-of-ethical-professional-practice

Don't meet the educational or professional experience requirements and want to get certified? There is an option for every situation. IMA offers a seven-year grace period for candidates in this situation. You can sit for the exam and then finish your bachelor's degree or two years of professional experience within the next seven years from the date of the exam. Once you do, you'll automatically become an active CMA.

Take the CMA Exam

The CMA exam is broken into two parts, which are both computer-based and administered in hundreds of testing facilities worldwide. With three two-month testing windows each year, you can sit for each exam part at a time and place convenient for you.

Examination Windows:

Exams are offered only during these two-month periods:

1. January and February
2. May and June
3. September and October

> **Note**
> While the testing windows here are typical, Covid-19 has affected test windows, with some windows expanding to accommodate disruptions in testing. For example, the May and June window in 2021 was expanded to April, May, and June. Check for updated dates and other testing news at https://www.prometric.com/test-takers/search/icma

Register for the CMA Exam

Follow these easy steps to fulfill the examination requirement for your CMA certification:

Step 1: Register for the exam at https://www.imanet.org/en/IMA-Certifications/CMA-Certification

Step 2: Receive confirmation of your registration, which provides your authorization number(s), testing window(s), and the Instructions for Candidates.

Step 3: Schedule your exam appointment(s) with Prometric, IMA's testing partner: www.prometric.com.

Step 4: Show up for your scheduled exam appointment(s) with the required identification documents.

> **Tip**
> Be sure to schedule your appointment as soon as possible. Your authorization number is only valid for the testing window you selected. You can't postpone your exams.

Exams are administered via Prometric Testing Centers throughout the world and are available in accordance with local customs. To locate a Testing Center and schedule exam appointments, visit www.prometric.com/ICMA

Exam Fees

Professional Member Fees

Non-refundable CMA Entrance Fee: $250*

Exam Fee: $415 per part

Rescheduling Fee**: $50

Student/Academic Member Fees

Non-refundable CMA Entrance Fee: $188*

Exam Fee: $311 per part

Rescheduling Fee**: $50

Total Cost to Earn Your CMA with No Exam Retakes:

Non-Student/Professional: $1080

Student (still in school): $810

*The CMA Entrance Fee covers:

- Credential review for educational qualification
- Credential review for experience qualification
- Six months access to the CMA Exam Support package, which includes printable practice questions
- Final Score Report
- Performance feedback reports for candidates who do not pass
- Personalized, numbered certificate for office display
- Congratulatory notification to employer or others, if desired[1]

CMA Exam Scoring

The CMA Exam has a unique scoring system that can sometimes be confusing for candidates. Here's everything you need to know to correctly interpret your CMA Exam score.

Release of CMA Exam Scores

Essays are graded offline by the ICMA, the certifying body of IMA, so do not expect to see your results the day of your exam. Instead, the ICMA will e-mail your exam results to you approximately six weeks from the end of the month in which you've taken your test.

---

*Please note there are no official, set score release dates.
**You must reschedule your exam more than 30 days prior to your scheduled appointment. You can only move the date to a later date within the same two-month testing window.

At the time grades are released, results are also available online in your myIMA Dashboard.

Exam Window	Score Release Window
January and February	3rd week of February–1st week of April
May and June	3rd week of June–2nd week of August
September and October	3rd week of October–2nd week of December

Weighting of the CMA Exam

- The multiple-choice questions section is worth 75% of the total score.
- Essays are worth 25% of the total score.
- To be able to take the essay section, you must score at least 50% on the multiple-choice section.

CMA Exam Scoring Scale

Parts 1 and 2 of the CMA Exam are scored on a scale of 0 to 500.

In order to equate all scores for all forms of the exam, the scores for each part are placed on a scale from 0 to 500. On this scale, a score of 360 represents the minimum passing scaled score. The scaled score allows candidates to know how they performed in relation to the passing standard of 360. (Source: IMA)

Your Performance Report

Performance Reports are sent via e-mail from Prometric to all candidates who take an exam part.

The performance reports are e-mailed approximately 14 days after exam results are posted to the candidate's profile.

Candidates who do not pass the exam will receive a report that indicates their performance on each of the key topic areas in the multiple-choice section as well as their overall performance on the essay section of the exam. There are three performance ratings: Satisfactory, Marginal, and Unsatisfactory.

Introduction

Welcome to Part 2, "Strategic Financial Management." The study text aligns perfectly with your UWorld CMA Exam Review Course so that you can follow along and make notes as you review the lectures. To test yourself after your study, take a lesson or session assessment; practice questions in the comprehensive test bank; or take a practice exam to get the test-day experience and hone your skills.

This study guide covers the following sections from the Institute of Certified Management Accountants (ICMA®) Content Specification Outline, which you will find in the Appendix.

Section A, "Financial Statement Analysis" (20%)

Section B, "Corporate Finance" (20%)

Section C, "Decision Analysis" (25%)

Section D, "Risk Management" (10%)

Section E, "Investment Decisions" (10%)

Section F, "Professional Ethics" (15%)

Section A: Financial Statement Analysis

Topic 1. Basic Financial Statement Analysis

Common-Size Financial Statement Analysis (Vertical Analysis)

After studying this lesson, you should be able to:

- For the balance sheet and income statement, prepare and analyze common-size financial statements; i.e., calculate percentage of assets and sales, respectively; also called vertical analysis (2.A.1.a).

The four basic financial statements are prepared for external and internal users. The external users need them prepared for their decision-making usefulness. Internal users use them for a variety of reasons, including performance evaluations. Using the statements alone will not give full insight to the operating results and financial position. That's where the vertical analysis of both the income statement and balance sheet come into play.

I. Basic Financial Statements

A. Financial statements are used by a variety of users with an economic interest in the organization. Their purpose is to provide financial information that has decision-making usefulness for each of the users described.

1. Direct interest users include the following groups:

a. Investors and owners

b. Management

c. Suppliers

d. Creditors

e. Employees

f. Customers

2. Indirect interest users include the following groups:

a. Regulatory agencies

b. Stock markets

c. Financial analysts

3. Internal users who make decisions impacting the operations and long-term viability of an organization include:

a. Board of directors

b. Company management

c. Employees

4. External users who determine whether they will invest in or do business with the organization include:

a. Investors

b. Suppliers

c. Customers

d. Stock exchanges

e. Regulatory agencies

B. Every organization, especially publicly traded corporations, prepares four basic financial statements to report their financial position. The following four statements are required by GAAP in the United States:

1. The income statement reports revenues, expenses, gains and losses, and other factors that have impacted the organization's profitability for a period of time, such as a month, quarter, or year. In addition, there will be a statement of comprehensive income that can be combined with the income statement or prepared as a separate statement immediately following it. The statement of comprehensive income starts with net income and then reports other items, net of taxes, such as the unrealized gain or loss on available-for-sale securities or the gain or loss on foreign currency translations.

2. The balance sheet, or statement of financial position, reports the assets, liabilities, and equity at a given point in time. It depicts the accounting equation

$$\text{Assets} = \text{Liabilities} + \text{Stockholders' Equity}$$

3. The statement of changes in equity position reports the changes from one time period to another. The statement will show the changes to stockholders' equity by major accounting category such as common stock, additional paid-in-capital, retained earnings, and treasury stock.

4. The statement of cash flows provides information about the sources and uses of cash, over a period of time.

C. The statement of cash flows reconciles the organization's beginning cash balance plus/minus the net increase/decrease to cash during the period to get the ending cash balance.

CHICAGO CEREAL COMPANY
Condensed Statements of Cash Flows
For the Years Ended December 31 (in thousands)

	Year 2	Year 1
Cash flows from operating activities		
Cash receipts from operating activities	$11,695	$10,841
Cash payments for operating activities	10,192	9,431
Net cash provided by operating activities	1,503	1,410
Cash flows from investing activities		
Purchases of property, plant, and equipment	(472)	(453)
Other investing activities	(129)	8
Net cash used in investing activities	(601)	(445)
Cash flows from financing activities		
Issuance of common stock	163	218
Issuance of debt	2,179	721
Reductions of debt	(2,011)	(650)
Payment of dividends	(475)	(450)
Repurchase of common stock and other items	(645)	(612)
Net cash provided (used) by financing activities	(789)	(773)
Increase (decrease) in cash and cash equivalents	113	192
Cash and cash equivalents at beginning of year	411	219
Cash and cash equivalents at end of year	$ 524	$ 411

Source: Kimmel, Paul D. *Financial Accounting: Tools for Business Decision Making*. Hoboken, NJ: John Wiley & Sons, 2015.

1. This statement is important because a company can have net income and be profitable, but still go bankrupt if doesn't have net cash inflows to pay employees, suppliers, and other creditors.
2. The statement of cash flows is divided into three sections:
   - **a.** First is the operating activities section and relates to the firm's day-to-day business as reported in the income statement. It also includes an analysis of current assets and current liabilities as they relate to the income statement.
     - **i.** The operating activities section is prepared using the indirect or direct method. The choice of methods has no impact on the preparation of the investing and financing activities sections.
       1. Most organizations use the indirect method that adjusts net income to net cash flow in the following way:
          - **a.** Start with net income.
          - **b.** Add depreciation and amortization expense.
          - **c.** Subtract gains and add back losses from the sale of assets.
          - **d.** Adjust for the changes (increase or decrease) to current assets and current liabilities (excluding cash and investments) as follows:
            - **i.** Increases to current assets are subtracted and decreases are added to net income.
            - **ii.** Increases to current liabilities are added and decreases are subtracted from net income.
       2. The direct method is less widely used. It lists the sources of cash received and the uses of cash paid.
   - **b.** Investing activities include the cash flows from buying and selling long-term assets and the debt or equity securities (investments) of other entities. The following are examples of investing activities:
     - **i.** Property, plant, and equipment
     - **ii.** Debt investments
     - **iii.** Equity securities in other entities in the form of common or preferred stock
   - **c.** Financing activities relate to how the organization funds the assets used in operations. These activities are taken from the long-term liability and stockholders' equity sections of the balance sheet. Note that interest payments are reported as interest expense on the income statement and are included in net income in the operating activities section. Examples are:
     - **i.** Issuing long-term debt
     - **ii.** Retiring (paying back) long-term debt
     - **iii.** Issuing common stock and preferred stock
     - **iv.** Paying dividends
     - **v.** Buying and selling of treasury stock
   - **d.** The total of the net cash provided and used by the three activities are added to the beginning cash balance to arrive at the ending cash balance.

e. Significant non-cash investing and financing activities is the last part of the statement. Changes to long-term liabilities and stockholders' equity are reported here. Examples include the conversion of debt to common stock and using long-term debt to finance the purchase of property, plant, and equipment.

II. Common-Size Financial Statement Analysis

A. The power of financial statements is in the ability to show results over multiple months, quarters, or years.

1. A single set of financial statements does not show relationships or trends from period to period

2. All users want to examine the financials in order to make optimal decisions concerning investing in or doing business with the organization.

B. Common-size financial statement analysis allows the user to compare financial statements from different time periods to analyze trends and review the organization's future growth prospects. Common-size analyses are vertical analyses.

1. Vertical analysis calculates financial statement amounts in each statement as a percentage of a base amount for that statement.

2. The base amount is set at 100%. All of the other line items on the financial statement are calculated as a percentage of the base amount. The formula is:

$ Amount of the Line Item ÷ $ Amount of the Base

C. A look at the Chicago Cereal Company's condensed income statements below shows data for Year 2 and Year 1. When analyzing the income statement, the base amount is Net Sales and is 100%. The Year 2 Net Sales are $11,776 and are stated in thousands.

CHICAGO CEREAL COMPANY
Condensed Income Statements
For the Years Ended December 31 (in thousands)

	Year 2		Year 1	
	Amount	**Percent***	**Amount**	**Percent***
Net sales	$11,776	100.0	$10,907	100.0
Cost of goods sold	6,597	56.0	6,082	55.8
Gross profit	5,179	44.0	4,825	44.2
Selling and administrative expenses	3,311	28.1	3,059	28.0
Income from operations	1,868	15.9	1,766	16.2
Interest expense	319	2.7	307	2.8
Other income (expense), net	(2)	.0	13	.0
Income before income taxes	1,547	13.2	1,472	13.4
Income tax expense	444	3.8	468	4.3
Net income	$ 1,103	9.4	$ 1,004	9.1

*Numbers have been rounded to total 100%.

Source: Kimmel, Paul D. *Financial Accounting: Tools for Business Decision Making*. Hoboken, NJ: John Wiley & Sons, 2015.

1. The first calculation is cost of goods sold and is calculated as: \$6,597 ÷ \$11,776 = 56.0%.
2. The next calculation is gross profit and is calculated as: \$5,179 ÷ \$11,776 = 44.0%.
3. The remaining line items on the statement are divided by \$11,776 to get their percent.
4. It is important to note that the percentages will add and subtract on the statement in the same way the dollar amounts do.

Condensed Income Statements
For the Years Ended December 31 (Chicago Cereal), and May 25 (General Mills)

	Chicago Cereal (in thousands)		General Mills, Inc. (in millions)	
	Amount	**Percent***	**Amount**	**Percent***
Net sales	\$11,776	100.0	\$17,910	100.0
Cost of goods sold	6,597	56.0	11,540	64.4
Gross profit	5,179	44.0	6,370	35.6
Selling and administrative expenses	3,311	28.1	3,474	19.4
Non-recurring charges and (gains)	0		(62)	(0.3)
Income from operations	1,868	15.9	2,958	16.5
Other expenses and revenues (including income taxes)	765	6.5	1,134	6.3
Net income	\$ 1,103	9.4	\$ 1,824	10.2

*Numbers have been rounded to total 100%.

Source: Kimmel, Paul D. *Financial Accounting: Tools for Business Decision Making*. Hoboken, NJ: John Wiley & Sons, 2015.

1. Vertical analysis allows the analysis of multiple time periods, in Chicago Cereal Company's case the comparison of Year 2 to Year 1. This is called an intracompany analysis.
2. This analysis also enables an intercompany comparison of companies of different sizes, and to industry averages, because it eliminates the impact of the size difference.
3. The income statements shown above compare Chicago Cereal to General Mills, Inc. using a vertical analysis. Comparing the dollar amounts of these two companies is meaningless because Chicago Cereal is in thousands while General Mills is in millions.
4. We see that Chicago Cereal is more profitable than General Mills at the gross margin level, but not as profitable at the profit margin level.

D. Next is the vertical analysis of the balance sheet. We continue with Chicago Cereal for Year 2 and Year 1 and the balance sheet that is shown below. When analyzing the balance sheet, the base amount is Total Assets and is 100%. For Year 2 the Total Assets are \$11,397 and are stated in thousands.

CHICAGO CEREAL COMPANY
Condensed Income Statements
For the Years Ended December 31 (in thousands)

	Year 2		Year 1	
Assets	**Amount**	**Percent***	**Amount**	**Percent***
Current assets	$ 2,717	23.8	$ 2,427	22.6
Property assets (net)	2,990	26.2	2,816	26.3
Other assets	5,690	50.0	5,471	51.1
Total assets	$11,397	100.0	$10,714	100.0
Liabilities and Stockholders Equity				
Current liabilities	$ 4,044	35.5	$ 4,020	37.5
Long-term liabilities	4,827	42.4	4,625	43.2
Total liabilities	8,871	77.9	8,645	80.7
Stockholders equity				
Common stock	493	4.3	397	3.7
Retained earnings	3,390	29.7	2,584	24.1
Treasury stock (cost)	(1,357)	(11.9)	(912)	(8.5)
Total stockholders' equity	2,526	22.1	2,069	19.3
Total liabilities and stockholders' equity	$11,397	100.0	$10,714	100.0

*Numbers have been rounded to total 100%.

Source: Kimmel, Paul D. *Financial Accounting: Tools for Business Decision Making*. Hoboken, NJ: John Wiley & Sons, 2015.

1. The first calculation is for the line item current assets and is calculated as: $2,717 ÷ $11,397 = 23.8%.
2. The second calculation is property assets (net) and is calculated as: $2,990 ÷ $11,397 = 26.2%.
3. The third calculation is other assets and is calculated as: $5,690 ÷ $11,397 = 50.0%.
4. These three percentages are added to come to 100%. As with the income statement, the percentages for the line items of the balance sheet will add in the same way the dollar amounts do.
5. This analysis continues in the same way with the calculations for the liability and stockholders' equity sections. The base amount used is still Total Assets. The reason is this, it is the same amount as Total Liabilities and Stockholders' Equity.
6. Note that treasury stock is a reduction to stockholders' equity and the dollar amount is in parenthesis. The percentage is shown the same way as the dollar amount.

Summary
The four basic financial statements are the income statement, the statement of retained earnings (or stockholders' equity), the balance sheet, and the statement of cash flows. These statements are prepared for the external user with decision-making usefulness in mind. They are also used by internal users. Be sure to understand how they are related to each other. The income statement and balance sheet can be evaluated using a vertical analysis. Knowing and understanding the format and interrelationship of the statements is critical for understanding Section A, as well as accounting.

Horizontal Financial Statement Analysis

After studying this lesson, you should be able to:

- For the balance sheet and income statement, prepare a comparative financial statement horizontal analysis; i.e., calculate trend year over year for every item on the financial statement compared to a base year (2.A.1.b).
- Calculate the growth rate of individual line items on the balance sheet and income statement (2.A.1.c).

A horizontal, or trend analysis, of the financial statements provides insight to the company's performance over many time periods. For example, two years of income statements can highlight if there have been increases or decreases in key line items such as sales, cost of goods sold, and net income. Longer term analyses can be done for sales, let's say, over the past five years to see how sales have trended. Focus on understanding this type of analysis and interpreting the data.

I. Horizontal Analysis

A. Financial statements are evaluated over a period of time. Horizontal analysis is also called trend analysis. It determines the increase or decrease from one time period to another.

B. A base period is determined in order to perform the analysis. This can be the immediate prior period or go back further in time.

C. The increase or decrease can be expressed as either a percent or as an amount. The basic calculations are:

1. Amount of change method: Current Period – Prior Period = Amount of Change
2. Percent change method: (Current Period – Prior Period) ÷ Prior Period = Growth Rate
3. Percent of prior period method: Current Period ÷ Prior Period = % Increase or Decrease

D. The following information for Chicago Cereal Company will be used for our calculations. The base year in the following calculations is the second time period given. For example, 1.a. the base year is Year 1. In 1.c. the base year is Year 3.

CHICAGO CEREAL COMPANY
Net Sales (in Thousands)
Base Period: Year 1

Year 5	Year 4	Year 3	Year 2	Year 1
$ 11,776	$ 10,907	$ 10,177	$ 9,614	$ 8,812

1. Amount of change method:
   - **a.** Year 2 from Year 1: $9,614 – $8,812 = $802
   - **b.** Year 5 from Year 1: $11,776 – $8,812 = $2,964
   - **c.** Year 4 from Year 3: $10,907 – $10,177 = $730
2. Percent change method:
   - **a.** Year 2 from Year 1: ($9,614 – $8,812) ÷ $8,812 = 9.1%
   - **b.** Year 5 from Year 1: ($11,776 – $8,812) ÷ $8,812 = 33.6%
   - **c.** Year 4 from Year 3: ($10,907 – $10,177) ÷ $10,177 = 7.2%

3. Percent of prior period method:
   a. Year 2 from Year 1: $9,614 ÷ $8,812 = 109.1%
   b. Year 5 from Year 1: $11,776 ÷ $8,812 = 133.6%
   c. Year 4 from Year 3: $10,907 ÷ $10,177 = 107.2%

The complete horizontal analysis of net sales follows:

CHICAGO CEREAL COMPANY
Net Sales (in Thousands)
Base Period: Year 1

Year 5	Year 4	Year 3	Year 2	Year 1
$11,776	$10,907	$10,177	$9,614	$8,812
133.6%	123.8%	115.5%	109.1%	100%

Source: Kimmel, Paul D. *Financial Accounting: Tools for Business Decision Making*. Hoboken, NJ: John Wiley & Sons, 2015.

E. The horizontal analysis can be used to analyze both the income statement and the balance sheet. The horizontal analysis of the comparative income statements for Chicago Cereal Company follows:

CHICAGO CEREAL COMPANY
Condensed Income Statements
For the Years Ended December 31 (in thousands)

			Increase (Decrease) during Year 2	
	Year 2	**Year 1**	**Amount**	**Percent**
Net sales	$11,776	$10,907	$869	8.0
Cost of goods sold	6,597	6,082	515	8.5
Gross profit	5,179	4,825	354	7.3
Selling and administrative expenses	3,311	3,059	252	8.2
Income from operations	1,868	1,766	102	5.8
Interest expense	319	307	12	3.9
Other income (expense), net	(2)	13	(15)	(115.4)
Income before income taxes	1,547	1,472	75	5.1
Income tax expense	444	468	(24)	(5.1)
Net income	$ 1,103	$ 1,004	$ 99	9.9

Source: Kimmel, Paul D. *Financial Accounting: Tools for Business Decision Making*. Hoboken, NJ: John Wiley & Sons, 2015.

The comparative income statements show the changes from Year 1 to Year 2. From these statements we can see that the Year 2 net sales increased from Year 1 by $869 thousand; this is calculated as $11,776 – $10,907.

This represents an 8.0% increase from Year 1, calculated as $869 ÷ $10,907.

It is important to note that the Increase (Decrease) Amount column is additive, the same as the income statement amounts are; however, the Increase (Decrease) Percentages *are not*.

F. Next is the horizontal analysis of comparative balance sheets for Chicago Cereal Company:

CHICAGO CEREAL COMPANY
Condensed Balance Sheets
December 31 (in thousands)

			Increase (Decrease) during Year 2	
Assets	**Year 2**	**Year 1**	**Amount**	**Percent**
Current assets	$ 2,717	$ 2,427	$ 290	1 1.9
Property assets (net)	2,990	2,816	174	6.2
Oilier assets	5,690	5,471	219	4.0
Total assets	$11,397	$10,714	$683	6.4
Liabilities and Stockholders' Equity				
Current liabilities	$ 4,044	$ 4,020	S 24	0.6
Long-term liabilities	4,827	4,625	202	4.4
Total liabilities	8,871	8,645	226	2.6
Stockholders' equity				
Common stock	493	397	96	24.2
Retained earnings	3,390	2,584	806	31.2
Treasury stock (cost)	(1,357)	(912)	(445)	48.8
Total stockholders' equity	2,526	2,069	457	22.1
Total liabilities and stockholders' equity	$ 11,397	$10,714	$ 683	6.4

Source: Kimmel, Paul D. *Financial Accounting: Tools for Business Decision Making*. Hoboken, NJ: John Wiley & Sons, 2015.

The amount change for current assets from Year 1 to Year 2 is $290,000, which represents an 11.9% increase.

The calculations are performed in the same way as done on the income statement. The Year 1 current asset amount of $2,427 is subtracted from the Year 2 amount of $2,717 to get the $290 increase. Then the increase of $290 is divided by $2,427 to get the 11.9% increase.

G. Using the horizontal analysis will show trends in the financial results from one time period to another. As we saw for Chicago Cereal Company, the net sales increased each and every year from Year 1 to Year 5. The intracompany comparison for Chicago Cereal Company's income statement and balance sheet for Year 1 and Year 2 was also able to be done. A horizontal analysis also makes comparisons to other companies, an intercompany basis, and industry averages possible. This is a useful tool.

Summary
Sometimes known as a trend analysis, a horizontal analysis can be performed to evaluate an individual financial statement or a specific line item on one of the statements. This analysis is useful to understand how the entity has performed from one time period to another by calculating growth rates or increases and decreases. Two or more time periods or years of data can be analyzed this way.

Topic 2. Financial Ratios

Liquidity Ratios

After studying this lesson, you should be able to:

- Calculate and interpret the current ratio, the quick (acid-test) ratio, the cash ratio, the cash flow ratio, and the net working capital ratio (2.A.2.a).
- Explain how changes in one or more of the elements of current assets, current liabilities, and/or unit sales can change the liquidity ratios and calculate that impact (2.A.2.b).
- Demonstrate an understanding of the liquidity of current liabilities (2.A.2.c).

The ability of a company to pay its current obligations as they come due, as well as have cash to meet unexpected needs, is what the liquidity ratios help assess. Focus on remembering the formulas as well as their interpretation for insight on the company's ability to pay current liabilities.

I. Understanding and Using Financial Ratios

A. Ratios measure a comparative relationship between two components of a financial statement or statements.

B. Financial ratios are an effective method for analyzing company performance.

1. Ratios can measure the relationship between different components of a single financial statement or between components on different financial statements.
2. Management and other users with limited financial knowledge usually can understand ratios.
3. Ratios can be charted or graphed over time to measure a company's performance in an easy-to-follow visual format.

C. Ratios are classified into three types of analysis of financial statements. The analyses are (1) liquidity, (2) solvency, and (3) profitability. Liquidity will be reviewed in this lesson. Solvency and profitability will be reviewed in subsequent lessons.

II. Liquidity Ratios

A. Liquidity measures the company's ability to pay its short-term obligations and meet any unexpected needs for cash with its current assets. The current liabilities represent the company's short-term obligations.

1. Liquidity is based on the ability of the company to convert its current assets into cash.
2. A profitable company can have liquidity problems, or even go bankrupt, if they cannot convert their sales into cash, as needed, to pay the short-term obligations.

B. Basic Concepts

1. Current assets include cash and other assets expected to convert to cash within one year, or the company's operating cycle, whichever is longer.
2. Current liabilities are the short-term obligations of the company that are expected to be paid within one year, or the company's operating cycle, whichever is longer.
3. Liquidity goes beyond the two basic concepts given above to include:
   - **a.** Conversion of inventory into sales
   - **b.** Conversion of credit sales in accounts receivable (AR) into cash

   c. Payment of purchases in accounts payable (AP)
   d. Payment of other current liabilities
4. The operating cycle of a company represents the time it takes to go from the receipt of inventory **to** the sale of inventory on account **to** the receipt of cash from the customer.
   a. A service provider incurs expenses for salaries, wages, and supplies in order to provide their service. Once the service is provided, the customer is invoiced and then cash comes **in**. A service provider has a relatively short operating cycle.
   b. A retailer and a manufacturer receive inventory to sell as is, or to produce a finished product, and then sell it. The inventory can be held for varying lengths of time. Once the sale is made, the customer is invoiced and then cash comes **in**. A retailer and a manufacturer have longer operating cycles than the service provider does.
5. Working capital usually refers to amount of cash or current assets a company has.
6. Firms need to balance the need for cash and liquidity, with the need for increasing shareholder wealth and growing the business. This leads to financial statement users questioning low current ratios, as well as high current ratios.

C. Key Liquidity Measures

1. Net Working Capital is the difference between current assets and current liabilities and is measured as a dollar amount:
   a. Net Working Capital = Current Assets – Current Liabilities
2. The Net Working Capital Ratio is a variation of net working capital. The ratio is an additional way to evaluate net working capital and its relationship to total assets. It is calculated as:
   a. Net Working Capital Ratio = Net Working Capital ÷ Total Assets
   b. It is expressed as a percent (%)
   c. This ratio is most meaningful when net working capital is a positive amount. A negative amount indicates that the current liabilities are greater than the current assets the company has. In this situation, the percent would be expressed as a negative.
3. Current Ratio measures the relationship between current assets and current liabilities:
   a. Current Ratio = Current Assets ÷ Current Liabilities
   b. It is expressed as X.X:1. This means that there are X.X dollars and cents in current assets for every dollar of current liabilities.
4. Quick Ratio (aka Acid-Test Ratio) measures the firm's ability to meet its current obligations with its cash, marketable securities, and AR.
   a. Quick Ratio = (Cash + Marketable Securities + AR) ÷ Current Liabilities
   b. Also expressed as X.X:1
5. Cash Ratio reduces the amount in the numerator to cash and marketable securities. It's a tougher measure of liquidity than the quick ratio and the current ratio are.
   a. Cash Ratio = (Cash + Marketable Securities) ÷ Current Liabilities
   b. Also expressed as X.X:1
6. Cash Flow Ratio measures how efficiently the cash provided from operations covers the current liabilities.
   a. Current Cash Debt Coverage Ratio = Cash Provided by Operations ÷ Current Liabilities
   b. Expressed as a percent (%)

D. Liquidity Calculations for Chicago Cereal Company

CHICAGO CEREAL COMPANY
Balance Sheets
December 31 (in thousands)

Assets	**Year 2**	**Year 1**
Current assets		
Cash	$ 524	$ 411
Accounts receivable	1,026	945
Inventory	924	824
Prepaid expenses and other current assets	243	247
Total current assets	2,717	2,427
Property assets (net)	2,990	2,816
Intangibles and other assets	5,690	5,471
Total assets	$11,397	$10,714
Liabilities and Stockholders' Equity		
Current liabilities	$ 4,044	$ 4,020
Long-term liabilities	4,827	4,625
Stockholders' equity—common	2,526	2,069
Total liabilities and stockholders' equity	$11,397	$10,714

Source: Kimmel, Paul D. *Financial Accounting: Tools for Business Decision Making*. Hoboken, NJ: John Wiley & Sons, 2015.

1. Net Working Capital = Current Assets – Current Liabilities

- **a.** Year 2 = $2,717 – $4,044 = $(1,327)
- **b.** Year 1 = $2,427 – $4,020 = $(1,593)
- **c.** In both years the company had fewer current assets than current liabilities. The deficit improved slightly from Year 1 to Year 2.

2. Net Working Capital Ratio = Net Working Capital ÷ Total Assets

- **a.** Year 2 = $(1,327) ÷ $11,397 = (11.6)%
- **b.** Year 1 = $(1,593) ÷ $10,714 = (14.9)%
- **c.** In a way, these ratios are meaningless because the net working capital is a negative amount. The ratios do express, however, the extent of this deficit as compared to total assets.

3. Current Ratio = Current Assets ÷ Current Liabilities

- **a.** Year 2 = $2,717 ÷ $4,044 = .67 = .67:1
- **b.** Year 1 = $2,427 ÷ $4,020 = .60 = .60:1
- **c.** General Mills Year 2 = .67:1 and the Industry Average = 1.06:1
- **d.** The intracompany analysis for Chicago Cereal shows the current ratio improved from Year 1 to Year 2. Generally the ratio should be a minimum of 1:1. In both years, Chicago Cereal had fewer current assets than current liabilities. The question is: Where will they get the cash to pay for the current liabilities as they come due?
- **e.** When compared to General Mills, both companies have a ratio of .67:1. However, both companies are below the industry average of 1.06:1.

4. Quick Ratio = (Cash + Marketable Securities + AR) ÷ Current Liabilities

- **a.** Year 2 = ($524 + 0 + 1,026) ÷ $4,044 = .38:1
- **b.** Year 1 = ($411 + 0 + 945) ÷ $4,020 = .34:1

c. As seen in the current ratio, Chicago Cereal's quick ratio improved from Year 1 to Year 2. However, both ratios are well below the 1:1 benchmark.

5. Cash Ratio = (Cash + Marketable Securities) ÷ Current Liabilities

   a. Year 2 = ($524 + 0) ÷ $4,044 = .13:1

   b. Year 1 = ($411 + 0) ÷ $4,020 = .10:1

   c. Both cash ratios decreased from the quick ratios.

6. Cash Flow Ratio = Cash Provided by Operations ÷ Average Current Liabilities. The cash provided by operating activities are Year 2 = $1,503 and Year 1 = $1,410.

   a. Year 2 = $1,503 ÷ $4,044 = .372 = 37.2%

   b. Year 1 = $1,410 ÷ $4,020 = .351 = 35.1%.

   c. The Year 2 and Year 1 cash flow ratio provided only 37.2% and 35.1%, respectively, of the cash needed to pay for the average current liabilities. Year 2 did improve from Year 1.

7. The six calculations used to analyze the liquidity of Chicago Cereal Company reveal that liquidity changed very little from Year 1 to Year 2. This suggests the company has liquidity problems and might struggle to pay its current obligations as they come due. If true, the company would need to take on short-term debt to be able to pay its current liabilities.

E. The Impact of Changes in Current Assets and Current Liabilities on Liquidity

1. In general, an increase in current assets, while keeping current liabilities the same, will improve the liquidity of a company. However, the increase in some current assets can make a stronger difference than others.

   a. When cash and accounts receivable increase there will be increases in the current ratio and the quick ratio.

   b. However, increases in inventory and prepaid expenses will improve the current ratio, but not the quick ratio and cash ratio. Remember that prepaid expenses will never convert to cash. They will be expensed, most often, with the passage of time.

2. The opposite is true for an increase in current liabilities. This will decrease all three of the ratios. Any increase, regardless of the line item or category, will decrease the ratios.

3. There will be improvements to liquidity when current assets increase, current liabilities decrease, or the cash provided by operating activities increases. There will be a decline in liquidity when current assets decrease, current liabilities increase, or the cash provided by operating activities decreases.

Summary

Ratio analysis looks at comparative relationships between two financial statement components. Specifically, liquidity ratios measure the entity's ability to pay its short-term obligations and meet any unexpected cash needs. There are a number of ratios and calculations used to assess liquidity. Be sure to remember each formula so you can perform the calculation. It is also important to be able to interpret the results of the calculations.

Solvency Ratios

After studying this lesson, you should be able to:

- Define solvency (2.A.2.d).
- Calculate and interpret the following ratios: debt-to-equity, long-term debt-to-equity, and debt-to-total assets (2.A.2.i).
- Define, calculate, and interpret the following ratios: fixed charge coverage (earnings to fixed charges), interest coverage (times interest earned), and cash flow to fixed charges (2.A.2.j).

A next step in analyzing a company's financial health is to determine how solvent it is. Solvency ratios assess the ability of the company to survive for the long term. Remembering and understanding this set of ratios is important. They focus on all liabilities, not just current liabilities. This lesson will focus on understanding and interpreting solvency ratios.

I. Solvency Ratios

A. Solvency is the ability of a company to survive over a long period of time. In other words, the ability of the company to pay not only its current liabilities as they come due but also its long-term liabilities.

1. An analysis of solvency uses components from the balance sheet, income statement, and the statement of cash flows.

B. Key Solvency Measures: it is important to understand the terminology that is used when referring to financial statement items. Debt, total debt, liabilities, and total liabilities are interchangeable terms. Long-term debt, long-term liabilities are interchangeable and can be calculated as total debt minus current liabilities. Equity, stockholders' equity, and total stockholders' equity are interchangeable terms.

1. Debt to Equity measures the relationship between total liabilities and stockholders' equity:

a. Debt to Equity = Total Debt ÷ Equity

2. Long-term Debt to Equity measures the relationship between only the long-term liabilities and stockholders' equity:

a. Long-term Debt to Equity = (Total Debt – Current Liabilities) ÷ Equity

3. Debt to Total Assets measures the relationship between total liabilities and total assets. The percentage can be interpreted as how much of the assets are financed, and therefore owned by, the creditors of the company. The difference between this percent and 100% is the amount of assets owned by the stockholders.

a. Debt to Total Assets = Total Debt ÷ Total Assets

4. Fixed Charge Coverage (aka Earnings to Fixed Charges Ratio) is a way to measure how well earnings can cover fixed charges. The earnings amount used is earnings before fixed charges and taxes. Fixed charges include interest, required principal repayment of loans, and leases.

a. Fixed Charge Coverage = Earnings before Fixed Charges and Taxes ÷ Fixed Charges

5. Interest Coverage (aka Times Interest Earned Ratio) is a way to measure how well earnings can cover interest expense.

a. Interest Coverage = EBIT ÷ Interest Expense

6. The cash flow to fixed charges ratio recognizes that payments for fixed charges must be made from cash and not from earnings. It answers the question, does the company have enough cash to pay for the fixed charges they incur.

a. Cash Flow to Fixed Charges = (Cash from Operations + Fixed Charges + Tax Payments) ÷ Fixed Charges

b. Note that cash from operations is an after-tax amount that is found on the statement of cash flows.

C. Solvency Calculations for Chicago Cereal Company

CHICAGO CEREAL COMPANY
Balance Sheets
December 31 (in thousands)

Assets	**Year 2**	**Year 1**
Current assets		
Cash	$ 524	$ 411
Accounts receivable	1,026	945
Inventory	924	824
Prepaid expenses and other current assets	243	247
Total current assets	2,717	2,427
Property assets (net)	2,990	2,816
Intangibles and other assets	5,690	5,471
Total assets	$11,397	$10,714
Liabilities and Stockholders' Equity		
Current liabilities	$ 4,044	$ 4,020
Long-term liabilities	4,827	4,625
Stockholders' equity—common	2,526	2,069
Total liabilities and stockholders' equity	$11,397	$10,714

Source: Kimmel, Paul D. *Financial Accounting: Tools for Business Decision Making.* Hoboken, NJ: John Wiley & Sons, 2015.

1. Debt to Equity = Total Debt ÷ Equity

a. Year 2 = $8,871 ÷ $2,526 = 351.2%

b. Year 1 = $8,645 ÷ $2,069 = 417.8%

2. Long-term Debt to Equity = Long-term Debt ÷ Equity

a. Year 2 = $4,827 ÷ $2,526 = 191.1%

b. Year 1 = $4,625 ÷ $2,069 = 223.5%

Both debt to equity and long-term debt to equity are similar calculations and just slightly different ways of measuring the relationship. For Chicago Cereal, the relative use of borrowed money to the resources invested by the owners is very high. This is a risky position for the company to be in. However, both percentages decreased from Year 1 to Year 2, which shows improvement.

3. Debt to Total Assets = Total Debt ÷ Total Assets

a. Year 2 = $8,871 ÷ $11,397 = 78%

b. Year 1 = $8,645 ÷ $10,714 = 81%

In both years, the debt to assets is very high and indicates a large degree of financial leverage. In spite of the slight decrease from Year 1 to Year 2, Chicago Cereal is highly leveraged and has a high risk that it will not be able to pay its maturing obligations as they come due.

CHICAGO CEREAL COMPANY
Condensed Income Statements
For the Years Ended December 31 (in thousands)

	Year 2	Year 1
Net sales	$11,776	$10,907
Cost of goods sold	6,597	6,082
Gross profit	5,179	4,825
Selling and administrative expenses	3,311	3,059
Income from operations	1,868	1,766
Interest expense	319	307
Other income (expense), net	(2)	13
Income before income taxes	1,547	1,472
Income tax expense	444	468
Net income	$ 1,103	$ 1,004

Source: Kimmel, Paul D. *Financial Accounting: Tools for Business Decision Making.* Hoboken, NJ: John Wiley & Sons, 2015.

4. Fixed Charge Coverage = Earnings before Fixed Charges and Taxes ÷ Fixed Charges. Before this calculation can be done for Chicago Cereal, the required repayment of principal and the amount of the lease payments are not known and need to be estimated. Let's assume that repayment of principal in Year 2 is $200 and Year 1 is $75. Let's also assume that there are no lease payments being made.

a. Year 2 = ($1,103 + $319 + $200 + $444) ÷ ($319 + $200) = 4.0 times

b. Year 1 = ($1,004 + $307 + $75 + $468) ÷ ($307 + $75) = 4.9 times

The fixed charge coverage rate decreased from Year 1 to Year 2, coming down almost one percentage point. This is not a good indication about Chicago Cereal's ability to cover their fixed charges at the current adjusted earnings levels. Reviewing the issuance of debt and the reductions to debt on the statement of cash flows for both years can give more information. It appears that they refinanced the debt in both years. However, in both years, the issuance of debt is greater than the reductions to debt.

5. Interest Coverage = EBIT ÷ Interest Expense

a. Year 2 = ($1,103 + $444 + $319) ÷ $319 = 5.8 times

b. Year 1 = ($1,004 + $468 + $307) ÷ $307 = 5.8 times

Chicago Cereal's EBIT was 5.8 times the amount of interest expense in both years. We don't know if this is a good indication or not. Comparing it to General Mills' 9.9 times shows that Chicago Cereal is not as able to cover interest expense as well as General Mills can. However, when we compare Chicago Cereal's 5.8 times to the industry average of 5.5, it shows that it is slightly better.

CHICAGO CEREAL COMPANY
Condensed Statements of Cash Flows
For the Years Ended December 31 (in thousands)

	Year 2	**Year 1**
Cash flows from operating activities		
Cash receipts from operating activities	$11,695	$10,841
Cash payments for operating activities	10,192	9,431
Net cash provided by operating activities	1,503	1,410
Cash flows from investing activities		
Purchases of property, plant, and equipment	(472)	(453)
Other investing activities	(129)	8
Net cash used in investing activities	(601)	(445)
Cash flows from financing activities		
Issuance of common stock	163	218
Issuance of debt	2,179	721
Reductions of debt	(2,011)	(650)
Payment of dividends	(475)	(450)
Repurchase of common stock and other items	(645)	(612)
alNet cash provided (used) by financing activities	(789)	(773)
Increase (decrease) in cash and cash equivalents	113	192
Cash and cash equivalents at beginning of year	411	219
Cash and cash equivalents at end of year	$ 524	$ 411

Source: Kimmel, Paul D. *Financial Accounting: Tools for Business Decision Making*. Hoboken, NJ: John Wiley & Sons, 2015.

6. Cash Flow to Fixed Charges = (Cash from Operations + Fixed Charges + Tax Payments) ÷ Fixed Charges

a. Year 2 = ($1,503 + 519 + $444) ÷ $519 = 4.8 times

b. Year 1 = ($1,410 + 382 + $468) ÷ $382 = 5.9 times

The cash flow to fixed charges is giving a better indication of Chicago Cereal's ability to pay the cash needed for the fixed charges than the fixed charge coverage did. Similar to the fixed charge coverage results, these calculations show that the result has come down just over one percentage point from Year 1 to Year 2. Remember that these fixed charges must be paid with cash.

Overall Chicago Cereal's solvency is acceptable, although not very good. Most of the calculations improved from Year 1 to Year 2, which indicates that its solvency has improved.

Summary
Solvency ratios assess the ability of an entity to survive for the long term. This means that it will stay in business long enough to repay all liabilities, not only short-term, but long-term, too. It is important to remember the formulas to perform the calculations, be able to interpret the results, and provide an assessment of an entity's solvency.

Operating Leverage and Financial Leverage

After studying this lesson, you should be able to:

- Define operating leverage and financial leverage (2.A.2.e).
- Calculate degree of operating leverage and degree of financial leverage (2.A.2.f).
- Demonstrate an understanding of the effect on the capital structure and solvency of a company with a change in the composition of debt vs. equity by calculating leverage ratios (2.A.2.g).
- Calculate and interpret the financial leverage ratio, and determine the effect of a given change in capital structure on this ratio (2.A.2.h).
- Discuss how capital structure decisions affect the risk profile of a firm (2.A.2.k).

There are two types of leverage that can be calculated to assess the riskiness of a business. Focus on operating leverage and you are measuring how much operating income (earnings before interest and taxes) will change if there is a change in sales. This looks at the cost structure of the company. Focus on financial leverage to understand the company's balance between debt and equity financing for raising capital.

I. Operating Leverage

A. Operating leverage is the extent that a company's operating income (earnings before interest and taxes) will change, based on a change in sales. The company's cost structure is based on the relative amount of fixed costs to variable costs. The higher the fixed costs, relative to the variable costs, the higher the operating leverage. Fixed costs include depreciation of property, plant, and equipment. A high operating leverage can be a good or bad thing. It's good when sales increase because profits will be much higher. It's not so good when sales decrease because profits will be much lower.

1. The degree of operating leverage (DOL) is calculated using one of the following formulas:

a. DOL = % Change in Earnings Before Interest and Taxes (EBIT) ÷ % Change in Sales

This formula is used when two time periods are available, such as a year.

b. DOL = Contribution Margin ÷ EBIT

This formula is used when only one time period is available and the variable and fixed costs are known.

2. DOL = % Change in Earnings Before Interest and Taxes (EBIT) ÷ % Change in Sales

CHICAGO CEREAL COMPANY
Condensed Income Statements
For the Years Ended December 31 (in thousands)

	Year 2	Year 1
Net sales	$11,776	$10,907
Cost of goods sold	6,597	6,082
Gross profit	5,179	4,825
Selling and administrative expenses	3,311	3,059
Income from operations	1,868	1,766
Interest expense	319	307
Other income (expense), net	(2)	13
Income before income taxes	1,547	1,472
Income tax expense	444	468
Net income	$ 1,103	$ 1,004

Source: Kimmel, Paul D. *Financial Accounting: Tools for Business Decision Making*. Hoboken, NJ: John Wiley & Sons, 2015.

a. Year 2 EBIT = \$1,103 + \$444 + \$319 = \$1,866

b. Year 1 EBIT = \$1,004 + \$468 + \$307 = \$1,779

c. % change in EBIT = (\$1,866 – \$1,779) ÷ \$1,779 = 4.8%

d. % change in Sales = (\$11,776 – \$10,907) ÷ \$10,907 = 8.0%

e. DOL = 4.8% ÷ 8.0% = 0.6

f. Interpretation: For every 1% change in sales there will be a 0.6% change in EBIT. The higher the DOL, the greater the risk because fixed costs must be covered regardless of the amount of sales.

3. DOL = Contribution Margin ÷ EBIT. Not knowing Chicago Cereal's total variable and total fixed costs, assume the following:

	Company A	**Company B**
Sales	\$900,000	\$900,000
Variable Costs	\$500,000	\$200,000
Contribution Margin	\$400,000	\$700,000
Fixed Costs	\$225,000	\$525,000
EBIT	\$175,000	\$175,000

a. DOL for Company A = \$400,000 ÷ \$175,000 = 2.29

b. DOL for Company B = \$700,000 ÷ \$175,000 = 4.00

c. Company B's DOL is higher than that of Company A due to the difference in their cost structures. Company B has higher fixed costs relative to their variable costs, which is an indication of a higher level of risk. The opposite is true for Company A, with higher variable costs as compared to the fixed costs.

4. Now assume that both companies have a 10% increase in sales. The effect of the different DOLs looks this way:

a. Company A's EBIT will increase by 22.9% (2.29 times 10%).

b. Company B's EBIT will increase by 40% (4.00 times 10%).

For both companies this is good, but it's even better for Company B.

5. Now let's assume that both companies have a 10% *decrease* in sales. The effect of the different DOLs now looks like this:

a. Company A's EBIT will *decrease* by 22.9%.

b. Company B's EBIT will *decrease* by 40.0%.

Not so good for either company, but even worse for Company B.

II. Financial Leverage

A. Financial Leverage looks at a company's capital structure, which is the balance between debt and equity financing. Debt financing results in tax deductible interest expense. Equity financing results in dividend payments that are *not* an expense reported on the income statement. A high degree of financial leverage equates to a greater degree of risk for the company. This is true because the interest expense must be paid with cash regardless of the amount of earnings.

1. The degree of financial leverage (DFL) is calculated using one of the following formulas:

a. DFL = % Change in Net Income ÷ % Change in EBIT

b. DFL = EBIT ÷ EBT

2. DFL = % Change in Net Income ÷ % Change in EBIT
    a. % Change in Net Income = ($1,103 – $1,004) ÷ $1,004 = .10 = 10%
    b. % Change in EBIT = 4.8% (see I.A.2.c.)
    c. 10% ÷ 4.8% = 2.1
    d. For every 1% change in EBIT there will be a 2.1% change in net income. An increase in EBIT will result in an increase in net income. As seen before, the opposite can also occur.
3. DFL = EBIT ÷ EBT
    a. Year 2 DFL = $1,866 ÷ $1,547 = 1.2
    b. Year 1 DFL = $1,779 ÷ $1,472 = 1.2

B. The financial leverage ratio is another way to evaluate the capital structure of a firm.
1. Financial Leverage = Total Assets ÷ Equity
2. Chicago Cereal Year 2 financial leverage = $11,397 ÷ $2,526 = 4.5
3. Chicago Cereal Year 1 financial leverage = $10,714 ÷ $2,069 = 5.2
4. For both Years 1 and 2, Chicago Cereal had high ratios. This means that the assets are primarily funded using debt instead of equity. This is very risky for Chicago Cereal.

III. The degree of total leverage measures the total level of risk faced by an organization. The following is the calculation for Chicago Cereal:
1. Degree of Total Leverage = DOL × DFL
2. Degree of Total Leverage = 0.6 × 2.1 = 1.26

A company's capital structure is directly related to its level of risk. An increase in debt will increase the amount of cash outflows and will increase the DFL and therefore risk. Increased debt also increases fixed costs in the form of interest expense. An increase in fixed costs will increase the degree of total leverage.

Summary

Leverage provides two ways to assess the riskiness of a business. This lesson explained both operating and financial leverage. Operating leverage looks at the extent operating income (earnings before interest and taxes) will change based on a change in sales, due to the entity's cost structure. Financial leverage looks at the capital structure and the balance between debt and equity financing. Be sure to focus on learning the formulas, as well as understanding the interpretation of the results, to evaluate the risk of the entity.

Efficiency Ratios

After studying this lesson, you should be able to:

- Calculate and interpret accounts receivable turnover, inventory turnover, and accounts payable turnover (2.A.2.l).
- Calculate and interpret days' sales outstanding in receivables, days' sales in inventory, and days' purchases in accounts payable (2.A.2.m).
- Define and calculate the operating cycle and the cash cycle of a firm (2.A.2.n).

The operating activities of a company indicate efficiency or inefficiency, along with measurements useful for cash management. Assessing accounts receivable gives information about the average time it takes the company to collect cash from a credit sale. A company needs to have inventory on hand, but there is a balance between too much and too little inventory for meeting customer demand. The last piece of the puzzle is to measure how long it takes the company to pay its accounts payable. Focus on the interrelationship of these three pieces.

I. Operating Efficiency Ratios

A. Three activities are analyzed to determine the operating efficiency of a company. They are: 1) inventory, 2) accounts receivable, and 3) accounts payable. This analysis is performed to determine the length of the *operating cycle*, which is the time between when goods are put into inventory (purchased) and when the cash is received from the sale of those goods. In addition, a further analysis can be performed to determine the length of the *cash cycle*. This represents the amount of time that the company's cash is tied up in inventories and accounts receivable.

1. Inventory is analyzed using the inventory turnover ratio and the number of days sales in inventory. A higher inventory turnover means there are fewer days sales in inventory.

a. Inventory Turnover Ratio = Cost of Goods Sold ÷ Average Inventory

b. Days Sales in Inventory = 365 days ÷ Inventory Turnover

c. An ***alternative*** calculation for Days Sales in Inventory = Average Inventory ÷ (Cost of Goods Sold ÷ 365)

2. Accounts receivable is analyzed using the accounts receivable (AR) turnover ratio and the number of days sales in receivables. A higher AR turnover means there are fewer days sales in accounts receivable.

a. AR Turnover Ratio = Credit Sales ÷ Average Gross AR

b. Days Sales in Receivables = 365 days ÷ AR Turnover

c. An ***alternative*** calculation for Days Sales in Receivables = Average Gross AR ÷ (Credit Sales ÷ 365)

3. Accounts payable is analyzed using the accounts payable (AP) turnover ratio and the number of days of purchases in AP. A higher AP turnover means there are fewer days of credit purchases in accounts payable.

a. AP Turnover Ratio = Credit Purchases ÷ Average AP

b. Days Purchases in AP = 365 days ÷ AP Turnover

c. An ***alternative*** calculation for Days Purchases in AP = Average AP ÷ (Credit Purchases ÷ 365)

B. Operating Activity Calculations for Chicago Cereal Company for Year 2:

Chicago Cereal Company				
Select Financial Statement Data				
	Year 2	**Year 1**	**Average**	**Increase**
Net Sales	$ 11,776	$ 10,907		
Cost of Goods Sold	$ 6,597	$ 6,082		
AR	1,026	945	986	81
Inventory	924	824	874	100

1. Inventory:

a. Inventory Turnover Ratio = Cost of Goods Sold ÷ Average Inventory

b. Inventory Turnover = $6,597 ÷ $874 = 7.5 times

c. Days' Sales in Inventory = 365 days ÷ Inventory Turnover

d. Days' Sales in Inventory = 365 ÷ 7.5 = 48.7 or 49 days

So what does the 49 days indicate? First you would compare this to management's targeted days' sales in inventory to see if the target is being met or not. A second comparison would be made to the industry average. In this case, that is 54.5 days. Chicago Cereal's days' sales in inventory at 49 days is lower than the industry average of 54.5 days. Managing inventory levels means finding a balance between increased inventory and incurring additional costs and decreased inventory and the risk of losing sales.

2. Accounts Receivable:

Most often the credit sales are not available, so in this case use net sales. The average cash collection of credit sales:

a. AR Turnover Ratio = Credit Sales ÷ Average Gross AR

b. AR Turnover = $11,776 ÷ $986 = 11.9 times

c. Days' Sales in Receivables = 365 days ÷ AR Turnover

d. Days' Sales in Receivables = 365 ÷ 11.9 = 30.7 or 31 days

These ratios measure the company's ability to convert AR into cash. First compare the 31 days to the credit terms of Chicago Cereal's sales invoice. If the invoice terms are net 30 days, then it seems that customers are waiting to pay until the end of the credit term. If the days' sales were lower than the 30 days, then customers would be paying before the end of the credit term. A high number may indicate collection issues or that there is poor customer credit management. A comparison to the industry average can also be made.

3. Accounts Payable:

a. AP Turnover Ratio = Credit Purchases ÷ Average AP

b. Not knowing what the credit purchases are, we can calculate an estimate by taking the cost of goods sold ± the change in inventory from Year 1 to Year 2: $6,597 + 100 = $6,697. Now assume that average AP is $800.

AP Turnover = $6,697 ÷ $800 = 8.4

c. Days Purchases in AP = 365 days ÷ AP Turnover

d. Days Purchases in AP = 365 ÷ 8.4 = 43.5 or 44 days

The interpretation is that Chicago Cereal pays for their credit purchases, on average, in 44 days. Again, a comparison would be made to the payment terms on the vendor's invoice to determine if they were paying their bills on time.

C. Now the calculation of the operating cycle can be made.

1. Operating Cycle = Days Sales in AR + Days Sales in Inventory
2. Operating Cycle = 31 + 49 = 80 days

   This means that it takes Chicago Cereal 80 days to realize its inventory in cash. This cycle continuously repeats itself as long as Chicago Cereal is in operation.

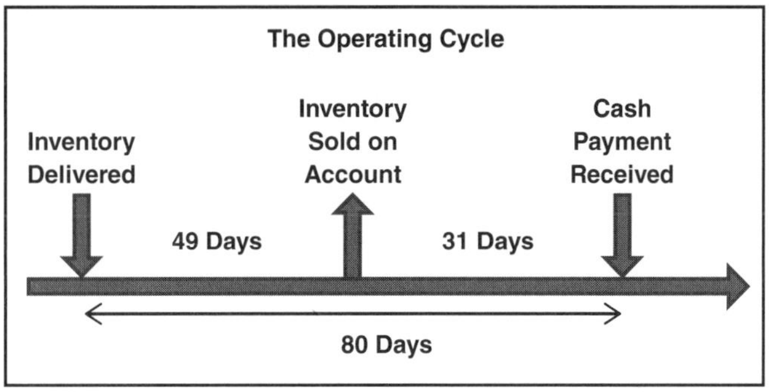

Figure 1

D. Now the calculation of the cash cycle (or cash conversion cycle) can be made.

1. Cash Cycle = Days Sales in AR + Days Sales in Inventory – Days Purchases in AP

   Or Cash Cycle = Operating Cycle – Days Purchases in AP
2. Cash Cycle = 31 + 49 – 44 = 36 days

   Or Cash Cycle = 80 – 44 = 36 days

This means that Chicago Cereal must finance 36 days' worth of purchases through retained earnings or a line of credit. A shorter cash cycle is better than a longer one.

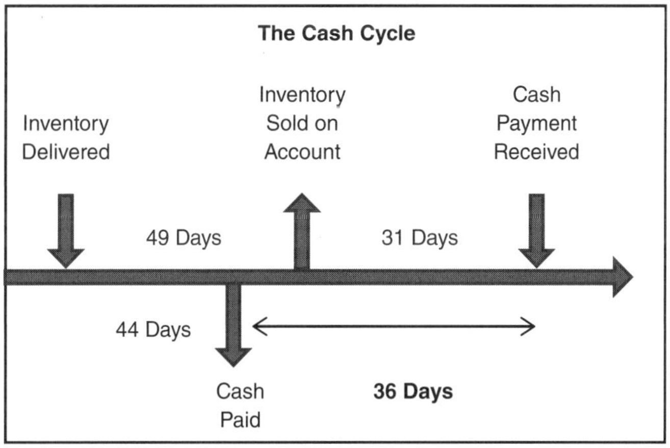

Figure 2

The analyses performed here are very important to assess a company's net working capital and cash management.

Summary
There are three operating activities that need to be analyzed to determine the efficiency of a company's operations. They are also important from a cash management point of view. This lesson described the formulas to evaluate (1) accounts receivable to determine the timing of the cash collection of credit sales, (2) inventory for the time it takes to sell what is on hand, and (3) accounts payable to determine when cash is disbursed for payments. Once these are known, the operating cycle and the cash cycle can be calculated and assessed. Be sure to spend time on these calculations and concepts until they are clear to you.

Efficiency Ratios—Use of Assets

After studying this lesson, you should be able to:

- Calculate and interpret total assets turnover and fixed asset turnover (2.A.2.o).

One measure of profitability is through the use of turnover ratios. This is based on the entity's use of its assets to generate sales. Focus on the calculations as well as the interpretation of the results of the calculations. Notice there is a difference between the calculations. One uses total assets while another uses fixed assets.

I. Turnover Ratios

A. Turnover ratios evaluate how well the company uses assets to generate sales. There are two common calculations to evaluate this:

1. Asset turnover:

a. Asset Turnover = Net Sales ÷ Average Total Assets

2. Fixed asset turnover:

a. Fixed Asset Turnover = Net Sales ÷ Average Net Property, Plant, and Equipment

B. Turnover Ratio Calculations for Chicago Cereal Company for Year 2:

CHICAGO CEREAL COMPANY
Select Financial Statement Data

	Year 2	Year 1	Average
Net Sales	$11,776	$10,907	
Total Assets	11,397	10,714	11,056
Net PP & E	2,990	2,816	2,903

1. Asset Turnover:

a. Asset Turnover = Net Sales ÷ Average Total Assets

b. Asset Turnover = $11,776 ÷ $11,056 = 1.1 times

2. Fixed Asset Turnover:

a. Fixed Asset Turnover = Net Sales ÷ Average Net Property, Plant, and Equipment

b. Fixed Asset Turnover = $11,776 ÷ $2,903 = 4.1 times

Interpret the asset turnover of 1.1 times as $1.10 of sales is generated by every $1.00 invested in assets. Chicago Cereal has a very low turnover, which indicates that it is not using its assets in an efficient way to generate sales.

The fixed asset turnover is better at 4.1 times. Fixed assets are considered to be productive assets because they are used in the daily operations of the company. This indicates an improvement from the asset turnover rate and is interpreted the same way.

Summary

The use of turnover ratios is one way to measure profitability. An entity will invest in resources in the form of assets that will then be used to generate sales revenues. This profitability measure evaluates the dollar amount of sales, generated by one dollar of assets. Remember, there are different definitions of assets that can be used in these formulas.

Topic 3. Profitability Analysis

Profitability—Vertical Analysis Revisited and Return Ratios

After studying this lesson, you should be able to:

- Calculate and interpret gross profit margin percentage, operating profit margin percentage, net profit margin percentage, and earnings before interest, taxes, depreciation, and amortization (EBITDA) margin percentage (2.A.2.p).
- Calculate and interpret return on assets (ROA) and return on equity (ROE) (2.A.2.q).

Another look at the vertical analysis reveals the importance of generating gross profit, operating profit, as well as net income, as we work our way down the income statement. Profitability can also be evaluated based on the return, meaning net income, on assets and equity. Most often management will have target numbers they want to achieve during the year.

I. Vertical Analysis Revisited

   A. As seen in the lesson "Common-Size Financial Statement Analysis (Vertical Analysis)," an analysis of profitability begins with a vertical analysis of the income statement. Chicago Cereal's ratios that have already been calculated are given here. There are four vertical analysis ratios used to evaluate different levels of profit or return on sales:

      1. Gross Margin = Gross Profit ÷ Net Sales. *Chicago Cereal = 44.0%*
      2. Operating Profit Margin = Operating Income ÷ Net Sales. *Chicago Cereal = 15.9%*
      3. Profit Margin = Net Income ÷ Net Sales. *Chicago Cereal = 9.4%*
      4. Earnings before Interest Taxes Depreciation and Amortization (EBITDA) Margin = EBITDA ÷ Net Sales. This cannot be calculated for Chicago Cereal because depreciation and amortization are not given in the information provided.

   B. Interpretation:

      1. Gross margin is an important ratio because of the strong influence it has on profit margin. It is an indicator of the adequacy of the selling price to cover cost of goods sold.
      2. Operating margin indicates the percent of profit from the operations of the business.
      3. Profit margin is also an important ratio, indicating the results of the company's performance for the time period. One company goal is to operate at a profit.
      4. EBITDA is an *estimate* of cash provided by operations. The EBITDA margin measures this amount as a percent of sales.
      5. For Chicago Cereal, all of the margins seem to be very good.

II. Return on Assets and Return on Equity

   A. Return on assets indicates the overall profitability of assets. The calculation is:

      1. Return on Assets = Net Income ÷ Average Total Assets
      2. Chicago Cereal's return on assets:

         a. Year 2 = 10.0%

         b. Year 1 = 9.4%

3. Compare to:

   a. General Mills Year 2 = 6.2%

   b. Industry Average Year 2 = 5.3%

   Chicago Cereal's return on assets increased from Year 1 to Year 2. The returns look good, but a comparison to General Mills and the industry average will be better indicators. Comparing Chicago Cereal's Year 2 return of 10.0% to General Mills' Year 2 return of 6.2% shows that Chicago Cereal performed better than General Mills. Also, Chicago Cereal performed much better than the industry average of 5.3%. Both companies' returns on assets were higher than the industry average.

B. Return on Equity is an indication of the profitability of the investment by common stockholders:

1. Return on Equity = Net Income ÷ Average Equity

2. Chicago Cereal does not have any preferred stock outstanding, and therefore no preferred dividend payments. The total stockholders' equity amounts can be used as is. Chicago Cereals' return on equity:

   a. Year 2 = 48%

   b. Year 1 = 46%

3. Compare to:

   a. General Mills Year 2 = 25%

   b. Industry Average Year 2 = 19%

   Chicago Cereal's return on equity is very high and increased from Year 1 to Year 2. Comparing Chicago Cereal's Year 2 return of 48.0% to General Mills' Year 2 return of 25% shows that Chicago Cereal performed much better than General Mills. Also, Chicago Cereal performed much better than the industry average of 19%. Both companies' returns on assets were higher than the industry average.

Summary

This lesson revisited the vertical analysis of the income statement to reinforce the importance of each level of profit and the corresponding percentage of net sales: gross profit, operating income, and net income. The return on assets assessed the return on the investments the entity made while the return on equity assessed the return on the investment the stockholders made.

Profitability—Market Value Ratios

After studying this lesson, you should be able to:

- Calculate and interpret the market/book ratio and the price/earnings ratio (2.A.2.r).
- Calculate and interpret book value per share (2.A.2.s).
- Identify and explain the limitations of book value per share (2.A.2.t).

Investors highly value successful companies. Just how high that value is can be assessed through the understanding of book value per share and earnings per share and how these amounts compare to the current market price of the company's stock. This lesson will teach ratios to use to evaluate a company's market value.

I. Market Value Ratios

A. Market value ratios are an indication of how highly investors value a publicly traded company. The calculations combine accounting data with stock market data. There are two calculations to assess this:

1. Market-to-Book Ratio = Current Stock Price ÷ Book Value per Share

a. Book Value = (Total Stockholders' Equity – Preferred Equity) ÷ Number of Common Shares Outstanding

2. Price/ Earnings Ratio (P/E) = Market Price per Share ÷ Earnings Per Share (EPS)

B. Information needed to perform these calculations:

1. The market price of Chicago Cereal's stock at the end of Year 2 was $52.92.

2. Chicago Cereal's Year 2 Common Stockholders' Equity is $2,526, as found on the balance sheet.

3. The average number of common shares outstanding in Year 2 was 418,700 shares.

4. Chicago Cereal's Year 2 EPS was $2.63.

C. Calculations and interpretations.

1. Before the calculation for the Market-to-Book Ratio can be made, book value needs to be determined. This calculation is only for common stockholders' equity. The formula for this is total stockholders' equity minus preferred equity.

a. Chicago Cereal's Year 2 Book Value = $2,526 ÷ 418.7 = $6.03 per Share

b. Interpretation: Book value represents the amount of **net assets** owned by the common stockholders. The book value could be low compared to the market value of the firm due to historical cost and accrual accounting used to record transactions. The amounts recorded for transactions also include management's estimates and assumptions. Book value is most relevant for certain types of businesses:

i. Financial companies with high cash and other assets for investing

ii. Manufacturing or other companies with high fixed assets

c. Chicago Cereal's Year 2 Market-to-Book Ratio = $52.92 ÷ $6.03 = 8.8

d. Interpretation: This means that Chicago Cereal is worth 780% (8.8 – 1.0) more than the amount that past and present stockholders have put into the firm. This example gave an extremely high Market-to-Book Ratio, and is not typical of most corporations.

2. Price/ Earnings Ratio (P/E)

a. Chicago Cereal's Year 2 P/E = \$52.92 ÷ \$2.63 = 20.1

b. Interpretation: The P/E ratio is an investor's assessment of the future earnings of the company. A high P/E might indicate that the company has good growth opportunity *or* that earnings are relatively safe. Both make the company more valuable. It is valid to compare this to the industry average, as well as to another firm in the industry.

Summary

Market value ratios are a way of determining how investors in common stock view the company. A key metric is the current stock price. This market price is measured against the book value and earnings per share of the company to better understand the market value of the company.

Profitability—EPS, Yields, and Shareholder Return

After studying this lesson, you should be able to:

- Calculate and interpret basic and diluted earnings per share (2.A.2.u).
- Calculate and interpret earnings yield, dividend yield, dividend payout ratio, and shareholder return (2.A.2.v).

Investors and other analysts want to know how well the company performed from a shareholder return point of view. Focus on the formulas as well as interpreting the results. Once again the market price per share is incorporated into the formulas used for this analysis. It puts into perspective the returns based on market price as well as focusing on the real return to investors, which is dividends.

I. Earnings per Share

A. Basic earnings per share (EPS) is calculated for common shareholders only, even if the company has preferred stock issued and outstanding. It represents the net income earned on each share of common stock that is outstanding. There are two formulas for calculating earnings per share:

1. EPS = (Net Income – Preferred Dividends) ÷ Weighted Average Common Shares Outstanding

2. Diluted EPS = (Net Income – Preferred Dividends) ÷ Diluted Weighted Average Common Shares Outstanding

a. The dilution comes from the shares of stock that could have been exercised or converted to common stock on the closing date of the financial statements. These shares come from:

i. Stock options

ii. Stock warrants

iii. Convertible bonds

iv. Convertible preferred stock

b. By including these additional shares as if they were issued and outstanding, the denominator in the equation is increased. This lowers the EPS amount. Therefore, diluted EPS will always be a lower amount than EPS.

c. When calculating diluted EPS, adjustments to the basic formula shown in number 2 above are required. This uses the "if-converted method." These are:

i. Stock Options: only increase the weighted average common shares outstanding amount.

ii. Stock Warrants: only increase the weighted average common shares outstanding amount.

iii. Convertible Bonds: increase the weighted average common shares outstanding amount. In addition, increase the net income (numerator) by the amount of the after-tax interest saved.

iv. Convertible Preferred Stock: increase the weighted average common shares outstanding amount. In addition, preferred dividends are no longer subtracted from net income.

B. Information needed to perform these calculations for Chicago Cereal:

1. Chicago Cereal's Year 2 Net Income is $1,103 (in thousands), as found on the income statement.
2. Chicago Cereal's preferred stock dividend is zero. They only have common stock.
3. The average number of common shares outstanding in Year 2 was 418.7 thousand shares.

C. Calculations and interpretation for Chicago Cereal:

1. Chicago Cereal's Year 2 EPS = ($1,103 – 0) ÷ 418.7 = $2.63
   - **a.** By itself, EPS doesn't have a lot of meaning so it is best to compare the amount to a forecasted amount, to a prior period EPS, or to the EPS of a competitor. Note that there will *not* be an industry average to compare it to, due to the large variations in the number of shares outstanding for individual companies within the industry.
   - **b.** Chicago Cereal's Year 1 EPS was $2.40. The Year 2 EPS increased from the prior year by $0.23 per share. This is a 9.6% increase. This is good.
   - **c.** General Mills' EPS for Year 2 was $2.90. Chicago Cereal's EPS in Year 2 was lower by comparison.
2. Diluted EPS. Due to lack of information, this cannot be calculated for Chicago Cereal.

D. A more detailed look at both of the EPS calculations will be based on the following data:

Net Income	$1,000,000
Tax rate	30%
Average stock price per share	$50.00
<u>Common stock:</u>	
Shares outstanding Jan. 1	240,000
2 for 1 stock split June 30	
New issue of CS on Oct. 1	80,000
<u>Preferred stock cumulative, convertible:</u>	
Dividend rate	5%
Par value per share	$100
Shares outstanding Jan. 1	2,000
Convertible to shares of CS	3
<u>Stock options:</u>	
Number of options outstanding during the year	5,000
Right to purchase shares of CS per bond	10
Exercise price per share	$40
<u>Stock warrants:</u>	
Number of warrants outstanding during the year	8,000
Right to convert to shares of CS	1
Exercise price per share	$30
<u>Convertible bonds:</u>	
Interest rate	5%
Number of bonds outstanding during the year	150
Issue price	$1,000
Right to convert to shares of CS	20

1. Calculate Basic EPS:

   a. Calculate the *numerator* of the equation: Net Income – Preferred Dividends = \$1,000,000 – (\$100 × 2,000 shares × 5%) = \$1,000,000 – \$10,000 = \$990,000. When adjusting for the dividends, even when the preferred stock is cumulative, only the current year dividends (paid or not) should be deducted from net income.

   b. Calculate the *denominator* of the equation: Weighted-Average Common Shares Outstanding

Shares outstanding Jan. 1	240,000
2 for 1 split on June 30	+240,000
Issue 80,000 × 25%	+ 20,000
Total weighted-average CS	500,000

   There are two things to recognize in this calculation. The first is that when a stock split occurs, regardless of when during the year, it is assumed to have occurred at the beginning of the year. The second is that any new issue of stock needs to be prorated for the amount of time during the year that these new shares were outstanding. In this example, 80,000 shares were issued on October 1st. This means they were outstanding for three months during the year. Prorated, this becomes 80,000 shares times (3/12) = 80,000 shares times 25% = 20,000 shares.

   c. Calculate Basic EPS:

      i. \$990,000 ÷ 500,000 = \$1.98

2. To calculate the Diluted EPS consider the following:

   a. Convertible **preferred stock** is convertible into 3 shares of common stock for each share of preferred stock. This conversion is calculated as 2,000 × 3 = 6,000 shares of common stock. Remember that the preferred dividends were subtracted from the net income when calculating basic EPS. Now that the preferred stock is converted into common stock, no preferred stock dividends will be paid, and therefore deducted from net income in the calculation.

   b. There were 5,000 **stock options** outstanding that could be exercised for 10 shares of common stock each. This mean there are 50,000 shares of common stock to consider in the dilution. However, the exercise of these options will generate a cash inflow to the company of 50,000 shares × \$40 = \$2,000,000. This cash will be used to purchase shares on the open market. This results in 40,000 shares (\$2,000,000 ÷ \$50 average stock price) of CS being purchased. The company only needs to issue an additional 10,000 shares of CS. This is calculated as 50,000 minus 40,000 = 10,000 shares. When the exercise price is greater than the average stock price the options would not be exercised because the holder could purchase the stock at a lower price on the open market. This makes the stock options antidilutive and would not change the diluted weighted-average number of shares outstanding.

   c. The 8,000 **stock warrants** are convertible to 1 share of CS so the total converted number of shares is 8,000. An important note about stock warrants is that warrants are only dilutive if the exercise price is less than the average stock price. This is true in this example because the exercise price is \$30/share and the average stock price is \$50/share. When the exercise price is greater than the average stock price the warrants would not be exercised because the holder could purchase the stock at a lower price on the open market than through the warrant. This would make the stock warrants antidilutive and would not change the diluted weighted-average number of shares outstanding.

   d. The **bonds** would be converted into 3,000 shares of CS. This is calculated as 150 bonds multiplied by 20 shares per bond. If the bonds are converted, then no interest would be paid to the bondholders. An adjustment is needed to net income for this. Start by calculating the interest expense per year. This is $1,000 × 150 bonds × 5% = $7,500 in interest. Next convert the interest expense to an after tax interest expense amount by taking $7,500 and multiplying it by 1 minus the tax rate. This results in $7,500 × (1 – 0.30) = $5,250 of after tax interest expense that is added back to net income.

e. Now we can calculate the diluted weighted-average number of shares outstanding:

Weighted-average shares outstanding	500,000
+ Converted preferred stock	6,000
+ Converted stock options	10,000
+ Converted stock warrants	8,000
+ Converted bonds	3,000
Diluted weighted-average shares outstanding	527,000

f. Calculate the diluted EPS as follows:

($1,000,000 + $5,250) ÷ 527,000 = $1.91

II. Yields

A. In this context, *yields* refers to the returns to shareholders. The following formulas are applicable:

1. Earnings Yield = EPS ÷ Market Price per Share
   a. This is the inverse calculation of the P/E ratio.
2. Dividend Yield = Annual Dividend per Share ÷ Market Price per Share
3. Dividend Payout Ratio = Common Dividends ÷ Earnings Available to Common Shareholders

B. Information for Chicago Cereal needed to perform these calculations:

1. Year 2 EPS is $2.63.
2. Year 2 Net Income (earnings) is $1,103 (in thousands).
3. Year 2 Market Price is $52.92.
4. Year 2 Dividend per Share is $1.13.
5. Year 2 Total Dividends were $475 (in thousands).

C. Calculations and interpretation:

1. Chicago Cereal's Year 2 Earnings Yield = $2.63 ÷ $52.92 = .0496 = 5.0%
   a. Earnings yield is the percent of a dollar invested that was earned by the company. For Chicago Cereal, 5.0% of the market stock price was earned in Year 2.
2. Chicago Cereal's Year 2 Dividend Yield = $1.13 ÷ $52.92 = .0214 = 2.1%
   a. This calculation isolates the yield from the dividend payment. Chicago Cereal's dividend yield is 2.1%.
3. Chicago Cereal's Year 2 Dividend Payout Ratio = $475 ÷ $1,103 = 43.1%
   a. Dividend payout represents the percentage of earnings that was paid out in dividends to common stockholders. Chicago Cereal paid out 43.1% of its earnings in dividends. There are a few things to keep in mind when assessing dividend payout and yield:
      i. Most companies are reluctant to cut dividends, even if there is an earnings shortfall.
      ii. The amount of dividends, and whether they are paid or not, are at the discretion of the board of directors.

III. Shareholder Return

A. The shareholder return ratio is calculated for a time period, most often one year, as follows:

1. Shareholder return = (Ending stock price – Beginning stock price + Annual dividend per share) ÷ Beginning stock price

2. Assume the following:

a. Beginning stock price = $52.00

b. Ending stock price = $60.00

c. Annual dividend/share = $3.00

3. Shareholder return = ($60.00 – $52.00 + $3.00) ÷ $52.00 = 21.2%

B. The shareholder return on common stock is evaluated using basic and diluted EPS, the yield calculations, and the shareholder return ratio. All of these evaluations take into consideration net income (earnings), dividends, and the market price per share at various points in time. The overall return to the shareholder is based on a combination of all of these variables.

Summary
Focus on remembering the calculations presented in this lesson. The calculations, as well as the interpretation of them, are important to evaluating profitability from the shareholder's perspective. Earnings per share is important; however, the tangible dividend payout is almost more important because it is a return the shareholder actually receives.

Limitations of Ratio Analysis

After studying this lesson, you should be able to:

- Identify the limitations of ratio analysis (2.A.2.w).

Ratio analysis is a valuable tool for analyzing the operating performance and financial strength of an entity. It requires many calculations and assessments to be made. This lesson will discuss many of the shortfalls and limitations of ratio analysis. Pay close attention to the words of caution in this lesson that emphasize that what we think are common terms can actually take on different definitions.

I. Limitations of Ratio Analysis

A. Ratio analysis is an excellent way to analyze the financial results of a firm to determine the liquidity, solvency, profitability, and operating efficiency. As seen from the analyses so far, it is not enough to calculate one ratio and make a determination about the financial health of the firm. Multiple calculations must be made and analyzed to come to any valid determination.

B. It is also important to compare the results of the current year's ratio analysis to the results from the firm's prior year(s). These horizontal analyses can reveal changes in the form of increases and decreases that have occurred. Comparisons to industry averages, when they are available and applicable, will also add insight.

C. Caution needs to be used when comparing one firm with another. The two firms must be in the same industry or the comparisons can be misleading. An example is that the commodity industry often has very low gross margins while the high-technology industry often has very high gross margins. To compare these two would give the impression that the high-technology firm is outperforming the commodity firm.

D. Ratio analysis is a great way to compare businesses of different sizes. But, their usefulness is limited as seen in these examples:

1. *Choice of inventory valuation method.* If one firm uses FIFO (first in, first out), it will have a higher inventory value and a lower cost of sales than a firm that uses LIFO (last in, first out), all else being equal. This choice will also give different results when calculating days' sales in inventory and return on assets.
2. *Composition of current assets.* The reason for the different variations on the current ratio (current assets ÷ current liabilities) is to recognize that not all current assets are created equal when it comes to liquidity and the ability to pay back current liabilities. Prepaid expenses are a current asset; however, they will never be converted to cash. They are simply used up over time. Inventory will hopefully be sold. This does not equate to an immediate inflow of cash.
3. *Choice of depreciation method.* Using the straight-line method of depreciation will result in higher operating and net income when compared to using an accelerated method of depreciation.
4. *Earnings per share.* EPS is calculated as (net income minus preferred dividends) divided by the weighted average number of common shares outstanding. Management can change the denominator in this equation with the purchase of treasury stock. This reduces the denominator, which results in higher earnings per share.
5. *Return on assets.* Unless you are doing the calculations yourself, you need to know and understand what numbers were used. The "return" can be net income, operating income, or some other definition. The "assets" can be total assets, PP&E (property, plant, & equipment), or some other definition.

E. The key to a successful analysis using ratios is to know what amounts are used in the calculations and that the components of the calculations are consistent from time period to time period.

Summary

There are limitations to using ratios to analyze an entity. To start, never look at just one ratio to evaluate the entity. Multiple ratios must be used. Ratios give the ability to compare companies of different sizes. Focus on knowing how the amounts were derived in order to make valid comparisons. For example, inventory can be valued using one of a variety of methods and each company may not have chosen the same method to use. Understanding the impact the different methods have on income and assets will be helpful to develop a useful analysis.

Sources of Financial Information and Their Use in Evaluating a Company's Financial Strength

After studying this lesson, you should be able to:

- Demonstrate a familiarity with the sources of financial information about public companies and industry ratio averages (2.A.2.x).
- Evaluate the financial strength and performance of an entity based on multiple ratios (2.A.2.y).

Analysts take their evaluation of a company farther, for better understanding and interpretation of the numbers, by looking outside the company. This lesson discusses the many resources found on the Internet that are used to obtain information about the company's competitors and industry information. This lesson also discusses how a complete analysis includes an assessment of the company's liquidity, solvency, profitability, and leverage.

I. Sources of Financial Information

A. Information about publicly traded companies is available from a wide range of sources. The information ranges from financial statements, to stock market trading, to the latest news reports.

B. Public companies are required by the SEC (Securities and Exchange Commission) to file quarterly statements, an annual report, and other required filings such as insider stock trading activity.

1. Most of this information can be found on the *company's website* under *investor relations*. Sometimes you might be redirected to the SEC's website.
2. The SEC website has the Edgar database, which contains all of the company's filings, and can be found at http://www.sec.gov/edgar.shtml.

C. There are other financial websites available that provide free information or are accessed through paid subscriptions. The following are a few examples:

1. CNN Money at http://money.cnn.com/data/markets.
2. Google Finance at http://www.google.com/finance.
3. Yahoo! Finance at www.finance.yahoo.com.
4. The *Wall Street Journal* has information available for free, with much more information available with a paid subscription, at www.wsj.com.
5. *Financial Times* has information available for free, with much more information available with a paid subscription, at www.ft.com.
6. Bloomberg has information available for free, with much more information available with a paid subscription, at www.bloomberg.com.
7. Reuters has information available for free, with much more information available with a paid subscription, at www.reuters.com.
8. Morningstar offers only a paid subscription service at www.morningstar.com.

D. Industry averages are more difficult to find. However, information can be found on most of these sites by looking for "sector" information.

II. Evaluation of the Financial Strength and Performance of an Entity based on Multiple Ratios

A. Smart investors and managers use a wide variety of ratios to both measure and manage financial health. There is *no single ratio* that can predict the success or failure of a company. The following are areas of focus for financial analysis:

1. ***Liquidity Ratios*** assess the ability of the company to pay short-term liabilities as they come due.

a. The Current Ratio = Current Assets ÷ Current Liabilities. It shows the amount of current assets as compared to current liabilities. The current assets, such as accounts receivable and inventory, will be turned into cash to pay for the liabilities coming due in the coming year.

b. The quick ratio, also called the acid-test ratio, is a more rigorous evaluation than the current ratio is. This is because only certain current assets are included in the calculation and others are excluded.

$$\text{Quick Ratio} = (\text{Cash} + \text{Marketable Securities} + \text{Accounts Receivable}) \div \text{Current Liabilities}$$

The current assets excluded are inventory and prepaid expenses.

c. A company with poor liquidity must find ways to raise cash to pay for current liabilities. This can be done by establishing a line of credit and/or taking a short-term loan for cash.

2. ***Solvency ratios*** assess the ability of the company to survive over a long period of time and pay all liabilities as they come due.

   a. The Debt to Total Assets Ratio = Total Debt ÷ Total Assets. This measures the percentage of assets financed by creditors. From this ratio the percentage of assets owned by the stockholders can be determined.

   b. A similar ratio is the Debt to Equity Ratio = Total Debt ÷ Stockholders' Equity. This shows the percent of total liabilities, or borrowed funds, compared to the resources invested by the owners.

   c. The times interest earned ratio, also called the interest coverage ratio, is an indication of the ability to pay all interest payments as they come due.

3. Evaluation of both liquidity and solvency is important because it is possible for a company to have good liquidity ratios and poor solvency ratios. The opposite could also be true.

4. ***Profitability ratios***. The basic gross margin, operating margin, and profit margin ratios demonstrate the firm's ability to control expenses and generate profit per dollar of sales. There are a variety of ratios that can be used to help determine a firm's profitability.

   a. *Earnings per share*. EPS = (Net Income – Preferred Dividends) ÷ Weighted Average of Common Shares Outstanding. Management can reduce the weighted average number of common shares outstanding by purchasing treasury stock. This reduces the denominator, which results in higher earnings per share.

   b. *Return on assets*. Unless you are doing the calculations yourself, you need to know and understand what numbers were used. The "return" can be net income, operating income, or some other definition. The "assets" can be total assets, PP&E (property, plant, & equipment), or some other definition.

   c. *The depreciation method used*. Using the straight-line method of depreciation results in higher operating income and net income than the use of an accelerated method of depreciation. This is true because the depreciation expense taken in the early years in the life of the asset is much higher when an accelerated method is used as compared to the straight-line method.

5. ***Leverage ratios*** assess the amount of fixed costs, or required interest payments, used by a firm as part of its overall financing structure.

   a. Operating leverage is based on the company's cost structure: the relative amount of fixed costs to variable costs. In general, the higher the fixed costs relative to variable costs, the riskier the business. The reason is that higher sales volumes will be needed to cover the higher amount of fixed costs.

   b. This is closely related to the CVP (Cost Volume Profit) analysis and the determination of the breakeven point.

c. Financial leverage looks at the company's capital structure and the balance between debt and equity financing. A high degree of financial leverage means a greater degree of risk for the company. Higher debt will increase the amount of required cash outflows to pay interest expense and repay the debt.

B. The key to a successful analysis using ratios is to know what amounts are used in the calculations and that the components of the calculations are consistent from time period to time period. The analyst needs to be aware of and/or perform additional analysis.

1. Compare the current-year results to prior-year results, a competitor firm's results, and industry averages to have enough data to determine the financial health and make predictions about the company.
2. Determine if there have been any changes in accounting methods from year to year.
3. Determine if there have been any acquisitions or divestitures during the year.
4. Be familiar with the industry, sector, and market the company operates in.

Summary

An evaluation of an entity's operating performance and financial strength would not be complete if the results weren't compared to a competitor's results and to industry averages. There are many sources of this *external* information available on the worldwide web. The entity analysis may look good, but just how good or bad it really is cannot be determined unless it is compared to competitors' or industry results. An analyst needs to be familiar with the industry and market, not just the entity itself, because sometimes the numbers will not paint the whole picture. Additionally, an analyst should have a good understanding and be able to assess the company's liquidity, solvency, profitability, and leverage in order to perform a complete analysis.

ROA and ROE—A Closer Look

After studying this lesson, you should be able to:

- Demonstrate an understanding of the factors that contribute to inconsistent definitions of "equity," "assets," and "return" when using ROA and ROE (2.A.3.a).
- Determine the effect on return on total assets of a change in one or more elements of the financial statements (2.A.3.b).
- Calculate and interpret sustainable equity growth (2.A.3.j.)

In this lesson, the ROA and ROE calculations are expanded to separate the impact of two components in each of the resulting returns. Focus on the elements of the financial statements to see how a change in one will impact ROA and ROE. This increases your understanding of the relationship between the financial statements.

I. Return Ratios

   A. Return on Assets (ROA) and Return on Investment (ROI) measure how well a firm uses its asset base to generate profits.

      1. Both ratios are key measures of the success of chief executive officers (CEOs) and business unit leaders. These individuals are responsible for profitability as well as investments in assets.

      2. Business managers use return ratios to compare the returns generated on one investment with other potential investments.

      3. Investors also use return ratios to assess profitability of a company.

      4. Return on Equity (ROE) measures the amount of profit in relation to common shareholders' equity.

   B. The formulas to calculate **ROA** and **ROE** are:

      1. **ROA** = Net Income ÷ Average Total Assets = **$1,103 ÷ $11,056 = 10%** Year 2 for Chicago Cereal

         a. The DuPont Model is an expanded version of this basic ROA calculation.

         b. **ROA** = (Net Income ÷ Sales) × (Sales ÷ Average Total Assets)

         ($1,103 ÷ $11,776) × ($11,776 ÷ $11,056) = 10%

         9.4% × 1.1 times = 10%

         c. Said another way, **ROA** = Net Profit Margin × Total Asset Turnover

         d. This breakdown allows for more detailed analysis of ROA by isolating the impact that the net profit margin has on ROA. For Chicago Cereal, it improves ROA. This is good because the Total Asset Turnover is a very low number.

      2. **ROE** = Net Income ÷ Average Equity = $1,103 ÷ $2,298 = 48%

         a. The DuPont Model is an expanded version of this basic ROE calculation.

         b. **ROE** = (Net Income ÷ Average Total Assets) × (Average Total Assets ÷ Average Equity)

         ($1,103 ÷ $11,056) × ($11,056 ÷ $2,298) = 48%

         10% × 4.8 times = 48%

c. Said another way, this is **ROE** = ROA × Financial Leverage

i. Financial Leverage = Assets ÷ Equity

d. This breakdown allows for more detailed analysis of ROE by showing the financial leverage. The ROA at 10% is increased substantially by the financial leverage ratio at 4.8 times.

C. By using the DuPont model to calculate ROA and ROE management has more insight as to why the percentages are what they are. This information can be used to develop plans to improve both returns by focusing on the weakest/lowest amounts.

II. Investors and managers *must be careful* when using the above formulas because there can be different meanings or definitions for *assets*, *equity*, and *income*. Unless you have done the calculation yourself, you may not know exactly what numbers have been used to calculate the return.

A. **Assets** can be defined as:

1. Average total assets for a two-year time period.
2. Total assets for a specific time period.
3. Operating assets, meaning property, plant and equipment. These are the assets used to generate income.

B. **Equity** can be defined as:

1. Average common stockholders' equity for a two-year time period. This is the amount that is most commonly used. Using this definition is in sync with the Earnings per Share (EPS) calculation, which uses only common stock outstanding.
2. Common stockholders' equity for a specific time period.
3. Total stockholders' equity that includes both preferred and common stockholders' equity. This definition is less frequently used.

C. **Income** or the **return** can be defined as:

1. Net income.
2. Net income minus preferred stock dividends. The deduction of preferred dividends brings the net income back to a return to common shareholders.
3. Operating income is used to remove income taxes, other gains and losses, and the impact of interest expense on loans outstanding.

D. In all cases, the key to understanding ratios is to know what the analyst is using for the calculations and to make sure that the components of the calculations are consistently used. If not used consistently, then comparisons to other time periods and/or competitor companies will not be valid.

III. The results of ROA and ROE calculations will be impacted by changes in the amounts of individual components on both the income statement and the balance sheet. The following chart lists individual components or items on a financial statement. The second column shows the change in the component that will increase ROA. The third column shows the change in the component that will increase ROE. For example, an increase in sales will increase both ROA and ROE.

Component	Will Increase ↑ ROA	Will Increase ↑ ROE
Sales	Increase	Increase
Cost of Sales	Decrease	Decrease
Operating Expenses	Decrease	Decrease
Selling, General, & Administrative Expenses	Decrease	Decrease
Interest Expense	Decrease	Decrease
Income Taxes	Decrease	Decrease
Assets	Decrease	No impact
Liabilities	No impact	No impact
Preferred Stock, including additional paid in capital	No impact	No impact
Common Stock, including additional paid in capital	No impact	Decrease
Retained Earnings	No impact	Decrease
Treasury Stock	No impact	Increase

IV. It is important to recognize that ROE, in combination with the dividend payout ratio, can be used to determine the sustainable growth rate (SGR). The SGR is the maximum rate a firm can grow at using its own revenue. Said another way, it is how much a firm can grow without having to borrow money for this growth. The formula is:

A. SGR = ROE × (1 – Dividend Payout Ratio)

B. The assumptions behind this formula are:

1. The firm will maintain its target capital structure: debt and equity.

2. The dividend payout ratio remains the same.

3. The firm will maintain or increase its revenues.

C. Recall that Chicago Cereal's ROE for year 2 is 48% and its dividend payout ratio for the same year is 43.1%. Using these percentages, the following is the calculation for Chicago Cereal's SGR:

1. SGR = .48 × (1 – .431)

2. SGR = .48 × .569

3. SGR = .273 or 27.3%

D. This tells us that Chicago Cereal can grow at a rate of 27.3% without having to take on new debt or sell more shares of common stock.

V. Return ratios are a valuable tool when analyzing the returns of a company. Understanding the definition of the components used will go a long way in developing a valid analysis.

Summary

This closer look at ROA and ROE expanded the basic equations for both of these calculations. This gave the ability to evaluate the components of each equation to determine the causes of the resulting ROA and ROE. Be sure to focus on the components of each equation to understand how the increase or decrease in one will increase or decrease the final result. Also remember the additional use of ROE to calculate the SGR. This is an important percentage to know when managing the company's finances.

Revenues and Its Relationship to Current Assets

After studying this lesson, you should be able to:

- Demonstrate an understanding of the relationship between revenue and receivables and revenue and inventory (2.A.3.e).
- Determine and analyze the effect on revenue of changes in revenue recognition and measurement methods (2.A.3.f).

The selling process results in transactions that change both the income statement and the balance sheet. Sales revenue and accounts receivable or cash are used to recognize the revenue. Cost of goods sold and inventory are used to record the movement of inventory to the customer. Understand the criteria for recognizing revenue to determine when these entries would be recorded.

I. Revenues and accounts receivable, as well as cost of sales and inventory, are related to each other through the sales process.

A. When inventory is sold and transferred to the customer, the sale is recorded as a sale on account. This means that accounts receivable, and not cash, will be increased. When the perpetual inventory method is used the journal entry to reduce inventory and increase cost of sales will be made at the same time as the recording of the sale. Let's assume that the selling price is higher than the cost of inventory, so there is gross profit. The two required journal entries are:

Debit: Accounts Receivable	xxx	
Credit: Sales		XXX
Debit: Cost of Sales	xxx	
Credit: Inventory		XXX

B. When these entries are made the dollar amount of sales minus cost of sales will create gross profit. There will be an increase to both gross profit and operating income for the amount of the gross profit.

C. At the same time, assets will increase by the amount of the gross profit as well. This is true because there is a reduction in the inventory account and an increase in the accounts receivable account. The change in assets is the same as the change on the income statement.

D. The increase in income from this transaction is higher in *percentage terms* than the increase in assets will be. Therefore, each sale will increase the return on assets, all things being equal.

II. Aspects of Accounting Standards Update (ASU) 2014-09, Revenue from Contracts with Customers (Topic 606)

A. Revenue is recognized to show the transfer(s) of promised goods or services to the customer in an amount that reflects the consideration the company expects to be entitled to for the transfer(s). This means that revenue is equal to the amount of consideration. There are five steps to be followed:

1. Identify the contract(s) with the customer
2. Identify the contract's performance obligation(s)
3. Determine the transaction price
4. Allocate the transaction price to the performance obligation(s) in the contract
5. Recognize revenue as the performance obligation is satisfied

B. It is the *transfer of control* of the promised goods or services to the customer that triggers the *recognition of revenue.*

C. The transfer of control to the customer can be:

1. At a point in time, or
2. Over time

D. When transferred over time, there are two methods than can be used to allocate revenues:

1. Output methods:
   - **i.** Performance completed to date
   - **ii.** Appraisals of results achieved
   - **iii.** Units produced or delivered
   - **iv.** Time elapsed
2. Input methods:
   - **i.** Resources consumed
   - **ii.** Labor hours expended
   - **iii.** Costs incurred
   - **iv.** Time elapsed
   - **v.** Machine hours used

E. Once a method is chosen, it is used for the term of the contract. There may be differences in recognized revenue from year to year, only to the extent of the changes in the activity from year to year. For example, when the actual labor hours in year 1 are different from the hours in year 2.

F. There are no longer industry differences that were used in the past for construction, software, real estate, and telecommunications.

G. A contract based on the transfer of control over time will create a contract asset on the balance sheet of the seller. The contract asset will be classified as current or long term based on the terms of the contract.

Summary

Focusing on understanding the relationships between the income statement and the balance sheet will increase your ability to analyze these statements. Remember: If the entity makes sales on account (credit sales), there will be accounts receivable; if they are a merchandiser or manufacturer, they will have inventory that, when sold, moves to cost of sales. A basic understanding of the Accounting Standards Update can give insight into the current and future recognition of revenues, and therefore cost of sales.

Cost of Sales and the Different Profit Margins

After studying this lesson, you should be able to:

- Analyze cost of sales by calculating and interpreting the gross profit margin (2.A.3.g).
- Distinguish between gross profit margin, operating profit margin, and net profit margin and analyze the effects of changes in the components of each (2.A.3.h).
- Define and perform a variation analysis (percentage change over time) (2.A.3.i).

Cost of sales has a big impact on the profits a company generates. Profit margins are revisited from the perspective of how three different expense components impact these margins. This recognizes that it's not enough to generate sales to earn a profit. Good cost management can improve profits.

I. Let's look at manufacturing company Chicago Cereal Company's income statement. This analysis can also be used for a merchandising company. The manufacturer will "purchase" the materials used to make the products they sell. The merchandiser will "purchase" the products they sell.

CHICAGO CEREAL COMPANY
Condensed Income Statements
For the Years Ended December 31 (in thousands)

	Year 2		Year 1	
	Amount	**Percent***	**Amount**	**Percent***
Net sales	$11,776	100.0	$10,907	100.0
Cost of goods sold	6,597	56.0	6,082	55.8
Gross profit	5,179	44.0	4,825	44.2
Selling and administrative expenses	3,311	28.1	3,059	28.0
Income from operations	1,868	15.9	1,766	16.2
Interest expense	319	2.7	307	2.8
Other income (expense), net	(2)	.0	13	.0
Income before income taxes	1,547	13.2	1,472	13.4
Income tax expense	444	3.8	468	4.3
Net income	$ 1,103	9.4	$ 1,004	9.1

*Numbers have been rounded to total 100%.

Source: Kimmel, Paul D. *Financial Accounting: Tools for Business Decision Making*. Hoboken, NJ: John Wiley & Sons, 2015.

The percentages have already been calculated for us on this statement. As a reminder, this vertical analysis uses Net Sales as the base amount.

A. **Gross Margin** = Gross Profit ÷ Net Sales = $5,179 ÷ $11,776 = 44.0%

1. Gross Margin measures the amount of each sales dollar available to cover operating expenses, including selling and administrative expenses, other expenses, and income tax expense. Chicago Cereal has $0.44 of every sales dollar available.
2. A company operating in a competitive market will not be able to set the selling price. In this situation, the only way the company can improve the gross margin is to manage its manufacturing costs, including purchasing costs. They will be highly motivated to reduce the cost of inventory.
3. When the company has flexibility in setting the selling price, it is able to cover cost increases in direct materials, direct labor, and manufacturing overhead *or* merchandise inventory included in cost of sales. This company may not be as motivated to lower these costs.

B. Operating Margin = Income from Operations ÷ Net Sales = \$1,868 ÷ \$11,776 = 15.9%

1. Operating Margin measures the amount of each sales dollar available to cover interest expense, other expenses, and income tax expense. Chicago Cereal has \$0.159 of every sales dollar available.

2. Operating Margin is a key metric for ***service*** *firms*. The reason is that service firms do not have cost of sales, and therefore have no Gross Margin. The primary expense incurred to provide their services are professional service fees. The service firm will look to reduce the cost of professional services as well as operating expenses.

C. Profit Margin = Net Income ÷ Net Sales = \$1,103 ÷ \$11,776 = 9.4%

1. Profit Margin measures the amount of each sales dollar earned for the common stockholders of the company. Chicago Cereal earned \$0.094 of every sales dollar for its stockholders.

D. Each margin has more meaning when it is compared to the prior period, a competitor's margins, or an industry average. Managing/reducing costs is an important way to increase profit margins. Cost reductions should not be done if it means the quality standards are not met.

II. Each ratio is determined by the expense component used to calculate it. The following chart identifies each cost category and its impact on each ratio.

Ratio	Cost of Sales	Operating Expenses Including Selling & Admin	Interest Expense Non-operating Gains/(Losses) Income Taxes
Gross Margin	Yes	No	No
Operating Margin	Yes	Yes	No
Profit Margin	Yes	Yes	Yes

Understanding the income statement, and how the different margins are determined, is extremely important for both the managers of the company and the external users of the statement. The managers use this information to focus on costs that may need to be reduced. The external users of this information want to determine how profitable the company is at each level.

Summary

This revisit to the three profit margins shown on the income statement focuses more on the impact that the different costs/expenses have on them. The calculations should be very familiar to you by now. Cost of goods sold is extremely important because this amount impacts gross margin, operating margin, as well as profit margin. Make sure to understand the impact each cost/expense item has on the different levels of income/margin.

Considerations when Measuring Income

After studying this lesson, you should be able to:

- Identify factors to be considered in measuring income, including estimates, accounting methods, disclosure incentives, and the different needs of users (2.A.3.c).

Four factors impact the measurement of income. It is important to understand how the use of estimates, choice of accounting methods, corporate disclosures in the annual report, as well as the different needs of internal and external users will change how income is measured. All of this can change the amounts reported on both the income statement and the balance sheet. Ultimately, they change the ratios.

I. The amount of expense and the resulting amount of income reported on the income statement are based on management decisions regarding the choices of accounting methods and estimates used. The FASB Accounting Standards Codification (ASC) requires four financial statements to be prepared for external users. The four financial statements and the required disclosures are a major part of a publicly traded company's annual report. The FASB ASC provides authoritative literature organized by topic.

A. There are four factors that need to be considered when measuring income:

1. **Estimates**—income is based on the use of estimates about future events. The management of a publicly traded company makes estimates based on history, current economic decisions, and other factors. The company's auditors will verify the estimates for reasonableness. These estimates can impact the amount of reported income significantly. Common estimates are:

   a. *The useful life of a depreciable asset.* The longer the life, the lower the annual depreciation expense, and therefore the higher the income.

   b. *The estimate of allowance for doubtful accounts.* The estimated percentage of uncollectable accounts determines the amount of bad debt expense reported on the income statement. The higher the bad debt expense, the lower the reported income.

2. **Accounting Methods**—the accounting method management chooses to use will affect the amount of reported income. The auditors will verify that the method is one of the generally accepted accounting methods and ensure that the chosen method is used consistently from year to year. For example:

   a. *The use of straight-line versus an accelerated depreciation method.* The accelerated method will report higher depreciation expense in the early years of the life of the asset. This results in a lower amount of income, as compared to the straight-line method.

   b. *The use of first-in, first-out (FIFO) versus last-in, last-out (LIFO) to value inventories will determine the amount of cost of goods sold.* During periods of inflation, the FIFO method will report higher inventory values and lower cost of goods sold compared to the use of LIFO. The lower cost of goods sold used by FIFO will report a higher amount of income before tax, a higher income tax expense, and higher net income than LIFO would report.

   The CMA candidate needs to understand how each method will impact the reported income. An extension of this is to also understand the impact the reported income and the relevant balance sheet amounts will have on common ratios. For example, the use of FIFO increases the amount of income, but also increases the value of the inventory. Both the income and inventory amounts will have an effect on the return on assets (ROA) calculation.

3. **Disclosure**—The FASB ASC provides the detail of the required disclosures. In addition, the SEC can require additional disclosures be made. The purpose of disclosures is to provide more detailed information than what is found in the numbers themselves on the financial

statements. Seeing the amount of inventory and cost of goods sold on the balance sheet and the income statement, respectively, does not tell you the valuation method management used to arrive at the numbers. The information provided in the notes is for the external users for their decision-making usefulness.

   a. It is up to the company to draft the disclosures. The level of detail provided by companies can range from the minimum required by FASB ASC to overwhelming amounts of detail. It is up to the individual external user to decipher and understand the information disclosed.

   b. Management is cautious to disclose any information that can be used by its competitors against the company.

   c. Management's focus is to increase shareholder value. The amount and content of the disclosures can have an impact on the stock price, as well as the perception of the company by investors and creditors.

4. **Different Needs of Users**—The users of the financial statements have different needs.

   a. The **internal users**, or management, use the financial statements to make business decisions to run the company. The four financial statements oftentimes are a starting point for them. Reports prepared using cost and managerial accounting concepts and techniques are often more important, especially when trying to manage the costs of running the business. Remember that the cost and managerial reports are prepared for *internal use only* and do not always follow GAAP guidelines.

   b. The **external users** of the financial statements have very different needs from the internal users, as well as from each other.

      i. Investors use the information to decide whether to invest, hold, or divest themselves of the company's stock. Investors will analyze the data to determine historical trends of sales and income, for example. They will also use ratio analysis to determine the financial and operational health of the company. These analyses help them make predictions about the future of the company, which they use to make their decision.

      ii. Creditors look for information to help them decide whether to extend credit to the company. This decision also includes a determination of the amount of credit to extend if they have decided to extend the firm credit. Based on the length of time of any credit or loans made, the use of liquidity and/or solvency ratios will help creditors do this. All creditors look for the principal amount to be repaid to them, as well as any interest expense that goes with the loan. Their goal is to minimize the risk of not being repaid.

      iii. Government reviews the financial statements from a tax and regulatory point of view.

      iv. Labor unions review the financial statements from the point of view of the firm's ability to give raises and provide benefits to its employees.

Summary

A thorough understanding of the use of estimates and different accounting methods in the preparation of the financial statements will enhance an analysis of a company. These estimates and methods are allowed under U.S. GAAP. But, management's decisions can and will impact the resulting net income and balances reported on the balance sheet. This ultimately determines the results of the ratio calculations.

Topic 4. Special Issues

Sales and Revenues — Important Considerations

After studying this lesson, you should be able to:

- Explain the importance of the source, stability, and trend of sales and revenue (2.A.3.d).

Revenue is recognized when certain conditions have been met. Once recognized, analysts are interested in the source of the revenues, the stability of sales, and the period-to-period trend in sales. These factors improve understanding of the reported revenues and form a basis for making future predictions of revenues.

I. The new guidelines from the FASB and the Securities and Exchange Commission (SEC) of the United States state that revenue from a contract with a customer is recognized when control of the good or service is transferred to the customer.

- **A.** These conditions are met with an obligation satisfied at a *point in time*. For a service provider, revenue is recognized when the service has been provided or with the passage of time. The passage of time condition gets met when the firm, such as an insurance company, is prepaid the insurance premiums by their customer. They record a liability such as unearned insurance premium revenue when their customer pays in advance for insurance coverage. On a monthly basis, revenue is recognized in the amount of the one month's premium and the liability is decreased.
- **B.** In addition, the following must be met for revenue to be recognized:
  1. The firm has a present right to payment for the asset.
  2. The customer has legal title to the asset *or* the service has been provided.
  3. The firm has transferred physical possession of the asset.
  4. The customer has the significant risks and reward of ownership of the asset.
  5. The customer has accepted the asset.

II. There are three factors whose importance needs to be explained when it comes to sales and revenues.

- **A.** The *Source* of the revenue from operating activities refers to the product or service being offered by the firm. Sales can also come from extended warranties paid for by the customers with the purchase of a product. Management decides which products and services the firm will offer. They will also develop a corporate strategy that will guide them to new product or service development that will be offered in future years. The firm can also have non-operating income of cash dividends from investments in the stock of other firms or interest revenue.
- **B.** Sales *Stability* comes from repeat customers who continually purchase the product or service. A solid base of repeat customers will provide a continuous stream of sales. This is supplemented by new customers who may be purchasing the product or service for the first time or who may not have purchased the product or service in a while. Sales become more stable when the first- or second-time customer gets converted to a repeat customer.
- **C.** Sales *Trends* are developed when sales are analyzed using a horizontal analysis. This analysis compares the dollar amount of sales from one time period to another. This can be done over a period of time such as years, quarters, over even weeks. Firms usually hope for a constant increase of sales over the periods of time. This is preferred to an up-and-down trend of sales fluctuations over the periods of time.

III. Additional considerations include:

A. The elasticity of demand for the product or service: This explains how customers respond to a change in the selling price.

a. When demand is highly elastic and the selling price increases, total sales will decrease. Customers will seek out substitutions to buy instead.

b. Elasticity of demand is relevant to analyzing sales trends.

c. When demand is highly inelastic and the selling price decreases, total sales will decrease. Lower prices will not increase the demand.

B. The level of competition in the market the firm competes in: The more competitive the market, the harder it is for a firm to maintain its level of revenues.

C. The amount of customer concentration: Does the firm have few or many customers they sell to?

a. Having many customers increases sales stability. If one or two customers stop buying from the firm there are many other customers to continue selling to. Sales would remain relatively stable.

b. Having only one or just a few customers decreases sales stability. If one customer stops buying from the firm there won't be any other customers to continue selling to. Sales would decrease drastically.

D. The degree of dependence on a few good sales representatives or many representatives: This analyzes the percentage of sales that come from each of the sales representatives.

a. When one or a few sales representatives are generating the majority of sales there is a risk if one or a few leave the firm. Often when this happens, customers will follow that sales representative to the new company they go to. This will decrease sales stability.

E. The level of geographical diversification of the market in which the firm competes: the greater the diversification, the more stability.

a. Greater diversification will improve sales stability because if sales decrease in one market, it will likely be offset by an increase in another market.

Summary

The recognition of revenue, especially from sales to customers, is guided by relatively strict criteria by the FASB in its Accounting Standards Update (ASU) 2014-09, *Revenue from Contract with Customers (Topic 606)*. Focus on the criteria and their application. Important factors when evaluating a company's sales revenues are the source of the sale, sales stability, and sales trends. Remember the other considerations based on supply and demand, level of competition, and other factors given.

Foreign Exchange Fluctuations

After studying this lesson, you should be able to:

Demonstrate an understanding of the impact of foreign exchange fluctuations (2A.4.a):

1. Identify and explain issues in the accounting for foreign operations (e.g., historical vs. current rate and the treatment of translation gains and losses).
2. Define functional currency.
3. Calculate the financial ratio impact of a change in exchange rates.
4. Discuss the possible impact on management and investor behavior of volatility in reported earnings.

There are many things to know and remember about foreign exchange fluctuations. This lesson will focus on the five accounting transactions and adjustments for reporting that these fluctuations impact. The basis for this is to understand both the direct and indirect currency quotes and how to apply them to the transactions and adjustments. Familiarity with ASC Topic 830 will help with this.

I. There has been rapid expansion of U.S. companies operating globally that exposes them to transactions denominated in foreign currencies. For the purpose of this lesson we will assume that a U.S. company is the parent company and the subsidiary is operating in a foreign country.

   A. U.S. companies operating globally will be recording the following accounting transactions:

      1. Accounting for *sales* made abroad and denominated in a foreign currency
      2. Accounting for *purchases* made abroad and denominated in a foreign currency
      3. Accounting for *assets* held abroad and valued in a foreign currency
      4. Accounting for *liabilities* held abroad and valued in a foreign currency
      5. Accounting for a foreign subsidiary that will be *consolidated* with the U.S. parent company's financial statements

   B. These businesses will have multiple transactions in many currencies during the year. When the U.S. company's consolidated financial statements are prepared these transactions, as well as the financial statements of their foreign subsidiary, must be converted to U.S. dollars. Once the conversion is done the amounts can be added together.

   C. The conversion is done using an *exchange rate*. The rates are quoted as a spot rate, meaning the rate that day. Sometimes it is referred to as the rate on the date of the balance sheet, for example. The exchange rates are given in either a *direct* or *indirect* quote.

      1. *Direct quote*: states the number of units of the domestic currency that can be converted into one unit of a foreign currency: $1.20 to £1 means one U.S. dollar and 20 cents can be exchanged for one British pound.
      2. *Indirect quote*: states the number of units of the foreign currency that can be converted into one unit of the domestic currency: £.83 to $1.00 means .83 British pounds can be exchanged for one U.S. dollar. Said another way, one U.S. dollar will get you .83 British pounds. This is calculated as £1 divided by $1.20 = £.83.

   D. The exchange rate of a specific currency can be allowed to fluctuate based on supply and demand *or* fixed by a government. When a currency *falls* relative to another currency it has *weakened* against that other currency. When a currency *rises* relative to another currency it has *strengthened* against that other currency. These are called currency fluctuations. These fluctuations result in gains or losses being recorded.

1. A sale denominated in a foreign currency means the accounts receivable is denominated in the foreign currency as well. If the dollar weakens, an exchange gain is recorded on the balance sheet date. Accounts receivable increases and the gain increases stockholders' equity through the other comprehensive income account.

   If a US Company makes a sale of €30,000, the sale is denominated in the foreign currency. The following are the calculations for the US dollar amounts, reflecting the different changes in the foreign exchange rates.

The sale is made when the spot rate is €1 : $1.05	**If the € *Strengthens*: €1 : $1.10**	**If the € *Weakens*: €1 : $1.02**
$31,500 is debited to AR (€30,000 × $1.05 = $31,500)	New AR balance is $33,000 (€30,000 × $1.10 = $33,000)	New AR balance is $30,600 (€30,000 × $1.02 = $30,600)
AR ↑ resulting in a **Gain**	$33,000 − $31,500 = **$1,500**	
AR ↓ resulting in a **(Loss)**		$30,600 – $31,500 = **$(900)**

2. For a purchase denominated in a foreign currency, the accounts payable is denominated in the foreign currency also. If the dollar weakens, an exchange loss is recorded on the balance sheet date. Accounts payable increases and the loss decreases stockholders' equity through the other comprehensive income account.

   If a US Company makes a purchase of €10,000, the purchase is denominated in the foreign currency. The following are the calculations for the US dollar amounts, reflecting the different changes in the foreign exchange rates.

The purchase is made when the spot rate is €1 : $1.05	**If the € *Strengthens*: €1 : $1.10**	**If the € *Weakens*: €1 : $1.02**
$10,500 is credited to AP (€10,000 × $1.05 = $10,500)	New AP balance is $11,000 (€10,000 × $1.10 = $11,000)	New AP balance is $10,200 (€10,000 × $1.02 = $10,200)
AP ↑ resulting in a **(Loss)**	$10,500 – $11,000 = **$(500)**	
AP ↓ resulting in a **Gain**		$10,500 – $10,200 = **$300**

E. Imports and exports are the most common type of foreign currency transactions. ASC Topic 830, has two requirements for foreign currency transactions:

1. At the date of a foreign currency transaction each account used in the recording of the transaction will be measured using the functional currency (most often the reporting currency) using the exchange rate on that date.

2. At each balance sheet date, all balances will be adjusted to reflect the exchange rate on that balance sheet date.

   Transactions recorded to accounts receivable and accounts payable will require an additional adjustment if the exchange rate has changed from the balance sheet date in item D. above to the payment date. This adjustment results in a gain or loss on the income statement.

F. There are two different translation methods identified in ASC Topic 830 to convert a foreign subsidiary's financial statements into U.S. dollars for consolidation. The method used is determined by the functional currency used by the subsidiary. The company has no choice. A *functional currency* is the currency of the primary economic environment the subsidiary operates in. Therefore, the subsidiary's local currency is its functional currency based on its sales market, how selling price is determined, where expenses are incurred, source of financing, and extent of intercompany transactions.

1. When the subsidiary has transactions that were conducted in a local or multiple currencies, these transactions must first be translated to the subsidiary's functional currency.
2. Once the subsidiary's currency is adjusted to the functional currency, re-measure the financial statements into parent's currency using the **historical rate/temporal method**.
   a. Nonmonetary accounts are translated at historical rate. These accounts are marketable securities carried at cost; inventories carried at cost and cost of sales; prepaid expenses; property, plant and equipment as well as depreciation expense.
   b. Monetary accounts are cash, receivables, and payables. These are translated using the current exchange rate on the balance sheet date.
3. If the subsidiary's currency *is* the functional currency, translate the financial statements into the parent's currency using the **current rate method**. All assets and liabilities are translated using the exchange rate on the balance sheet date. The income statement items are translated using the weighted average rate for the year.

G. There are three steps to consolidate a foreign subsidiary into the parent's financial statements:
   1. Modify the subsidiary's financials to conform to U.S. GAAP.
   2. Re-measure the trial balance into the functional currency only when the subsidiary has conducted transactions in multiple currencies.
   3. Translate the financials from the functional currency into the reporting currency. This requires the parent to prepare worksheet eliminations before they consolidate the foreign subsidiary into the parent company.

H. The income statement and accompanying notes should provide information about the aggregate gains or losses from foreign subsidiaries during the accounting period. The translation adjustments are usually presented showing the beginning amount of cumulative translation adjustments, plus or minus the aggregate adjustment, and the resulting ending amount of cumulative translation adjustments. The amount of the current year adjustment is reported on the statement of comprehensive income.

Summary

Global expansion of so many companies exposes them to foreign exchange fluctuations. Both sales and purchases made abroad are denominated in a foreign currency. Fluctuations can have a positive or negative impact on the actual dollars exchanged for these transactions. Focus on how currencies are quoted to be able to calculate the amounts and any fluctuations between transaction dates. ASC Topic 830 specifies two important dates. The first is the foreign currency transaction date and the second is at the subsequent balance sheet date.

Inflation and the Financial Ratios

After studying this lesson, you should be able to:

- Demonstrate an understanding of the impact of inflation on financial ratios and the reliability of financial ratios (2.A.4.b).

Understand that the main impact of inflation is on sales, expenses, income, and the cost of inventory. Period-to-period comparisons will be distorted during multiple periods of high inflation. Focus on how horizontal analyses can be used to remove the impact of this distortion so the real increases or decreases from period to period can be recognized.

I. Inflation will impact sales, expenses, income, and the cost of inventory. This can cause distortions when comparing year-to-year financial statements.

- **A.** During inflationary times the cost of items will increase to the firm, as will the price they sell their products or services for. The questions to ask:
  - **1.** Are expenses increasing from year-to-year because we are using more *or* are we paying more?
  - **2.** Are sales increasing due to increased volume *or* are we charging more?
- **B.** The use of horizontal analysis to measure growth, in sales or income, from a base year is useful because the results can be adjusted for and restated to remove the impact of inflation.
  - **1.** An analysis of sales can be done to measure the percent increase from year-to-year.
  - **2.** However, if sales increased by 10% based solely on increasing the selling price, and the rate of inflation was 12%, the firm did not see sales increase in real terms. This would be a bad sign for the firm because the increase due to inflation exceeds the increase in selling price.
  - **3.** Now let's assume that sales went from $1,000 in Year 1 to $1,100 in Year 2. This would be a sales growth in absolute dollars of 10%. Now let's assume that inflation is 12%. The Year 2 sales can be adjusted for inflation by dividing the Year 2 sales of $1,100 by 1.12. This results in $982, which is a decrease of $18 from the Year 1 sales. This means there was an actual decline in sales from Year 1 to Year 2.
- **C.** The use of vertical analysis can measure how growth in one financial metric relates to another metric. This can also help highlight the impact of inflation.
- **D.** Inflation can have a significant impact on key ratios because of its effect on price and cost increases. As revenues and expenses increase over time during periods of inflation, ratios such as return on assets can show increases that are not necessarily due to the firm performing better, but rather because income is higher due to inflation.
- **E.** Inflation has been relatively low in the United States, Western European countries, and the United Kingdom during the past several years. The issues discussed so far have a minimal impact on these countries and the firms doing business there. However, in South America where there has been much higher inflation the impact will be considerable.

Summary

The rate of inflation will impact the income statement as well as the carrying cost of inventory. This means that key ratios, such as return on assets, will be impacted also. Horizontal analysis is useful to separate out real growth from increases simply due to inflation.

Changes in Accounting Treatment

After studying this lesson, you should be able to:

- Describe how to adjust financial statements for changes in accounting treatments (principles, estimates, and errors) and how these adjustments impact financial ratios (2.A.4.c).

Financial statement adjustments are required when there are changes in accounting principle, changes in accounting estimates, and changes in reporting entities. Each has a specifically described way of reporting these changes and providing year-to-year comparative statements. Errors will be corrected based on the time period that error is discovered. Keep in mind that errors are unintentional mistakes.

I. Accounting Changes

A. *Changes in Accounting Principles* require retrospective application. This requires the adjustment of prior-period financial statements to incorporate the effect of the new principle "as if" the new principle had been used in the prior periods. The beginning retained earnings of the earliest period presented is adjusted to reflect the effect of the change. It is not appropriate to record the cumulative effect of the change in the current year's net income. Changes in accounting principle will change the financial ratios, so the financial ratios need to be recalculated for any prior-period adjustments.

1. One type of change is the result of new guidance in the Accounting Standards Codification from the Financial Accounting Standards Board (FASB).

2. Another type of change is the result of management's election to change from one generally accepted accounting principle (GAAP) method to another, when a choice is allowed. A common example of this type of change is management electing to change from the last-in, first-out (LIFO) method of valuing inventories to the first-in, first-out (FIFO) method.

B. *Changes in Accounting Estimates* are changes in an estimated amount based on new information. This change is reported prospectively, meaning in the current period and future periods only. Prior-period statements are *not* restated for a change in estimate. Changes in accounting estimates will not change the financial ratios of prior periods, so no recalculation is needed.

1. One example of a change in accounting estimate is to change the bad-debt percentage from 4% down to 3%. This change would be made when economic conditions have improved.

2. Another example is to change the useful life of a depreciable asset from seven to ten years.

C. *Changes in Reporting Entities* occur when the financial statements represent a different reporting entity. This type of change is reported retrospectively, similar to how changes in accounting principle are reported. Prior-period financial statements are updated to reflect the financial information for the new reporting entity "as if" the new entity existed all along. The beginning retained earnings of the earliest period presented is adjusted to include the cumulative earnings differences. Changes in reporting entity will change the financial ratios, so the ratios will need to be recalculated for any prior-period adjustments.

1. Some examples include:

a. Presenting consolidated financial statements in place of individual ones

b. A change in subsidiaries through acquisition

c. A change to, or from, the equity method of accounting for an investment

II. Error Corrections. Errors are unintentional mistakes:

A. The discovery of a material error that was made in a prior period requires the correction of the error to reflect accurate retained earnings balances. This means that an error made that affected the reporting of net income or loss in a prior period be corrected by adjusting the beginning balance of retained earnings. The adjustment is made net of income taxes. Any prior-period financial statements presented for comparison purposes need to be restated to include the correction. The correction of an error will change the financial ratios for the prior-period financial statements that are presented, so the ratios need to be recalculated for any prior periods presented.

1. Some examples include:

a. Misapplication of US GAAP or IFRS

b. Journal entries made to the wrong general ledger accounts or for the wrong dollar amounts

c. Journal entries that should have been made, but were not

B. Errors have to be corrected when they are discovered. When an error is made and discovered in the current time period the correction is made at that time. This does not require any adjustments to be made other than the correction itself.

The following summarizes the changes in accounting treatment:

Type of Change:	**Accounting Principle**	**Reporting Entity**
Application	Retrospective	Retrospective
Required *Reporting* Adjustment	• Apply to the beginning of the earliest period presented in the financial statements • Cumulative effect to the beginning retained earnings	• Apply to the beginning of the earliest period presented in the financial statements • Cumulative effect to the beginning retained earnings
Example	• Newly issued Accounting Standards Codification (US ASC) • Change from one US generally accepted accounting principle to another US GAAP principle	• Presenting consolidated financial statements in place of individual ones • Changing specific subsidiaries that make up the group of entities presented • Changing the entities included in combined financial statements

Type of Change:	**Accounting Estimate**	**Errors**
Application	Prospective	Retrospective
Required *Reporting* Adjustment	• None	Restate and reissue financial statements if error is material to the prior period financials
Example	• Change to the useful lives of assets • Change in estimate of uncollectible receivables or warranty obligations	• Material error in a previously issued financial statements • Includes: errors in recognition, measurement, presentation, or disclosure from mathematical errors or mistakes in the application of generally accepted accounting principles (US GAAP)

Summary

When taking the CMA Exam it is important to know why accounting changes are made and how to report them. Accounting changes take the form of changes in accounting principle, changes in accounting estimates, and changes in reporting entities. Also important is when the discovery of the error is made as this will dictate how to correct it. Focus on the *why* and the *how* regarding these issues.

Book vs. Market Value and Accounting vs. Economic Profit

After studying this lesson, you should be able to:

- Distinguish between book value and market value; and distinguish between accounting profit and economic profit (2.A.4.d).

Focus on understanding the accounting terminology as it relates to book value and market value. These valuations are done for assets, liabilities, the firm, as well as per share of common stock. Accounting profit is different from economic profit for only one reason: the inclusion of opportunity costs in the economic profit calculation.

I. Book Value vs. Market Value

A. Book Value vs. Market Value of an Asset or Liability

1. The book value of an asset is the amount that the asset is reported at on the balance sheet. This value is the original cost of the depreciable asset minus the accumulated depreciation of that asset. These assets are usually fixed assets such as buildings and equipment.
2. The market value of an asset is the amount the asset can be sold for.
3. The book value of a liability is also the amount it is reported at on the balance sheet. Using bonds as an example, the book value of a bond is its face value plus the premium or minus the discount.
4. The market value of a liability, such as a bond, is the trading price of the bond on the open market. This value will be stated as a discount (< 100), face value (= 100), or a premium (> 100).

Practice Question

In October, Year 4, Allen Company exchanged a used packaging machine having a book value of $120,000 for a different type of new machine and paid a cash difference of $15,000. The market value of the used packaging machine was determined to be $140,000. In its income statement for the year ended December 31, Year 4, how much gain should Allen recognize on the exchange?

Answer

Book value	$120,000
Market value	$140,000
(Gain) / Loss	$(20,000)

The cost of the new packaging machine is:

Market value of old machine	$140,000
Plus additional cash paid	15,000
Total cost of new machine	$155,000

Explanatory journal entry:

New machine	$155,000	
Cash		$15,000
Old machine		120,000
Gain on exchange		20,000

This question assumes the asset transaction has commercial substance. This is defined as "causing a significant change in the future cash flows of the company". If there was no commercial substance, then the asset exchange transaction would be recorded at book value of $120,000.

What if Allen Company sold the old machine instead of exchanging it for the new one?

Continues...

In October, Year 4, Allen Company purchased a new packaging machine for $150,000 in cash. The old machine had a book value of $30,000 and can be sold for $25,000. In its income statement for the year ended December 31, Year 4, how much (gain) or loss should Allen recognize on the exchange?

Book value of old machine	$30,000
Cash received	$25,000
(Gain) / Loss	$5,000

Explanatory journal entry:

New machine	$150,000	
Loss on sale	5,000	
Cash		$125,000*
Old machine		30,000

*Cash calculation:

Cash paid for new machine	$150,000
Cash received for old machine	25,000
Net cash paid out	$125,000

B. Book Value of the Firm

1. This value is calculated as the difference between total assets and total liabilities plus any preferred stock. This means that the book value of the firm is equal to the firm's common stockholders' equity.

C. Book Value per Share of Common Stock

1. Book value per share of common stock is the ratio of common stockholders' equity to the number of common shares outstanding. This value usually has no relation to the liquidation value or its market value or price.
2. The market value of a share of common stock is the price that investors buy and sell the stock on the open market, if a publicly traded company.

   Fair value financial reporting standards are more prevalent than before. Statement of Financial Accounting Standards 159 permits the use of fair value reporting of certain financial instruments. It's important to recognize and consider the impact fair value reporting has on financial reporting and ratio analysis.

II. Accounting Profit vs. Economic Profit

A. Accounting profit and economic profit are both used to evaluate a company's performance.

1. Accounting profit uses accrual accounting based on generally accepted accounting principles (GAAP). Accounting expenses are also called explicit costs.
   a. Accounting Profit = Accounting Revenues – Accounting Expenses
2. *Economic profit* also includes opportunity costs, which are also called implicit costs. These costs are defined as the benefits given up by choosing one alternative instead of another.
   a. Economic Profit = Accounting Revenue – Accounting Expenses – Opportunity Costs

B. It is possible to have a positive accounting profit and a positive economic profit, or a negative meaning an economic loss. A positive economic profit means the better alternative was chosen. When there is an economic loss it could mean that a different alternative should have been chosen.

Summary

Many values are used in the world of accounting. The ability to distinguish between them and recognize why and when each is used is important to understanding the financial statements and interpreting ratios and other calculations. Book value, market value, face value, and others need to be clear in your mind. The concepts of accounting profit and economic profit are also important when performing analyses.

Quality of Earnings

After studying this lesson, you should be able to:

- Identify the determinants and indicators of earnings quality, and explain why they are important (2.A.4.e).

It is important to understand that reported earnings are managed by the company's executives through the decisions they make about accounting methods. There are other decisions they make that also impact reported earnings and can have long-term operational consequences. This is the decision of how and when to maintain assets. All of these factors impact the quality of the earnings reported.

I. Quality of Earnings

The income reported by a company can be managed by the executives through their decisions about the assumptions and accounting principles used. The choice of one assumption and/or principle over another can change the amount of the reported income. Because of this, investors are very interested in the quality of the earnings reported. A *high* quality of earnings is preferred because it is assumed to provide complete and transparent information.

A. Selection of Accounting Methods

1. Management can choose from a variety of generally accepted accounting principles to prepare the financial statements. They can select principles that are conservative or aggressive.
2. A conservative management approach is to choose the principles and methods that will not overstate earnings. During times of inflation, the last-in, first out (LIFO) inventory valuation method is considered to be conservative. The higher amount of cost of sales will lower the reported income. On the balance sheet, this results in a lower inventory balance. Compare this to choosing the first-in, first-out (FIFO) method that reports higher income due to lower cost of sales. The balance sheet will report a higher inventory balance that will result in a higher current ratio.
3. The aggressive approach is not favorably considered. Excessive conservatism can also negatively impact earnings quality.
4. The notes to the financial statements will tell users of the statements the principles and methods used by management in preparing the financials. Full and transparent information adds to a high quality of earnings.

B. Asset Maintenance and Lack of Investments for the Future

1. Management has discretion on the amount spent on certain expense items. One of the most common is spending on repairs and maintenance of equipment and buildings. In the short term this reduction in spending can increase reported income. However, this cannot continue for the long term because of the risk the equipment will break down and the buildings will fall into disrepair. When this happens, it usually will cost more to fix the equipment and could disrupt the day-to-day operations of the business, possibly resulting in decreased sales. There is a trade-off between spending now and spending later.
2. Another area of discretionary spending is on research and development. As seen with the lack of asset maintenance, it will improve income in the short term but could have devastating effects on future earnings. Not spending on research and development, especially in a high-technology or a pharmaceutical company, will mean a lack of new products to generate future sales.

C. Impact of Economic Forces

1. Changing economic conditions are not the result of management decisions, but instead the result of outside forces. The management team can reduce the impact of economic cycles and other external factors that influence earnings by the activities they engage in.

II. Earnings persistence is the idea that current earnings can predict future earnings. Analysts look for stable earnings from year to year as a sign of a well-managed company. When the earnings are stable, they *can be used* as a predictor of future earnings. It is difficult to use earnings that vary from year to year to predict future earnings.

A. The idea of sustainable income goes along with the concept of earnings persistence. Sustainable income starts with the actual reported income and then excludes any unusual items, or onetime events, that were reported in revenues, expenses, gains, and losses. Their exclusion brings the reported income amount to a number that can now be used to predict future results. Examples of unusual items would be discontinued operations. Items that are reported in other comprehensive income would also be excluded and usually are due to the format of the report. The key is that most of these items are nonrecurring.

Investors and analysts need to read and understand the impact of what is reported in the notes to the financial statement. This gives them insight into the earnings that are reported and how well the reported earnings can be used to predict future earnings.

B. The following partial income statement begins with Patel Company's income before tax. During this year, Patel operated a division at a loss up until the time that the division was sold. The income statement needs to report the gain or loss from the actual disposal (sale) of the division *and* the gain or loss from operating the division. Both of these amounts are presented below the *income from continuing operations*, which is an after tax amount. This means the loss from the disposal of the division and the loss from the operations of the division must be reported as after tax amounts. If there were no discontinued operations the line item labelled "Income from Continuing Operations" would have been labelled "Net Income".

Patel Company **Partial Year End Income Statement**		
Income Before Tax		$1,500,000
Income Tax Expense (30% tax rate)		450,000
Income from Continuing Operations		1,050,000
Discontinued Operations:		
Loss from Disposal of Division, Net of Tax $300,000 × (1 – 30%) = $210,000	$210,000	
Loss from Operations of Division, Net of Tax $500,000 × (1 – 30%) = $350,000	$350,000	560,000
Net Income		$490,000

To understand earnings persistence, and therefore the quality of earnings, to be able to predict future earnings, the income from continuing operations would be the amount to use in the analysis.

Summary
Earnings, that bottom-line number, is the focus of much attention. It is used to assess operating results, predict future earnings, as well as assess the impact of costs. The ideas of high-quality earnings and persistent earnings are valuable concepts to understand. It is also important to be able to identify the things that will impact both quality and persistence.

Section A Review Questions

aq.sales.revenues.0004_1710

1. Diamond, Inc. (Diamond) has a 5-year construction contract to build a canal for $600,000. The estimate of total costs is $400,000. Year 1 and Year 2 incurred costs are, respectively, $100,000 and $20,000. If the ultimate payment is assured, the cost estimate is reliable, and Diamond uses an input method of costs expended to recognize revenue, which of the following realized profits would Diamond report for Year 1 and Year 2, respectively?

   A. $0; $0
   B. $40,000; $40,000
   C. $50,000; $60,000
   D. $50,000; $10,000

aq.liquid.ratios.0006_1904

2. Cash that normally would have been used to pay the firm's accounts payable is used instead to pay off some of the firm's long-term debt. This will cause the firm's:

   A. current ratio to rise.
   B. payables turnover to rise.
   C. quick ratio to fall.
   D. cash conversion cycle to lengthen.

aq.horiz.financial.0001_1710

3. In which scenario would a horizontal analysis be the best choice?

   A. A bank wishes to compare progress among different companies.
   B. A company wishes to market its growth to potential stockholders.
   C. A vendor wishes to evaluate financial statement data in a given year.
   D. An investor wishes to evaluate financial statement data by expressing each item in a financial statement as a percentage of a base amount.

aq.solvency.rat.0004_1710

4. The following data pertain to Ruhl Corp.'s operations for the year ended December 31, Year 1:

Operating income	$800,000
Interest expense	100,000
Income before income tax	700,000
Income tax expense	210,000
Net income	$490,000

   The times interest earned ratio is:

   A. 8.0 to 1.
   B. 7.0 to 1.
   C. 2.1 to 1.
   D. 4.9 to 1.

aq.common.size.0001_1710

5. Which of the following would **not** be included on a balance sheet?

   A. Prepaid rent
   B. Retained earnings
   C. Cost of goods sold
   D. Accumulated depreciation

aq.cost.sales.0005_1710

6. Given the following information about a firm, what are the gross and operating profit margins, respectively?

- Net Sales = \$1,000
- Cost of Goods Sold = \$600
- Operating Expenses = \$200
- Interest Expenses = \$50
- Tax Rate = 34%

A. 20%; 15%
B. 40%; 20%
C. 40%; 10%
D. 20%; 10%

aq.inflation.fin.0003_1710

7. If the consumer price index is 135 and was 122 a year ago, the rate of inflation was:

A. 9.6%.
B. −9.6%.
C. 10.7%.
D. −10.7%.

aq.profit.market.0003_1710

8. Which ratio must be calculated using an amount external to a company's financial statements?

A. Current ratio
B. Times interest earned
C. Price-earnings ratio
D. Inventory turnover

aq.eff.ratios.0003_1710

9. Early in 20x7, Rivers Company switched to a JIT (just-in-time) inventory system. Financial information for the two most recent years are listed here.

	20x6	20x7
Net sales revenue	\$2,000,000	\$1,800,000
Cost of goods sold	800,000	788,000
Beginning inventory	200,000	130,000
Ending inventory	130,000	30,000

How many times did inventory turnover increase by as a result of the switch to the JIT system?

A. 2.1 times
B. 5.1 times
C. 20.1 times
D. 3.8 times

aq.eff.ratios.0008_1710

10. The cash conversion cycle is the:

A. length of time it takes to sell inventory.
B. length of time it takes the firm to pay the credit extended to it for purchases.
C. sum of the time it takes to sell inventory and the time it takes to collect accounts receivable.
D. sum of the time it takes to sell inventory and collect on accounts receivable, less the time it takes to pay for credit purchases.

aq.profit.eps.0006_1710

11. All else being equal, which of the following will help decrease a company's total debt-to-equity ratio?

A. Buying Treasury stock
B. Paying cash dividends to stockholders
C. Converting long-term debt to short-term debt
D. Lowering the dividend payout ratio

aq.profit.vertical.0006_1710

12. Four home decor stores have net income and average total assets as shown here.

	Net Income	Average Total Assets
Store 1	$186,000	$2,250,000
Store 2	$342,000	$4,700,000
Store 3	$4,900,000	$58,000,000
Store 4	$2,300,000	$29,500,000

Which store has the *lowest* return on assets?

A. Store 2
B. Store 1
C. Store 3
D. Store 4

aq.book.vs.market.0002_1710

13. The following data pertains to a machine owned by Showman Corporation:

- Historical cost: $35,000
- Accumulated depreciation: $30,000
- Showman uses straight-line depreciation
- 7 years is the useful life of the machine
- No estimated salvage value was used

The machine is being sold to another company for $4,000. What amount needs to be recognized as a gain/loss to Showman Company?

A. Loss of $5,000
B. Loss of $1,000
C. $0
D. Gain of $4,000

aq.forex.fluctuations.0003_1710

14. On November 15, Year 1, Celt, Inc., a U.S. company, ordered merchandise FOB shipping point from a German company for 200,000 Euros. The merchandise was shipped and invoiced to Celt on December 10, Year 1. Celt paid the invoice on January 10, Year 2. The spot rates for Euros on the respective dates are as shown here.

November 15, Year 1	$0.4955
December 10, Year 1	$0.4875
December 31, Year 1	$0.4675
January 10, Year 2	$0.4475

In Celt's December 31, Year 1, income statement, the foreign exchange gain is:

A. $9,600.
B. $4,000.
C. $8,000.
D. $1,600.

aq.op.lev.0010_1710

15. Which of the following is *likely* to encourage a firm to increase the amount of debt in its capital structure?

A. The firm's assets become less liquid.
B. The corporate tax rate increases.
C. The firm's earnings become more volatile.
D. The personal tax rate increases.

Section B: Corporate Finance

Topic 1. Risk and Return

Calculating Return

After studying this lesson, you should be able to:

- Calculate rates of return (2.B.1.a).
- Demonstrate an understanding of the relationship between risk and return (2.B.1.d).

Investment and financing decisions focus on the risk and return an investor or organization faces. The more risk posed by an investment, the more return investors will expect in return. This lesson reviews the concepts of risk and return, how to calculate rates of returns, and the different levels of risk investors may want to assume in their decision making.

I. Risk and Return

a. An investment's rate of return, or the amount of money earned, depends on the risk associated with that investment. Risk is the possibility of loss of value. When investments pose a greater risk, investors require a higher rate of return to compensate for bearing the greater risk. Thus, investors often face a tradeoff between risk and reward when evaluating investment options.

b. For example, an investor is likely to expect a greater return for an investment in an unproven, startup company than from an investment in a well-established company. The startup company could be considered a higher risk investment because it has a greater probability for loss of value while also having an increased potential for gain. The well-established company could be considered a lower risk investment because it has a lower probability for loss of value while also having a smaller potential for gain.

c. Risk is often measured by the uncertainty related to a specific investment. One measure of uncertainty is how variable the return on investment is. For example, the return on a savings account will typically not vary much over time. In contrast, the return on the stock of a technology firm could change from small returns and large returns over time.

Examples of Investment Risks

Low-Risk Investments, Lower Returns

Bank savings accounts, money market accounts, government bonds.

High-Risk Investments, Higher Returns

Corporate bonds, stock, mutual funds, exchange-traded funds, real estate.

Time and Risk

Investments that take more time require a higher rate of return. For example, the U.S. government issues T-bills, which have little to no default risk and mature within less than a year. The U.S. government also issues government bonds, which also have little to no default risk, but which mature in 10 to 30 years depending on the bond. The longer investment period on U.S. government bonds means they pay more than U.S. T-bills, even though both have similar default risk.

d. Investors are often categorized based on their risk preferences. A *risk-averse* investor is someone who tries to limit risk exposure and has lower expectations for returns. A *risk-neutral* investor is someone who is indifferent about trying to limit or seek out risk and has balanced expectations for returns. A *risk-seeking* investor is willing to take on greater risk exposure in the hopes of gaining greater returns.

Examples of Risk Tolerance

Suppose an investor will win $200 if a coin flip is heads and lose $100 if the coin flip is tails. The investor would expect to gain $50 from this opportunity. This is determined by multiplying the probability of each outcome by the expected outcome amount: (50% × $200) + (50% × − $100) = $50. If the investor could either take the coin flip or a certain amount of cash, then the investor would be:

Risk-Averse Investor

If an investor would accept an amount less than $50 instead of taking the coin flip, then the investor is risk averse. This investor will accept less than the expected value to avoid the risk of losing.

Risk-Neutral Investor

If the investor is willing to take $50 instead of the coin flip, then the investor is risk neutral.

Risk-Seeking Investor

If the investor would only take an amount greater than $50 instead of the coin flip, the investor is risk seeking. The investor would rather take his or her chances with the coin flip instead of accepting the expected value of the investment in hopes of getting a larger return.

II. Calculating Return

a. Returns are calculated as the amount received from an investment over a given period of time compared to the initial investment. The period of time over which an investment return is calculated can be any period of time, from one day to many years.

b. The rate of return considers two factors related to investor value: first, capital appreciation, which is an increase in the price of the asset over the investment period; and second, any income that the investment might pay out such as dividends or interest payments. The total return is the sum of the capital appreciation and income divided by the original investment amount.

Calculating Rate of Return

Return = (Capital Appreciation + Income) ÷ Investment

Or,

$\text{Return} = [(\text{Investment}_{t+1} - \text{Investment}_t) + \text{Income}] \div \text{Investment}_t$

c. Evaluating risk and possible returns is often done by measuring the returns on a given investment as a random variable with a probability distribution. The expected return is the measure of the investment's possible returns multiplied by the probability of each return occurring. This calculation is similar to the coin-flip example above, but likely with more possible outcomes and their associated probabilities.

d. Along with the expected return value, the standard deviation of returns is another useful statistical measure which shows the variability of returns in relation to the expected return value. The higher the standard deviation of returns, the greater the volatility of the investment's returns. Two investments could have the same expected return, but one could have a higher standard deviation than the other. The greater standard deviation means that the investment is riskier because the expected return value is less certain.

Volatility of Returns

The volatility of a return is measured as the standard deviation, which is the dispersion or range of potential outcomes for the return. The standard deviation is useful because it provides the probability that an outcome will take place.

A large standard deviation means that the return outcome could take place over a broad range of outcomes. Thus, the investment is more risky because the outcome is less certain.

A small standard deviation means that the return outcome is likely to take place closer to the expected value. Thus, the investment is less risky because the outcome is more certain.

Summary

Investors often face a tradeoff between risk and return. Typically, the greater the risk to the investor, then the greater the rate of return the investor receives. Risk is also often measured by the amount of uncertainty related to an investment. Investors are categorized according to their risk preferences: risk averse, risk neutral, or risk seeking. Calculating returns is done by looking at the amount received from an initial investment over time (this includes both the increase in the initial asset and the income paid out) compared to the initial investment. Two key measures are used in calculating risk and possible returns: expected return and standard deviations of returns.

Further Reading

Parrino, R., Kidwell, D., and Bates, T. (2017). *Fundamentals of Corporate Finance*, 4th Edition. Hoboken, NJ: John Wiley & Sons.

Types of Risk

After studying this lesson, you should be able to:

- Identify and demonstrate an understanding of systematic (market) risk and unsystematic (company) risk (2.B.1.b).
- Identify and demonstrate an understanding of credit risk, foreign exchange risk, interest rate risk, market risk, industry risk, and political risk (2.B.1.c).
- Distinguish between individual security risk and portfolio risk (2.B.1.e).
- Demonstrate an understanding of diversification (2.B.1.f).

Risk is a broad concept that can be broken down into several types of risk. Understanding what each type of risk means is important to evaluating how it can affect business operations and financial performance. This lesson reviews key terms and definitions for understanding risk in its various forms.

I. Unsystematic (Company) Risk and Systematic (Market) Risk

a. *Unsystematic risk* refers to the risk to an investor from owning stock in one particular company. It is a broad term that encompasses any type of risk that may affect the returns of a company's stock. Unsystematic risk comes from company-specific factors such as the company's financial leverage, effectiveness of business operations, strategy, sales cycle and seasonality, credit risk of customers, labor stoppages, and overall company management. Each company faces a unique set of risks. Investors can reduce their exposure to risk arising from one company by diversifying their equity investments across different industries and companies.

b. A diversified portfolio is one with a mix of investments from different industries. In a diversified portfolio, the chances of all investments performing very well or very poorly is small. Thus, a diversified portfolio can effectively eliminate unsystematic risk.

c. *Systematic risk* is the risk that arises from high-level economic cycles and political environments. Systematic risk is affected by macroeconomic factors such as interest rates, inflation, growth rates of gross domestic product (GDP), currency exchange rates, government rules and regulations, and public policies. Investors cannot diversify away systematic risk. Systematic risk is often called nondiversifiable or market risk. A measure of systematic risk is called *beta*, which measures how correlated an individual stock's returns are with the broader market returns.

II. Portfolio Risk

a. When evaluating a single investment, risk is often measured as the standard deviation of returns. However, investors normally invest in a variety or portfolio of assets. In order to measure the risk of assets in a diversified portfolio, other measures than standard deviation are used. In a diversified portfolio, the only risk of an individual asset comes from systematic risk. This is measured as the correlation between returns on an individual asset and the returns of the broader stock market.

b. Assets whose stock prices move in the same direction are said to have a positive correlation. Stocks in the same industry will generally move in the same direction and have a positive correlation. This happens because the macroeconomic factors related to systematic risk will typically affect companies in the same industry in similar ways. In contrast, stocks in very different industries, such as a utility stock and a technology stock, could move in opposite directions and have a negative correlation.

c. Correlation is measured as a number between –1 and +1. The closer the correlation is to –1 or +1, the stronger the relationship between the two variables. A +1 correlation means the two variables move in the same direction and in an exact measurable amount. A –1 correlation means the two variables move in the opposite direction and in an exact measurable amount. A zero correlation means there is no linear relationship between the two variables.

d. Diversified portfolios are typically less risky for a given level of expected returns than an individual asset. This reduction in risk comes from eliminating the unsystematic risk associated with an individual asset.

III. Types of Risk

a. *Credit risk or default risk*—The risk that a borrower will not repay the investor as promised. When there is a greater probability that a borrower will default, the lender will charge a higher interest rate to compensate for the higher risk.

b. *Interest rate risk*—The risk that market interest rates will vary and impact the value of interest-bearing securities, such as bonds.

c. *Foreign exchange risk or currency risk*—The risk that economic value will be lost due to fluctuations in exchange rates. Companies exporting goods and services benefit when their home currency weakens relative to a foreign currency. More goods and services will be purchased by those using a foreign currency because the goods and services are relatively less expensive. In contrast, companies importing goods and services benefit when their home currency strengthens relative to a foreign currency because they can acquire the goods and services for relatively less money.

d. *Industry risk*—The risk associated with the factors specific to a given industry. For example, agricultural companies are likely to face the risk of a drought negatively affecting their performance, whereas financial companies would not be as affected by the risk of a drought.

e. *Political risk*—The risk that political influence and decisions may affect the profitability and effectiveness of an organization. For example, environmental regulations may affect the operations and costs of chemical producers and manufacturing firms.

Summary

There are many types of risk that an organization may face every day. Understanding risk in its various forms is important to evaluating how it can affect an organization. Unsystematic risk (or company risk) is related to company-specific factors while systematic risk (or market risk) is related to macroeconomic factors. Portfolio risk is related to the diversity or lack of diversity of assets within a particular portfolio. Other types of risk to be familiar with are credit or default risk, interest rate risk, foreign exchange or currency risk, industry risk, and political risk.

Further Reading

Parrino, R., Kidwell, D., and Bates, T. (2017). *Fundamentals of Corporate Finance*, 4th Edition. Hoboken, NJ: John Wiley & Sons.

Capital Asset Pricing Model

After studying this lesson, you should be able to:

- Define beta and explain how a change in beta impacts a security's price (2.B.1.g).
- Demonstrate an understanding of the Capital Asset Pricing Model (CAPM) and calculate the expected risk-adjusted returns using CAPM (2.B.1.h).

The Capital Asset Pricing Model (CAPM) is a common framework used to understand the relation between risk and expected return. The model is often used to measure a firm's cost of equity capital. This lesson reviews the components of CAPM and how companies use it.

I. Capital Asset Pricing Model (CAPM)

a. The Capital Asset Pricing Model (CAPM) describes the relationship between risk and expected return. It is used to determine how much return investors require for an investment given its systematic risk (beta). This is often referred to as the cost of equity capital. CAPM measures an investment's rate of return as a function of three market conditions:

i. Risk-free rate of return (R_f)

ii. Market risk premium ($R_m - R_f$)

iii. Beta (β) of the investment, which measures the investment's sensitivity to changes in the market

b. The risk-free rate typically refers to the current rate of return on a risk-free security such as U.S. Treasury bill.

c. The market rate of return is expected return of the broader stock market such as the S&P 500 or Dow Jones Industrial Average. It is used to calculate a market risk premium ($R_m - R_f$). The "premium" refers to the amount of return expected from the market above and beyond the return that could be earned from a risk-free security. The premium is the additional return to compensate investors for bearing greater risk.

d. Beta indicates how much, and in what direction, a rational investor expects an investment to move given a 1% change in the market.

Comparing Betas

Beta (β) = 0: A beta of zero indicates a fixed return with no sensitivity to market changes, in other words, no systematic risk. An example of a security with a zero beta is U.S. T-bills, whose value does not change based on stock market changes.

Beta (β) > 1: A beta greater than 1 indicates more systematic risk than the market. A stock with a beta of 1.5 is expected to increase 1.5% if the market increases 1.0%. Technology stocks often have a beta greater than 1.

Beta (β) < 1: A beta less than 1 indicates less systematic risk than the market. A stock with a beta of 0.5 is expected to increase 0.5% if the market increases 1.0%. Utility companies often have a beta less than 1.

Beta (β) = 1: A beta equal to 1 indicates the same systematic risk as the market. A stock with a beta of 1.0 is expected to increase 1.0% if the market increases 1.0%. An index fund that tracks the S&P 500 would have a beta close to 1.0.

e. The CAPM is used to calculate the expected return on an investment, given the level of market risk and sensitivity of the investment relative to the market. The equation for the CAPM is:

$$K_e = R_f + \beta(R_m - R_f)$$

where:

i. K_e = Investment's required rate of return or Cost of Equity Capital

ii. R_f = Risk-free rate

iii. R_m = Market rate of return

iv. β = systematic risk or the investment's sensitivity to changes in market prices.

Example of CAPM

Consider the following information:

$R_f = 4\%$

$R_m = 12\%$

$\beta = 1.5$

Plugging these into the CAPM results in an expected return of:

$$K_e = R_f + \beta(R_m - R_f)$$

$$16\% = 4\% + 1.5 \times (12\% - 4\%) = 4\% + 12\%$$

Summary
The relationship between risk and expected return is described by the Capital Asset Pricing Model (CAPM) and is used to determine how much return investors require for a particular investment. This model uses three factors (risk-free rate of return, market rate of return risk premium, and beta of the investment) to measure an investment's rate of return. The CAPM equation is: $K_e = R_f + \beta(R_m - R_f)$.

Further Reading
Parrino, R., Kidwell, D., and Bates, T. (2017). *Fundamentals of Corporate Finance*, 4th Edition. Hoboken, NJ: John Wiley & Sons.

Topic 2. Long-Term Financial Management

Term Structure of Interest Rates

After studying this lesson, you should be able to:

- Describe the term structure of interest rates and explain why it changes over time (2.B.2.a).
- Demonstrate an understanding of the relationship among inflation, interest rates, and the prices of financial instruments (2.B.2.p).

This lesson reviews the structure of interest rates for debt instruments. It also discusses the various risk characteristics of debt instruments that can affect how the debt instrument is priced.

I. Term Structure of Interest Rates

a. A key feature of debt-based financial instruments, such as bonds, mortgages, or business loans, is how the interest rate is structured. Each financial instrument will have a unique structure that is negotiated between the debtholder and the debt issuer. Furthermore, economic factors will influence the interest rate of each debt instrument.

b. The *term structure of interest rates* refers to the relationship between the time until the principal balance of the debt instrument is due and how much the debt instrument pays in interest. *Term to maturity* is the amount of time, whereas *yield to maturity* is the interest rate being paid. This relationship is often shown graphically with a *yield curve.*

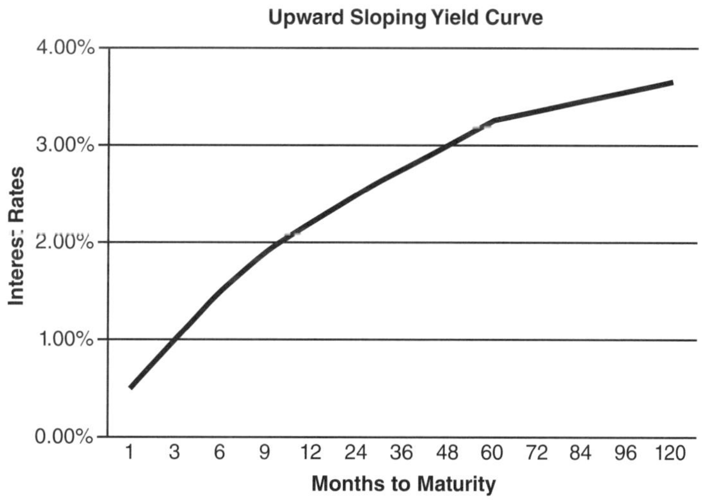

c. In general, yield curves have an upward slope, which means that longer-term securities have a higher yield than shorter-term securities. This is a result of time being a risk factor such that debt instruments whose term to maturity is more distant have higher risk, or more uncertainty about the future.

d. It is possible to have a downward-sloping yield curve, meaning that shorter-term securities have a higher yield than longer-term securities. While not as common, downward-sloping yield curves are often a sign that an economy is going into a recession.

e. There are three common factors that influence both the shape and level of yield curves. These factors include: the real rate of interest, the expected rate of inflation, and the interest rate risk.

  i. *Real rate of interest* is the base interest rate in the economy. It affects the level, but not the slope, of the yield curve because it is not affected by the term to maturity. It is affected by individuals' preferences for saving versus spending, with higher rates when the economy is growing and lower rates when the economy is receding.

  ii. *Expected rate of inflation* is the belief about whether prices will be increasing in the future and by how much. It affects the slope of the yield curve.

  iii. *Interest rate risk* is the uncertainty about future bond prices that arises from future interest rates being unpredictable. Bond prices move inversely with interest rates, meaning that if interest rates go up, bond prices go down. It affects the shape of the yield curve.

Summary
The structure of the interest rate is a key feature in debt-based financial instruments. The term structure of interest rates is the relationship between the term to maturity and the yield to maturity of the debt instrument. This relationship can be shown graphically through the yield curve, which generally has an upward slope. The shape and level of yield curves are influenced by the real rate of interest, the expected rate of inflation, and the interest rate risk.

Further Reading
Parrino, R., Kidwell, D., and Bates, T. (2017). *Fundamentals of Corporate Finance*, 4th Edition. Hoboken, NJ: John Wiley & Sons.

Types of Financial Instruments: Bonds

After studying this lesson, you should be able to:

- Identify and describe the basic features of a bond such as maturity, par value, coupon rate, provisions for redeeming, conversion provisions, covenants, options granted to the issuer or investor, indentures, and restrictions (2.B.2.c).
- Identify and evaluate debt issuance or refinancing strategies (2.B.2.d).
- Demonstrate an understanding of duration as a measure of bond interest rate sensitivity (2.B.2.f).

Bonds are a commonly used debt instrument, though they can vary greatly in their features. This lesson reviews the basic features of bonds and how companies use them as part of their debt structure.

I. Features of Bonds

a. Bonds are the primary form of long-term debt financing for government institutions and corporations. Bonds can be understood as a contractual obligation to repay a principal amount plus interest over time. The issuer of a bond agrees to repay the principal amount, referred to as the *face value* or *par value* of the bond, at a future date. Many bonds also require the payment of periodic interest payments over the life of the bond, referred to as the *coupon rate*.

b. An *indenture* is the contract made between a bondholder and bond issuer. The indenture delineates the key features of a bond such as the maturity date, when interest payments are to be made, how interest will be calculated, and other features. The other features could specify whether the bond is *callable*—the bond issuer can repay the bond earlier than the maturity date—or *convertible*—exchanges debt-obligations for equity shares in a company.

c. Bonds can also have *covenants*, which place restrictions on activities of a bond issuer. Covenants are used to help protect the financial interest of bondholders. *Negative or restrictive covenants* limit the bond issuer from certain activities, whereas *positive or affirmative covenants* require the bond issuer to meet specific requirements.

d. Bonds can be backed by *collateral*, which is the property or asset the bond issuer will forfeit to the bondholder if the bond issuer can no longer repay the debt. Some bonds require that a *sinking fund* be used which requires the bond issuer to make periodic payments in order to repay the bond principal.

e. Bonds can vary greatly in their duration. Short-term bonds typically have a maturity date 2 to 5 years into the future. Medium or intermediate-term bonds have a maturity date 5 to 10 years into the future. Long-term bonds have a maturity date more than 10 years into the future.

II. Bond Ratings

a. Bonds are often rated by credit rating agencies. The ratings help investors assess the riskiness of bonds. Moody's, S&P, and Fitch ratings are the three major rating agencies for bonds. They provide a grade or rating to a bond which indicates the credit quality of the bond issuer.

b. Highly rated bonds are known as investment-grade bonds. These bonds are perceived to be safer because the bond issuer is highly likely to be able to pay interest payments and ultimately repay the bond principal. An example of the most highly rated bond, an AAA rating, is U.S. Treasury bonds. Higher rated bonds have lower interest rates due to the lower amount of default risk.

c. Low-rated bonds are known as junk bonds. These bonds have a higher default risk. Junk bonds have higher interest rates to compensate investors for the increased likelihood that the bond issuer may not be able to make interest payments or repay the bond principal.

d. Bond ratings refer to a specific bond issuance. A single company may have several bond issuances, each of which will receive a bond rating. While a single company's bonds are likely to be similarly rated, they may receive different ratings based on the bonds' characteristics, such as time to maturity and coupon rate.

e. Credit rating agencies assess the credit quality of bonds based on factors such as the company's financial position, the future financial outlook, and any collateral securing a bond. If a company has positive cash flows and prospects of continued favorable financial performance, the bonds will receive a higher rating. If a bond is backed by collateral, it lowers the riskiness of the bond because the bondholder could seize the collateral if needed.

f. A bond rating can change over the lifetime of the bond. As circumstances change for a company, either favorably or unfavorably, the rating agencies may update their ratings. Macroeconomic factors may also come into play if they affect a company's ability to repay its debt.

g. Bond rating example: see exhibit below.

Corporate Bond Rating Systems

Explanation	Moody's	Standard & Poor's/ Fitch	Default Risk Premium	Regulatory Designation
Best quality, smallest degree of risk	Aaa	AAA		
High quality, slightly more long-term risk than top rating	Aa	AA		
Upper-medium grade, possible impairment in the future	A	A	Lowest	Investment Grade
Medium grade, lacks outstanding investment characteristics	Baa	BBB		
Speculative, protection may be very moderate	Ba	BB	Highest	Noninvestment Grade
Very speculative, may have small assurance of interest and principal payments	B	B		
Issues in poor standing, may be in default	Caa	CCC		
Speculative to a high degree, with marked shortcomings	Ca	CC		
Lowest quality, poor prospects of attaining real investment standing	C	C		

Moody's has a slightly different notation in its ratings of corporate bonds than do Standard & Poor's and Fitch, but the interpretation is the same. Bonds with the highest credit standing are rated Aaa (or AAA) and have the lowest default risk. The credit rating declines as the default risk of the bond increases.

Source: Parrino, R., Kidwell, D., and Bates, T. (2015). *Fundamentals of Corporate Finance*, 3rd Edition. Hoboken, NJ: John Wiley & Sons, p. 256. ISBN: 978-1-118-84589-9.

III. Bond Yields

a. Bonds pay a stated interest rate, or *coupon rate*. However, the value of a bond can change daily with interest rate fluctuations in the market.

b. Bonds are bought and sold in the market. Often they are sold at a *discount* or *premium* to the stated face value of the bond. While the structure and amounts of the bond's interest and principal payments will not change, investors can adjust the value at which they sell the bond to make its effective interest rate different. Bonds sold above par value are *premium* bonds, which takes place when the market interest rate is below the coupon rate of the bond. In contrast, bonds sold below par value are *discount* bonds, which takes place when the market interest rate is above the coupon rate.

c. *Yield to maturity* is the discount rate at which the bond's principal and interest payments are equal to the price of the bond. Bonds are sold at a discount or premium in order to create a desired yield to maturity.

IV. Debt Issuance

a. When companies issue debt, the debt may be either *secured* or *unsecured* debt. A *secured* bond means that the principal is backed by the companies' assets as collateral. For example, a bond to finance a new factory may have the factory itself as collateral. If the company cannot repay the debt, the debt holder has the right to seize ownership of the factory. An *unsecured* bond does not have collateral, but rather is simply backed by the company's promise to repay the debt. In the event of default on unsecured debt, the only recourse available to the debt holder is legal action.

b. In the event of a company's bankruptcy, the company's debt is ranked in order to determine who will be paid first. Secured debtholders are paid first from the collateral backing the loans they made. If the company has any remaining funds, either from asset holdings or liquidation of assets, then unsecured debtholders are paid alongside any other general creditors that the company may have.

c. Organizations have the ability to refinance debt by paying off existing debt and issuing new debt. When determining whether to refinance debt, organizations should consider the following factors:

i. *Credit rating*—Credit ratings change over time. If a company's credit rating has improved, it may be able to issue debt at lower interest rates.

ii. *Macroeconomic conditions*—Interest rates change in the global economy in expansionary and recessionary periods. If market interest rates have changed, a company may be able to refinance at lower interest rates than its current debt is at.

iii. *Cash position*—When a company needs cash for a project, investment, or general expenses, it can raise money in various ways, including issuing debt, issuing equity (stock ownership), or internally generated funds (retained earnings). Companies often chose to use debt-financing when they can obtain favorable interest rates and loan conditions.

iv. *Covenants*—Existing covenants on a company's debt may have restrictions on the company's debt-to-assets and debt-to-equity ratios. These restrictions may prevent the amount which a company can take on in additional debt.

v. *Earnings*—Companies must make money to repay debt. Income coverage ratios, such as the times interest earned ratio, indicate the company's ability to pay interest expense from operating income.

vi. *Risk*—Companies vary in their risk appetite for debt. Having a highly leveraged company, that is, one with a high amount of debt compared to equity, can be financially rewarding inasmuch as the debt obligations can be met. However, this can also pose a high amount of default risk, and ultimately, bankruptcy, if the company cannot generate cash flow to make payments.

Summary

Bonds are a contractual obligation to repay a principal amount plus interest over time and are a primary form of long-term debt financing for government institutions and corporations. Bonds have specific covenants, can be backed by collateral, and vary greatly in duration. Bond ratings help investors assess the riskiness of bonds. They pay a stated interest rate but can be sold at a premium or a discount to the stated face value of the bond. When issuing debt, a company may issue either secured or unsecured debt.

Further Reading

Parrino, R., Kidwell, D., and Bates, T. (2017). *Fundamentals of Corporate Finance*, 4th Edition. Hoboken, NJ: John Wiley & Sons.

Types of Financial Instruments: Stock

After studying this lesson, you should be able to:

- Define and identify the characteristics of common stock and preferred stock (2.B.2.b).

This lesson reviews two types of equity capital: common stock and preferred stock. Stock ownership represents a major avenue by which companies raise funds for the business. Stock ownership and exchanging ownership also plays a large role in the economy in the form of stock markets.

I. Common Stock

a. Ownership shares in a company are referred to as *equity* or *stock*. Common stock is the most important type of stock. Common stockholders have ownership rights which include:

i. *Right to vote*—Common stockholders can vote on corporate matters such as election of board of directors, approving mergers or acquisitions, and approval of executive compensation plans.

ii. *Preemptive right*—If a company issues additional shares to raise capital, current common stockholders are allowed to purchase new shares proportional to the shares they currently own. This allows owners to maintain the same ownership percentage.

iii. *Dividends*—Common stockholders have the right to receive dividends, if they are paid. Unlike bondholders who hold a contractual obligation to receive interest payments, common stockholders do not have a contractual right for dividends to be paid. In other words, companies do not have to pay dividends.

iv. *Residual claim*—In the event a company is liquidated, the common stockholders have the right to all remaining assets after creditors and preferred stockholders have been paid.

b. The *common stock account* on the balance sheet is comprised of two accounts. The first is the *Common Stock* account, which is listed at the par value of the stock issued. The par value is typically listed as $1 and has nothing to do with the actual amount per share at which the stock was issued. The *Additional Paid-in Capital* account is the amount of money received from issuing stock above and beyond the par value.

c. Stock may be purchased in the primary or secondary capital market. The primary market, also known as an initial public offering (IPO), refers to the first time at which a company offers ownership in the company to the general public through stock exchanges. The company receives the cash proceeds from an IPO. The secondary market refers to the buying and selling of a company's stock on a stock exchange. The company is not directly involved and does not receive any proceeds from secondary market exchanges. Rather, the ownership shares and money are exchanged between investors.

II. Preferred Stock

a. Preferred stock is a unique financial instrument that has characteristics of both common stock and debt. Preferred stock is like debt because it has a fixed dividend amount that does not change with the company's earnings. However, as with common stock, companies are not required to pay a preferred stock dividend in a given financial period.

b. That being said, preferred stock dividends are often cumulative, which means that if a dividend was skipped, it must be made up in the future before dividends can be paid to common stockholders.

i. *Example*—Consider a preferred stock with cumulative dividends that pays a dividend of $10/share per year. If the company has not paid the dividend in the last two years, then the company must pay preferred stockholders $20/share ($10 × 2 years) before it can pay a common stock dividend.

c. Preferred stockholders do not have voting rights unless certain pre-specified events take place. For example, if a company defaults on a loan or cannot pay a preferred stock dividend, this may trigger voting rights for preferred stockholders.

d. In the event of a liquidation, preferred stockholders are paid after bondholders but before common stockholders.

e. Preferred stock often has previsions to convert shares of preferred stock into shares of common stock. The terms of conversions are established at the initial offering of the preferred stock.

Summary

Ownership shares in a company are referred to as equity or stock. Common stock has specific features such as right to vote, preemptive right, no contractual right to dividends, and residual claim in the event of liquidation. Stocks can be purchased in the primary market (initial public offering) and in the secondary market (the stock market). Preferred stock is unique as it has characteristics of both common stock (no requirement to pay dividends in a given financial period) and debt (fixed dividend amount that does not change with earnings).

Further Reading

Parrino, R., Kidwell, D., and Bates, T. (2017). *Fundamentals of Corporate Finance*, 4th Edition. Hoboken, NJ: John Wiley & Sons.

Other Financial Instruments

After studying this lesson, you should be able to:

- Define and demonstrate an understanding of derivatives and their uses (2.B.2.h).
- Identify and describe the basic features of futures and forwards (2.B.2.i).
- Distinguish a long position from a short position (2.B.2.j).
- Define options and distinguish between a call and a put by identifying the characteristics of each (2.B.2.k).
- Define exercise price, strike price, option premium, and intrinsic value (2.B.2.l).
- Define interest rate and foreign currency swaps (2.B.2.n).
- Define and identify characteristics of other sources of long-term financing, such as leases, convertible securities, and warrants (2.B.2.o).
- Describe lease financing, explain its benefits and disadvantages, and calculate the net advantage to leasing using discounted cash flow concepts (2.B.3.g).

I. Options

a. Options are the most common and best-understood derivatives, with the value of the option deriving from another item, such as a stock price or a commodity price. An option is a contract between parties where the option buyer has the right, but not the obligation, to buy or sell a given amount of the underlying asset. The buyer of an option pays the seller or writer of an option a premium or fee in order to buy the right to exercise the contractual agreement at a future date.

b. Important terms and definitions for understanding options:

i. The *underlying asset* of an option is the asset upon which the value of the option is based. The underlying asset may be tangible (such as a building or stock) or intangible (such as an interest rate or the value of a stock index).

ii. A *call option* allows the owner to buy the underlying asset at a specified price.

iii. A *put option* allows the owner to sell the underlying asset at a specified price.

iv. A *short position* is taken when an investor expects the price of an underlying asset to fall.

v. A *long position* is taken when an investor expects the price of an underlying asset to rise.

vi. The *strike (or exercise) price* is the fixed value at which the owner can buy or sell the underlying asset.

vii. *Exercise date* is the last day on which the buyer can exercise the option. An *American option* contract allows the owner to exercise the option at any time during the option period. In contrast, a *European option* is allowed to be exercised only on the maturity date. Most options that are traded on exchanges are American options.

viii. *In the money* means that an owner of an option will benefit from exercising the option.

ix. *Out of the money* means that an owner of an option will not benefit from exercising the option.

Example of a Call Option

Consider an investor who paid a $3 premium for a stock call option. If the strike price is $30, then the value of the option would be as follows:

- If the stock is at $30, the stock price is at the money. The option holder does not gain or lose value by exercising the option. The net loss to the investor is $3.
- If the stock is at $35, the option holder exercises the option because it is in the money and gains $5. The net gain to the investor is $2.
- If the stock is at $20, the option holder does not exercise the option because it is out of the money. The option holder loses the $3 premium but does not lose the $10 if he or she exercised the option to buy at $30.

Example of a Put Option

Consider an investor who paid a $3 premium for stock put option. If the strike price is $30, then the value of the option would be as follows:

- If the stock is at $30, the stock price is at the money. The option holder does not gain or lose value by exercising the option. The net loss to the investor is $3.
- If the stock is at $35, the option holder does not exercise the put option because it is out of the money. The net loss to the investor is $3.
- If the stock is at $20, the option holder exercises the put option because it is in the money. The option holder will gain $10 from exercising the option and selling at $30 instead of the market price of $20. The net gain to the investor is $7.

II. Forwards and Futures

a. A *forward contract* between two parties requires one party to buy or sell a specified asset on a specified day at a predetermined price. Unlike options where a premium is paid for the option contract, no initial payment is made in a forward contract upon signing the contract. A forward contract legally obligates the parties to act according to contract terms.

b. Much like an option, the *underlying asset* may be tangible (stock, currency, commodity) or intangible (interest rate, stock market index). The *delivery price* is the contractually obligated price in the contract. Delivery of the underlying asset occurs on the contract's *delivery date.*

c. The party who will buy the underlying asset under contract terms is considered to have a long position. The party who will deliver the underlying asset is considered to have a short position. The payoff structure for a forward contract depends on the underlying asset's change in value. The buyer of the underlying asset gains value when the underlying asset's price rises and loses value when the underlying asset's price falls. Thus, companies who plan to buy an asset in the future and believe that the asset's price could increase can reduce their costs by entering into a forward contract to lock in the asset's price.

d. A *futures contract* is similar to a forward contract, but the parties execute the contract differently. Forward contracts are agreements made directly between two parties. Futures contracts, on the other hand, are agreements actively traded on organized exchanges. Thus, the counterparty is generally unknown in a futures contract.

e. Futures contracts usually do not carry the expectation of actual delivery of a physical asset, but rather parties exchange the monetary value of the contract. This usually takes place as a daily settling up of the monetary values among the parties. This money is not paid directly to the parties but is paid through an exchange-regulated clearing house.

Example of a Forward Contract

Many firms use forward contracts to remove the volatility and risk associated with changes in commodity prices. Consider an airline firm that wants to fix the price of its jet fuel. In order to do so, it enters a 90-day forward contract with a jet fuel supplier on June 1. On September 1, the supplier will deliver the fuel to the airline at the price specified in the contract. The value of the forward contract is as follows:

- If the jet fuel price rises between June 1 and September 1, the airline gains value and the supplier loses value because the supplier must deliver the fuel to the airline at the forward contract price.
- If the jet fuel price falls between June 1 and September 1, the airline loses value and the supplier gains value. The airline would have to pay a higher price than the market price.

III. Swaps

a. A *swap* is an agreement between two parties to exchange future cash payments related to underlying assets.

b. Examples of types of commonly used swaps:

i. *Currency swap* is an agreement to exchange cash in one currency for cash in another currency at some future date.

ii. *Interest rate swap* is an agreement to exchange cash flows from one type of interest rate structure for cash flows in another type of interest structure. The most common interest rate swap is to swap cash flows from a variable rate of interest for cash flows of a fixed rate of interest. Interest rate swaps are extremely customized between parties and can be based on many different interest rates.

iii. A *credit default swap* requires one party to indemnify (or reimburse) the other party in the event of default by a third party. Credit default swaps act similar to insurance. For example, two banks may enter into a credit default swap agreement for one of Bank A's debtors. Bank A would make payments to Bank B as a premium for the credit default swap. If the debtor defaults, then Bank B would pay Bank A the amount of the lost value. One of the most well-known credit default swaps is for mortgage-backed securities.

IV. Leases

a. A *lease* can be thought of like a rental agreement. A *lessee* pays the owner of an asset, the *lessor*, for the right to use the asset for a specified period. Leases are a very common form of financing used by most firms. Firms lease assets such as buildings, office space, furniture, computers, copy machines, vehicles, and equipment.

b. Firms choose to lease assets because it can be less expensive than purchasing the asset outright. Leases can also reduce information and transaction costs associated with buying and selling assets. Many lease agreements contain a termination clause that allows the lessee to terminate the contract with 60 to 90 days' notice. This provision provides the lessee with greater operational flexibility.

c. Financial accounting rules (GAAP) distinguish between two types of leases:

i. *Operating Lease*—These leases are thought of as rentals.

ii. *Finance Lease*—While termed a lease, these arrangements are more like purchases. A lease is considered to be a finance lease if any of the following conditions are true:

1. The lease transfers ownership of the asset to the lessee at the end of the lease term.

2. The lease contains a bargain purchase option, that is, an option to buy the asset at a low price below the expected market value of the asset.

3. The lease term is for a major part of the remaining economic life of the underlying asset. The FASB does not provide a rule, but rather a guideline of the lease term being 75% of the estimated useful life of the asset.

4. The present value of the minimum lease payments exceeds substantially all of the fair value of the underlying asset. The FASB does not provide a rule, but rather a guideline of 90% of the fair market value of the asset.

5. The underlying asset is a specialized asset for the lessee that is not expected to have any alternative future use to the lessor at the end of the lease term.

iii. For both types of leases, the lessee records the lease as a right-of-use asset and corresponding liability on its balance sheet. However, the treatment of the amortization of the asset and liability will differ slightly between the two lease types.

d. Conflicts can arise between lessees and lessors. For example, the lessee may use the asset more intensely than the lessor desires or may not maintain the asset as needed. Lessors can protect themselves against these conflicts by charging premiums for assets known to be treated poorly, charge a deposit that will not be returned until the asset is inspected, or place explicit restrictions on the asset's use.

e. While there are nonfinancial reasons to lease or buy an asset, a useful tool in evaluating the decision to lease or buy is doing a net present value (NPV) calculation. The comparison made is the NPV of the incremental cash flows from leasing compared to current purchase price of the asset.

Example of an (Operating) Lease or Purchase Decision

Consider a firm that needs a machine for its production process. The firm can purchase the machine outright for $25,000. Alternatively, the firm can lease the machine for $6,000 for five years. Assume that none of the five conditions for a finance lease is met, so the firm will record the lease as an operating lease. Also, assume that if the machine is purchased, the firm will use straight-line depreciation with no salvage value. If the firm has a 25% marginal tax rate and a 10% cost of capital, should the firm purchase or lease the machine?

Cash Flows if Leased

The annual after-tax cash flows are $4,500 = $6,000 × (1 – 25%).

Using a Present Value Table, the present value annuity factor for 5 years at 10% is 3.7908[1].

The Net Present Value of the lease payments is $17,058.60.

Cash Flows if Purchased

The initial cash outflow is $25,000. The firm will receive a tax benefit from depreciation on the machine. The annual cash benefit from the depreciation expense is $1,250 ([$25,000 ÷ 5 years] × 25% marginal tax rate)

Using a Present Value Table, the present value annuity factor for 5 years at 10% is 3.7908[2]. Thus, the net present value of the tax benefit is $4,738.50.

The Net Present Value of purchasing taking into account the tax-benefit from depreciation is $20,261.50 ($25,000 – $4,738.50).

The firm will incur a lower net present value cost by leasing the machine ($17,058.60) than it would by purchasing the machine ($20,261.50).

[1] Solutions are computed using present value tables. Due to rounding errors, the solution may be slightly different if a calculator is used.

[2] Solutions are computed using present value tables. Due to rounding errors, the solution may be slightly different if a calculator is used.

V. Warrants

a. Warrants are long-term options for the holder to purchase stock directly from the issuing corporation. Warrants are similar to options, but warrants are issued by a company, whereas options are issued on stock exchanges. A warrant contract allows the holder to purchase stock at a specified price, quantity, and future time. If the stock price rises beyond the price in the warrant contract, holders will earn value by exercising the warrants.

Summary

There are various financial instruments used by companies and investors besides stock and bonds. Options are a derivative that derive their value from another item such as a stock price or commodity price. A forward contract is between two parties where one party is required to buy or sell a specified asset on a specified day. A futures contract is similar to a forward contract but is actively traded on organized exchanges and does not usually include physical assets. A swap is an agreement to exchange future cash payments related to underlying assets. Leases are contracts where an asset's owner grants a second party use of the asset in exchange for payments. Leases come in two forms: operating and finance. Finally, warrants are long-term options for the holder to purchase stock.

Further Reading

Parrino, R., Kidwell, D., and Bates, T. (2017). *Fundamentals of Corporate Finance*, 4th Edition. Hoboken, NJ: John Wiley & Sons.

Taxes and Capital Structure

After studying this lesson, you should be able to:

- Explain how income taxes impact financing decisions (2.B.2.g).
- Demonstrate an understanding of how income taxes impact capital structure and capital investment decisions (2.B.2.v).

Decisions about capital structure are affected by taxes. This lesson reviews the effect of taxes on financing and capital investment decisions.

I. Effect of Taxes on Capital Structure Decisions

a. *Capital structure* is the mix of debt and equity that a company uses to finance its activities. Taxes can play a significant role in the decision process of whether to finance projects or investments with debt or with equity. Taxes can change the level, timing, and risk of free cash flow available to investors, and as such, can influence firm value.

b. Payments made to equity holders and debtholders are treated differently for tax purposes. Companies can deduct interest payments on debt on their taxes, but cannot deduct dividend payments. This *tax shield* for interest payments reduces the cost of debt. This can result in a lower cost of capital to the firm. It follows that companies' decisions about capital investments could be influenced if their cost of capital is lower.

c. When firms have higher leverage (i.e., more debt), it can lead to higher firm value because the tax-deductible interest payments reduce the amount of income reported for tax purposes. This leads to lower tax payments and higher after-tax free cash flow.

d. Issuing debt is generally less expensive than issuing stock. This is because the underwriting fees charged to facilitate raising capital are lower for debt than equity.

Example of Tax Shield Benefits

Capital structures with debt can affect a firm's after-tax cash flows because interest payments are tax deductible. Consider a firm with no debt and annual earnings before interest and taxes (EBIT) of $100. Assume the current tax rate is 35%.

If the firm takes out $1,000 of debt at 5% interest, it will pay $50 per year in interest, in which case the firm will have taxable income of $50 ($100 EBIT – $50 interest). Assuming the same tax rate of 35%, the firm will pay $17.50 in taxes. In contrast, assume the firm could raise $1,000 in preferred stock that paid a 5% dividend. The $50 per year in dividends would not be tax deductible. As such, the firm will have a lower tax obligation and higher after-tax cash flow if it used debt instead of preferred stock for the $1,000 in capital. Because the firm has greater free cash flow when using debt in these two scenarios, the firm value would be higher using debt. However, the risk is that the firm must generate sufficient income to cover debt obligations.

Summary

Taxes can affect decisions about a company's capital structure. Capital structure is the mix of debt and equity a company chooses to use to finance its activities. Interest payments on debt can be deducted from taxes, whereas dividend payments cannot. Additionally, companies with higher leverage (more debt) can have a higher firm value because of the tax-deductible interest payments. Finally, issuing debt is generally less expensive than issuing stock. All of these factors may influence a company's decisions about capital investments.

Further Reading

Parrino, R., Kidwell, D., and Bates, T. (2017). *Fundamentals of Corporate Finance*, 4th Edition. Hoboken, NJ: John Wiley & Sons.

Cost of Capital

After studying this lesson, you should be able to:

- Define the cost of capital and demonstrate an understanding of its applications in capital structure decisions (2.B.2.q).
- Determine the weighted-average cost of capital and the cost of its individual components (2.B.2.r).
- Calculate the marginal cost of capital (2.B.2.s).
- Explain the importance of using marginal cost as opposed to historical cost (2.B.2.t).
- Demonstrate an understanding of the use of the cost of capital in capital investment decisions (2.B.2.u).

This lesson discusses the cost of capital, which is a critical factor used in firms' investment decision making. The cost of capital is affected by the cost of debt, the cost of equity, and tax rates. This lesson reviews these terms and their definitions.

I. Defining the Cost of Capital

a. Firms incur costs in order to raise funds for their business activities. Firms raise funds from two primary sources: (1) debt and (2) equity. The cost of capital for a firm will depend on the proportion of the source of its funds and their respective costs. The cost of capital for a firm is the required rate of return the firm must earn in order to meet investors' and debtholders' expectations.

b. A firm's *cost of debt* is the amount of interest the firm must pay to service its debt. Cost of debt generally refers to a firm's long-term debt, meaning that debt which has a maturity of longer than one year. A firm's debt can come in various forms such as lines of credit, bank loans, or bonds.

c. The cost of debt is determined after-tax because interest payments are tax deductible. For example, if the average interest rate of a firm's various debt obligations is 10% and the current tax rate is 35%, then the firm's cost of debt is equal to 6.5% because 35% of the interest payments are tax-deductible.

d. A firm's *cost of equity* is the amount a firm pays to equity holders to compensate them for their investment. The return does not need to be in cash, as with debtholders, but could come in the form of stock price appreciation or dividends. The cost of equity is a blended average of return required of each type of equity holder, such as common stockholders and preferred stockholders. A firm's cost of equity is commonly determined using the *Capital Asset Pricing Model*. Other valuation models, such as the *Dividend Growth Model*, can be used. CAPM is most commonly used in practice.

e. The *weighted-average cost of capital* (WACC) is the blended average of the different types of capital used to finance a firm.

II. Calculating the Weighted-Average Cost of Capital

a. Once a firm's cost of debt and cost of equity are determined, the costs are weighted proportionate to the amount of each component to determine the weighted-average cost of capital. The WACC is sometimes referred to as a firm's *hurdle rate* or *discount rate*, which is the amount of return on a project, investment, or business operations the company must earn in order to satisfy its debt and equity holders.

$$\text{WACC} = (\text{Proportion of Debt} \times \text{Rd} \times (1 - \text{Tax Rate}) + (\text{Proportion of Equity Category} \times \text{Re})$$

Where:

Proportion of Debt = Debt ÷ (Debt + Equity)

Proportion of Equity Category = Equity ÷ (Debt + Equity)

R_d = Cost of Debt

R_e = Cost of Equity

Example

Consider a company with the following capital structure and costs:

20% Debt with a cost of debt of 10%

10% Preferred stock with a 5% dividend

70% Common stock with cost of equity of 12%

If the income tax rate is 35%, the company's weighted-average cost of capital is 10.2%, calculated as follows:

$$\begin{aligned}\text{WACC} &= [20\% \times (10\% \times (1 - 35\%))] + (10\% \times 5\%) + (70\% \times 12\%)\\ &= 0.013 + 0.005 + 0.084 = 0.102\end{aligned}$$

III. Marginal versus Historical Cost of Capital

a. A firm's *marginal cost of capital* is the cost of each new dollar in capital raised. When making decisions about future projects or investments, the marginal cost of capital should be used instead of the historical cost of capital. Firms change over time concerning their capital structure, profitability, growth, risk, and more. Historical cost of capital rates may not adequately reflect changes in these factors. As such, a forward-looking determination should be made of the cost of capital when making decisions and evaluations of future projects and investments. The basic calculations remain the same, but are made with future projections rather than relying on historical rates and calculations.

IV. Use of Cost of Capital in Investment Decisions

a. Firms often use the cost of capital as an evaluation tool to determine if a project or investment will increase firm value. Such an approach can make sense at times, but each project should be evaluated with some cautions. First, WACC should only be used if the new project has a similar risk profile as the firm's current projects upon which the calculation of WACC was based. Second, WACC should only be used if the new project has the same capital structure—financing mix—as the firm as a whole. For example, consider a firm that previously had funded projects using equity capital such as common stock or preferred stock, but now would like to fund a new project using debt. This firm would not want to evaluate the new project using its historical cost of capital, but rather would look to what its new, marginal cost of capital would be based on the new capital mix of equity and debt.

Summary

Cost of capital is the required rate of return that a firm must earn in order to meet investors' and debtholders' expectations and is a critical factor in investment decisions. Debt and equity are the two primary sources of funds used by a firm. The weighted-average cost of capital (WACC) is the blended average of the different types of capital used and is often used to help make future decisions for a company.

Further Reading

Parrino, R., Kidwell, D., and Bates, T. (2017). *Fundamentals of Corporate Finance*, 4th Edition. Hoboken, NJ: John Wiley & Sons.

Valuation of Financial Instruments: Valuing Debt and Equity

After studying this lesson, you should be able to:

- Value bonds, common stock, and preferred stock using discounted cash flow methods (2.B.2.e).
- Use the constant growth dividend discount model to value stock and demonstrate an understanding of the two-stage dividend discount model (2.B.2.w).
- Demonstrate an understanding of relative or comparable valuation methods, such as price/earnings (P/E) ratios, market/book ratios, and price/sales ratios (2.B.2.x).

This lesson reviews valuation methods for debt and equity. The discounted cash flow method is a valuation technique that can be used to value bonds, common stock, and preferred stock. Other valuation methods are discussed, including the dividend growth model and relative valuation method.

I. Discounted Cash Flow Valuation Method

a. The *discounted cash flow (DCF) method* is based on the principle that the value of any asset is the present value of its future cash flows. The DCF method takes into account the *time value of money*, which is that a dollar today is worth more than a dollar in the future. This is because a dollar today can earn interest to increase its value in the future. The DCF also takes into account the risk involved with investing a dollar. The *discount rate* used in the DCF method thus compensates investors for their time and risk. The rate used for the discount rate in DCF models depends on the type of asset being valued.

b. In order to value any asset using the DCF method, the following steps are taken:

i. Estimate the expected future cash flows.

ii. Determine the discount rate to be used.

iii. Calculate the present value of the future cash flows.

II. Bond Valuation

a. Valuing bonds using the DCF method is straightforward because the cash flows are known both in magnitude and in timing. When bonds are issued, their principal value and coupon rate are specified. With the cash flows known, the remaining piece of information needed is the discount rate. For bonds, this is usually the market interest rate for bonds with similar time to maturity and credit ratings.

b. When the market interest rate and a bond's coupon rate are the same, the bond will sell at *par value*. When a bond has a coupon rate below the market interest rate, it will sell as a *discount bond* in order to make the bond's cash flows yield the higher market interest rate. In contrast, when a bond has a coupon rate above the market interest rate, it will sell as a *premium bond* in order to make the bond's cash flows yield the lower market interest rate.

III. Common Stock Valuation Using DCF

a. The DCF method can also be used to value common stock. However, valuation of common stock is more complex for three reasons.

i. The expected cash flows from the stock, known as dividends, are less certain both in size and in timing. Dividends are subject to approval by boards of directors. Without the obligatory payment of dividends as with interest payments for bonds, estimating the expected cash flows is more difficult with common stock.

ii. Common stock does not have a final maturity date as with bonds. Common stock is a true perpetuity in that the owners never have to redeem the asset for cash.

iii. The discount rate used in a DCF for common stock is not directly observable. The cost of capital can be estimated, but it is more difficult to group common stock in risk classes than with bonds.

b. Common stock can be valued using a firm's stock price, estimated growth rate, and current dividend. The obvious restriction of this method is that if a firm does not pay a dividend, this valuation method will not work. This valuation method is known as the Dividend Discount Model (DDM), which is essentially a DCF model.

c. The DDM values a stock based on the present value of future cash flows. The DDM considers these factors in the analysis of stock value:

i. Cash flow—dividends paid to stockholders

ii. Expected holding period of the stock

iii. Pattern of dividend growth, which may be one of the next patterns:

1. Constant dividend (zero growth)
2. Constant growth of dividend
3. Variable growth of dividend

d. The Zero-Growth Dividend Model assumes that dividends will not increase over time. In which case, the value or price of a stock is expressed by the following equation:

$$P_0 = \text{Constant Dividend} \div \text{Discount Rate.}$$

For example, if a firm pays a constant dividend of \$5 and the required rate of return or discount rate is equal to 10%, then the price of the stock per share is equal to \$5 ÷ 10% = \$50 per share.

e. The Constant Growth Dividend Model assumes that dividends will increase over time at an equal growth rate, in which case the value or price of a stock can be expressed with the following equation:

$$P_0 = \text{Dividend}_1 \div (\text{Discount Rate} - \text{Dividend Growth Rate}).$$

In other words, the price of a stock is equal to next period's dividend divided by the difference between the required rate of return and the growth rate of the dividends. For example, if a firm paid a \$5 dividend in the current period, has plans to increase dividends by 5% each period, and has a required rate of return of 10%, then the price of the stock per share is equal to (\$5 × 1.05) ÷ (10% – 5%) = \$105 per share.

f. When a firm has a variable growth dividend, the valuation technique requires that future dividends be projected on a year-to-year basis. Each of these projected dividends is then discounted to the present value. The valuation model also requires a terminal value, which is assumed to have a constant growth in the dividend into the future. Thus, the valuation model for a variable growth dividend is a combination of discounting individual dividends and the constant-growth dividend model. The general equation for a variable growth dividend is as follows:

$$P_0 = [D_1 \div (1 + R)] + [D_2 \div (1 + R)^2] + \ldots + [D_3 \div (1 + R)^3] + [P_t \div (1 + R)^t]$$

Where:

P_t can be determined by $[D_{t+1} \div R - g]$

D = Dividend

R = Discount rate or required rate of return

g = Dividend growth rate

For example, consider a firm that plans to pay a dividend of \$2.00 in period 1, \$4.00 in period 2, and \$5.00 in period 3. Thereafter, the firm plans to have a dividend growth rate of 5%. If the firm has a required rate of return of 15%, then the value of the stock at period 3 is equal to:

$$P_3 = [D_{3+1} \div R - g] = (\$5 \times 1.05) \div (15\% - 5\%) = \$52.50.$$

We can now calculate the present value of the stock as follows:

$$P_0 = [D_1 \div (1 + R)] + [D_2 \div (1 + R)^2] + [D_3 \div (1 + R)^3] + [P_3 \div (1 + R)^3]$$

$$P_0 = [\$2.00 \div (1 + 15\%)] + [\$4.00 \div (1 + 15\%)^2] + [\$5.00 \div (1 + 15\%)^3] + [\$52.50 \div (1 + 15\%)^3]$$

$$P_0 = \$1.74 + \$3.03 + \$3.29 + \$34.52 = \$42.58$$

IV. Common Stock Valuation using Relative Methods

- **a.** Stocks can also be valued with other methods than the DCF. These methods rely on comparisons or ratios. In order to be effective, comparison firms must be chosen careful so that they are similar in factors such as industry, product offerings or services, and size.
- **b.** Three of the most common valuation ratios are the following:
  - **i.** Price-to-earnings (P/E) ratio
  - **ii.** Market-to-book (M/B) ratio
  - **iii.** Price-to-sales (P/S) ratio

V. Preferred Stock Valuation

- **a.** Preferred stock can be valued similar to bond valuation because it has a fixed cash flow. Thus, the DCF model can be used to map out the future cash flows and discount them back to present value. In this sense, preferred stock can be treated like an annuity and calculated as follows:

$$P_0 = \text{Dividend} \div \text{Required Rate of Return}$$

For example, a \$100 stock paying a 7% dividend with a 10% required rate of return has the equation of

$$P_0 = (\$100 \times 7\%) \div 10\%$$
$$= \$7 \div 10\% = \$70$$

Bond Valuation Example

Consider a \$1,000,000 bond that pays annual interest payments of 5% for 10 years. What is the present value of this bond? The first step is to map out the cash flows.

At time 1 through 10, there will be a \$50,000 cash flow as interest payments are made.

At time 10, there will be a \$1,000,000 cash flow to repay the principal.

Par-Value Bond

By definition, a par value bond means the present value of the cash flows is equal to the face value of the bond, or \$1,000,000.

Discount Bond

If the market interest rate is 8%, then the price of the bond will be reduced below face value so that the cash flows yield 8%. The price of the bond can be calculated as follows:

Determine the present value of the 10-year stream of \$50,000 cash flows. Using a present value table, the annuity factor at 8% for 10 years is 6.7101[1]. Then, multiply \$50,000 by 6.7101 to get \$335,505.

Continues...

Determine the present value of the repayment of the $1,000,000 principal at year 10. Using a present value table, the discount factor at 8% for 10 years is 0.4632[2]. Then, multiply $1,000,000 by 0.4632 to get $463,200.

Finally, add the two values together ($335,505 + $463,200) to determine the present value price of the bond: $798,705.

Premium Bond

If the market interest rate is 2%, then the price of the bond will be increased above face value so that the cash flows yield 2%.

Determine the present value of the 10-year stream of $50,000 cash flows. Using a present value table, the annuity factor at 2% for 10 years is 8.9826[3]. Then, multiply $50,000 by 8.9826 to get $449,130.

Determine the present value of the repayment of the $1,000,000 principal at year 10. Using a present value table, the discount factor at 2% for 10 years is 0.8203[4]. Then, multiply $1,000,000 by 0.8203 to get $820,300.

Finally, add the two values together ($449,130 + $820,300) to determine the present value price of the bond: $1,269,430.

---

[1]Solutions are computed using present value tables. Due to rounding errors, the solution may be slightly different if a calculator is used.

[2]Solutions are computed using present value tables. Due to rounding errors, the solution may be slightly different if a calculator is used.

[3]Solutions are computed using present value tables. Due to rounding errors, the solution may be slightly different if a calculator is used.

[4]Solutions are computed using present value tables. Due to rounding errors, the solution may be slightly different if a calculator is used.

Summary

The valuation of debt and equity can be done using various different techniques. A common method is the discounted cash flow (DCF) method, which is based on the principle that the value of any asset is the present value of its future cash flows. Bonds and preferred stock can use the DCF method for valuation purposes. The valuation of common stock is more complex. The Dividend Discount Model is the most commonly used valuation method for common stock. The three most common variations of this model are the Zero-Growth Dividend Model, the Constant Growth Dividend Model, and the Variable Growth Dividend Model.

Further Reading

Parrino, R., Kidwell, D., and Bates, T. (2017). *Fundamentals of Corporate Finance*, 4th Edition. Hoboken, NJ: John Wiley & Sons.

Valuation of Financial Instruments: Valuing Options

After studying this lesson, you should be able to:

- Demonstrate an understanding of the interrelationship of the variables that comprise the value of an option (e.g., relationship between exercise price and strike price and the value of a call) (2.B.2.m).

The lesson reviews how options can be valued prior to the option expiration date. Factors that affect option values are discussed.

I. Valuing Options

a. Option values are readily and easily determined when the option expires. The value is simply the difference between the exercise price and the value of the underlying asset. Whether an option is a put or call option determines if the option is in the money for the option holder.

b. Options are much more difficult to value prior to the expiration date. This is because the value of the underlying asset at the option expiration date can change over time. In this situation, the following five factors affect the value of an option:

i. Current price of the underlying asset

ii. Exercise price

iii. Volatility of the value of the underlying asset

iv. Time until the option expires

v. Risk-free rate of interest

These five factors mean that the value of an option will depend on current spread between the underlying asset's value and the exercise price, how likely the underlying asset is to change in price, how long until the option is exercised, and the time value of money.

Two popular models used to value options are the *Black-Scholes model* (BSM) and the *binomial model*. Calculations using these models are not required for the CMA exam, but an understanding of the models' assumptions is expected.

c. The Black-Scholes model (BSM) is a popular method for pricing options. The BSM's key assumptions include:

i. The stock pays no dividends during the option's life.

ii. The option is a European option, which means the option can be exercised only on the maturity date.

iii. The stock is traded in an efficient market.

iv. There are no transaction costs, taxes, or commissions.

v. The risk-free rate exists, is constant across the life of the option, and is the same for all maturity dates.

vi. The underlying stock's returns are normally distributed.

d. The binomial model values an option through a different, but still complex, mathematical computation. The model is based on a binomial tree where there are a number of decision points. The key assumptions of the binomial model are:

- **i.** The investor is risk neutral.
- **ii.** The underlying stock's price can only either decrease or increase with time (in other words, the stock cannot remain constant).
- **iii.** The possibility of arbitrage (immediate buying and selling of the asset in different markets to earn a profit) is zero.
- **iv.** The market is perfectly efficient.
- **v.** The duration of the option is shortened.

Summary

Options are easily valued after the expiration date but are much more difficult to value prior to the expiration date. The value of an option is affected by the following factors: current price of the underlying asset, exercise price, volatility of the underlying asset, time until the option expires, and risk-free rate of interest. The Black-Scholes model and the binomial model are two popular models for valuing options.

Further Reading

Parrino, R., Kidwell, D., and Bates, T. (2017). *Fundamentals of Corporate Finance*, 4th Edition. Hoboken, NJ: John Wiley & Sons.

Topic 3. Raising Capital

Financial Markets and Regulation

After studying this lesson, you should be able to:

- Identify the characteristics of the different types of financial markets and exchanges (2.B.3.a).
- Define insider trading and explain why it is illegal (2.B.3.l).

Financial markets come in various forms and sizes. This lesson reviews different types of financial markets and their role in the economy. This lesson also discusses regulation of financial markets, including restrictions on insider training.

I. Financial Markets

a. Financial markets exist to facilitate the flow of money from investors (those looking to obtain a return on capital) and users (those seeking to obtain capital in order to fund business operations). The assets being exchanged on financial markets can include stocks, bonds, options, commodities, and more.

b. A *primary market* is a market in which new security issues, either debt or equity, are sold directly to investors. A key characteristic of primary markets is that issuance of the new security results in new money for the issuing firm. Primary markets are often less accessible for everyday investors because they are wholesale markets taken up by large institutional investors.

c. A *secondary market* is a market in which owners of securities can sell them to other investors. Secondary markets are more familiar to most people.

i. Examples of secondary markets for stocks include the New York Stock Exchange, NASDAQ, London Stock Exchange, Euronext, Hong Kong Stock Exchange, Shanghai Stock Exchange, and many other exchanges throughout the world.

ii. Examples of secondary markets for commodities (oils, metals, food, etc.) include the Chicago Mercantile Exchange, Hong Kong Mercantile Exchange, London Metal Exchange, and many others.

iii. Examples of secondary markets for futures include the Chicago Board of Trade and New York Board of Trade while for options the major market is the Chicago Board Options Exchange.

d. A *money market* is a specific type of secondary market wherein short-term debt instruments, meaning those with a maturity within one year, are traded. The largest money markets are in New York City, London, and Tokyo. Money markets exchange large amounts of money, with a $1 million minimum transaction limit. Money market instruments are highly liquid, almost like cash. The advantage of a money market instrument is that it can earn a higher interest rate than regular cash holdings while maintaining a high level of liquidity.

e. A few key terms to understanding financial markets:

i. *Marketability*—How easily a security can be converted into cash. Financial exchanges facilitate greater marketability for financial instruments.

ii. *Liquidity*—The ability to convert an asset into cash quickly without loss of value. This term is similar to marketability, but carries additional meaning in that when a security is sold, its value is preserved.

iii. *Broker*—Market specialists who facilitate exchanges between buyers and sellers. They receive a commission fee as a market matchmaker. Brokers do not bear any risk of ownership.

iv. *Dealer*—Market specialists who facilitate exchanges by buying and selling securities from their own holdings. Dealers do bear risk of ownership. Dealers gain profit by selling securities at prices above that which they paid themselves to acquire the securities.

II. Regulation

a. Insider trading is an illegal practice where individuals with confidential or nonpublic information trade on investments for profits. In many cases, company management or influential investors with significant ownership percentages have access to information the public does not have. If these individuals trade on investments with this knowledge, they have broken the law and are subject to fines, jail time, or both.

b. Firms have blackout period policies that specify when employees holding company shares are forbidden to buy or sell. These periods are often around the time of quarter-end or month-end closings, when management has knowledge about a company's financial performance that has not yet been released to the public.

c. In the United States, when corporate insiders buy and sell securities of their own firm, they must report their trades to the Securities and Exchange Commission. This practice is legal; however, it can become illegal if trades are made while the individual has material, nonpublic information. The illegal practice also includes "tipping," which takes place when an insider provides information that is material and nonpublic to another individual who proceeds to trade based on that information.

Summary

Financial markets exist to facilitate the flow of money from investors and users. They come in various forms and sizes. Primary markets sell debt or equity directly to investors and are usually less accessible to everyday investors. Secondary markets are familiar to most people and are a market where owners of securities sell to other investors. Regulation on financial markets includes restrictions on insider trading and blackout period policies for employees holding company shares.

Further Reading

Parrino, R., Kidwell, D., and Bates, T. (2017). *Fundamentals of Corporate Finance*, 4th Edition. Hoboken, NJ: John Wiley & Sons.

Market Efficiency

After studying this lesson, you should be able to:

- Demonstrate an understanding of the concept of market efficiency, including the strong form, semi-strong form, and weak form of market efficiency (2.B.3.b).

Financial markets facilitate exchange between buyers and sellers. This lesson reviews the efficiency of financial markets, which is the extent to which a financial market reflects information in securities' prices.

I. Market Efficiency

a. Markets depend on information between buyers and sellers. In an ideal state, the price of a security would reflect its true value, or the future cash flows an investor can reasonably expect to receive. In order for this to take place, the price of a security would need to incorporate all available information about the size, timing, and riskiness of the cash flows. Furthermore, as new information becomes available, the price would need to adjust accordingly. When prices appropriately reflect the knowledge and expectations of all investors, the market is said to be *efficient*. Public markets help facilitate more efficient markets by allowing investors to observe transaction prices and volume while also allowing them to inexpensively trade in the market if desired.

b. The *Efficient Market Hypothesis* (EMH) is an underlying theory about how well markets are able to reflect information in security prices. The degree to which this theory applies is often described in three forms.

i. *Strong-Form Efficiency*—Security prices reflect all available information. This form is more of an ideal than reality. If this form held true, then it would not be possible to earn returns greater than market averages based on private information.

ii. *Semistrong-Form Efficiency*—Security prices reflect all public information but not all private information. For examples, investors who have private information could acquire such information through analysis of the firm or discussions with a firm's customers. This form is a reasonable representation of how most large stock markets function.

iii. *Weak-Form Efficiency*—Securities prices reflect all past information but not all private or public information. Under this form, investors could not earn returns greater than market averages based on historical patterns in security prices, but rather only by trading based on public or private information.

Summary
A financial market is efficient when prices appropriately reflect the knowledge and expectations of all investors. Investors are able to observe transaction prices and volumes as well as inexpensively trade through the use of public markets. The Efficient Market Hypothesis (EMH) is a theory about how well markets are able to reflect information in security prices and has three forms (strong, semi-strong, and weak) which describe how well the theory applies.

Further Reading

Parrino, R., Kidwell, D., and Bates, T. (2017). *Fundamentals of Corporate Finance*, 4th Edition. Hoboken, NJ: John Wiley & Sons.

Financial Institutions

After studying this lesson, you should be able to:

- Describe the role of the credit rating agencies (2.B.3.c).
- Demonstrate an understanding of the roles of investment banks, including underwriting, advice, and trading (2.B.3.d).

This lesson discusses the role that financial institutions play in financial markets. Financial institutions are key intermediaries between firms and investors. The roles of credit rating agencies and investment banks are described and discussed.

I. Financial Institutions

  a. Financial institutions play a significant role in the flow of cash through the financial system. They provide cash from debt and equity issuances in the primary exchange market while also facilitating secondary exchange markets where debt and equity holders trade securities. The graphic below shows the flow of cash through the financial system:

Cash Flows between the Firm and the Financial System

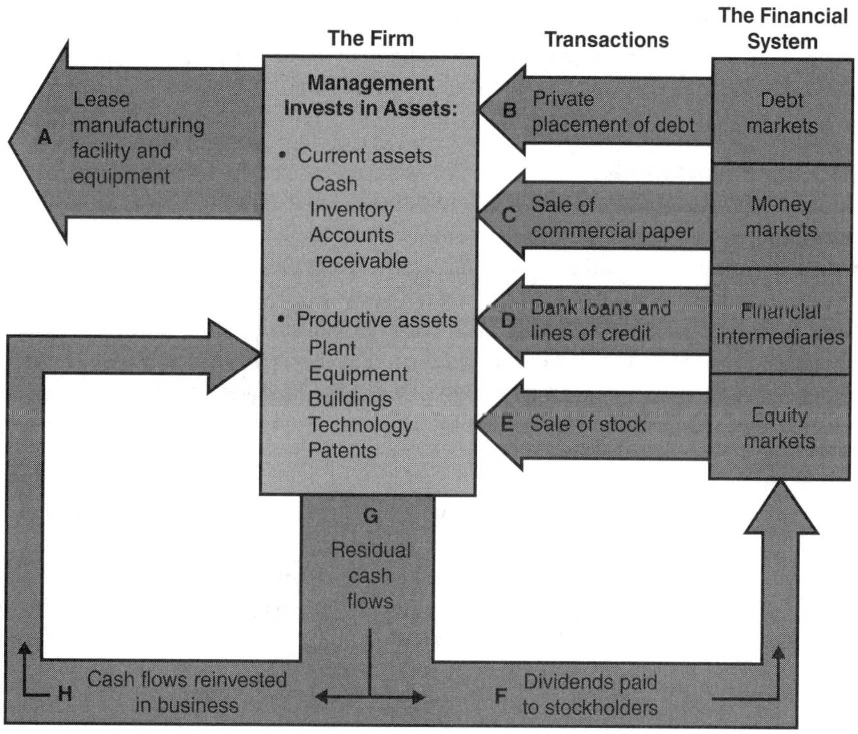

This exhibit shows how the financial system helps businesses finance their activities. The arrows in the exhibit indicate the major cash flows into and out of a firm over a typical operating cycle Money obtained from the Financial system, combined with reinvested cash flows from operations, enables a firm to make necessary investments and fund any other requirements.

Source: Parrino, R., Kidwell, D., and Bates, T. (2015). *Fundamentals of Corporate Finance*, 3rd Edition. Hoboken, NJ: John Wiley & Sons, p. 39. ISBN: 978-1-118-84589-9.

II. Credit Rating Agencies

a. Credit rating agencies provide assessments of the risk that a company will default on its debt obligations. They play an important role in financial markets by reducing *information asymmetry*—where one party in a transaction has more information than the other party—between firms and debtholders. When firms issue new public debt, they obtain a credit rating on that issuance. The credit rating communicates to investors the riskiness of the debt and helps determine an appropriate interest rate.

b. Moody's, S&P, and Fitch ratings are the three major credit rating agencies. See *Part 2 Section B.2.2 Types of Financial Instruments: Bonds* for related information about credit ratings.

III. Investment Banks

a. *Investment banks* are banks whose specialty is helping companies sell new debt and equity in the primary markets. Investment banks can sometimes also play a role as brokers and dealers, creating their markets and profiting from trading securities.

b. *Origination* is the process by which investment banks ready a security for sale, either debt or equity. Investment bankers help companies determine the feasibility of selling debt or equity with regards to the amount and type of capital. As part of this process, the investment bank helps companies obtain a credit rating for the security (if debt), establishes the sale date, obtains necessary legal approvals, and creates the securities.

c. *Underwriting* is the process by which investment banks help a company complete the sale of a security. Typically, this takes place by the investment bank buying the new security from the company and then reselling the security to investors. This two-step process allows the company to obtain a fixed price for the security while allowing the investment bank to benefit from the potential of selling the security for higher than it paid. The spread between these two prices is referred to as the *underwriting spread*. Investment banks bear a risk in the underwriting process that they will not be able to sell the security at the price they paid.

d. *Commercial banks* are banks that offer financial services such as checking accounts, savings accounts, lines of credit, and term-loans. Government regulations have varied over time as to whether commercial banks could engage in investment banking activities. Investment banking carries higher risk than traditional financial services. To protect the financial system, these two types of banking have been separated at times. However, regulations have also been passed to eliminate the distinction. Following current legislation is the best way to know whether commercial banks are presently allowed to engage in investment banking activities.

Summary

Financial institutions are key intermediaries between firms and investors by providing cash from debt and equity issuances in the primary market and also by facilitating secondary exchange markets. Credit rating agencies help reduce information asymmetry between firms and debtholders. Investment banks specialize in helping companies sell new debt and equity in primary markets by providing origination and underwriting services. Commercial banks offer financial services.

Further Reading

Parrino, R., Kidwell, D., and Bates, T. (2017). *Fundamentals of Corporate Finance*, 4th Edition. Hoboken, NJ: John Wiley & Sons.

Initial and Secondary Public Offerings

After studying this lesson, you should be able to:

- Define initial public offerings (IPOs) (2.B.3.e).
- Define subsequent/secondary offerings (2.B.3.f).

This lesson describes public offerings by firms. The process of a firm's initial public offering is described. Additional public offerings of firms that already have public traded securities is also discussed.

I. Initial Public Offerings

a. *Initial public offerings (IPOs)* refer to an event of a firm "going public" or offering ownership shares in the firm to the general public for the first time. There are several reasons why a firm can benefit from going public:

i. *Size of capital raised*—Firms can raise larger amounts of equity capital in the public equity market than from private sources. The public markets provide access to millions of investors who can easily participate in established financial market exchanges.

ii. *Ease of additional offerings*—Once a firm's stock is publicly listed, it becomes easier for the firm to raise additional capital through equity offerings. Investors value the liquidity of publicly held stock and will therefore accept lower yields, meaning higher prices paid to the firm issuing stock.

iii. *Funding with control*—Firms can determine the proportion of ownership shares they would like to make available to the public. An entrepreneur who is in need of additional capital to fund business operations or projects can sell a portion of the firm in the public market while also maintaining majority ownership in the firm.

iv. *Diversify personal portfolio*—Going public allows a firm's stock to trade on secondary market exchanges. This helps entrepreneurs and business managers to conveniently sell some of their shares now and then in order to diversify their own portfolios and to capture gains from appreciated firm value.

b. Going public can also have drawbacks. The process of an IPO is costly due to legal fees, auditing fees, consulting fees, and regulatory filing fees. Furthermore, firms may not always be able to sell stock in an IPO at what they believe is the firm's value. This happens because less information is known about private firms and investors may be hesitant to invest when the firm value is uncertain.

c. Going public also requires a firm to comply with disclosure and filing requirements by the Securities and Exchange Commission (SEC). Among the many requirements, firms are required to produce detailed financial statements on a quarterly basis. Firms must also provide disclosures on executive compensation, strategic initiatives, and other material information that could potentially erode some of the firm's competitive advantage in the marketplace.

d. The *origination process* of an IPO involves the firm's management working with an investment banker to determine how much money the firm needs to raise and what proportion of the ownership shares will be offered. The firm must also evaluate its financial performance and future strategic initiatives. Once a firm has determined it will go public, it must register with the SEC. The first step to register is a *preliminary prospectus* that contains detailed information about firm's business activities and financial performance and position.

e. Once a firm is registered and receives approval from the SEC, it may begin the *underwriting process*. Underwriting is the process by which an investment bank agrees to buy the firm's securities and then resell the securities to investors. This is often accomplished by a group of investment banks, or underwriting syndicate, in order to spread out the risk that the securities will not sell at the price paid by the underwriters. The securities then begin trading as the underwriter sells the securities to investors.

II. Secondary Public Offerings

a. A *secondary public offering* or *seasoned public offering* takes place when a firm that already has publicly traded securities engages in a sale of additional securities. The advantage for firms issuing additional securities is that investors typically will pay higher prices for a second offering as opposed to a first offering. This is because the stock is better known and has higher liquidity.

Summary

When a firm offers ownership shares to the general public for the first time, it is called an initial public offering (IPO). A firm may go public for various reasons such as the ability to raise large amounts of equity capital, the ease of raising additional capital, the ability to control the proportion of public ownership, and the ability to trade on the market. Going public can also have drawbacks such as the high cost of going public, the risk of not selling the stock at the believed value, and the new disclosure and filing requirements. After an IPO, a firm can offer additional securities in a secondary public offering.

Further Reading

Parrino, R., Kidwell, D., and Bates, T. (2017). *Fundamentals of Corporate Finance*, 4th Edition. Hoboken, NJ: John Wiley & Sons.

Dividend Policy and Share Repurchases

After studying this lesson, you should be able to:

- Define the different types of dividends, including cash dividends, stock dividends, and stock splits (2.B.3.h).
- Identify and discuss the factors that influence the dividend policy of a firm (2.B.3.i).
- Demonstrate an understanding of the dividend payment process for both common and preferred stock (2.B.3.j).
- Define share repurchase and explain why a firm would repurchase its stock (2.B.3.k).

This lesson discusses the various types of dividends that firms can pay. These include cash dividends, stock dividends, and stock splits. The process by which dividends are paid is reviewed. The lesson also covers share repurchases and discusses why a firm does this.

I. Dividend Policy

a. Organizations pay dividends to shareholders as a means to return profits to them. When deciding whether to pay a dividend, firms consider several factors, including the following:

i. *Cash Availability*—Firms often have cash commitments that necessitate cash to be used for something besides dividends. This can include debt principal and interest payments, capital investment projects, and payroll expenses.

ii. *Covenants*—Covenant requirements imposed by financial institutions, such as debt-to-assets ratios, debt-to-equity ratios, or other measures of liquidity or insolvency, can limit a firm's ability to pay a cash dividend.

iii. *Performance*—Whether the firm can generate higher returns by investing in the business compared to what shareholders could earn by investing money should the dividend be distributed to them. All else being equal, if a firm can earn its investors higher returns by investing in projects to grow revenue and profits, it will often simply reinvest cash in the business instead of paying dividends.

b. Dividends are paid differently to common stockholders and preferred stockholders. Preferred dividends are paid to owners of preferred stock on a priority basis compared to common shareholders. Preferred dividends can also be paid in arrears if they are specified as cumulative preferred stock. This means that if preferred shareholders are owed dividends for the last two years, both years' dividends must be paid before dividends are paid to common shareholders.

c. All dividends require approval from the board of directors. The date the company announces that the board has approved a dividend is called the *declaration date*. Included in the dividend announcement will be the *ex-dividend date*, which is the first day the stock will trade without the rights to the recently declared dividend. The *record date* is two business days after the ex-dividend date and represents the day on which the investors who are shareholders of record are determined to receive the dividend. Finally, the dividend is distributed to shareholders on the *payable date*, which is usually a couple of weeks after the record date.

d. Most dividends are paid as a cash dividend. Dividends are taxable to the dividend recipient.

II. Stock Repurchases

a. Firms can also distribute value to their shareholders by using *stock repurchases*. Stock repurchases, also known as *treasury stock,* take place when a company buys shares of its own stock on the open market. When a company repurchases its own shares, those shares are removed from circulation. This reduction in the shares outstanding means that the remaining owners of the company's stock have a larger claim on the company's value and dividends.

b. For example, if a firm has 100,000 shareholders and has determined it will pay a dividend totaling $1,000,000, then each shareholder would receive $10 per share. If the firm decided to use other cash to repurchase 20,000 shares, resulting in a new total of 80,000 shares outstanding, then the $1,000,000 dividend would be $12.50 per share. Thus, if a firm repurchases its stock, the shareholder benefits from an increase in the firm's share price and from a greater dividend amount.

c. Shareholders can often choose if they want to participate in a company's stock repurchases. This can happen by the shareholder selling shares on the open market, which the company in turn buys, or through a tender offer in which the company announces a price that it will pay for shares.

III. Stock Dividends and Stock Splits

a. A *stock dividend* takes place when a company distributes new shares to existing shareholders on a pro-rata basis. This means that each shareholder maintains the same proportion of ownership.

b. Stock dividends do not change the value of a company's assets. Stock dividends are simply accounting changes that result in shareholders' shares being more in number but worth the same amount.

c. A *stock split* is similar to a stock dividend, but is larger in scale. In a stock split, each share is divided into multiple shares.

d. While the value of the company's assets does not change with stock dividends or stock splits, there are reasons why firms would want to use these accounting techniques. One often-cited reason is the trading range argument, which is that firms want to keep their stock within a certain trading range value, say between $5 and $100. This benefit has not received much support in academic research. The main benefit is that stock splits send a positive signal about the firm's outlook.

e. Reverse stock splits, where shares outstanding are reduced as opposed to increased, often take place when a firm's stock price trades at low values. The NYSE and NASDAQ have requirements that a stock's price stay above a specified threshold ($5 and $1, respectively).

Summary

Firms pay dividends to shareholders as a means of returning profits to them. Before paying a dividend a firm must consider cash availability, covenant requirements, and firm performance. Dividends are paid to preferred stockholders first (including any dividends in arrears on cumulative preferred stock) and then to common stockholders. Firms can distribute value to their shareholders by repurchasing their own shares from the open market (known as stock repurchases or treasury stock). Stock dividends and stock splits create more shares on the open market while not changing the value of the company's assets.

Further Reading

Parrino, R., Kidwell, D., and Bates, T. (2017). *Fundamentals of Corporate Finance*, 4th Edition. Hoboken, NJ: John Wiley & Sons.

Topic 4. Working Capital Management

Working Capital Terminology

After studying this lesson, you should be able to:

- Define working capital and identify its components (2.B.4.a).
- Calculate net working capital (2.B.4.b).
- Explain the benefit of short-term financial forecasts in the management of working capital (2.B.4.c).
- Recommend a strategy for managing current assets that would fulfill a given objective (2.B.4.gg.).

This lesson reviews the key terms and concepts for working capital. Definitions are provided along with discussion of managing working capital accounts.

I. Working Capital Terms and Definitions

a. The following key terms are important to understanding what working capital is and how it is managed:

i. *Current Assets*—Comprised of cash and other assets which a firm expects to convert to cash within one year or less. These can include marketable securities, accounts receivable, inventory, and various miscellaneous accounts such as prepaid expenses. Current assets are sometimes referred to as *Gross Working Capital*.

ii. *Current Liabilities*—Comprised of obligations that a firm expects to pay within one year or less. These can include short-term notes payable, current maturities of long-term debt, accounts payable, deferred revenue, and various miscellaneous accounts such as accrued expenses.

iii. *Net Working Capital* refers to the difference between Current Assets and Current Liabilities. Net working capital is a measure of a firm's liquidity[1]. When people refer to "working capital," they are usually referring to "net working capital."

iv. *Liquidity*—The ability to convert assets into cash without a loss of value.

II. Managing Working Capital

a. A firm's working capital management policy is the set of decisions made to manage the firm's short-term cash inflows and cash outflows. The general goal of managers is to manage working capital in such a manner that the company can maintain normal business operations with the smallest possible net investment in working capital.

b. Firms face tradeoffs with each type of working capital:

i. *Cash and Cash Equivalents*—Cash on hand means a firm is likely to meet its financial obligations. Without enough cash, a firm is at greater risk to not be able to pay its bills. However, cash holdings have low rates of return and thus holding an excessive amount of cash can be an opportunity cost to the firm.

ii. *Receivables*—Extending credit to customers can help increase a firm's sales. However, evaluating customers' credit can be costly and accounts can go uncollected, resulting in losses to the firm.

[1] If you're preparing for the CMA© exam, you should note that this formula is on the ICMA formula sheet.

iii. *Inventory*—Maintaining large inventories can benefit a firm because the product will be available when customers want to purchase it and the firm will have the materials needed for production. However, costs are incurred to finance, warehouse, and protect inventories.

iv. *Payables*—Trade credit is appealing because it is a short-term financing mechanism usually with no interest. However, penalties can be incurred if not paid on time and future credit may be limited.

Summary

Working capital is a measure of a firm's liquidity and refers to the difference between current assets and current liabilities. Current assets are cash and other assets expected to be converted to cash within a year. Current liabilities are obligations that a firm expects to pay within a year. Firm managers set policies for managing working capital with the general goal of maintaining normal operating procedures with the smallest net investment in working capital.

Further Reading

Parrino, R., Kidwell, D., and Bates, T. (2017). *Fundamentals of Corporate Finance*, 4th Edition. Hoboken, NJ: John Wiley & Sons.

Cash Management

After studying this lesson, you should be able to:

- Identify and describe factors influencing the levels of cash (2.B.4.d).
- Identify and explain the three motives for holding cash (2.B.4.e).
- Prepare forecasts of future cash flows (2.B.4.f).
- Identify methods of speeding up cash collections (2.B.4.g).
- Calculate the net benefit of a lockbox system (2.B.4.h).
- Define concentration banking (2.B.4.i).
- Demonstrate an understanding of compensating balances (2.B.4.j).
- Identify methods of slowing down disbursements (2.B.4.k).
- Demonstrate an understanding of disbursement float and overdraft systems (2.B.4.l).

This lesson reviews how firms can manage their cash holdings. Cash facilitates exchange in business transactions and is a critical component of any business. Techniques for managing the flow of cash are discussed.

I. Cash Management

a. Cash management is the process by which a firm collects, invests, and administers its cash. Accounting, finance, and treasury departments work together to ensure the organization uses cash efficiently and that cash is available for operating and capital investment needs.

b. Cash management policies are focused on managing a firm's *liquidity* needs, that is, the ability of a firm to convert assets into cash without loss of value when needed. Efficient cash management optimizes the timing of cash inflows and cash outflows.

c. Cash management systems are built around the *cash conversion cycle*, which is the period of time over which a firm converts its cash outflows for its products and services into cash inflows. The diagram below depicts this cycle:

The Cash Conversion Cycle

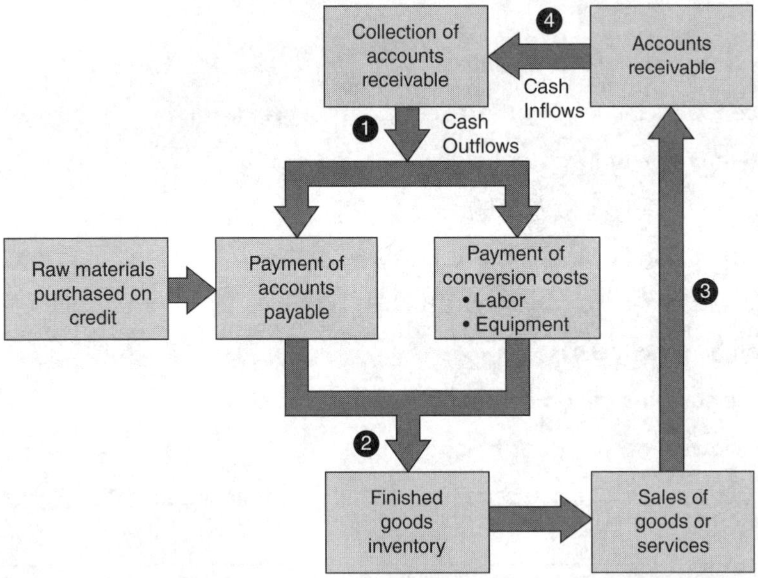

A typical cash conversion cycle begins with cash outflows for raw materials and conversion costs and goes through several stages before these resources are turned back into cash. The cash conversion cycle reflects the average time from the point that cash is used to pay for raw materials until cash is collected on the accounts receivable associated with the product produced with those raw materials. One of the main goals of a financial manager is to optimize the time between the cash outflows and the cash inflows.

Source: Parrino, R., Kidwell, D., and Bates, T. (2015). *Fundamentals of Corporate Finance*, 3rd Edition. Hoboken, NJ: John Wiley & Sons, p. 447. ISBN: 978-1-118-84589-9.

II. Holding Cash

a. Firms maintain cash balances, sometimes very large cash balances, for a variety of reasons.

i. The *transaction motive* means that firms have cash reserves in order to make payments related to their business operations. Firms pay cash for materials, labor, operating expenses, and many other expenses. Without cash to engage in financial transactions, firms struggle to maintain continuing business operations.

ii. The *precautionary motive* means that firms have cash reserves for unexpected or emergency cash needs. Firms can forecast expected cash needs; however, it is difficult to be accurate in forecasting. Having extra cash available allows firms to experience unanticipated cash needs without damaging business operations.

iii. The *compliance motive* means that firms have cash reserves in order to comply with cash balance requirements from loans and other bank services. Referred to as *compensating balances*, these requirements benefit the bank providing the loan or service by providing access to the firm's deposit interest free.

III. Forecasting Cash Flows

a. A key tool for managing cash flow is to make forecasts of cash inflows and cash outflows. Anticipating the timing of cash flows can help firms determine their cash needs and where their cash will be invested. The *cash budget* is a budgeting tool that helps firms map out their expected cash collections and cash disbursements along with any financing needs.

b. When preparing cash flow forecasts, the following are important considerations:

i. *Credit Terms Received*—The terms such as interest rates and payment-due dates vendors or suppliers are willing to extend on accounts payable. These terms affect the timing of cash outflows.

ii. *Credit Terms Extended*—In like manner, firms extend credit to their customers. The interest rates and payment-due dates extended to customers affect the timing of cash inflows.

iii. *Payment form*—Firms have a variety of options to complete financial transactions that affect the timing of cash flows. Paying hard cash is the quickest cash outflow, followed by checks, and then by credit cards. The variation in processing time from payment type can make a significant difference in a firm's cash flow management.

iv. *Inventory Needed*—Inventory represents a more illiquid asset. It requires cash be invested and then held as inventory until the product is sold. The average time that inventory is held before being converted into cash affects the timing of a firm's forecasted cash flows.

IV. Collecting Cash

a. Firms create collection systems to gather and deposit cash. Firms can collect payments in many forms such as cash, check, debit or credit card, and electronic transfers.

Collection float is a measure of the time from when a transaction is initiated until the cash is available for use. For example, when a check is mailed to a firm, the collection float is broken down as follows:

i. *Mail float*—The time from when the check is mailed to when the firm receives the check

ii. *Processing float*—The time from when the firm receives the check to when it is deposited

iii. *Availability float*—The time from when the check is deposited to when the funds are made available to the organization

b. A *lockbox system* is an arrangement between a bank and a firm that allows geographically dispersed customers to send their payments to a post office box near them. The payments are then collected and processed by the bank. Because the payment skips the firm's location, the collection float is reduced. In the case of mailed checks, the bank generally provides photocopies or electronic scans of the checks along with payment remittance forms to the firm. The primary drawback of a lockbox system is the cost of administering the system, which can include post office box rental fees, account or deposit fees, and processing fees.

c. The net benefit of a lockbox system is the dollar value of reduced mail and processing float less the costs of the system. A firm benefits from a lockbox by accelerating cash collections, which allow the firm to earn interest on the cash sooner than it otherwise would.

Example

Value of a Lockbox

Consider a firm that uses a lockbox system that costs $0.30 per processed check. The firm receives an average of 100 checks per business day with an average value of $1,000. The firm estimates the lockbox reduces processing by 2 days. If there are 270 business days per year and the firm's account receivable costs 5% in interest to the firm, what is the net benefit of the lockbox system?

Cost of the Lockbox

$$100 \text{ checks} \times \$0.30 \text{ per check} \times 270 \text{ days} = \$8{,}100$$

Savings from the Lockbox

$$2 \text{ days} \times 5\% \times (\$1{,}000 \text{ per check} \times 100 \text{ checks}) = \$10{,}000$$

The net benefit to the firm is $1,900 per year by using the lockbox system.

d. Electronic payment systems use digital means to bypass the traditional system of mailing checks for payment. Automated clearinghouse (ACH) transactions process and settle payments electronically. In the United States, the Federal Reserve is the primary ACH operator. Fedwire, operated by the Federal Reserve, provides financial institutions the ability to transfer funds through their respective Federal Reserve bank accounts.

e. Firms will often use a *concentration banking system*. This system transfers all funds from a variety of regional banks into a single central banking account. It simplifies the cash management process because firms can focus on one bank account rather than multiple accounts.

V. Disbursing Cash

a. Organizations use disbursement systems to pay employees, suppliers, tax agencies, and other external stakeholders. *Disbursement float* is a measure of the time between when a firm initiates payment and when the funds are deducted from the firm's bank account. Disbursement float is similar to collection float, but it also adds *clearing float*, which is the time between when the other party deposits the firm's check and when the amount is officially deducted from the firm's bank account.

b. Firms can use a variety of methods to control disbursement activities.

i. A *zero-balance account (ZBA)* allows a bank to write checks against an account with no money in it. A daily transfer from the bank's master account covers any checks written. Firms may have multiple ZBAs for supplier payments, tax payments, wages, etc. ZBAs allow for decentralized payables activity and the elimination of excess cash in multiple bank accounts.

ii. *Centralized payables* allows a firm to use a single bank account and take advantage of economies of scale from a single payment location.

iii. A *payable through draft (PTD)* requires a bank to present the instrument to the firm for final acceptance. The firm then will deposit funds to cover the draft. This service incurs higher charges for the firm but allows the firm greater management over its cash funds.

iv. *Electronic commerce (e-commerce)* facilitates relationships and transactions digitally. Processing payments online reduces cycle time and has lower error rates.

Summary
The process by which a firm collects, invests, and administers its cash is referred to as cash management. Cash management is a critical component of any business. Firms need to maintain cash balances in order to make payments related to business operations, to have reserves in case of unexpected or emergency needs, and to meet compliance requirements. Firms use cash budgets to help forecast the timing of cash flows. Collection float (the measure of time from the initiation of a transaction until cash is available) and disbursement float (the measure of time from when a payment is initiated and when funds are deducted from the firm's bank account) also influence cash inflow and outflow.

Further Reading
Parrino, R., Kidwell, D., and Bates, T. (2017). *Fundamentals of Corporate Finance*, 4th Edition. Hoboken, NJ: John Wiley & Sons.

Marketable Securities Management

After studying this lesson, you should be able to:

- Identify and describe reasons for holding marketable securities (2.B.4.m).
- Define the different types of marketable securities, including money market instruments, T-bills, treasury notes, treasury bonds, repurchase agreements, federal agency securities, bankers' acceptances, commercial paper, negotiable CDs, Eurodollar CDs, and other marketable securities (2.B.4.n).
- Evaluate the trade-offs among the variables in marketable security selections, including safety, marketability, yield, maturity, and taxability (2.B.4.o).
- Demonstrate an understanding of the risk-and-return trade-off (2.B.4.p).

This lesson reviews various types of marketable securities and how firms manage their holdings. Marketable securities represent an important part of a firm's asset management and its liquidity needs.

I. Holding Marketable Securities

a. Holding excessive levels of cash is generally discouraged because cash accounts earn very low rates of interest. As an alternative, firms can invest in short-term securities to earn additional income while sacrificing little with regards to liquidity.

b. Firms should consider the following factors when deciding whether to use marketable securities and what type of marketable security to use:

i. *Risk*—Marketable securities vary in their risk level. While they generally have lower risk exposure than stocks or long-term bonds, they do have more risk compared to a savings account. The yields on marketable securities are higher than a savings account to compensate for the additional risk exposure.

ii. *Liquidity*—Marketable securities vary in how quickly they can be converted into cash without loss of value. Their maturity is generally less than one year, but can be illiquid over short-term periods.

iii. *Maturity*—Related to liquidity, firms should consider the time to maturity of marketable securities. Firms should manage marketable securities' maturity to match the timing of firm's cash needs.

iv. *Taxes*—Some marketable securities do not require payment of taxes, such as municipal bonds.

II. Types of Marketable Securities

a. Marketable securities come in various forms. The following table provides examples of marketable securities:

Instrument	Description
U.S. Treasury securities	Direct obligations of the U.S. Treasury; backed by the full faith and credit of the U.S. government. Interest rates provide a reference point and market indicator for other securities. Considered "safe" investments because they are free of default risk, are actively traded on a large secondary market, and are highly marketable.

Continues...

Instrument	Description
U.S. Treasury securities (cont.)	Common types include: • Treasury bills (T-bills): Do not bear interest; sold at a discount and mature to face value in 1 year or less. • Treasury notes (T-notes): Bear interest semiannually; mature within 1 to 10 years. • Treasury bonds (T-bonds): Similar to T-notes but have maturities longer than 10 years; generally not purchased for a short-term portfolio except when the bond is close to maturity.
Federal agency securities (agency securities)	Interest-bearing securities usually offered and redeemed at face value. Generally not backed by the full faith and credit of the U.S. government but still considered relatively safe investments and free of default risk. Typically smaller issues than Treasury securities; not quite as marketable but still highly liquid. Limited tax exposure; many are exempt from state/local income taxes but not state franchise taxes.
Repurchase agreements (repos)	Purchase of a security from another party, usually a bank or security dealer who agrees to buy it back at a specified date for a fixed price. Commonly involve U.S. Treasury securities as the underlying security to be repurchased at a rate slightly less than the U.S. Treasury securities offer. Varying maturity, starting with overnight repurchase agreements. Generally considered a relatively safe investment (because of the government underlier). Often transferred to a third party to ensure that securities are available for sale if the issuer defaults.
Bankers' acceptances (BAs)	Essentially time drafts that result from commercial trade financing; frequently involve international transactions. Involve a letter of credit "accepted" by a bank; typically implies the BA is backed by that bank. Varying maturities and denominations. Liquidity is provided by an active secondary market of dealers.
Commercial paper	Unsecured short-term loan issued by a corporation. Negotiable instrument but typically held to maturity because of a weak secondary market; typically higher yield than similar securities because of its low marketability. Maturity ranges from 1 to 270 days. May be interest bearing or discounted; usually are discounted. Generally rated by credit rating agencies (e.g., Moody's or Standard & Poor's) to help investors assess risk.
Negotiable certificates of deposit (CDs)	Interest-bearing deposits issued by banks or savings-and-loan institutions that can be traded in money markets; generally sold at face value in denominations of \$1 million. Most mature between 1 and 3 months, though can be for several years. Offer fixed and variable interest rates. Not guaranteed by the Federal Deposit Insurance Corporation if in excess of \$250,000. *Continues...*

Instrument	Description
Negotiable certificates of deposit (CDs) (cont.)	Highly marketable if issued by a large, established bank. Common types include: • Eurodollar (or euro) CDs—dollar-denominated CDs issued by foreign branches of U.S. banks and foreign banks, primarily in London • Yankee CDs—CDs issued by U.S. branches of foreign banks • Thrift CDs—CDs issued by savings and loan associations, savings banks, and credit unions
Eurodollar deposits	Typically nonnegotiable dollar-denominated time deposits held by banks outside the United States (although not necessarily in Europe); not subject to U.S. banking regulations. May be purchased through most large U.S. banks. Maturities range from overnight to several years; most are 6 months or less.
Short-term municipals	State and local government issues. Often exempt from state or local taxes.

Summary

Cash accounts generally earn low interest rates so firms will often invest in short-term marketable securities that can earn additional income while still being fairly liquid. When deciding what type of marketable security to use, firms should consider the risk, liquidity, maturity, and tax requirements related to each security. There are many types of marketable securities, including U.S. treasury securities, federal agency securities, repurchase agreements, bankers' acceptances, commercial paper, negotiable certificates of deposit, Eurodollar deposits, and short-term municipals.

Further Reading

Parrino, R., Kidwell, D., and Bates, T. (2017). *Fundamentals of Corporate Finance*, 4th Edition. Hoboken, NJ: John Wiley & Sons.

Accounts Receivable Management

After studying this lesson, you should be able to:

- Identify the factors influencing the level of receivables (2.B.4.q).
- Demonstrate an understanding of the impact of changes in credit terms or collection policies on accounts receivable, working capital, and sales volume (2.B.4.r).
- Define default risk (2.B.4.s).
- Identify and explain the factors involved in determining an optimal credit policy (2.B.4.t).

This lesson discusses how firms can manage their accounts receivable. Firms have choices about the credit terms they offer customers. Factors affecting credit policies are discussed.

I. Managing Accounts Receivable

a. Firms often extend credit to customers by delivering the product or services now in exchange for a promise of future payment. This arrangement benefits firms because it makes it easier and more likely that customers will make purchases, and depending on the credit terms, the firm can earn interest.

b. The amount of accounts receivable a firm has is affected by several factors, including the following:

i. *Credit Screening*—Firms can evaluate customers' creditworthiness. For example, firms may require customers have a minimum credit score in order to receive financing. Firms incur costs for credit screening, and as such, firms vary in the extent to which they screen customers.

ii. *Credit Terms*—Firms can determine the interest and term length. Lower interest rates and longer payment periods will increase the likelihood customers use credit to finance their purchases. For example, a common credit term is 2/10, net 30, which means a customer receives a 2% discount if it pays in 10 days, and it must pay its receivable in 30 days.

iii. *Monitoring Collections*—Once credit is extended to a customer, the firm must make efforts to collect the promised money. Firms vary in how actively they remind customers to pay.

iv. *Default Risk*—The risk that customers will not pay their bill. This is related to the initial credit screening, but can also be affected by subsequent events that affect a customer's ability to pay their bills.

c. The goal of a firm's credit policy is to increase sales while also realizing cash collections. Firms expect a portion of their credit sales to be uncollectible, but the firm's credit policy should seek to optimize the tradeoff between increasing sales and the amount of cash not recovered by collection.

d. The *average collection period* (or the *days sales in receivables*) measures how much time passes between a sale and the time a customer pays[1]. A firm can measure average collection period as a weighted average of the times customers pay.

i. For example, if 20% of customers pay in 10 days, 60% pay in 30 days, and 20% pay in 60 days, the average collection period is $(20\% \times 10) + (60\% \times 30) + (20\% \times 60) = 2 + 18 + 12 = 32$ days.

e. The firm's average balance in receivables is calculated as the *Average Daily Sales* × *Average Collection Period.*

[1] If you're preparing for the CMA© exam, you should note that this formula is on the ICMA formula sheet.

i. For example, if the firm's average collection period is 32 days and average daily sales are \$20,000, the average balance in A/R is (\$20,000 × 32 days) = \$640,000.

f. The *Accounts Receivable Turnover Ratio* measures the number of times the company cycles its A/R each year. The formula is *Annual Net Credit Sales ÷ Average Receivables Balance*[2].

i. For example, if a firm had \$7,200,000 in credit sales and had an average receivables balance of \$640,000, the accounts receivable turnover ratio would be 11.25 = (\$7,200,000 ÷ \$640,000).

g. A common tool use to manage accounts receivable is an *aging schedule*. This schedule maps out the accounts receivable by how far past the initial sale they are. It is used to help identify and track delinquent accounts. The older a receivable is, the greater likelihood that it will not be collected.

Summary

Firms often extend credit to customers by delivering the product or service now in exchange for a future promise of payment. The amount of accounts receivable a firm has is affected by credit screening of customers, terms of credit extended by the firm, monitoring of the extended credit, and the risk of default of payment. Firms expect a portion of their accounts receivable to be uncollectible. It is important for firms to evaluate and manage their accounts receivable as the older a receivable is, the greater likelihood that it will not be collected.

Further Reading

Parrino, R., Kidwell, D., and Bates, T. (2017). *Fundamentals of Corporate Finance*, 4th Edition. Hoboken, NJ: John Wiley & Sons.

[2] If you're preparing for the CMA© exam, you should note that this formula is on the ICMA formula sheet.

Inventory Management

After studying this lesson, you should be able to:

- Define lead time and safety stock; identify reasons for carrying inventory and the factors influencing its level (2.B.4.u).
- Identify and calculate the costs related to inventory, including carrying costs, ordering costs, and shortage (stockout) costs (2.B.4.v).
- Explain how a just-in-time (JIT) inventory management system helps manage inventory (2.B.4.w).
- Identify the interaction between high inventory turnover and high gross margin (calculation not required) (2.B.4.x).
- Demonstrate an understanding of economic order quantity (EOQ) and how a change in one variable would affect the EOQ (calculation not required) (2.B.4.y).

This lesson discusses the management of a firm's inventory. Inventory management starts with the purchase of raw materials and ends with the sale of finished goods. Tools and techniques are discussed and defined.

I. Managing Inventory

a. Inventory management starts with the purchase of raw materials and ends with the sale of finished goods. Firms have inventory on hand or in storage facilities for several reasons, such as the following:

i. Protect against suppliers' financial uncertainty or shipping delays.

ii. Mitigate the risk of stock-outs because of high demand.

iii. Ensure the firm can operate in an efficient and effective manner.

b. Firms attempt to minimize total inventory cost while carrying sufficient inventory to maintain operations. This can be a difficult managerial problem due to the complexity of forecasting sales demand, availability of raw materials, and production processing. Firms must balance several costs when determining the optimal inventory level to carry. These costs include the following:

i. *Purchasing costs*—The actual amount that a firm pays for materials. This can include shipping and taxes on the goods purchased.

ii. *Carrying costs*—The warehouse space, handling costs, insurance, taxes, and depreciation associated with storing inventory.

iii. *Ordering costs*—The costs of purchasing departments, administrative support, and other fixed costs associated with placing orders with suppliers.

iv. *Stock-out costs*—The lost revenue (an opportunity cost) associated with not being able to fulfill customers' orders in a timely manner.

c. Firms spend considerable time and resources to determine the right quantity of inventory to carry because inventory is a significant investment and can result in reduced cash flow if not managed well. If a business wants to minimize stock-out costs, it will incur higher carrying and ordering costs. In contrast, firms seeking to minimize carrying and ordering costs will risk incurring larger stock-out costs from not having the right inventory on hand.

d. The following key terms are important to understanding how firms design their inventory purchasing and management strategies.

i. *Lead-time* is the time between when a firm places an order with a supplier and when the goods arrive at the business.

ii. *Safety stock* is protection against increased demand and should be calculated to balance the volatility of demand with the risk the firm wishes to incur for stock-out costs. It is the amount of inventory a firm has on hand beyond the projected sales amount.

iii. The *reorder point* is calculated as:

(Average Daily Demand in Units × Lead Time) + Safety Stock

For example, a firm has daily demand of 1,000 units, requires lead-time of 30 days, and wants a safety stock of 3 days' worth of inventory.

The reorder point is (1,000 × 30 days) + 3,000 units = 33,000 units.

II. Just-in-Time Inventory Management

a. Just-in-time (JIT) systems help firms manage inventory and reduce cost. Firms contract with suppliers to deliver inventory only on order when the firm requires it. In other words, JIT can be considered a "pull" inventory system wherein demand is the trigger for inventory ordering rather than predetermined inventory levels. The philosophy behind a JIT system is different from traditional inventory systems in that it regards inventory storage as a non-value-added activity. Thus, JIT attempts to reduce or eliminate the carrying costs of inventory.

b. JIT systems were pioneered by Japanese firms like Toyota Motor Company. Most auto manufacturers now employ a JIT system. Firms with JIT systems benefit from having little to no carrying costs and not having the risk of inventory obsolescence. However, firms with JIT systems are very dependent upon their suppliers and their ability to deliver goods as needed.

III. Inventory Turnover

a. Firms can also manage inventory costs by increasing their inventory turnover. High inventory turnover ratios mean that firms move their inventory from raw materials to sales more quickly. When firms have high inventory turnover ratios, they incur fewer overhead expenses in these areas:

i. Fewer employees required to handle and move material

ii. Lower utility costs because the firm requires less space to store inventory

iii. Less depreciation expense or rent expense related to handling equipment, such as forklifts

Lower overhead expenses from having high inventory turnover means cost of goods sold will be lower, which in turn improves a firm's gross margin.

IV. Economic Order Quantity

a. Firms can use the *economic order quantity (EOQ)* model to calculate the order quantity that minimizes the total costs incurred to order and hold inventory. If a firm carries less inventory, it will order more and have higher ordering costs. Firms carrying more inventory may make fewer orders, but these firms will have more costs with warehousing, handling, and depreciation required to store and carry inventory.

b. The formula for EOQ is given as follows:

$$EOQ = \sqrt{[(2 \times \text{Reorder Costs} \times \text{Sales per Period}) \div \text{Carrying Costs}]}$$

c. The EOQ model has several key assumptions: (1) demand remains uniform, (2) ordering costs and carrying costs are constant, and (3) no quantity discounts are allowed.

d. Calculations using the EOQ are not required on the CMA exam, but an understanding of the concept and its features is expected.

Summary

A difficult managerial problem is managing inventory that consists of minimizing total inventory costs while carrying sufficient inventory to maintain operations. When determining optimal inventory level, firms must balance purchasing costs, carrying costs, ordering costs, and stock-out costs. Firms use various techniques such as just-in-time inventory management, inventory turnover calculations, and the economic order quantity model in order to determine the right quantity of inventory to carry.

Further Reading

Parrino, R., Kidwell, D., and Bates, T. (2017). *Fundamentals of Corporate Finance*, 4th Edition. Hoboken, NJ: John Wiley & Sons.

Types of Short-Term Credit

After studying this lesson, you should be able to:

- Demonstrate an understanding of how risk affects a firm's approach to its current asset financing policy (aggressive, conservative, etc.) (2.B.4.z).
- Identify and describe the different types of short-term credit, including trade credit, short-term bank loans, commercial paper, lines of credit, and bankers' acceptances (2.B.4.aa).
- Demonstrate an understanding of factoring accounts receivable and calculate the cost of factoring (2.B.4.dd).

This lesson reviews the types of short-term credit firms can use to finance their working capital. The costs and benefits of each type of financing are discussed.

I. Sources of Short-Term Financing

- **a.** Short-term credit to finance working capital requirements comes from several sources: (1) trade credit, (2) short-term bank loans, (3) commercial paper, and (4) accounts receivable financing.

II. Trade Credit

- **a.** Trade credit, or accounts payable, takes place when a firm makes and receives delivery of a purchase, but does not pay for it upon purchase. Instead, the firm is extended credit by the counterparty. Often the credit terms for accounts payable are written as 2/10, net 30; that means the purchasing firm receives of 2% discount if it pays the bill within 10 days but must pay the full amount within 30 days. Penalties and fees are charged after the 30-day period.

III. Short-Term Bank Loans

- **a.** Firms have a variety of financing agreements available from banks.
  - **i.** *Term loans* are payable by a certain date. Common bank loans are generally term notes. The promissory note that includes the amount, maturity, interest rate, and debt covenants is sometimes called a *promissory note*.
  - **ii.** *Lines of credit* allow businesses to borrow given amounts to a certain ceiling level assuming the firm makes minimum payments each month. Lines of credit sometimes carry commitment fees that a firm must pay on the unused portion of the credit line. A line of credit may either be an *informal line of credit*, which is a verbal agreement that a firm can borrow an agreed-upon amount of money, or a *formal line of credit*, which is an agreement with a legal obligation for the bank to lend an agreed-upon amount of money.
  - **iii.** *Secured* versus *unsecured* loans—*secured loans* are backed by *collateral*, meaning that if the borrower defaults on the loan, the bank can seize the asset serving as collateral for the loan. Secured loans carry lower interest rates than unsecured loans because the collateral reduces the cost of default risk to the bank.

IV. Commercial Paper

- **a.** Commercial paper is short-term, unsecured notes payable issued by large firms with high credit ratings. Commercial paper is usually issued in very large denominations (usually exceeding $100,000).
- **b.** Pension funds, institutional investors, and insurance companies usually purchase commercial paper as a secure, low-risk investment.
- **c.** Commercial paper is not secured; however, a related financial instrument called *bankers' acceptances* are short-term notes payable issued by firms yet backed or guaranteed by a commercial bank.

V. Accounts Receivable Financing

a. Firms finance their accounts receivable in two ways. The first way is by obtaining a bank loan using the accounts receivable as collateral. The firm is able to accelerate the availability of cash while waiting to collect on the accounts receivable. Once collected, the firm pays off the bank loan. If there is a shortfall in collecting the accounts receivable, the firm is still legally obligated to repay the full amount of the loan.

b. The second way is to sell the rights to the accounts receivable, referred to as *factoring*. Factoring takes place when a bank or financial institution buys a firm's accounts receivable without recourse. The accounts receivable are sold at a discount, typically 2% to 5%. The firm benefits because it receives cash more quickly and discharges the risk of default to someone else. The bank benefits from the discount received inasmuch as the accounts receivable are collected.

c. The cost of factoring can be quite high. For example, consider a firm with \$10,000 in accounts receivable. The firm sells the accounts receivable to a bank at a 2% factor. The accounts receivable collection period is one month. This means that the firm receives \$9,800 cash while incurring a \$200 expense. This translates into a simple annual interest rate of 24.48% $= (\$200 \div \$9,800) \times 12$.

Summary
Firms often use short-term credit to finance their working capital. Trade credit (accounts payable) occurs when a firm makes and receives delivery of a purchase but does not pay for it right away. Banks offer various short-term loans such as term loans, formal or informal lines of credit, and secured loans. Large firms issue commercial paper, which are short-term, unsecured notes. Finally, firms will sometimes finance their accounts receivable by using their accounts receivable as collateral for a bank loan or factoring (selling their rights to) their accounts receivable.

Further Reading
Parrino, R., Kidwell, D., and Bates, T. (2017). *Fundamentals of Corporate Finance*, 4th Edition. Hoboken, NJ: John Wiley & Sons.

Short-Term Credit Management

After studying this lesson, you should be able to:

- Estimate the annual cost and effective annual interest rate of not taking a cash discount (2.B.4.bb).
- Calculate the effective annual interest rate of a bank loan with a compensating balance requirement and/or a commitment fee (2.B.4.cc).
- Explain the maturity matching or hedging approach to financing (2.B.4.ee).
- Demonstrate an understanding of the factors involved in managing the costs of working capital (2.B.4.ff).

This lesson discusses how firms can manage their short-term credit. Financial managers have several strategies available to them depending on their risk preferences.

I. Managing Short-Term Credit

a. Working-capital needs fluctuate over time. This can happen due to economic cycles and business seasonality. Firms must develop strategies of how they will fund working capital needs. *Permanent working capital* is the minimum level of working capital that a firm will always have on its books. Fluctuations in working capital above that amount need to be financed and managed. Three common alternatives for financing working capital needs are:

i. *Maturity matching*—This strategy tries to match the maturities of liabilities to the assets that they fund.

ii. *Long-term funding*—This strategy uses long-term debt and equity to fund working capital and fixed assets.

iii. *Short-term funding*—This strategy uses short-term debt to finance working capital, and at times, a portion of fixed assets.

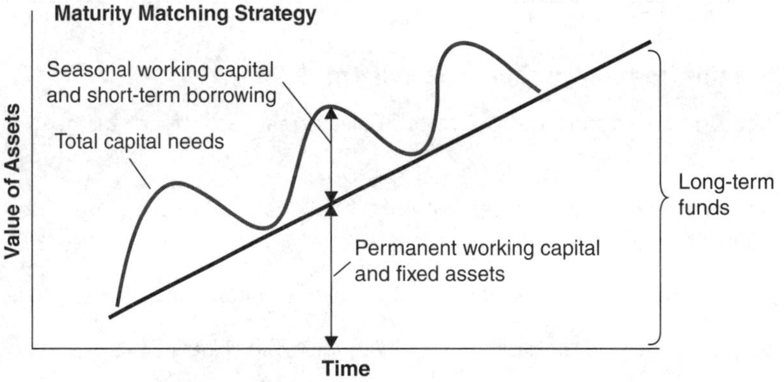

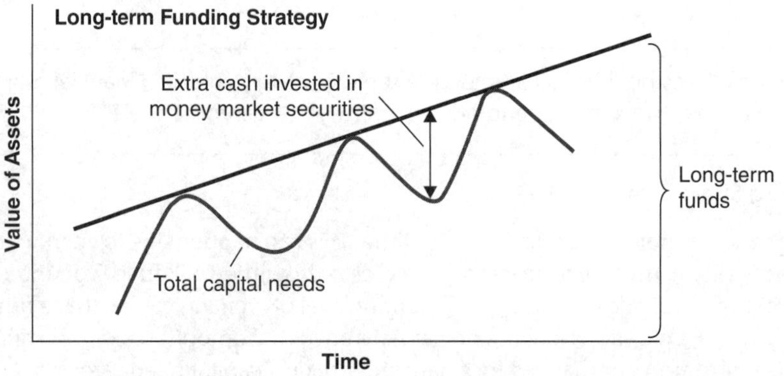

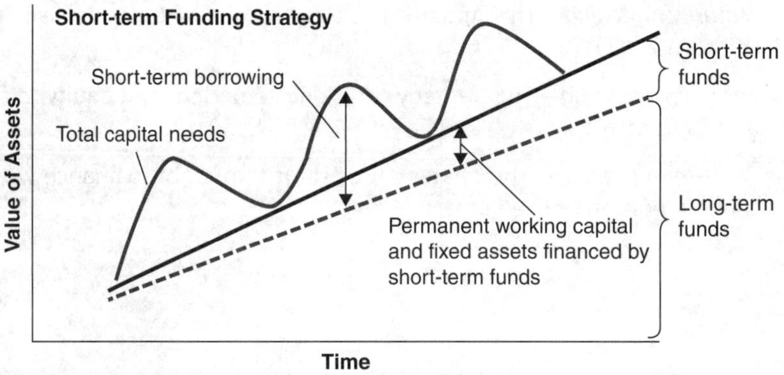

Source: Parrino, R., Kidwell, D., and Bates, T. (2015). *Fundamentals of Corporate Finance*, 3rd Edition. Hoboken, NJ: John Wiley & Sons, p. 461. ISBN: 978-1-118-84589-9.

II. Cash Discounts

a. Firms should calculate the cost of not taking a cash discount in payment terms to determine their ideal disbursement strategy. If a firm can obtain short-term financing at a lower cost than the cost of the discount, it should take the discount and obtain the short-term financing required to pay in the discount period.

b. The formula to calculate the cost of not taking a discount is:

$$\frac{(\text{Discount }\%) \div (100\% - \text{Discount}\%) \times (\text{Days in Year})}{(\text{Total Payment Period} - \text{Discount Period})}$$

For example, if a firm has 2/10, net 30 terms, the cost of not taking the discount is:

$$\frac{(2\% \div 98\%) \times (360)}{(30 - 10)} = .0204 \times (360 \div 20) = 36.72\%$$

If the firm chooses to finance a payable of $100,000 for 30 days instead of paying $98,000 for 10 days, it will cost the firm $2,000 (or 36.72%) to finance the payable for 20 days. Unless the organization is facing severe financial difficulty, it will be able to obtain short-term financing for less than $2,000 for 20 days.

III. Bank Loan Interest Rates

a. When a firm sets up a line of credit with a bank, it often has commitment fees that a business must pay on the unused portion of the credit line.

b. For example, consider a firm that is currently using $250,000 of a $1,000,000 credit line. The interest rate is 5% with a 1% commitment fee. The firm must pay interest of $12,500 ($250,000 × 5%) and a commitment fee of $7,500 ($750,000 Unused × 1%). The total expense on the line of credit is $20,000, which is an effective interest rate of 8.0% = $20,000 ÷ $250,000.

c. Some financial institutions require *compensating balances* to be held as part of loan requirements. *Compensating balances* are minimum balances that must be maintained in a bank account to offset the cost of a loan incurred by a bank. For a loan with a compensating balance, the total borrowing amount is calculated as:

Amount Needed ÷ (1 − Compensating Balance %)

d. For example, consider a firm that needs $500,000 for a project. The bank offers to fund this loan at 8% with a compensating balance of 20%. The firm must actually borrow $625,000 = ($500,000 ÷ (1 – 20%). The firm must pay 8% on the full $625,000 even though $125,000 of it will simply be held in an account at the bank. The total interest expense on the loan will be $50,000 = $625,000 × 8%. This makes the effective interest rate 10% = $50,000 ÷ $500,000.

Summary

Economic cycles and business seasonality cause working capital to fluctuate over time. Fluctuations above the permanent working capital amount must be financed and managed. Maturity matching, long-term funding, and short-term funding are three alternatives used for financing working capital needs. If the cost of obtaining short-term financing is lower than the cost of a discount, a firm should obtain the short-term financing to pay in the discount period. Firms need to include bank requirements (such as commitment fees and compensating balances) in their evaluations of short-term debt.

Further Reading

Parrino, R., Kidwell, D., and Bates, T. (2017). *Fundamentals of Corporate Finance*, 4th Edition. Hoboken, NJ: John Wiley & Sons.

Topic 5. Corporate Restructuring

Mergers and Acquisitions

After studying this lesson, you should be able to:

- Demonstrate an understanding of the following:
- Identify defenses against takeovers (e.g., golden parachute, leveraged recapitalization, poison pill (shareholders' rights plan), staggered board of directors, fair price, voting rights plan, white knight) (2.B.5.b).
- Identify possible synergies in targeted mergers and acquisitions (2.B.5.e).

Business combinations can take many forms. This lesson reviews the terms and definitions related to mergers and acquisitions. Possible actions to prevent takeovers are also reviewed.

I. Mergers and Acquisitions

a. An *acquisition* is when one firm buys a controlling interest, which is greater than 50% ownership, in another business. This takes place for several reasons. Firms may acquire competitors to increase their own market share and limit competition. Firms may acquire smaller firms with unique capabilities or product offerings to facilitate growth. Firms may acquire struggling firms with the hope of improving efficiencies due to their own size, scale, and management techniques. Whatever the reasons, acquisitions form a critical activity in the financial market.

b. A *merger* takes places when two firms combine into one. Mergers take several forms. A *horizontal merger* is when two firms in the same industry are combined. A *vertical merger* is when two companies that make parts for a finished good are combined. A *conglomerate merger* is when two companies are combined that are from different industries.

c. Mergers and acquisitions can be executed through various financial agreements involving cash, debt, and equity. A firm can pay all cash for another company. A firm could also exchange ownership shares whereby the owners of the firm being acquired are paid with shares in the acquiring company. A *leveraged buyout* is a merger where the buyer uses debt to finance a significant portion of the transaction. The assets of the business are collateral for the debt assumed to execute the leveraged buyout.

II. Defenses against Takeovers

a. Sometimes a firm does not want to be acquired or bought by another firm. In which case, acquisition targets can implement a number of protective actions against acquisition.

i. A *golden parachute* provides very large payouts to executives released as part of an acquisition. It serves as a defense against takeover because the acquiring firm would incur significant additional costs to complete the transaction.

ii. *Staggered board of directors* is a strategy wherein a firm elects only part of its board each year. By having staggered terms of service on the board of directors, it makes it more difficult for shareholders to select a majority of board members to vote current management out.

iii. The *white knight* defense involves the targeted company finding a friendly buyer to outbid the potential acquirer. The firm will still be acquired, but is able to have input as to who the acquiring firm will be.

iv. *Poison pills* are provisions that make a potential acquisition target less attractive. An example would be making all debt redeemable in the event of an acquisition. Another example is a *voting rights plan* in which the acquisition target issues stock with special voting rights to shareholders. This strategy can allow shareholders of an acquisition target to have special or unique privileges in the event of a takeover event.

v. A *leveraged recapitalization* makes a firm less attractive to acquiring firms by taking out a significant amount of debt and distributing large cash dividends to shareholders. The additional debt burden deters other firms from wanting to acquire the firm.

Summary

Mergers and acquisitions are types of business combinations. Acquisitions are when one firm buys a controlling interest, which is greater than 50% ownership, in another business. Mergers take place when two firms combine into one. Mergers can take the form of horizontal mergers, vertical mergers, or conglomerate mergers. Mergers and acquisitions can take place through various forms of financial agreements. When a firm does not want to be taken over by another firm, it can implement protective actions against acquisition.

Restructuring and Combining

After studying this lesson, you should be able to:

- Identify and describe divestiture concepts such as spin-offs, split-ups, equity carve-outs, and tracking stock (2.B.5.c).
- Evaluate key factors in a company's financial situation and determine if a restructuring would be beneficial to the shareholders (2.B.5.d).

This lesson discusses how firms sell off or eliminate a portion of their products and services. Various forms of restructuring are defined and discussed along with factors that influences a firm's decision to do so.

I. Restructuring and Combining

a. Companies can reduce or eliminate a portion of the company through a *divestiture*. Divestitures can come in various forms. A few of the most common types of divestitures are the following:

i. *Spin-offs*—A spin-off takes place when a firm forms a new company out of a portion of its current divisions or product lines. For example, if firm A decides to divest itself of one of its divisions, it could create a new firm that will function independently as its own entity. Spin-offs are typically accomplished by distributing a special stock dividend to current shareholders. The firm does not receive any cash consideration for the spin-off. Spin-offs often take place when a firm has become large and diverse, which can create management difficulties. Spin-offs allow firms to narrow their strategic focus. Another reason spin-offs take place is if a part of a business has become unprofitable. By spinning-off a portion of the firm, the remaining firm is no longer burdened by the costs and upkeep of the spun-off portion of the firm.

ii. *Equity carve-outs*—This is a similar restructuring to a spin-off, but the firm sells only a minority interest in the new firm instead of selling the entire ownership stake. The carve-out does create a new entity that has its own board of directors and financial statements, but the parent firm retains a controlling interest. Carve-outs can help a firm monetize the growth in a portion of their company by selling ownership shares in the market.

iii. *Split-ups*—This restructuring takes one firm and splits it into two separately run firms. Each firm is a standalone firm with independent management and boards of directors. Many split-ups occur because the government is concerned about monopolistic behavior. Companies also can split up when company management and the board of directors believe separate companies will provide greater value than a single company will.

iv. *Tracking stocks*—Ownership shares that are issued by a parent company to monitor the performance of one strategic business unit (SBU). Tracking stocks typically have limited or no voting rights. Companies use a tracking stock to measure the performance of a high-growth SBU held inside of a parent company. While the parent company maintains control of the SBU, the creation of a tracking stock provides a mechanism for investors to invest in a portion of the company. All financial results from the SBU are tracked separately from the parent company's overall financial results, which creates greater transparency for market participants to evaluate the SBU performance.

Summary

When a company reduces or eliminates a portion of its company it is called a divestiture. Some of the most common forms of divestitures are spin-offs, equity carve-outs, split-ups, and tracking stocks.

Evaluating Business Combinations

After studying this lesson, you should be able to:

- Value a business, a business segment, and a business combination using discounted cash flow method (2.B.5.f).
- Evaluate a proposed business combination and make a recommendation based on both quantitative and qualitative considerations (2.B.5.g).

This lesson reviews how to use the discounted cash flow method to evaluate business combinations. It also discusses quantitative and qualitative factors that are important to consider when evaluating proposed business combinations.

I. Evaluating Mergers and Acquisitions

a. As with any investment, firms must evaluate a potential acquisition or merger to determine if it will generate an appropriate return on investment. The discounted cash flow (DCF) method can be used to evaluate whether a proposed business combination will create value. Similar to valuing an investment or project, valuing a business combination is comprised of identifying cash inflows and cash outflows along with determining an appropriate discount rate.

b. Valuing a firm using the DCF does have its drawbacks. Whereas a project typically has an expected useful life, a firm is considered to have an indefinite life. The value of a firm's income can be projected for three to five years, but any projections past that point have a high degree of uncertainty. As such, the value of a business is estimated as the sum of the following three factors:

i. Present value of future cash flows over a short window of time. This is typically three to five years.

ii. Present value of all future cash flows thereafter. This is referred to as the *terminal value*.

iii. Present value of non-operating assets, which are the cash and other assets not required to support the business.

c. Business combinations are often done with the strategic goal of increasing revenues, decreasing costs, or expanding market share. The challenge with evaluating the potential value creation is in determining how revenue and expenses will change or grow in the future. The use of *what-if* analyses can be beneficial by evaluating the likelihood of various scenarios and outcomes. Rather than assuming the proposed model and its assumptions will hold true, a what-if analysis can identify what circumstances must hold true in order for the project to create value. This allows the management decision maker to evaluate the riskiness of a proposed business combination and understand what factors can influence the success of the merger or acquisition.

d. Examples of revenue-generation synergies from business combinations:

i. Selling more products through the companies' existing sales channels

ii. Creating new products from technologies developed in the acquired company

iii. Expanding into new geographic markets

iv. Extending a brand name to new products

e. Examples of cost-saving synergies from business combinations:

i. Closing facilities producing the same or similar products

ii. Reducing employee staff, such as sales teams or administration

iii. Consolidating information systems

   iv. Greater centralization of processes and activities, such as accounting centralized at a single corporate location

f. Businesses must evaluate a variety of quantitative and qualitative factors when deciding whether to acquire or merge with another company.

g. Examples of quantitative factors to consider when evaluating a business combination:
   i. Increased revenue from new products or markets
   ii. Increased margins from better pricing or lower costs of goods due to quantity discounts
   iii. Reduced costs from identifying duplicate departments or processes
   iv. Increased return on assets because of decreased duplicate assets

h. Examples of qualitative factors to consider when evaluating a business combination:
   i. Strength of the management team
   ii. Fit of the companies' cultures
   iii. Brand strength
   iv. Specialized expertise in a type of technology or in a business process

Summary
When considering a potential acquisition or merger a firm must evaluate whether it will generate an appropriate return on investment. The discounted cash flow (DCF) method is often used to evaluate whether a proposed combination will create value to the firm. What-if analyses are also used to evaluate how revenues and expenses will change in the future depending on various assumptions.

Further Reading
Parrino, R., Kidwell, D., and Bates, T. (2017). *Fundamentals of Corporate Finance*, 4th Edition. Hoboken, NJ: John Wiley & Sons.

Topic 6. International Finance

Fixed, Flexible, and Floating Exchange Rates

After studying this lesson, you should be able to:

- Demonstrate an understanding of foreign currencies and how foreign currency affects the prices of goods and services (2.B.6.a).
- Identify the variables that affect exchange rates (2.B.6.b).
- Calculate whether a currency has depreciated or appreciated against another currency over time, and evaluate the impact of the change (2.B.6.c).

The globalization of the business world gives rise to a need to understand international finance. This lesson reviews how foreign currencies affect economic transactions. Factors affecting exchange rates are discussed.

I. Foreign Exchange Rates

a. Foreign exchange rates influence how firms will source and sell their goods and services. Foreign exchange rates indicate how much of one currency can be exchanged for one unit of another country's currency.

b. Foreign exchange rates may be *fixed*, *flexible (floating)*, or *managed floating*.

i. A *fixed exchange rate* requires a country to maintain its currency at or near a benchmark value, such as another country's currency, or the value of a commodity, such as gold. The benefits of a fixed exchange rate system include (1) governments cannot take actions to artificially expand or contract their monetary supply, (2) no incentive to speculate in foreign exchange rates, and (3) reduced uncertainty exists for businesses working with foreign currencies.

ii. *Flexible* or *floating exchange rates* are set by market supply and demand for currencies. Most of the world's major currencies are floating currencies. The benefits from a floating exchange rate include (1) governments have more freedom to dictate their monetary policies, (2) trade balances can adjust more readily, allowing for a more flexible system of trading goods and services, and (3) opportunity to profit off of exchange rate fluctuations.

iii. A *managed floating exchange rate* system combines features of the fixed and floating exchange rate systems. In such a system, governments can intervene in markets when required, but market forces generally dictate foreign currency exchange rates. For example, central banks, such as the U.S. Federal Reserve, can purchase or sell currencies to adjust foreign exchange rates. Managed floating exchange rates can help prevent or mitigate economic turmoil from supply and demand; however, these systems can lack clear rules and policies, which results in more volatile exchange rates.

c. Factors that influence exchange rates include the following:

i. Inflation rates.

ii. Interest rates.

iii. Public debt—higher levels of debt will make a currency less valuable.

iv. Current account deficits—a negative current account will make a currency less valuable.

v. Ratio of imports to exports, also called terms of trade or balance of trade.

vi. Political and economic stability.

d. A currency that is less valuable than the currency of the importing country will make imports less expensive for the importing country. A country with a less valuable currency will benefit more from exporting to other countries. Countries with heavy importing activity will lose value in this scenario.

e. A currency that is more valuable than the currency of the importing country will make importing less expensive for the home country. A country with a more valuable currency will benefit more from importing from other countries. Countries with heavy exporting activity will lose value in this scenario.

Foreign Exchange Rate Example
Suppose a company buys steel for use in manufacturing its products. The price of steel per ton is 660 units of currency in Country A. Alternatively, the company can buy the same amount of steel from a foreign country, Country B, at the price of 1,320 units of currency in Country B.

The foreign exchange rate between the two countries is 1-to-2.

Now suppose that the price of a ton of steel in the two countries remains the same, but the foreign exchange rate has changed to be 1-to-1.8. The company will now be required to exchange 733 units of Country A's currency in order to purchase a ton of steel.

1,320 units of Country B's currency $\div$ 1.8 $=$ 733 units

Due to the change in the foreign exchange rate, the steel in country B is now more expensive.

Summary
Foreign currency exchange rates indicate how much of one currency can be exchanged for one unit of another country's currency. Foreign exchange rates can be fixed, flexible (floating), or managed floating and are influenced by a variety of factors. Companies with heavy exporting or importing activity need to carefully evaluate foreign exchange rates when deciding which countries to trade with.

Further Reading
Parrino, R., Kidwell, D., and Bates, T. (2017). *Fundamentals of Corporate Finance*, 4th Edition. Hoboken, NJ: John Wiley & Sons.

Managing Transaction Exposure

After studying this lesson, you should be able to:

- Demonstrate how currency futures, currency swaps, and currency options can be used to manage exchange rate risk (2.B.6.d).
- Calculate the net profit/loss of cross-border transactions, and evaluate the impact of this net profit/loss (2.B.6.e).
- Recommend methods of managing exchange rate risk and calculate the net profit/loss of your strategy (2.B.6.f).

Exchange rate risk arises because firms transact in different currencies than their normal operations. This lesson discusses strategies that firms can use to limit their exposure to exchange rate risk.

I. Managing Transaction Exposure

a. Investors and firms have a variety of options to reduce risk exposure associated with foreign currency exchange rates. The following instruments are used to either fix an exchange rate for a transaction or exchange one currency exchange rate for another.

i. *Currency futures* are contracts to fix a currency exchange rate at a given date.

1. For example, an American company importing goods from Europe may execute a currency futures contract to hedge, or reduce the risk, against volatility of the euro. An American company could enter into a futures contract to exchange a set amount of euros for every U.S. dollar three months from the present date. The futures contract allows the American company to forecast future cash flows and financial statements because the futures contract fixes the currency exchange rate.

ii. *Currency swaps* occur when two organizations contract to exchange or "swap" different currencies and assume the foreign exchange risk associated with the other party's home currency.

1. For example, assume that an American company and a European company need to borrow funds In the other company's currency. However, the two companles may be able to borrow money at lower rates in their home markets than they can borrow foreign currency in the other market. A possible solution is for these companies to borrow money from their local institutions and then execute a currency swap of their two loans at a prevailing exchange rate. The companies assume exchange risk in this transaction, but benefit from lower interest payments on their loans.

iii. *Currency options* give organizations the right, but not the obligation, to buy or sell foreign currency at a contractually obligated price during the option period.

1. Currency options differ from currency futures because futures require the company to comply with the terms of the contract. Options only give the party the right to execute the transaction. Buyers of currency options pay a premium for the ability to determine if the option is executed.

Example of Currency Swaps

This example shows how two organizations—one in the United States and one in Europe—can execute a currency swap to minimize the interest expense associated with borrowing foreign currency.

	Company A (USA—\$)	**Company B (Europe—€)**
Local interest rate	6%	8%
International borrowing interest rate	12%	10%
USD/EUR exchange rate	1.12	1.12
Currency borrowed	\$100,000	€100,000
Currency assumed	€100,000	\$112,000

In this example, Company A will pay \$6,000 of interest annually on \$100,000. Company B will pay €8,000 of interest annually on €100,000.

If the companies borrowed the foreign currency, Company A would pay \$13,440 of interest (€100,000 × 12% × 1.12 exchange rate). Company B would pay €8,928 (\$100,000 × 10% ÷ 1.12) of interest if it borrowed \$100,000 as foreign currency. In the swap example, each company pays less in interest but assumes the foreign exchange risk associated with the other nation's currency.

Example of Currency Futures

Suppose that an American firm sells a piece of equipment to a European firm for €100,000. The agreement is such that the European firm will pay for the equipment in 90 days when the equipment is delivered. At the time of the sale, the exchange rate is €1 = \$1.60.

In order to limit their exposure to exchange rate risk, the American firm can enter into a forward contract to exchange €1 for \$1.58 in 90 days.

If in 90 days the exchange rate is €1 = \$1.50, the American firm will benefit from the forward contract by exchanging €100,000 for \$158,000 even though the current exchange rate would have yielded only \$150,000.

If in 90 days the exchange rate is €1 = \$1.65, the American firm would still exchange €100,000 for \$158,000. The firm does not benefit from the increase in the exchange rate. The forward contract provided certainty and reduced exchange rate risk, but also removed the potential upside of the risk.

Summary

Firms that transact in different currencies than their normal operations face exchange rate risk. Currency swaps, currency options, and currency futures are a few strategies that investors and firms use to minimize their exposure to exchange rate risk.

Further Reading

Parrino, R., Kidwell, D., and Bates, T. (2017). *Fundamentals of Corporate Finance*, 4th Edition. Hoboken, NJ: John Wiley & Sons.

Financing International Trade

After studying this lesson, you should be able to:

- Identify and explain the benefits of international diversification (2.B.6.g).
- Identify and explain common trade financing methods, including cross-border factoring, letters of credit, banker's acceptances, forfeiting, and countertrade (2.B.6.h).

This lesson reviews issues facing firms with international projects. Common methods of financing international trade are also discussed.

I. International Capital Budgeting

a. Capital investment projects that take place in international countries make the determination of future cash flows more complicated. While the tools of capital budgeting and valuation are similar (e.g., NPV, DCF, etc.), estimating future cash flows is more difficult.

b. Foreign countries have different tax codes as well as different financial reporting standards. Estimating the after-tax cash flows requires familiarity with these systems that may lead firms to incur costs to hire consultants and tax experts.

c. Foreign governments often place restrictions on the amount of cash that can be moved out of a country. These are commonly referred to as *repatriation of earnings restrictions*. The restrictions are put in place by foreign governments to limit the outflow of capital from their country. In terms of forecasting cash flows, uncertainty about the limits and policies related to repatriation complicates the accuracy of estimating future cash flows.

d. Estimating future cash flows in a foreign currency requires an estimate of future exchange rates. As most major currencies are floating currencies, the current exchange rate is not a reliable indicator of future exchange rates. Forecast future exchange rates can be difficult due to the many factors that influence exchange rates such as politics, inflation, monetary policies, and macroeconomic conditions.

e. The stability of a country's political environment is an important consideration when evaluating foreign business activities. Politics can have a significant effect on a firm's ability to estimate future cash flows. Foreign governments may change tax laws, labor laws, tariffs, quotas, and repatriation laws. Practically speaking, the more uncertainty about a country's political environment, the higher the appropriate discount rate for capital budgeting purposes should be.

f. Despite the increased difficulty of estimating future cash flows on international projects, there are significant benefits to international diversification.

II. International Bank Lending

a. Organizations depend on a variety of payment methods to pay for global trade. These include:

i. *Letters of credit* are agreements sent from a lender to an exporter on behalf of an importer guaranteeing the lender will accept a draft for payment from the importer.

ii. *Sight drafts* are bills for imports payable upon receipt.

iii. *Time drafts* are bills that must be paid at a specific time or upon completion of an obligated action.

iv. *Consignment* takes place when an exporter sends goods to be sold to an importer. The importer will pay the exporter once the goods are sold.

v. *Open accounts* are similar to traditional accounts receivable and payable. There is a risk of default by the buyer if the buyer does not pay according to terms.

b. Additional financing methods for international trade:

  i. *Banker's acceptance* letters are short-term financing instruments issued by a firm and guaranteed by a financial institution. The letters are traded in secondary markets. A party buying a banker's acceptance can present the letter for payment at the bank issuing the letter.

  ii. *Foreign currency accounts* can be maintained by a firm in order to pay bills in that foreign currency.

  iii. In *countertrading* (also known as *bartering*), goods and services are exchanged instead of cash.

  iv. In *forfeiting*, the purchaser pays for receivables from an exporter at a discount for immediate cash. A forfeiting transaction usually includes these features:

    1. A credit period no shorter than 180 days
    2. The possibility of settling the transaction in most major currencies
    3. A letter of credit, promissory note, or other guarantee made by a bank

Summary
Firms with international projects face various difficulties that might include any of the following: different tax codes and financial reporting standards, restrictions on the amount of cash that can be moved out of a country, forecasting the future exchange rates, and the unknown stability of a country's political environment. Common methods of financing international trade include letters of credit, sight drafts, time drafts, consignment, open accounts, banker's acceptance letters, foreign currency accounts, countertrading, and forfeiting.

Further Reading
Parrino, R., Kidwell, D., and Bates, T. (2017). *Fundamentals of Corporate Finance*, 4th Edition. Hoboken, NJ: John Wiley & Sons.

Section B Review Questions

aq.acc.rm.0003_1710

1. The accounts receivable turnover ratio is a measure of:

   A. the number of times a customer made a purchase on account.
   B. the number of times the firm's inventory was replaced.
   C. the amount of credit sales within a reporting period.
   D. the number of times a company cycles its accounts receivable.

aq.bonds.0007_1710

2. For a bond issue which sells for less than its par value, the market rate of interest is:

   A. dependent on the rate stated on the bond.
   B. higher than the rate stated on the bond.
   C. equal to the rate stated on the bond.
   D. less than the rate stated on the bond.

aq.val.de.0004_1710

3. If a firm pays a constant dividend of $10 and the required rate of return or discount rate is equal to 10%, what is the price of the stock using the zero-growth dividend model?

   A. $1
   B. $10
   C. $50
   D. $100

aq.coc.0009_1710

4. When calculating the weighted-average cost of capital (WACC), an adjustment is made for taxes because:

   A. equity is risky.
   B. the interest on debt is tax deductible.
   C. preferred stock is used.
   D. equity earns higher return than debt.

aq.fff.er.0002_1710

5. Which type of foreign exchange system allows for governments to intervene and influence exchange rates?

   A. Managed floating exchange rate
   B. Flexible exchange rate
   C. Floating exchange rate
   D. Fixed exchange rate

aq.fff.er.0004_1710

6. Consider two countries: Country A and Country B. If Country A's currency is more valuable than Country B's, how will country A's imports from Country B be affected?

   A. Imports will increase.
   B. Imports will decrease.
   C. Imports will not be affected.
   D. Not enough information is given.

aq.cap.ass.0004_1710

7. Consider the information below. Using the capital asset pricing model, what is the firm's cost of equity (round to 2 decimals)?

   Risk-free rate of return = 0.05

   Market rate of return = 0.12

   Firm's beta = 1.2

   A. 13%
   B. 19%
   C. 8%
   D. 11%

aq.cap.ass.0003_1710

8. The capital asset pricing model (CAPM) is used to determine the cost of what?

   A. Cost of capital
   B. Cost of debt
   C. Cost of equity
   D. Cost of leasing

aq.mark.e.0002_1710

9. Which form of market efficiency is described below?

   Security prices reflect all public information but not all private information. For example, investors who have private information could acquire such information through analysis of the firm or discussions with a firm's customers. This form is a reasonable representation of how most large stock markets function.

   A. Strong-form efficiency
   B. Semistrong-form efficiency
   C. Weak-form efficiency
   D. Semiweak-form efficiency

aq.val.de.0003_0720

10. Schmidt, Inc. issues a $10 million bond with a 6% coupon rate, 4-year maturity, and annual interest payments when market interest rates are 7%. Time value of money factors are listed below.

    PV of $1 @ 7% for 4 years = 0.7629

    PV ordinary annuity @ 7% for 4 years = 3.38721*

    Solutions are computed using present value tables. Due to rounding errors, the solution may be slightly different if a calculator is used.

    What is the initial carrying value of the bonds?

    A. $9,661,326
    B. $9,400,000
    C. $10,000,000
    D. $10,338,721

aq.fin.it.0004_1710

11. Which of the following financial tools involves an exporter sending goods to an importer before the good has been sold to a customer?

    A. Letters of credit
    B. Countertrading
    C. Consignment
    D. Sight drafts

aq.mark.sm.0005_1710

12. Which of the following is best described as unsecured (without collateral), short-term borrowing by very large, creditworthy firms?

    A. Commercial paper
    B. Eurodollars
    C. Repurchase agreements
    D. Bankers' acceptances

aq.restruc.c.0003_1710

13. Which of the following types of business divestitures would a firm use in order to most effectively monitor the performance of a strategic business unit?

    A. Spin-off
    B. Equity carve-out
    C. Split-up
    D. Tracking stock

aq.eval.bc.0004_1710

14. When using the discounted cash flow method to evaluate a business combination, what is the appropriate assumption about longevity of the target firm?

    A. Three to five years
    B. Product's projected useful life
    C. Industry average firm life
    D. Indefinite life

aq.term.struc.0005_1710

15. The real rate of interest is:

    A. the nominal interest rate plus expected inflation.
    B. the risk-free rate plus expected inflation.
    C. the nominal interest rate minus expected inflation.
    D. the nominal interest rate plus the risk-free rate.

Section C: Decision Analysis

Topic 1. CVP Analysis

Cost Behavior and C-V-P Analysis

After studying this lesson, you should be able to:

- Demonstrate an understanding of how Cost-Volume-Profit (CVP) analysis (Breakeven analysis) is used to examine the behavior of total revenues, total costs, and operating income as changes occur in output levels, selling prices, variable costs per unit, or fixed costs. (2.C.1.a).

Sometimes known as Breakeven analysis, Cost-Volume-Profit (CVP) analysis is a classic, and very effective, tool for understanding and managing the relationship between costs, prices, sale volumes, and profits. This lesson introduces the basic C-V-P formula and visually demonstrates the relationships across costs, revenue, and volume. Be sure to focus on really understanding the formula and the CVP charts. The concepts should be clear to you.

I. The "One" Cost-Volume-Profit Formula and Its Formats

A. The *Cost-Volume-Profit (C-V-P) formula* is effectively the formula for profit in the organization. Profit analysis, including breakeven, can be derived from this basic formula, and this basic C-V-P formula can be expanded into two formats.

Revenue − Variable Cost − Fixed Cost = Profit

1. (Sales Price × Volume) – (Variable Cost per Unit × Volume) – Total Fixed Costs = Profit[1]
2. Revenue – (Variable Cost Ratio × Revenue) – Total Fixed Costs = Profit[2]

Note that Variable Cost Ratio = Variable Costs ÷ Revenue.

---

[1]If you're preparing for the CMA© exam, the ICMA formula sheet uses an abbreviation of this formula. It is: Breakeven point in units = fixed costs ÷ unit contribution margin

[2]If you're preparing for the CMA© exam, the ICMA formula sheet uses an abbreviation of this formula. It is: Breakeven point in dollars = fixed costs ÷ (unit contribution margin ÷ selling price)

B. Notice in the first format of the C-V-P formula that there are five factors: Sales Price (per unit), Volume, Variable Cost per Unit, Total Fixed Costs, and Profit. By setting Profit = 0 in this format and filling in values for three of the remaining four factors, you can determine the value of the final factor necessary to have breakeven ($0) profit.

C. Generally, when sales price and/or sales volume information isn't available, then the second format of the C-V-P formula is used, with the key input being the variable cost ratio.

1. This format is most often used to find the necessary revenue to have breakeven profit.
2. Note that the variable cost ratio can be determined by dividing current total variable costs by total revenue, or by dividing the variable cost per unit by the sales price.

D. Remember that these two formats of the C-V-P formula are essentially the same formula! For example, if you have the unit information to solve for breakeven volume (units) using the first format, then you can easily determine the breakeven point in sales dollars by multiplying the number of breakeven units by the sales price per unit.

II. Cost-Volume-Profit Charts

A. Visually show the relationship of revenue and costs across the volume of the key production activity.

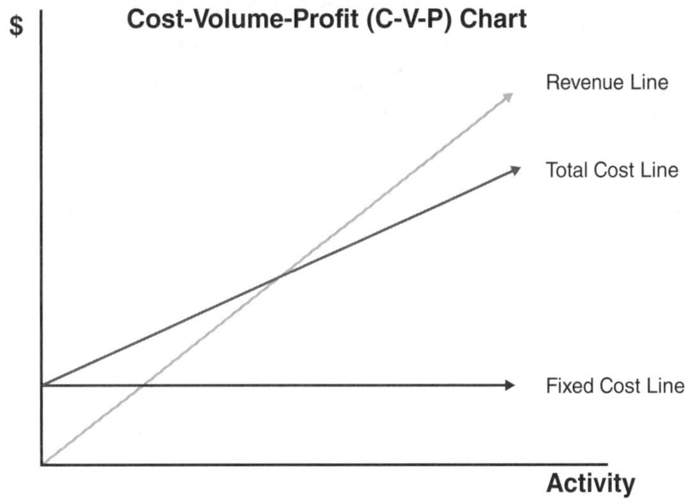

B. Variable costs per unit of activity are depicted in the C-V-P chart as the slope (rise over run) of the Total Costs line.

C. Fixed costs can certainly shift and change based on many different circumstances, but fixed costs are constant with respect to the volume of the key production activity and should always be stated in total.

D. *Breakeven* is defined as the level of sales and activity volume at which revenues exactly offset total costs, both fixed and variable. This is the point in the C-V-P chart where the Revenue line crosses over the Total Costs line.

E. The breakeven point usually can be expressed both in sales units (on the horizontal axis in the C-V-P chart) and in sales dollars (on the vertical axis in the C-V-P chart).

F. Profit and loss is defined by the difference between revenue and total cost above and below the breakeven point, respectively.

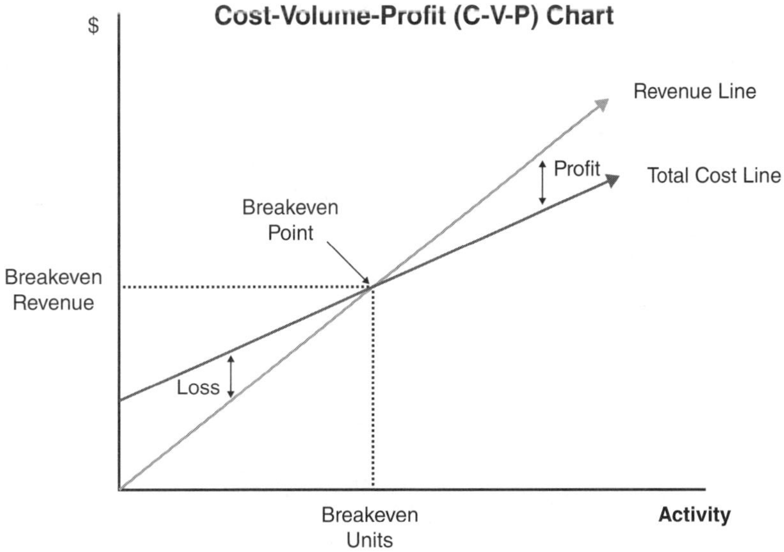

III. Cost Behavior

A. Cost behavior is based on the organization's *key activity*.

B. The *key activity* is what primarily drives costs and revenues and can be defined as almost anything for any organization (items sold for a retail store, feet drilled for an oil driller, billable hours for a law firm, etc.)

Practice Question
Parker Corporation sells a product for $15. Variable costs per unit are $5. Fixed costs are $700,000. What is Parker's breakeven point in units and in sales dollars?

Answer:

For breakeven point in units:

(Sales Price × Volume) – (Variable Cost per Unit × Volume) – Total Fixed Costs = Profit

($15 × Units) – ($5 × Units) – $700,000 = $0

($10 × Units) – $700,000 = $0

($10 × Units) = $700,000

Units = $700,000 ÷ $10 = 70,000 Units to breakeven

For breakeven point in sales dollars:

Revenue – (Variable Cost Ratio × Revenue) – Total Fixed Costs = Profit

Variable Cost Ratio = $5 ÷ $15 = 33.33% *or* 0.3333

(1 × Revenue) – (0.3333 × Revenue) – $700,000 = $0

(0.6667 × Revenue) – $700,000 = $0

(0.6667 × Revenue) = $700,000

Revenue = $700,000 ÷ 0.6667 = $1,050,000 Sales Dollars to breakeven

Alternatively,

70,000 Breakeven Units × $15 = $1,050,000 Sales Dollars to breakeven

Summary
Profit analysis in an organization is effectively evaluated with the Cost-Volume-Profit (C-V-P) formula. The basic formula of Revenue – Variable Cost – Fixed Cost = Profit can be used to derive breakeven as well as expanded into two other formats. Cost-Volume-Profit charts are used to visually show the relationship of revenue and costs. Cost behavior in any organization is based on the key activity of that organization. The key activity is any factor that primarily drives costs and revenues.

Contribution Margin

After studying this lesson, you should be able to:

- Calculate operating income at different operating levels (2.C.1.b).
- Differentiate between costs that are fixed and costs that are variable with respect to levels of output (2.C.1.c).
- Explain why the classification of fixed vs. variable costs is affected by the time frame being considered (2.C.1.d).
- Calculate contribution margin per unit and total contribution margin (2.C.1.e).

Another critical tool used by management to evaluate revenues and costs is contribution margin. Unlike gross margin, contribution margin focuses on the effects of fixed and variable costs on operating profit. This lesson will introduce you to the difference between contribution margin and gross margin as well as help you to understand how to use contribution margin to analyze a company's revenues and costs. Additionally, you will learn how to apply contribution margin to the basic C-V-P formula.

I. The Contribution Margin Statements and Calculations

A. The contribution margin statement

1. The traditional view of the cost's function *is not* the cost's behavior.

2. GAAP (Generally Accepted Accounting Principles) and IFRS (International Financial Reporting Standards) income statements generally classify operating costs into two groups: Cost of Goods Sold and Administrative & Sales Expense, which are useful for tracking product costs through inventory on the balance sheet.

3. On the other hand, contribution margin income statements classify operating costs into Variable Costs and Fixed Costs, which is useful for effective management of profit.

Traditional View of the Cost's Function
is not the Cost's Behavior!

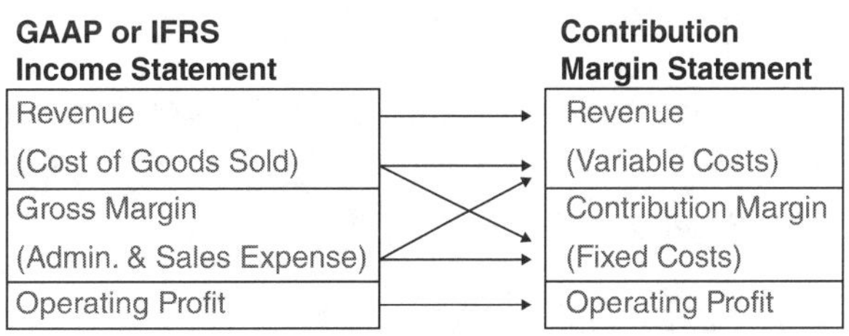

4. Note that with either type of income statement, we are reporting on the same overall operating costs, but classifying costs using different criteria. The contribution margin approach is focused on *cost behavior.*

a. Costs are classified as variable if they proportionally increase and decrease based on changes in the volume of the organization's key production activity.

b. Fixed costs don't change based on the key production activity (though these costs can certainly shift based on other factors, including management discretion).

B. Contribution margin calculations

1. It is useful to break down revenue, variable costs, and contribution margin to unit values (i.e., price per unit, variable cost per unit, contribution margin per unit). However, it's important to *not* reduce fixed costs and operating profit to unit values. This is because these two numbers do not remain constant with increases and decreases in sales volume.

2. A common-size analysis is another useful tool. In a common-size analysis, variable costs ratios and contribution margin ratios are analyzed in relation to Revenue. Fixed costs and operating profit should not be analyzed in relation to revenues. Again, these ratios do not remain constant with increases and decreases in sales volume.

Contribution Margin Calculations

Revenue	Price per Unit	100%
(Variable Costs)	(VC per Unit)	(VC%)
Contribution	CM per Unit	CM%
(Fixed Costs)	(FC per Unit) N	(FC%) N
Operating Profit	Profit per Unit N	Profit% N

II. Computing Income using the Contribution Margin Approach

A. Contribution margin in the C-V-P formula

1. Variable costs are best measured and managed in their unit amount while fixed costs are best measured or managed in their total amount. This is why the contribution margin statement is represented very well by all versions of the C-V-P formula.

2. Contribution margin represents the portion of revenues that are available to cover fixed costs. It can be expressed on a per-unit basis or as a ratio (percentage) of revenue.

> Sales Revenue − Variable Costs = Contribution Margin
>
> Sales Price per Unit − Variable Costs per Unit = Contribution Margin Rate
>
> Contribution Margin ÷ Revenue = Contribution Margin Ratio

3. Contribution margin calculations can be used to provide an easy way to shorten the C-V-P formula.

> Revenue − Variable Cost − Fixed Cost = Profit
>
> 1. (Sales Price × Volume) – (Variable Cost per Unit × Volume) – Total Fixed Costs = Profit
> 2. Revenue – (Variable Cost Ratio × Revenue) – Total Fixed Costs = Profit
>
> Contribution Margin − Fixed Cost = Profit
>
> 1. (Contribution Margin Rate × Volume) – Total Fixed Costs = Profit
> 2. (Contribution Margin Ratio × Revenue) – Total Fixed Costs = Profit

B. Computing income at different levels of operating volume

1. There are many different ways to compute income with varying levels of operating volume; however, the most efficient approach is based on contribution margin numbers.

2. Consider an item with a unit sales price of \$1.50, a variable cost per unit of \$1.00, and total fixed costs of \$5,000. The contribution margin rate is \$0.50 per unit (\$1.50 – \$1.00). With this rate, we can easily compute income at 5,000 units sold, 10,000 units sold, and 15,000 units sold.

> (Contribution Margin Rate × Volume) – Total Fixed Costs = Profit
> (\$0.50 × 5,000) – \$5,000 = –\$2,500
> (\$0.50 × 10,000) – \$5,000 = \$0
> (\$0.50 × 15,000) – \$5,000 = \$2,500

3. Note the pattern of the profit increasing by \$2,500 for every 5,000 units. Using this method, a pattern emerges that can be followed to compute subsequent incomes.

C. Calculating breakeven with the **simplified** C-V-P formula

1. If unit information is available, breakeven point in sales dollars can be determined easily by calculating the breakeven point in units and then multiplying the number of units by the sales price per unit.

2. Sometimes no unit sales price or unit variable cost information is available. In these cases, it is not possible to calculate the breakeven point in units. It is, however, still possible to calculate the breakeven point in sales dollars, but a slightly different approach must be used.

3. When no unit information is available, but total sales revenue, total variable costs, and total fixed costs are known, the breakeven point in sales dollars can be determined by calculating the contribution margin ratio. The contribution margin ratio represents the **percentage of each sales dollar that is available to cover fixed costs**.

   a. If total sales are \$100 and variable costs are \$40, then the contribution margin is \$60. This means that for every \$100 of sales, \$60 is available to cover fixed costs.

   b. If we **express the contribution margin as a ratio (or percentage) of sales dollars**, then we can say that 60% (\$60 ÷ \$100) of each sales dollar is available to cover fixed costs. If total fixed costs are \$300, then we can calculate the number of sales dollars necessary to cover fixed costs and to break even shown below.

   > (Contribution Margin Ratio × Revenue) – Total Fixed Costs = Profit
   > (60% × Breakeven Revenue) – \$300 = \$0
   > 60% × Breakeven Revenue = \$300
   > Breakeven Revenue = \$300 ÷ .60
   > Breakeven Revenue = \$500

   c. The variable cost ratio and the contribution margin ratio are complements to each other. The contribution margin ratio is always 1 – variable cost ratio (and vice versa).

   d. To check to see if a breakeven answer is correct, verify that net income is zero when variable costs and fixed costs are deducted from breakeven sales. This is shown below with the example continued from above.

Breakeven Sales	**\$500**	**100%**
– Variable Costs	(\$200)	40%
= Contribution Margin	\$300	60%
– Fixed Costs	(\$300)	
= **Operating Profit**	**\$0**	

4. Thus, the "One" C-V-P formula introduced in the previous lesson can be simplified to calculate breakeven in sales volume or sales dollars using the contribution margin rate and the ratio as follows (note that this simplified formula saves a few math steps):

Breakeven Point in Sales Volume = Total Fixed Costs ÷ Contribution Margin Rate
(where Contribution Margin Rate = Sales Price per Unit – Variable Cost per Unit)

Breakeven Point in Sales Dollars = Total Fixed Costs ÷ Contribution Margin Ratio
(where Contribution Margin Ratio = Contribution Margin ÷ Sales Revenue)

Practice Question
Given the following facts, calculate breakeven in sales dollars:

- Current sales revenue and current variable costs are $120,000 and $90,000, respectively.
- Fixed costs are $40,000.

Answer:

(Contribution Margin Percentage × Revenue) – Total Fixed Costs = Profit

(25% × Revenue) – $40,000 = $0

(25% × Revenue) = $40,000

Revenue = $40,000 ÷ 25% = $160,000

Or:

Breakeven Point in Sales Dollars = Total Fixed Costs ÷ Contribution Margin Ratio

Breakeven Point in Sales Dollars = $40,000 ÷ 25%

Breakeven Point in Sales Dollars = $160,000

To Verify Answer:

Breakeven Sales	$160,000	100%
- Variable Costs	($120,000)	75%
= Contribution Margin	$40,000	25%
- Fixed Costs	($40,000)	
= Operating Profit	$0	

III. Effect of Time-frame on the Classification of Fixed and Variable Costs

A. The C-V-P formula and the contribution margin approach to managing profit are based very much on the assumption that the variable cost per unit and the total fixed costs remain constant. That is, as we explore different levels of production volume activity in the analysis, these two numbers won't shift. The upper and lower boundary of production volume activity where variable cost per unit or total fixed costs start to change represents the **relevant range** of the management analysis.

B. *Relevant range* is a key assumption in C-V-P analysis. At some point in time as a business expands or contracts, variable costs per unit or total fixed costs will shift. When this happens, the current relevant range of production activity shifts, and we must reanalyze costs to identify the new variable cost per unit and/or the new total fixed costs. At that point, we use the new data for the C-V-P formula and the contribution margin approach.

Summary

Contribution margin is computed as Revenue – Variable Costs. On the other hand, gross margin is computed as Revenue – Cost of Goods Sold. It is crucial to understand the difference between contribution margin and gross margin. Contribution margin is used in management accounting analysis to quickly determine the effects of prices, costs, and volumes of activity on Operating Profit. It is important to note that cost structures (and prices) are only constant within a relevant range of time or activity. When operations move outside the relevant range of activity, the contribution margin analysis needs to be reset.

Targeted Profit and Taxes

After studying this lesson, you should be able to:

- Calculate the breakeven point in units and dollar sales to achieve targeted operating income or targeted net income (2.C.1.f).
- Demonstrate an understanding of the impact of income taxes on CVP analysis (2.C.1.l).

Most companies are not as interested in just breaking even as they are in achieving a particular after-tax income goal (often referred to as targeted profit). In this lesson, you will learn how to modify the basic C-V-P formula to evaluate for a targeted profit. You will also learn how to adjust the after-tax targeted profit to pre-tax targeted profit before using it in the C-V-P formula.

I. Targeted Profit and the Basic C-V-P Formula

A. Generally, organizations are much more interested in understanding how to achieve a certain level of profit versus achieving zero profit (i.e., breakeven). In this case, rather than using the C-V-P formula to do breakeven analysis, we instead use the formula to do targeted profit analysis.

B. There really isn't any adjustment to the basic C-V-P formula to incorporate targeted profit. Instead of setting Profit = \$0 to do breakeven analysis, now set (i.e., target) the Profit at whatever amount is desired, and solve the formula.

$$\text{Revenue} - \text{Variable Cost} - \text{Fixed Cost} = \textit{Profit}$$

$$(\text{Sales Price} \times \text{Volume}) - (\text{Variable Cost per Unit} \times \text{Volume}) - \text{Total Fixed Costs} = \textit{Profit}$$

$$\text{Revenue} - (\text{Variable Cost Ratio} \times \text{Revenue}) - \text{Total Fixed Costs} = \textit{Profit}$$

C. In fact, you should see that the basic C-V-P formula can be used to isolate and solve for any factor that management is interested in understanding. Sometimes this is referred to as "What-If" analysis. For example, what if we wanted a target profit at \$10,000? What would Volume need to be? Or what would Sales Price need to be? Or what would Variable Cost per Unit (or Total Fixed Costs) need to be?

D. To solve for any factor in the C-V-P formula, set that factor as "unknown" in the formula and hold all other input factors constant. Then solve the unknown in the formula.

Practice Question

Watson's Fish Company buys whole salmon from various fishermen at \$4 per pound and sells the fish to restaurants for \$6 per pound. Its fixed costs are \$20,000 per month. How many pounds must be sold to break even, and how many pounds to earn a profit of \$10,000 per month?

Answer for Breakeven:

$$\$6(\text{Volume}) - \$4(\text{Volume}) - \$20{,}000 = \$0$$
$$\$2(\text{Volume}) = \$20{,}000 \rightarrow \text{Breakeven Volume} = \$20{,}000 \div \$2 = 10{,}000 \text{ pounds}$$

Answer for Targeted Profit:

$$\$6(\text{Volume}) - \$4(\text{Volume}) - \$20{,}000 = \$10{,}000$$

$$\$2(\text{Volume}) = \$10{,}000 + \$20{,}000 \rightarrow \text{Targeted Profit Volume} = \$30{,}000 \div \$2 = 15{,}000 \text{ pounds}$$

What if Watson's is only able to purchase 12,000 pounds of fish each month, and it still targets monthly profit at \$10,000? What price would Watson's have to sell to the restaurants in order to maintain its targeted profit?

Continues...

Targeted Profit:

$$\text{Price}(12{,}000) - \$4(12{,}000) - \$20{,}000 = \$10{,}000$$

$$\text{Price}(12{,}000) = \$10{,}000 + \$20{,}000 + \$48{,}000 \rightarrow \text{Targeted Profit Price}$$

$$= \$78{,}000 \div 12{,}000 = \$6.50 \text{ per Pound}$$

II. Adjusting the C-V-P Formula for Income Taxes

A. It is important to remember that all the Revenue, Cost, and Profit factors in the C-V-P are in pre-tax dollars. Hence, you need to pay attention when income taxes are involved and bear in mind the difference between pre-tax operating profit and after-tax profit.

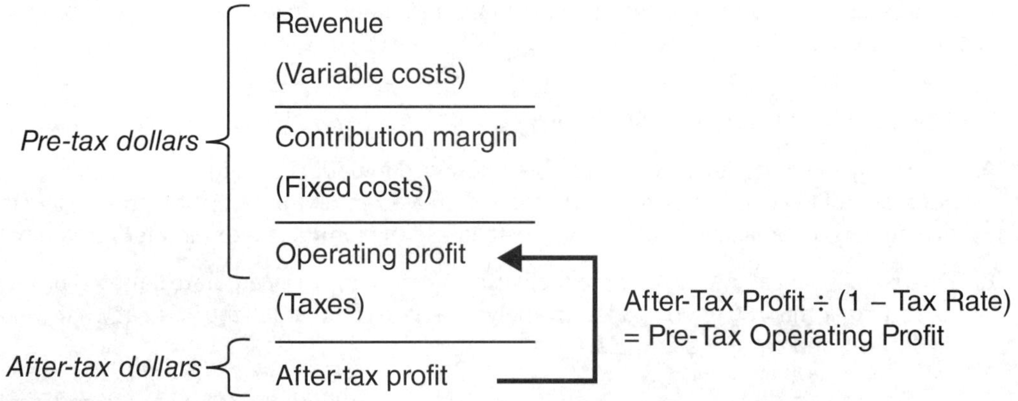

B. If the targeted profit is defined as an after-tax profit, then you need to convert after-tax profit to pre-tax profit before you run any C-V-P analyses. The conversion formula is:

$$\text{After-Tax Profit} \div (1 - \text{Tax Rate}) = \text{Pre-Tax Operating Profit}$$

Practice Question

Spelling Sports, Inc. is developing a new badminton racquet product for water sports. The following cost information relates to the product.

	Unit Costs
Direct Materials	$3.25
Direct Labor	4.00
Distribution	0.75

Direct Materials, Direct Labor, and Distribution are all variable costs. The company will also be absorbing $200,000 of additional fixed costs associated with this new product. A corporate fixed charge of $50,000 currently absorbed by other products will be allocated to this new product.

How many racquets must Spelling Sports sell at a price of $14 per racquet to increase after-tax income by $35,000? Spelling Sports' effective income tax rate is 30%.

Answer:

First the after-tax profit should be converted to a pre-tax profit amount.

$$\text{Pre-Tax Profit} = \text{After-Tax Profit} \div (1 - \text{Tax Rate}) = \$35{,}000 \div (1 - 0.3) = \$50{,}000$$

Next, add up the Variable Unit Costs. Then use the Pre-Tax Profit as the Targeted Profit in the C-V-P formula solution.

$$\text{Total Variable Unit Costs} = \$3.25 + \$4.00 + \$0.75 = \$8.00$$

Continues...

Finally, note that the $50,000 allocated corporate charge is not relevant to this analysis since this cost is not actually caused by the new product. Hence, fixed costs for the C-V-P analysis of racquets is limited to $200,000.

Revenue − Variable Costs − Fixed Costs = Profit

\$14(Volume) − \$8(Volume) − \$200,000 = \$50,000

\$6(Volume) = \$50,000 + \$200,000 → Targeted Profit Volume = \$250,000 ÷ \$6 = 41,666.67

Note: 41,666.67 can be rounded up to 41,667 racquets to generate $35,000 in after-tax profit.

Summary
The objective of C-V-P analysis is not always about getting to the breakeven point. In fact, it's almost always about achieving an income goal, which is referred to as the targeted profit. The transition from breakeven to targeted profit is simple. Just change "Profit" in the C-V-P formula from zero to the targeted profit amount. Typically, organizations are focused on achieving an after-tax income goal. Hence, we need to adjust the after-tax targeted profit to a pre-tax targeted profit before using it as "Profit" in the C-V-P formula.

Multiple Products C-V-P

After studying this lesson, you should be able to:

- Demonstrate an understanding of how changes in unit sales mix affect operating income in multiple-product situations (2.C.1.g).
- Calculate multiple-product breakeven points given percentage share of sales and explain why there is no unique breakeven point in multiple-product situations (2.C.1.h).

Up to this point, you have learned how to apply the C-V-P formula to organizations selling only one product. However, this is not the reality for most organizations. More often than not, organizations sell more than one type of product or service. This lesson will help you understand how to adapt the C-V-P formula to be used for more than one type of product or service.

I. Sales Mix Ratio

A. Most organizations sell more than one type of product or service into the market place. This reality complicates the C-V-P formula and contribution margin analysis, but not very much!

B. When working in a multiple product context, it is crucial to compute the current or desired *sales mix*. The sales mix is the sales of each product or service relative to total sales. It is critical to use the sales mix ratio consistently when solving C-V-P problems.

C. Remember that the sales mix is about how all the products' *sales* relate to each other. Don't use the products' costs or profits in determining the sales mix. This is a common mistake.

D. The sales mix can be computed either in terms of sales volume (units) or in terms of sales revenue (dollars). The sales mix ratio will be different when computed in units versus dollars.

E. Either type of sales mix ratio (units or dollars) can be used in the C-V-P formula, but it is crucial that one or the other sales mix ratio is used **consistently** throughout the analysis. Don't mix them up!

Practice Question

ComputerGuard offers computer consulting, training, and repair services. For the most recent fiscal year, sales were as follows:

	Consulting	Training	Repair	Total
Sales Volume (hours)	6,000	10,500	12,500	29,000
Sales Revenue	$600,000	$525,000	$375,000	$1,500,000

What is the sales mix?

Answer:

ComputerGuard's sales mix in terms of revenue dollars can be described as a ratio of percentages or as a ratio of smaller numbers. In terms of a percentage ratio, the sales mix in dollars is:

Consulting: $600,000 ÷ $1,500,000 = 40%

Training: $525,000 ÷ $1,500,000 = 35%

Repair: $375,000 ÷ $1,500,000 = 25%

This can be presented as 40% : 35% : 25%.

Alternatively, we can simply reduce the actual revenue values to smaller but consistent numbers—essentially, by dropping zeros from the larger numbers.

Continues...

One way to present this could be 60 : 52.5 : 37.5.

Either of these sales mix sets are equivalent to the other and either can be used in solving the C-V-P formula. Generally, for revenue dollars, the percentage ratio is easier to use.

ComputerGuard's sales mix in terms of volume of units can also be described as a ratio of percentages or as a ratio of smaller numbers. In terms of a percentage ratio, the mix is:

Consulting: 6,000 ÷ 29,000 = 20.7%

Training: 10,500 ÷ 29,000 = 36.2%

Repair: 12,500 ÷ 29,000 = 43.1%

This can be presented as 20.7% : 36.2% : 43.1%.

Alternatively, we can also reduce the actual sales volume values to smaller consistent numbers by dropping zeros from the larger numbers.

One way to present this would be 6 : 10.5 : 12.5. (Another example, 60 : 105 : 125, would also work).

Either of these sale mix sets is equivalent to the other and either can be used in solving the C-V-P formula. For volume of units, it's easiest to use the ratio of smaller number with the basket method, which is described below.

II. C-V-P Computations with Multiple Products

A. Once you've determined the organization's sales mix, then you can use that information to do C-V-P analysis. If you don't have data on unit prices and unit variable costs, or if you simply want to do breakeven or targeted profit analyses on the organization's sales revenue, you would use the variable cost ratio format of the C-V-P formula.

$$\text{Revenue} - (\text{Variable Cost Ratio} \times \text{Revenue}) - \text{Total Fixed Costs} = \text{Profit}$$

B. Alternatively, if you do have data on unit prices and unit variable costs, then you probably want to use the more traditional unit-based format of the C-V-P formula.

$$(\text{Sales Price} \times \text{Volume}) - (\text{Variable Cost per Unit} \times \text{Volume}) - \text{Total Fixed Costs} = \text{Profit}$$

This can be further simplified to:

$$\text{CM Rate}(\text{Volume}) - \text{Total Fixed Costs} = \text{Profit}$$

C. When solving for breakeven or targeted profit revenue using the variable cost ratio format of the C-V-P formula, be sure to use the sales mix for revenue, not the sales mix for units. The easiest version of the sales mix is the ratio of percentages.

Summary

Continuing with the ComputerGuard example, in addition to data on sales, the table below also provides information on total variable costs and total fixed costs for the most recent fiscal year:

	Consulting	**Training**	**Repair**	**Total**
Sales Volume (hours)	6,000	10,500	12,500	29,000
Sales Revenue	$600,000	$525,000	$375,000	$1,500,000
Variable Costs	$325,200	$250,950	$305,000	$881,150
Total Fixed Costs				$290,000

Remember that ComputerGuard's sales mix in terms of revenue dollars is 40% : 35% : 25% for Consulting, Training, and Repair, respectively.

Continues…

Note that ComputerGuard's total variable cost ratio is $881,150 ÷ $1,500,000 = 58.7433% (be careful about rounding!)

What is the total breakeven revenue and breakeven revenue for each product?

Answer:

Revenue − .587433(Revenue) − $290,000 = $0
.412567(Revenue) = $290,000 → Break even Revenue = $290,000 ÷ .412567 = $702,917

Now we need to break out this total revenue across the three product lines using the *sales mix in terms of revenue dollars.*

Consulting: $702,917 × 40% = $281,167

Training: $702,917 × 35% = $246,021

Repair: $702,917 × 25% = $175,729

D. When solving for breakeven or targeted profit volume using the more traditional unit-based format of the C-V-P formula, you should use the sales mix for volume of units, not the sales mix for revenue dollars. And the easiest way to approach this multiproduct C-V-P analysis is using the "basket method."

E. The "basket method" is a three-step process:

1. Make a basket with the sales mix.
2. Solve the C-V-P for the basket.
3. Multiply the basket solution with the sales mix.

Practice Question
Continuing with the ComputerGuard example, you can use the Sales Volume in hours to break out the Sales Revenue into price per hour, and the Variable Costs into variable cost per hour:

	Consulting	Training	Repair	Total
Sales Volume (hours)	6,000	10,500	12,500	29,000
Sales Revenue	$600,000	$525,000	$375,000	$1,500,000
Sales Price per Hour	$100.00	$50.00	$30.00	
Variable Costs	$325,200	$250,950	$305,000	$881,150
Variable Costs per Hour	$54.20	$23.90	$24.40	
Total Fixed Costs				$290,000

What is the breakeven in hours for each product and in total hours?

Answer:

Remember that Computer Guard's sales mix in terms of **volume of units** is 6 : 10.5 : 12.5 for Consulting, Training, and Repair, respectively.

First step is to make a basket with the sales mix and determine the total price and variable cost of this basket.

Continues...

	Consulting	Training	Repair	Total
Sales Mix (hours)	6	10.5	12.5	
Sales Price per Hour	$100.00	$50.00	$30.00	
Basket Price	$600.00	$525.00	$375.00	$1,500.00
Variable Cost per Hour	$54.20	$23.90	$24.20	
Basket Variable Cost	$325.20	$250.95	$305.00	$881.15

Solve for the total breakeven volume:

$1,500 (Volume) − $881.15(Volume) − $290,000 = $0
$618.85 (Volume) = $290,000 → break even Baskets = $290,000 ÷ $618.85 = 468.61 Baskets

Now we need to break out this total number of baskets across the three product lines using the *sales mix in terms of volume of units.*

Consulting:	468.61 × 6 = 2,812 hours
Training:	468.61 × 10.5 = 4,920 hours
Repair:	468.61 × 12.5 = 5,858 hours
Total hours:	13,590 hours

III. Crucial C-V-P Assumptions

A. We assume a constant sales mix in calculating C-V-P analysis. The sales mix is absolutely key to solving the C-V-P analysis with multiple products. Most organizations don't maintain the exact same sales mix from year to year, or even from month to month. Hence, the more the actual sales mix turns out to be different from the sales mix used in solving C-V-P equations, the more the results of the analysis won't be relevant to the actual sales situation.

B. Just because the actual sales mix is shifting from what the organization originally planned doesn't mean the organization won't break even or will fail to reach its targeted profit. When an organization has more types of products or services in its sales mix, it has more possible solutions to achieve breakeven or targeted profit. Hence, we need to be very careful when applying C-V-P solutions to manage profit in an organization with a shifting sales mix.

C. We assume constant prices, variable cost rates, and total fixed costs in C-V-P analysis. This is not a problem as long as the projected production volume stays within a "relevant range" for the organization.

Summary

C-V-P analysis for multiple products is a much more realistic management setting than the analysis on a single product. Most organizations have multiple products or lines of service. Using the basket method to compute multiproduct C-V-P solutions helps keep the analysis focused on the classic C-V-P formula, which simplifies the work. The key is to build the C-V-P solution around the sales mix using a three-step approach:

1. Make a basket with the sales mix.
2. Solve the C-V-P for the basket.
3. Open the basket and multiply the sales mix.

Risk and Uncertainty

After studying this lesson, you should be able to:

- Define, calculate, and interpret the margin of safety and the margin of safety ratio (2.C.1.i).
- Explain how sensitivity analysis can be used in CVP analysis when there is uncertainty about sales (2.C.1.j).
- Analyze and recommend a course of action using CVP analysis (2.C.1.k).

The C-V-P formula is based on very specific values for prices, volumes, variable costs, and fixed costs. In the business world, there is a lot of uncertainty around these four C-V-P inputs. Organizations also like to explore the impact on profit based on anticipated changes in these same inputs. In this lesson, you will learn how organizations build some "margin of safety" into their C-V-P analysis as well as how they explore the impact of anticipated changes through a process called Sensitivity Analysis.

I. Managing with Uncertainty

A. External environment factors create opportunities and threats, which in turn create uncertainties on an organization's prices, volumes, and costs. We don't manage uncertainty itself, but we manage within the context of uncertainty, particularly in C-V-P analysis.

B. There are many external factors that can affect the key inputs to C-V-P analysis. These external factors include the following (and you can certainly think of more than this list):

- Competitors
- Suppliers
- Customers
- Government
- Environment
- Society
- Technology

II. The Margin of Safety Computation

A. The concept of uncertainty connects directly with the margin of safety computation. Significant uncertainty involving one or more of the four key C-V-P inputs (price, volume, variable cost, fixed cost) requires a larger margin of safety.

B. *Margin of safety* is the difference between the current sales level and the breakeven point. That is, the margin of safety indicates how much sales volume (in units) or revenue (in dollars) can decrease before operating income becomes negative. The computation is

Current Sales − Breakeven Sales = Margin of Safety

Note: If you're preparing for the CMA© exam, you should note that this formula is on the ICMA formula sheet. Note that this formula can be based on either Current Sales or on Planned Sales.

For example, if sales are currently 200,000 units and the breakeven point is 150,000 units, the margin of safety would be 50,000 units. Alternatively, if sales are $180,000 and the breakeven point is $110,000, the margin of safety would be $70,000. Remember that, similar to breakeven or profit, margin of safety can be expressed in either sales units or revenue dollars.

C. Margin of safety can also be expressed as a percentage. The computation is

Margin of Safety ÷ Current Sales = Margin of Safety Percentage

Note: If you're preparing for the CMA© exam, the ICMA formula sheet uses this version of the Margin of Safety Percentage formula.

For example, if the margin of safety is \$70,000 and the current sales are \$110,000, the margin of safety percentage is \$70,000 ÷ \$110,000 = 63.6%. The margin of safety percentage (sometimes called the margin of safety ratio) can be computed using either sales units or revenue dollars. The margin of safety percentage can also be computed based on the percentage that sales can decline before hitting the breakeven point (though this approach is less typical). From that perspective, the computation is

Margin of Safety ÷ Breakeven Sales = Margin of Safety Percentage

Either percentage (based on breakeven sales or current sales) represents the margin of safety. Just be sure to clearly understand what perspective is important in the analysis, that is, how far current sales can decline before hitting the breakeven point or how far current sales are above the breakeven point.

D. Note that the margin of safety computation can also be used to measure the distance between current sales and the sales associated with some minimal profit target. The computation doesn't have to focus strictly on the sales margin above the breakeven point.

Practice Question

Michael Scott Paper Company produces office paper. The sales price per ream of paper is \$30, the variable cost per ream is \$14, and the total fixed cost is \$20,000. If the current sales volume is 2,000 reams of paper, what is the margin of safety? Compute in terms of units, dollars, and percentage based on breakeven sales.

Answer:

First, calculate the breakeven point.

$$\$30(\times) - \$14(\times) - \$20{,}000 = 0$$

$$\$16(\times) = \$20{,}000$$

$$\times = 1{,}250 \text{ reams of paper}$$

Then, calculate margin of safety.

Units: 2,000 – 1,250 = 750 reams

Dollars: 2,000(\$30) – 1,250(\$30) = \$60,000 – \$37,500 = \$22,500

Percentage: 750 reams ÷ 2,000 reams = \$22,500 ÷ \$60,000 = 37.5%

III. Sensitivity Analysis with C-V-P Inputs

A. Given the necessary uncertainty surrounding the four key C-V-P inputs (price, volume, variable cost, fixed cost), using sensitivity analysis you can determine the impact of changes in each input with respect to breakeven or some other minimal profit target.

B. The objective of sensitivity analysis is to identify the C-V-P input that has the greatest impact on the profit in terms of potential change in the input.

C. Holding the other C-V-P inputs constant, adjust each input by a percentage or dollar amount change, and then observe the change in profit. Higher effects on profit indicate higher sensitivity in the C-V-P analysis to that particular price, volume, or cost input.

Practice Question

Hanover, Inc. provides landscape design consulting. The rate is expected to be $56 per hour, but market demand leads to rate adjustments. Variable costs per hour are estimated at $32 and total fixed costs at $800,000. Annual sales volume is projected to be 40,000 hours.

Hanover management wants to understand how sensitive operating profit is to unexpected shifts down of prices and sales volumes, and unexpected cost increases, by as much as 5 percent.

Answer:

The analysis begins by using the C-V-P formula to determine expected profit based on current price, volume, and cost estimates:

$$\text{Price}(\text{Volume}) - \text{Variable Cost Rate}(\text{Volume}) - \text{Total Fixed Costs} = \text{Profit}$$

$$\$56(40{,}000 \text{ Hours}) - \$32(40{,}000 \text{ Hours}) - \$800{,}000 = \$160{,}000$$

Next, by adjusting each input by 5 percent and holding the other inputs constant, management can observe the change in profit related to each C-V-P input:

5% Price Decrease: $53.20(40,000 hours) – $32(40,000 hours) – $800,000 = $48,000 (a 70% change)

5% Volume Decrease: $56(38,000 hours) – $32(38,000 hours) – $800,000 = $112,000 (a 30% change)

5% VC Increase: $56(40,000 hours) – $33.60(40,000 hours) – $800,000 = $96,000 (a 40% change)

5% FC Increase: $56(40,000 hours) – $32(40,000 hours) – $840,000 = $120,000 (a 25% change)

Based on the sensitivity analysis, Hanover's profit is most sensitive to a 5 percent shift in price.

Practice Question

Zak & Company builds office chairs. Projected price, cost, and volume data for one of its chair lines are:

Price: $460 per chair

Variable cost: $380 per chair

Total fixed cost: $250,000

Sales volume: 4,000 chairs

Either the price or variable cost could differ as much as $10 per chair. Fixed costs may turn out to be 10% higher. And sales volume might be as many as 1,000 chairs lower. Management at Zak & Company needs actual profit on this line of chairs to at least break even.

How sensitive is the breakeven goal to the range of estimates on price, variable cost, fixed cost, or sales volume?

Answer:

Expected profit based on current price, volume, and cost estimates:

$$\$460(4{,}000\text{Chairs}) - \$380(4{,}000 \text{ Chairs}) - \$250{,}000 = \$70{,}000$$

Profit based on change in each estimate:

$10 Price decrease: $450(4,000 chairs) – $380(4,000 chairs) – $250,000 = 30,000

1,000 Volume decrease: $460(3,000 chairs) – $380(3,000 chairs) – $250,000 = ($10,000)

$10 Variable cost increase: $460(4,000 chairs) – $390(4,000 chairs) – $250,000 = $30,000

10% Fixed cost increase: $460(4,000 chairs) – $380(4,000 chairs) – $275,000 = $45,000

It appears that breakeven profit is most sensitive to the sales volume estimate.

Summary

In the business world, there is a lot of uncertainty around the four C-V-P inputs of prices, volumes, variable costs, and fixed costs. As a result, organizations typically need to build some margin of safety into their C-V-P analysis. Margin of Safety calculations represent the distance between current sales and breakeven sales (or some other projected sales level for the organization). In addition to Margin of Safety calculations, organizations can also explore the impact on profit based on anticipated changes or variance in the four C-V-P inputs. This process is called Sensitivity Analysis.

Topic 2. Marginal Analysis

Defining Relevant Costs

After studying this lesson, you should be able to:

- Identify and define relevant costs (incremental, marginal, or differential costs), sunk costs, avoidable costs, explicit and implicit costs, and relevant revenues (2.C.2.a).
- Calculate relevant costs given a numerical scenario (2.C.2.d).

Margin analysis in management accounting is based on a core ability to identify the relevant costs and revenues in a decision setting and not become confused by irrelevant costs and revenues. In particular, sunk costs represent costs already spent or committed to be spent in the future which can't be changed by the decision at hand. Sunk costs are irrelevant. Opportunity costs are not actually "spent," but are economic costs representing the cost (or value) of the next best alternative to the decision at hand.

I. What Costs Are Relevant?

A. Relevant costs are defined as the costs affected by the decision about to be made. Variable costs are almost always considered to be relevant, but be careful. If for any reason a variable cost will take place whether or not the decision facing the manager does take place, then that variable cost is not relevant to the decision.

B. Irrelevant costs are *not* affected by the decision. Often, fixed costs are unaffected and irrelevant to the decision. However, remember that fixed costs are defined as costs that *do not* change based on volume of production or sales. A fixed cost that is relevant to the decision goes away or takes place only if management determines to move forward with the decision, even though the fixed cost may not get incrementally larger or smaller depending on the scale of the decision.

II. Sunk Costs

A. Sunk costs are unchanged by the decision, and are never relevant. Typically, these are past costs made prior to the decision.

B. Sunk costs are not always in the past. Future costs can also be "sunk" if these costs are unavoidable and unchanged by the decision. For example, costs committed to be paid due to a contract signed for some old equipment are sunk costs, even if the old equipment is replaced by new equipment.

III. Opportunity Costs

A. Be careful with opportunity costs. These costs don't actually represent money paid or received by the organization. Opportunity costs represent money that *might* have been paid or received.

B. The economic definition of opportunity cost is "the value of the next best opportunity given up to make the current decision." Opportunity cost is the result of an incremental analysis on other options.

1. Value given up in the next best opportunity is a *cost* of the current decision. For example, in the decision to move forward to produce and sell a particular product (Product A), the profit given up by not producing and selling the next best alternative product (Product B) is a cost of the decision to sell Product A.

2. Alternatively, costs that would have been paid in the next best opportunity are actually a *value* of the current decision. For example, in a decision to spend money to satisfy an environmental regulation requirement (Solution A), the costs that would have been spent to satisfy the regulation requirement using a different solution (Solution B) are actually an economic savings that offsets Solution A.

Practice Question

Management at Tough Trucking is considering the purchase of a new delivery truck for $86,000. If they purchase the new truck, they will sell their current truck, which cost them $61,000 two years ago, for $48,000. General maintenance and insurance on the current truck is approximately $3,100 annually. The current truck is also due for a major overhaul that will cost $5,500. Straight-line depreciation on the current truck is $10,000 per year. General maintenance and insurance for the new truck will be approximately the same as for the current truck. If the new truck is purchased, depreciation on it will be $12,000 per year.

Which costs are relevant and irrelevant, and why?

Answer:

It is crucial to focus on the decision at hand, which is whether to purchase the new truck. Relevant costs are the costs affected if the decision to purchase the new truck is made.

Relevant Costs:

- The $86,000 purchase price of the new truck is obviously relevant, and is offset by the $48,000 opportunity cost (value) of selling the old truck.
- The overhaul cost of $5,500 is also relevant and offsets the purchase price of the new truck.

Irrelevant Costs:

- The old purchase price of the current truck ($61,000) is unchanged whether or not the new truck is purchased. This is a sunk cost.
- Because annual maintenance and insurance costs of both trucks are the same ($3,100), these are irrelevant costs. If the costs were different from each other, then the difference between the costs would be relevant.
- Even though the annual depreciation expense for each truck is different, these costs are irrelevant because they are non-cash expenses represented already by the purchase prices. However, if taxes were involved in this decision, then the tax savings created by depreciation expense would be relevant.

Summary

Understanding and distinguishing between relevant and irrelevant costs and revenues is the foundation of making smart, relevant decisions. Out-of-pocket costs in a decision being considered can be either variable or fixed, but that doesn't necessarily mean these costs are relevant or irrelevant. The key is whether the cost would be avoided if the decision at hand weren't made. Hence, "avoidable costs" are the "relevant costs." Unavoidable costs are sometimes called "sunk costs." In addition to out-of-pocket costs, managers also need to factor in the opportunity costs of making the decision. Whatever costs that would have been spent in the next best decision are actually saved by, and offset, the costs of the current decision. Also, and often more importantly, whatever value or profit that would have been received by making the next best decision must be considered a cost of the current decision—this is the core definition of "opportunity cost."

Sunk Costs, Opportunity Costs, and Capacity

After studying this lesson, you should be able to:

- Explain why sunk costs are not relevant in the decision-making process (2.C.2.b).
- Demonstrate an understanding of and calculate opportunity costs (2.C.2.c).

In this lesson we focus on the definition and application of sunk costs and opportunity costs. Sunk costs are never relevant to a decision, but often confuse decision makers. Opportunity costs, when present, are always relevant. Decision makers can miss including opportunity costs in the analysis. Understanding these two types of cost is crucial to relevant decision making.

I. The Irrelevance of Sunk Costs!

A. Remember that sunk costs are defined as costs that are unchanged by the decision. Typically, these are past costs made prior to the decision, and are never relevant.

B. Sunk costs can also take place in the future. If future costs are committed, and cannot be avoided by making the decision at hand, these future costs are considered "sunk" and are not relevant to the decision.

C. With practice, you can learn to identify and disregard sunk costs when doing relevant decision analysis.

Practice Question

Amazing.com is an e-commerce company that designs "business-ready" websites for small retail companies. The company committed to a \$3 million contract to build and support 300 individual retail websites as part of a larger service provided by a specialized industry association. To support this project, Amazing.com hired 30 additional programmers and invested in additional office space. The programming labor costs will be \$1.5 million, which is based on expected wages of \$50,000 for each programmer. Office equipment costs were \$200,000 and an office rental contract was signed for \$300,000.

After spending \$1.2 million in production costs (\$800,000 in programming, \$200,000 in equipment, and \$200,000 for rent), an economic recession pushed the specialized industry association into bankruptcy. At that point, 100 of the merchant websites had been fully developed, with the remaining 200 websites still in production.

Amazing.com individually contacted each of the retailers to determine their willingness to continue with the website build-and-support service. Not surprisingly, many of the merchants were unable or unwilling to individually contract with Amazing.com to have a retail website completed for \$10,000 (based on the original \$3 million ÷ 300 merchants). But 120 merchants did express interest in receiving their website at a \$3,000 price, for a total of \$360,000 in revenue.

Amazing.com will only need 10 programmers to finish the work. However, regardless of whether any more programing work is done, the company is contractually obligated to pay wages equal to the equivalent of 15 programmers (15 × \$50,000 = \$750,000). The office equipment not needed can be scrapped for \$30,000. The equipment needed to complete the 120 merchant websites has a scrap value of \$10,000. Fortunately, the office rental contract can be canceled at this point, saving \$100,000. The 10 programmers can be squeezed into Amazing.com's own office space without additional space costs.

Which costs are sunk and irrelevant, and which costs are relevant, to this decision to individually contract with 120 merchants for a total revenue of \$360,000?

Continues...

Answer:

Remember that sunk costs are defined as costs that are unaffected by the decision at hand. The decision for Amazing.com is whether to take on the work to complete 120 retail websites. Otherwise, Amazing.com will effectively walk away from this programming work and scrap the investment made thus far.

Sunk Costs:

- The $1.2 million spent thus far in programming, equipment, and rental space are certainly sunk costs.
- It will require 10 programmers to complete the websites. However, Amazing.com is obligated to pay salaries equal to 15 programmers. Because Amazing.com can't avoid paying these programmers, whether or not these retail websites are actually built, the $750,000 in programming costs used for these 120 websites are sunk costs.
- Total scrap value of equipment is $40,000 ($30,000 + $10,000). The $30,000 that can be scrapped right now would be scrapped whether or not the retail websites will be built and delivered. Hence, this $30,000 is irrelevant to the decision.
- Because the office rental contract will be canceled regardless of whether or not the retail websites are delivered, the $100,000 saved is irrelevant to the decision.

Relevant costs:

- The only relevant cost to making the decision to complete and deliver 120 retail websites for $360,000 is the scrap value of the equipment needed to complete the work, which is $10,000. Based on this one relevant cost, Amazing.com should make the decision to build these "cheap" retail websites.

II. The Relevance of Opportunity Costs!

A. Opportunity costs, if present, are always relevant to a business decision. The challenge, though, with opportunity costs is that there isn't a recorded transaction in the accounting records to indicate and put a dollar value on the cost.

B. Opportunity costs represent the value the organization could have received if resources to make the current decision were used instead for the next best opportunity given up. Typically, the opportunity cost is measured by the revenue less variable costs less any direct fixed costs that represent the next best opportunity.

C. One key characteristic to watch for in the current decision is "capacity." When the organization is running out of capacity, it has more opportunities than it has the capability to pursue. In those situations, the organization needs to make choices about how to best optimize the capacity. It is those situations with limited capacity where opportunity costs clearly occur.

D. Evaluating the profitability of a decision with opportunity costs often fits the following framework:

Revenues

–Variable costs

–Direct Fixed costs

–Opportunity costs

Practice Question

Kreature Komforts, Inc. makes high-quality portable stadium seats that fans can attach to bleachers. The company facilities can make 30,000 seats a year. A summary of operating results for last year follows:

Sales (18,000 seats at a sales price of $100)	$1,800,000
Variable costs	990,000
Contribution margin	$ 810,000
Fixed costs	495,000
Net operating income	$ 315,000

A foreign distributor has offered to buy 15,000 seats at $90 per seat next year. This is an all-or-nothing offer; that is, if Kreature Komforts accepts the offer, it must fill the entire order. Kreature Komforts expects its regular sales next year to be 18,000 units. If Kreature Komforts accepts the offer, what would be the impact on its operating income next year? (Assume that the total fixed costs would be the same no matter how many seats are produced and sold.)

Answer:

Kreature Komforts is currently planning to produce 18,000 seats. Taking on the 15,000 seat order would push the company past its 30,000 seat production capacity. In order to accept the new order, Kreature Komforts would have to forgo 3,000 seats of normal sales. The value, measured by the contribution margin, of these 3,000 seats is an opportunity cost of the new order. Note that variable cost per seat is 990,000 ÷ 18,000 = $55.

Additional Revenue = 15,000 × $90	$1,350,000
Additional Variable Cost = 15,000 × $55	(825,000)
Additional Contribution Margin	$ 525,000
Opportunity Cost = 3,000 × ($100 − $55)	(135,000)
Additional Operating Income	$ 390,000

Total Operating Income for Kreature Komforts with this additional order = $315,000 + $390,000 = $705,000

Summary

Understanding and identifying sunk costs and opportunity costs is crucial to successfully making relevant decisions. Sunk costs represent costs that have either already been made or are unavoidable in the future whether or not the current decision is made. These costs are never relevant and should not be considered in the decision. Opportunity costs, in contrast, are crucial to include in a relevant analysis of the decision. Opportunity costs represent the value given up by forgoing the next best alternative to the current decision. Opportunity costs are not always present in a decision. Opportunity costs are present when the organization is faced with a choice. Often that choice is present when the organization has limited capacity and is not able to take advantage of all opportunities presented. Hence, pay attention to capacity constraints when doing relevant decision analysis.

Marginal Analysis and Product Line Decisions

After studying this lesson, you should be able to:

- Define and calculate marginal cost and marginal revenue (2.C.2.e).
- Demonstrate proficiency in the use of marginal analysis for decisions such as (iv.) selling a product or performing additional processes and selling a more value-added product (2.C.2.g).
- Demonstrate proficiency in the use of marginal analysis for decisions such as (v) adding or dropping a segment (2.C.2.g).
- Calculate the effects on operating income of a decision to sell or process further or to drop or add a segment (2.C.2.k).
- Identify the effects of changes in capacity on production decisions (2.C.2.l).
- Identify and describe qualitative factors in make-or-buy decisions, such as product quality and dependability of suppliers (2.C.2.i).
- Demonstrate an understanding of the impact of income taxes on marginal analysis (2.C.2.m).

In this lesson we define margin costs and margin revenues as the incremental change in cost and revenue based on making the decision at hand. We also describe relevant costs as the costs that can be avoided if the decision is made. We then explore these concepts in three specific types of decisions: processing further a product for a higher price, adding or dropping a business division to increase overall profit, and prioritizing products based on a constraint in the organization.

I. Defining Marginal Costs and Marginal Revenues

A. Identifying marginal costs is tied directly to a fundamental concept in relevant decision making, which is that only the costs that will change if the decision is made are relevant to the decision. Further, the term *marginal cost* is essentially synonymous with the term *incremental cost.*

1. We basically follow a two-step process in analyzing relevant costs. First, we identify the cost affected by the decision as the relevant cost.

2. With the relevant cost identified, the second step is to determine the amount by which the relevant cost affects the decision—that is, how much additional (incremental) cost is created by the relevant cost. This is what is known as the marginal cost.

B. Marginal revenue is identified much the same way that we identify marginal costs. It is the incremental revenue that is directly associated with making the decision at hand.

II. Decisions to Process a Product Further

A. The concept of marginal cost and marginal revenue describes exactly the approach taken with decisions involving products or services that have multiple stages of development with a sales point available at each stage. The decision is about whether to continue processing the product further by adding more cost in order to sell at a higher (premium) price.

B. The math is straightforward. Compute the change in cost (i.e., the marginal cost) and compare to the change in revenue (i.e., the marginal revenue). If the marginal revenue exceeds the marginal cost, then process the product further to the next sales point.

C. Note that the incremental analysis of marginal costs and marginal revenues can be conducted using total costs and total revenues, or using cost per unit and price per unit.

D. When multiple products are involved, there is typically a joint production process or shared service that all the products or services will move through. However, the cost of the joint process or shared service *cannot* be directly tied to individual products. There are several methods available that can be used to allocate these joint costs. However, it is important to understand that the allocation of joint costs does *not* affect the decision to sell now or process further individual products or services.

Practice Question

A company manufactures three products using the same production process. The costs incurred up to the split-off point are $200,000. These costs are allocated to the products on the basis of their sales value at the split-off point. The number of units produced, the selling prices per unit of the three products at the split-off point and after further processing, and the additional processing costs are as follows.

Product	Number of Units Produced	Selling Price at Split-Off	Selling Price after Processing	Additional Processing Costs
D	3,000	$11.00	$15.00	$14,000
E	6,000	$12.00	$16.20	$16,000
F	2,000	$19.40	$24.00	$9,000

Which product(s) should be processed further and which should be sold at the split-off point?

Answer:

Product	Incremental Price	Incremental Revenue	Incremental Costs	Incremental Profit
D	$15.00 – $11.00 = $4.00	$4.00 × 3,000 = $12,000	$14,000	($2,000)
E	$16.20 – $12.00 = $4.20	$4.20 × 6,000 = $25,200	$16,000	$9,200
F	$24.00 – $19.40 = $4.60	$4.60 × 2,000 = $9,200	$9,000	$200

Products E and F should be processed further. Product D should be sold at the split-off point.

Note that this decision can also be analyzed using per-unit incremental costs, and comparing the per-unit costs to the incremental price per unit.

III. Decisions to Add or Drop a Product Line

A. Another term that can be used to describe relevant costs is *avoidable costs*. Similarly, irrelevant costs can be described as *unavoidable costs*. This terminology, of course, captures well the concept that only relevant costs are affected by the decision being considered.

B. When managers are considering a decision to add or drop a division or product line based on a desire to increase profits, it's very important that unavoidable costs are not included in the analysis of the division. Unavoidable costs are often allocated to divisions or product lines despite the fact that these business units don't actually create the costs.

C. When assessing the "true profitability" of a business unit, a contribution margin approach in the analysis is best. Variable costs belonging to a division or product line are almost always avoidable if the business unit is discontinued or dropped. And if the business unit has any direct fixed costs, (i.e., fixed costs that are directly caused by the business unit), those costs should also be included in the analysis.

D. A good template to use to assess the relevant revenues and costs of a division, product line, customer group, or another for-profit business unit is shown below.

Revenues
– Variable Costs
Contribution Margin
–Direct Fixed Costs
Business Unit Profit

Practice Question

You received a report on the operating performance of Wasson Company's six divisions. With the report came a recommendation that if the Ortiz Division were to be eliminated, total profits would increase by $23,870.

	Ortiz Division	The Other Five Divisions	Total
Sales	$96,200	$1,664,200	$1,760,400
Cost of Goods Sold	76,470	978,520	1,054,990
Gross Profit	19,730	685,680	705,410
Operating Expenses	43,600	527,940	571,540
Operating Income	$(23,870)	$157,440	$133,870

With a little more research, you learn that in the Ortiz Division cost of goods sold is $70,000 variable and $6,470 fixed, and its operating expenses are $15,000 variable and $28,600 fixed. None of the Ortiz Division's fixed costs will be eliminated if the division is discontinued.

What will be the effect on total profits if the Ortiz Division is eliminated?

Answer:

If Wasson Company's profit analysis on the Ortiz Division was organized to separate the variable and fixed costs, it would demonstrate the contribution margin of this division, which in this case is the incremental value provided by the Ortiz Division. As shown below, if this division were eliminated, Wasson Company profits would *not* increase by $23,870. Instead, it will *decrease* by $11,200. For this division, all fixed costs are unavoidable and, therefore, irrelevant to the analysis.

	Ortiz Division	
Sales		**$96,200**
Variable Costs (avoidable)		
Cost of Goods Sold	$70,000	
Operating Expenses	15,000	85,000
Contribution Margin	19,730	$11,200
Fixed Costs (unavoidable)		
Cost of Goods Sold	$6,470	
Operating Expenses	28,600	35,070
Operating Income		$(23,870)

IV. Decisions to Prioritize Products with Constraints

A. It is important to pay attention to constraints in the organization when analyzing relevant costs and revenues in decision making. When the organization's resources are constrained, limited, or bottle-necked, then choices need to be made to prioritize products or services in order to optimize profit for the organization.

B. The key focus is contribution margin. But the analysis should *not* be based on the units of *output* for the organization. Instead, identify the resource creating the constraint on total output, and compute contribution margin based on the units of *input*. Input for the constraint is defined in terms of whatever measure is used to identify how the constraint is consumed by the products or services.

C. The analysis process is done using two steps.

1. First, compute contribution margin per unit of output for each product or service using the constraint.

2. Then multiply contribution margin per unit of output by the number of outputs generated based on each unit of input.

D. The contribution margin per unit of input determines the priority of products or services using the constrained resource.

Practice Question

The Good Health Baking Company produces a salt-free whole-grain bread and a carob-chip cookie. The demand for these products is exceeding Good Health's production capacity. The company has only 80,000 direct labor hours available. A case of bread requires one direct labor hour while a case of cookies requires half a direct labor hour. The company estimates that it can sell 100,000 cases of bread and 50,000 cases of cookies in the next year. The following financial information is available:

	Bread	Cookies
Selling price per case	$60	$30
Variable costs per case		
Direct materials	$13	$4
Direct labor	8	4
Variable production overhead	2	1
Variable marketing costs	2	1
Total Variable costs	$25	$10

How should Good Health allocate its production capacity between bread and cookies? That is, how many cases of bread and how many cases of cookies should Good Health produce in order to maximize total profits?

Answer:

Direct labor hours represent the constrained resource for Good Health. Determine the priority of production by computing contribution margin per direct labor hour (the unit of input for the constrained resource).

	Bread	Cookies
Selling price per case	$60	$30
Variable cost per case	(25)	(10)
Contribution margin per case	$35	$20
Cases per direct labor hour	1	× 2
Contribution margin per direct labor hour	$35	$40

Good Health should prioritize cookies first in order to most profitably use its limited direct labor hours. Hence, it should produce and sell all the cookies possible to the market (50,000 cases). Then it should use the remaining direct labor hours to produce bread.

Continues...

Direct Labor Hours Needed:

50,000 cases of cookies × 0.5 direct labor hour = 25,000 direct labor hours used

80,000 available hours – 25,000 hours = 55,000 hours remaining to produce bread

55,000 direct labor hours × 1 case per hour = 55,000 cases of bread

	Bread	Cookies
Cases Produced	55,000	50,000
Contribution Margin per Case	× $35	× $20
Total Contribution Margin	$1,925,000	$1,000,000

This works out to total contribution margin for Good Health of $2,925,000. No other combination of production will generate more profit than this combination.

Summary

Working with marginal costs and marginal revenues involves carefully determining the incremental effect on costs and revenues based on making the decision at hand. In this regard, "marginal" and "incremental" are essentially describing the same concept. Relevant costs can also be synonymous with the concept of "avoidance." That is, costs that can be avoided by making the decision are relevant to the decision analysis. Remember that when resources are constrained in the organization, the focus in the decision needs to shift to identifying the most profitable use of the constrained input.

We considered three specific types of decisions in this lesson.

1. Decisions regarding the further processing of products for higher prices versus selling products at an earlier point are based on comparing the incremental (marginal) revenues and incremental (marginal) costs of processing further.
2. Decisions regarding the adding or dropping of business units such as product lines or customer groups are based on revenue of the business unit, its variable costs, and its direct fixed costs (if any).
3. Decisions regarding the most profitable use of constrained resources are based on computing the contribution margin per unit of input coming from the constrained resource, and prioritizing products or services based on how they use units of resource input.

Practice Problems

After studying this lesson, you should be able to:

- Identify and calculate total cost, average fixed cost, average variable cost, and average total cost (2.C.2.f).
- Calculate the effects on operating income of a decision to sell or process further, and of a decision to drop or add a segment (2.C.2.k).
- Demonstrate proficiency in the use of marginal analysis for decisions such as (iii) making or buying a product or service (2.C.2.g).
- Calculate the effect on operating income of a make-or-buy decision (2.C.2.j).
- Demonstrate proficiency in the use of marginal analysis for decisions such as (iv) selling a product or performing additional processes and selling a more value-added product (2.C.2.g).
- Demonstrate proficiency in the use of marginal analysis for decisions such as (v) adding or dropping a segment (2.C.2.g).
- Identify the effects of changes in capacity on production decisions (2.C.2.l).

This is a video lesson in the course that provides extra practice applying marginal analysis principles for three types of decisions: make-or-buy decisions, production prioritization decisions involving constraints, and sell-or-process-further decisions.

Comprehensive Problems with Opportunity Costs

After studying this lesson, you should be able to:

- Demonstrate proficiency in the use of marginal analysis for decisions such as (i) introducing a new product or changing output levels of existing products (2.C.2.g).
- Demonstrate proficiency in the use of marginal analysis for decisions such as (ii) accepting or rejecting special orders (2.C.2.g).
- Demonstrate proficiency in the use of marginal analysis for decisions such as (iii) making or buying a product or service (2.C.2.g).
- Calculate the effect on operating income of a decision to accept or reject a special order when there is idle capacity and the order has no long-run implications (2.C.2.h).
- Recommend a course of action using marginal analysis (2.C.2.n).
- Calculate the effect on operating income of a make-or-buy decision (2.C.2.j).

This is a video lesson in the course that provides extra practice applying marginal analysis principles to more comprehensive problems involving make-or-buy decision and a special-order decision. Both of these comprehensive problems involve opportunity costs. There is a special emphasis in these comprehensive problems to use incremental costs and revenues in the analysis of these decisions.

Topic 3. Pricing

Pricing Methods

After studying this lesson, you should be able to:

- Identify different pricing methodologies, including market comparables, cost-based, and value-based approaches (2.C.3.a).
- Differentiate between a cost-based approach (cost-plus pricing, markup pricing) and a market-based approach to setting prices (2.C.3.b).

Price, being at the core of how revenue is derived, is at the center of an organization's strategy. How an organization sets or accepts a price in the marketplace is a significant signal about the organization's product or service. This lesson introduces the topic of pricing and three overall methods of assessing and setting price in the marketplace.

I. Why Price Matters

A. Revenue forms the core of the business strategy $\rightarrow$ Price $\times$ Volume $=$ Revenue

1. "Setting" the price depends on the nature of the organization's business, the market the organization competes in, and the organization's overall strategy.

2. The price is a *signal* to the market about the organization's product or service. Hence, the organization needs to be very careful (strategic) about the price it brings to the marketplace.

B. There are three basic approaches (methods) that organizations use to set and accept prices in the marketplace.

1. Cost-based methods

2. Competition-based methods

3. Customer-based methods

II. Cost-Based Methods

A. Cost-based methods are based on the costs to produce the product or service. There are a number of ways to determine the cost basis for these methods. Remember that costs include the following:

1. Direct materials costs or cost of supplies.

2. Direct labor costs, which sometimes have to be averaged across units of product or service.

3. Overhead costs, which are often allocated across units of product or service.

B. Strategic goals that organizations may be pursuing when using a cost-based pricing method include achieving a certain profit margin percentage or profit dollar amount either per product or across the entire company.

III. Competition-Based Methods[1]

A. Competition-based methods require a careful assessment of what is happening in the organization's market. The marketplace can be generally described across three different levels of competition.

1. A highly competitive marketplace with a lot of competitors.

[1] Competition-based pricing is also referred to as market-based pricing.

2. A complex marketplace with several competitors working to differentiate (distinguish) their product or service as unique.
3. An isolated or insulated marketplace where the organization essentially delivers the product or service with little or no competition. Note that these kinds of "monopoly" marketplaces often have some kind of oversight to control or regulate how the organization prices and provides its product or service.

B. The classic economic model depicting Demand and Supply curves can be used to illustrate the nature and impact of competition on the organization's price strategy.

C. In addition to overall goals of making a profit, other strategic goals that organizations may be pursuing when using a competition-based pricing method include setting prices to achieve market share and longevity in the marketplace, or alternatively price skimming to capture immediate profits before exiting the market.

IV. Customer-Based Methods[2]

A. Customer-based methods require the organization to understand the value its customers want to receive by purchasing the organization's product or service, and what that value is worth to them.

B. Remember that price is a signal. It is a signal in the marketplace and to the customer about quality and value.

C. How do customers react to price changes? For example, when the price is increased, do customers buy more or less of the product? Customer reactions indicate to the organization how the customer perceives value in the product or service.

D. In addition to overall goals of making a profit, other strategic goals that organizations may be pursuing when using a customer-based pricing method include setting prices to capture new customers, retaining repeat customers, and establishing a clear market brand.

Summary
There are three basic approaches that organizations use to set and accept prices in the marketplace. Cost-based pricing involves identifying the cost of creating the product or service, and then using the cost information to establish a price. Competition-based pricing requires a clear assessment of supply and demand in the marketplace. Customer-based pricing is about a clear understanding of how the customer truly values the organization's product or service. Each of these methods is focused on helping the organization achieve goals with respect to short-term and long-term profitability.

[2] Customer-based pricing is also referred to as value-based pricing.

Cost-Based Pricing

After studying this lesson, you should be able to:

- Calculate selling price using a cost-based approach (2.C.3.c).
- Define and demonstrate an understanding of target pricing and target costing and identify the main steps in developing target prices and target costs (2.C.3.h).
- Calculate the target operating income per unit and target cost per unit (2.C.3.j).
- Define the pricing technique of cost plus target rate of return (2.C.3.l).

Some organizations use a price markup percentage on costs to set prices. This lesson will teach you how to build a markup percentage on each of the three cost types (variable costs, production costs, and total costs). You'll also learn about the risk of basing costs on price (the price death spiral). Finally, this lesson will reverse the price markup percentage formula in order to establish a targeted cost that achieves a profit goal in markets where the price is set and must be accepted by the organization.

I. The Cost Markup Formula

A. The cost markup formula to set price is straightforward:

Targeted Price = Cost × (1 + Markup%)

Note that "Cost" in this formula is a cost per unit (not a total cost). Using this formula requires two important steps:

1. First thing to do is decide which cost to use. There are several types of costs, including

a. Variable costs

b. Absorption costs (also known as product costs or costs of goods sold)

c. Total costs, including sales and administrative costs (also known as period costs)

2. The second thing to do is determine the markup percentage. This is actually a fairly challenging formulation that depends on the type of cost being using in the markup percentage.

B. Setting the markup percentage is based on using the C-V-P formula.

1. The C-V-P formula is basically represented as Revenue – Variable Cost – Fixed Cost = Profit.

2. One specific form of the C-V-P formula is: Sales Price(Volume) – VC Rate(Volume) – Total FC = Profit.

3. The key thing to note in the specific C-V-P formula is the presence of "Sales Price." Note above in the cost markup formula that Price = Cost × (1 + Markup%).

4. Assuming that we choose to base the price on the variable cost, we can then substitute the cost markup formula into the C-V-P formula and solve for the markup percentage as follows:

Sales Price(Volume) – VC Rate(Volume) – Total FC = Profit

VC Rate(1 + Markup%)(Volume) – VC Rate(Volume) – Total FC = Profit

VC Rate + VC Rate(Markup%)(Volume) – VC Rate(Volume) – Total FC = Profit

VC Rate(Volume) + VC Rate(Markup%)(Volume) – VC Rate(Volume) – Total FC = Profit

VC Rate(Markup%)(Volume) – Total FC = Profit

VC Rate(Markup%)(Volume) = Profit + Total FC

Markup% = (Profit + Total FC) ÷ (VC Rate × Volume)

C. The C-V-P formula for the markup percentage can be generalized to the other types of costs bases (absorption costs and total costs) with the following solutions.

1. Absorption (COGS) cost approach: Markup% = (Profit + Total Sales & Admin Costs) ÷ (COGS Rate × Volume)
2. Total cost approach: Markup% = (Profit) ÷ (Total Cost Rate × Volume)

D. Depending on the type of business the organization is in and the type of market it is pursing, organizations choose different costs on which to base their prices. Retail organizations tend to base their prices on variable costs (i.e., wholesale purchase costs). Public-reporting companies tend to base their prices on absorption costs (i.e., costs of goods sold). And many non-retail, non-public organizations tend to base their prices on total costs.

Practice Question

An engineering consulting firm has an annual profit goal of $250,000. Based on an expected annual volume of 15,000 billable consulting hours, the firm projects the following costs:

Variable costs of services: $600,000

Fixed costs of services: $750,000

Variable selling & administrative expense: $180,000

Fixed selling & administrative expense: $210,000

Compute the markup percentage based on variables costs, on costs of services, and on total costs. What is the targeted price to achieve the firm's profit goal?

Answer:

Cost markup formula: Price = Cost × (1 + Markup%)

General formula for Markup%: (Profit + Total costs to be covered)÷ (Cost basis per unit × Volume)

Costs per Unit:

Variable costs of services: $600,000 ÷ 15,000 hours = $40 per hour

Fixed costs of services: $750,000 ÷ 15,000 hours = $50 per hour

Variable selling & administrative expense: $180,000 ÷ 15,000 hours = $12 per hour

Fixed selling & administrative expense: $210,000 ÷ 15,000 hours = $14 per hour

Variable Costs Basis:

Cost Basis per Unit = $40 + $12 = $52 per Hour

Costs to be covered by the price: Fixed costs of service ($750,000) and Fixed selling & admin. expense ($210,000)

Markup Percentage = ($250,000 + $750,000 + $210,000) ÷ ($52 per Hour × 15,000 Hours) = 155.13%

Target Price = $52 per Hour × (1 + 1.5513) = $132.67 per Hour

Absorption Costs (Costs of Services) Basis:

Cost Basis per Unit = $40 + $50 = $90 per Hour

Costs to be covered by the price: Variable selling & admin. expense ($180,000) and Fixed selling & admin. expense ($210,000)

Continues…

Markup Percentage = ($250,000 + $180,000 + $210,000) ÷ ($90 per Hour × 15,000 Hours) = 47.41%

Target Price = $90 per Hour × (1 + 0.4741) = $132.67 per Hour

Total Costs Basis:

Cost Basis per Unit = $40 + $50 + $12 + $14 = $116 per Hour

Costs to be covered by the price: None. All costs are used in the cost basis per unit.

Markup Percentage = $250,000 ÷ ($116 per Hour × 15,000 Hours) = 14.37%

Target Price = $116 per Hour × (1 + 0.1437) = $132.67 per Hour

II. The Price Death Spiral

A. Organizations must be very careful when establishing markup formulas that automatically adjust prices based on costs. If increasing prices tend to drive down sales volumes in the organization's marketplace, then the organization needs to be very careful to not let the cost markup formula automatically increase the price, which then drives down sales volume even further, leading to the markup formula marking up prices even more. This kind of automatic price adjustment response in the cost markup formula can be disastrous for the organization, and is referred to as the price death spiral.

B. For example, in the Practice Question above, assume that setting the price for engineering consulting hours at $132.67 (or $133) per hour actually causes the volume of consulting hours to drop from 15,000 to 12,000 hours. The Total Cost Basis markup formula (or either of the other two markup formulas) would then establish a new price at $153.83 per hour as follows:

Markup Percentage = $250,000 ÷ ($133 per Hour × 12,000 Hours) = 15.66%

Target Price = $133 per Hour × (1 + 0.1566) = $153.83 (or $154) per Hour

Note that with a smaller volume of 12,000 hours, the fixed costs of services and fixed selling & administrative expense increase to $62.50 and $17.50 per unit, respectively.

This increased price will likely cause the volume of consulting hours the firm can sell in the marketplace to drop even further, leading to a price death spiral.

III. Target Costing

A. Many organizations actually do not have the ability (i.e., the power) to set prices in their marketplace. Instead of being "price makers," these kinds of organizations are "price takers." When the organization is essentially forced to accept the market price, then the only thing the organization can control to achieve the targeted profit is costs.

B. In these circumstances, the cost markup formula can be adjusted to take the market price and a desired markup percentage, and then establish a *targeted cost*. The Target Costing formula is very similar to the Cost Markup formula.

Targeted Cost = Price ÷ (1 + Markup%)

C. For example, in the Practice Question above, assume that in order to sell 15,000 engineering consulting hours into the marketplace, the firm will have to accept a billable rate of $110 per hour. Assuming that the firm desires a 14% markup on total costs per hour to achieve its profit goal, then the firm will need to target its total costs as follows:

Targeted Cost = $110 per Hour ÷ (1 + 0.14) = $96.49 per Hour

Current Total Costs = $116 per Hour

Cost Reduction Target = $116 – 96.49 = $19.51 per Hour

Practice Question

Referring to the Practice Question above, assume that the engineering consulting firm must accept a market price of \$110 per hour in order to sell 15,000 consulting hours. What would the firm's variable cost target need to be in order to maintain a markup percentage of 155% on variable costs? And what would the firm's costs of service target need to be in order to maintain a markup percentage of 47% on costs of services?

Answer:

Variable Costs Basis:

Targeted Cost = \$110 per Hour ÷ (1 + 1.55) = \$43.14 per Hour

Current Variable Costs = \$52 per Hour

Cost Reduction Target = \$52 – 43.14 = \$8.86 Variable cost per Hour

Absorption Costs (Costs of Services) Basis:

Targeted Cost = \$110 per Hour ÷ (1 + 0.47) = \$74.83 per Hour

Current Costs of Services = \$90 per Hour

Cost Reduction Target = \$90 – 74.83 = \$15.17 Service cost per Hour

Summary

One way to set price is based on costs. There are several specific approaches to cost-based pricing, including basing the price on variable costs, absorption (COGS) costs, and total cost. The basic Target Price formula is:

Targeted Price per Unit = (Profit + All Other Costs in Total)
÷ (Unit Rate for the Cost Basis Selected × Volume)

An important risk to consider when using cost-based pricing is the potential for a price death spiral, which happens when a declining sales volume drives price using a cost-based formula, which then subsequently drives down sales volume even further. Finally, when the organization is forced to accept the market price (rather than set the price in the market), a target costing approach can be used to establish the cost needed to achieve a desired profit margin percentage given the price established by the market. The Target Cost formula is:

Targeted Cost per Unit = Price ÷ (1 + Markup%)

Competition-Based Pricing

After studying this lesson, you should be able to:

- Demonstrate an understanding of how the pricing of a product or service is affected by the demand for and supply of the product or service, as well as the market structure within which it operates (2.C.3.d).
- Demonstrate an understanding of the impact of cartels on pricing (2.C.3.e).
- Demonstrate an understanding of the short-run equilibrium price for the firm in (1) pure competition, (2) monopolistic competition, (3) oligopoly, and (4) monopoly using the concepts of marginal revenue and marginal cost (2.C.3.f).
- Calculate the price elasticity of demand using the midpoint formula (2.C.3.m).
- Define and explain elastic and inelastic demand (2.C.3.n).
- Estimate total revenue given changes in prices and demand as well as elasticity (2.C.3.o).
- Discuss how pricing decisions can differ in the short run and in the long run (2.C.3.p).

The nature of economics and competition creates tremendous pressure in the marketplace to set price at the point where the quantity of goods and services demanded is equal to the quantity of goods and services supplied; otherwise, oversupply or shortages take place in the marketplace. This lesson will clarify how price affects the quantity demanded. Additionally, it will discuss the four different types of market structures and how the nature of demand is different across these structures.

Note: Competition-based pricing is also referred to as market-based pricing.

I. Supply and Demand Curves

A. Competition-based pricing is based on a clear view of how price is affected by demand and supply in the economy.

B. All else remaining equal, as the price of a good or service increases, the quantity of the *supply* will *increase*. Conversely, as the price of a good or service increases, the *quantity* of the demand will *decrease*.

C. The relationship between supply and demand with respect to price and quantity is demonstrated in the classic microeconomic diagram below. Note that Demand slopes downward, which means that quantity demanded increases as prices decrease. And note that Supply slopes upward, which means that quantity supplied decreases as prices decrease.

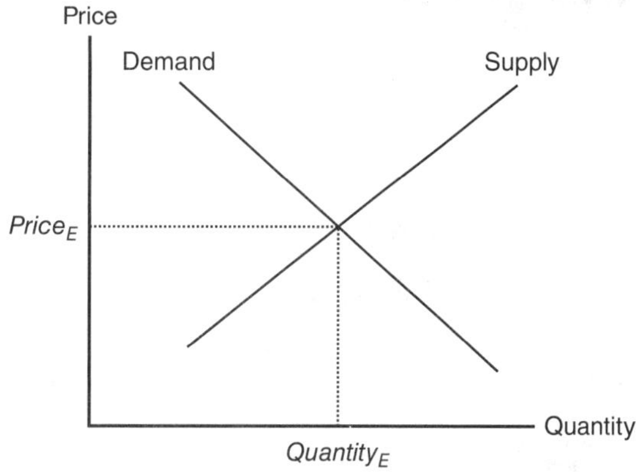

D. In a normal competitive market, supply and demand exerts pressure on the price to move it to "equilibrium," which is the price point where the quantity supplied will equal the quantity demanded. This is represented above by the equilibrium $Price_E$ and the equilibrium $Quantity_E$.

II. Oversupply and Shortages in the Market

A. Price can certainly be out of equilibrium, and often is for at least short periods of time. If the price is too high ($Price_H$), then there will be an *oversupply* of the product or service in the marketplace because suppliers will provide more ($Quantity_S$) than consumers will demand ($Quantity_D$). This is demonstrated below in the first diagram.

B. On the other hand, if the price is too low ($Price_L$), then there will be a *shortage* (or undersupply) of the product or service in the marketplace because consumers will demand more ($Quantity_D$) than suppliers will provide ($Quantity_S$). This is demonstrated below in the second diagram.

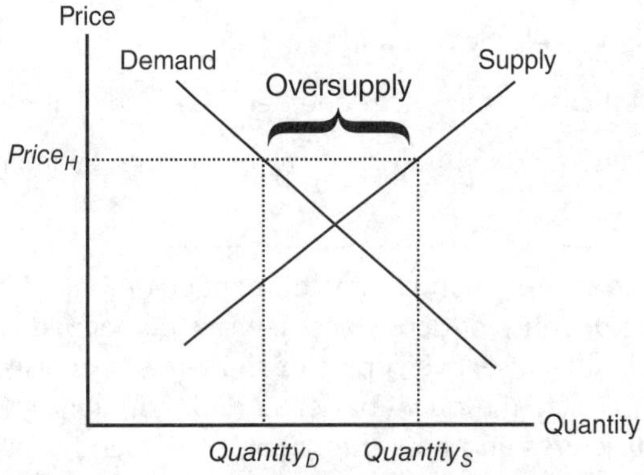

Note: Supply > Demand

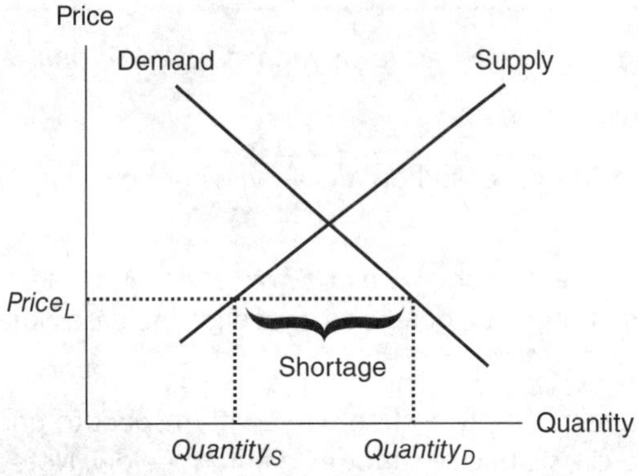

Note: Demand > Supply

C. In both of these situations, there will be natural pressure in the economic marketplace for Price and Quantity to move back to the equilibrium point.

III. Movements versus Shifts in Supply and Demand

A. According to the Law of Supply and Demand, the only cause of *movement* up and down the Supply or Demand curves is a change in price. It is very important to understand that a change in price does *not* change the supply or demand curve.

1. For example, if the price increases, this doesn't change the nature (or function) of demand in the marketplace. The quantity demanded simply moves down along the demand curve to a new (and lower) level of quantity.
2. Simultaneously, this same increase in price causes the quantity supplied to simply move up the supply curve to a new (and higher) level of quantity.

B. It's important to distinguish "movement in" Supply or Demand from "shift of" Supply or Demand. What causes an actual "shift" of Supply or Demand, leading to a new equilibrium price? In short, there are many things that might happen in the economy, *other than price changes*, that will cause either supply or demand to shift.

1. For example, fundamental changes that cause Supply to shift to the right (see below) include events such as improvements to the basic technology that creates the product, the reduction of the production costs, growth in the number of producers in the economy, or decreases in the price of *substitute* products that the supplier could alternatively sell. These events will shift Supply to the right (see below), and opposite events shift Supply to the left. Note below that Supply shifts to the right ($Supply_0$ to $Supply_1$) will increase the equilibrium quantity while *decreasing* the equilibrium price, which means price and quantity will settle and stabilize at a new level ($Quantity_1$ and $Price_1$), and Demand quantity will move down the curve to the new equilibrium price.

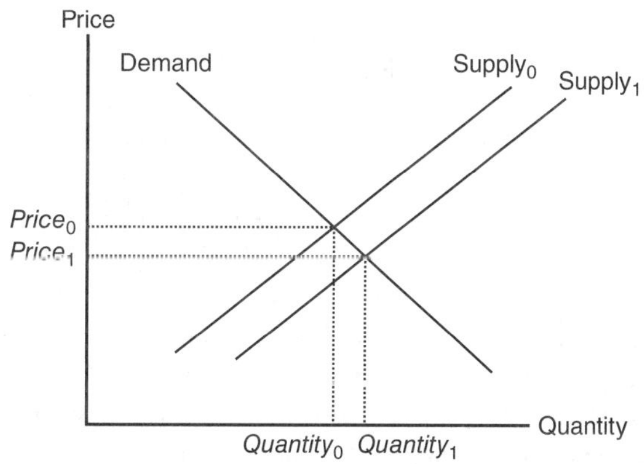

C. On the other hand, fundamental changes that cause Demand to shift to the right (see below) include events that lead to upsurges in the preference for the product (perhaps as a result of advertising or actual product improvements), price increases for substitute products that could be alternatively purchased, or price decreases for *complementary* goods or services (e.g., gasoline is a complementary good for vehicles). Income effects on demand shifts are particularly important to understand. As income increases, Demand for luxury goods will shift to the right, but Demand for inferior goods will shift to the left. Note below that Demand shifts to the right ($Demand_0$ to $Demand_1$) will increase the equilibrium quantity *and* increase the equilibrium price, leading to new price and quantity levels ($Quantity_1$ and $Price_1$) as Supply moves up the curve to the new equilibrium point.

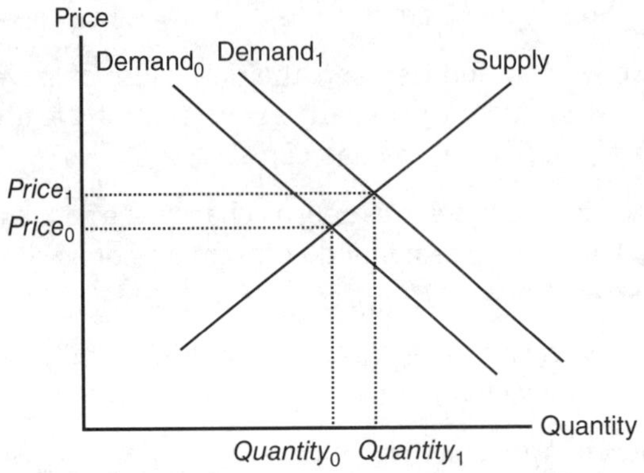

D. Understanding economic factors that *change* the demand for, or supply of, the organization's product or service in the marketplace is crucial to anticipating movements in price in the marketplace.

IV. Price Elasticity of Demand

A. The price elasticity of demand concept is focused on the relationship of demand to price. That is, we generally expect that as price goes up, demand goes down. Price elasticity of demand is used to describe (and compute) how much movement in demand the organization can expect from a movement in price.

B. The fundamental computation for price elasticity of demand is provided below, as well as how we describe the result of the computation.

$$\frac{\text{Demand \% Change}}{\text{Price \% Change}}$$

If > 1, then Elastic
If < 1, then Inelastic
If = 1, then "Unitary" Elastic

C. Price elasticity of demand basically describes the slope of the Demand curve. When elasticity is greater than 1, this means the Demand curve is more flat. When elasticity is less than 1, this means the Demand curve is more steep. Notice in the diagrams below that as the Demand curve becomes more steep (more inelastic), an increase in price has a smaller effect on the change in quantity demanded. (Unitary elasticity, a fairly uncommon circumstance, simply means that the Demand curve is at a perfect 45-degree angle, indicating that the percentage change in the price level is exactly equal to the percentage change in the quantity demanded.)

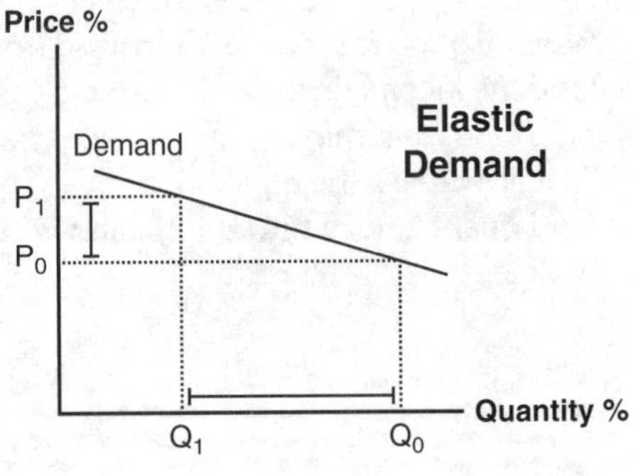

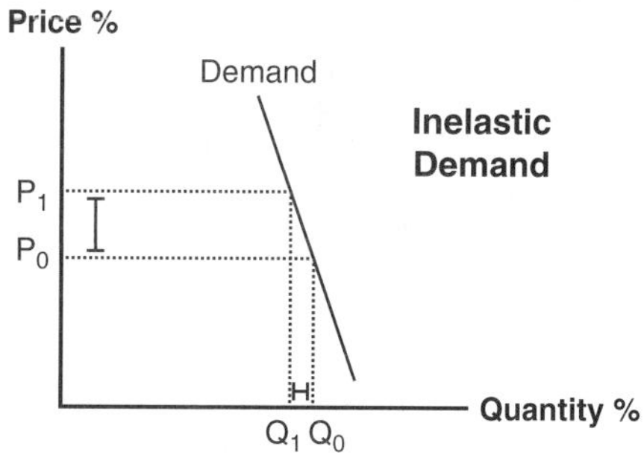

D. Understanding the price elasticity of demand is crucial to the price-setting process. If demand is elastic, then demand is very responsive to price, and increasing the price will *decrease* overall revenue. On the other hand, if demand is inelastic, then increasing the price will *increase* overall revenue. It is important to remember these relationships between price and revenue based on elasticity of demand, as summarized below.

If Elastic, then a price increase will decrease revenue

If Inelastic, then a price increase will increase revenue

If Unitary, then a price increase will not change revenue

E. When computing the price elasticity of demand, the percentage change should be done using the Midpoint Method. Otherwise, the computation result, and occasionally the identification of demand being either elastic or inelastic, is different when analyzing a price decrease versus a price increase. In addition, percentage change numbers used in computing the price elasticity of demand are taken at the absolute value.

1. Computing the percentage change using the Midpoint Method is done as follows:

$$\frac{\text{New} - \text{Old}}{(\text{New} + \text{Old})/2}$$

Note: If you're preparing for the CMA© exam, you should note that this formula is on the ICMA formula sheet. Note that format of the formula presented in this lesson demonstrates exactly how the ICMA formula is computed.

2. For example, assume the current demand is 100 units at the current price of \$10 per unit. If demand drops to 80 units when price is increased to \$11, then the percentage change in demand would be as follows:

$$\left|\frac{80\text{ units} - 100\text{ units}}{(80\text{ units} + 100\text{ units})/2}\right| = \left|\frac{-20\text{ units}}{90\text{ units}}\right| = |-22.22\%| = 22.22\%$$

Similarly, the percentage change in price would be 9.52% (be sure to compute this yourself).

3. Finally, the price elasticity of demand in this example would be computed as follows:

$$\frac{\text{Demand \% Change}}{\text{Price \% Change}} = \frac{22.22\%}{9.52\%} = 2.33 \rightarrow \text{which means that demand is elastic.}$$

F. The final characteristic to understand about price elasticity of demand is that the Demand curve is actually curved, as shown below. This indicates that price elasticity of demand is not constant, but shifts across different price points.

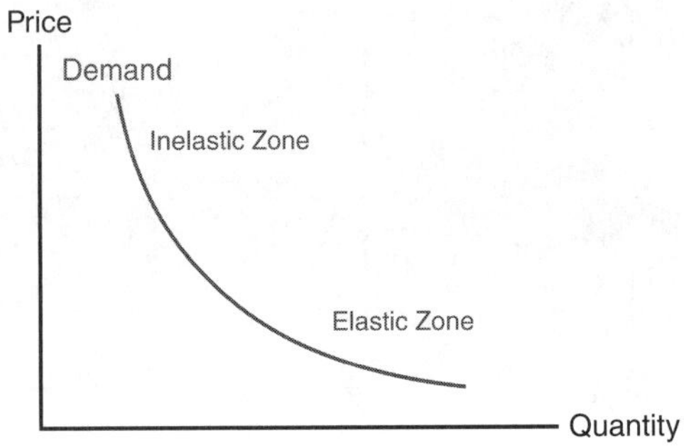

In the illustration above, demand becomes more inelastic as the firm increases price and demand shifts down. This means that there is a subset of the market that isn't price sensitive. As the firm decreases price, demand increases as consumers who are more price conscious enter the market. In other words, demand becomes more elastic at lower price levels.

Practice Question

A consumer technology company has developed a new electronic game and plans to bring it to market at a price of \$85. The first year of market is when early adopters will purchase the game, and management forecasts indicate that 10,000 early adopters will purchase the game at an \$85 price. Further forecast analysis suggests that at a \$100 price, demand by early adopters would drop to 9,000.

In the second year, demand is expected to surge as the majority of the available market begins purchasing the game. However, the company will need to aggressively reduce price in order to compete for the available market in the second year. Management is considering a price reduction in the second year to between \$45 and \$50. Market demand is forecasted to be 80,000 consumers at a \$45 price and 60,000 consumers at a \$50 price.

What is the price elasticity of demand in the first year and in the second year? Which price in the first year will maximize first-year revenue, and which price in the second year will maximize second-year revenue?

Answer

Price elasticity of demand in the first year:

$$\left|\frac{(9K - 10K) \div ((9K + 10K) \div 2)}{(\$100 - \$85) \div ((\$100 + \$85) \div 2)}\right| = 0.65 \text{ (Note that the demand is inelastic)}$$

Price elasticity of demand in the second year:

$$\left|\frac{(60K - 80K) \div ((60K + 80K) \div 2)}{(\$50 - \$45) \div ((\$50 + \$45) \div 2)}\right| = 2.71 \text{ (Note that the demand is elastic)}$$

Price effect on revenue in the first year:

$\$85 \times 10{,}000 \text{ units} = \$850{,}000$
$\$100 \times 9{,}000 \text{ units} = \$900{,}000$

(Note that when the price elasticity of demand is *inelastic*, price increases will *increase* revenue.)

Price effect on revenue in the second year:

$\$45 \times 80{,}000 \text{ units} = \$3{,}600{,}000$
$\$50 \times 60{,}000 \text{ units} = \$3{,}000{,}000$

(Note that when the price elasticity of demand is *elastic*, price increases will *decrease* revenue.)

V. Market Structures

A. Perfect Competition market structures are very difficult markets in which to compete profitably. In fact, as the market competition becomes increasingly more "perfect" (i.e., more and more firms competing on the same product or service), profitability becomes impossible. Firms in this market are "price takers" with no influence on the price as it is driven down to equal total cost. The Demand curve for each firm is effectively flat and absolutely elastic. Any effort by the firm to increase price will drive the quantity demand for that firm's product down to zero. There are not many examples of Pure Competition market structures. Markets for agriculture products, common stocks, and international currencies can approach a Perfect Competition structure.

Market Structure	Number of Firms	Type of Product	Barriers to Entry	Firm's Influence on Price
Perfect Competition	Many!	Identical	None	None

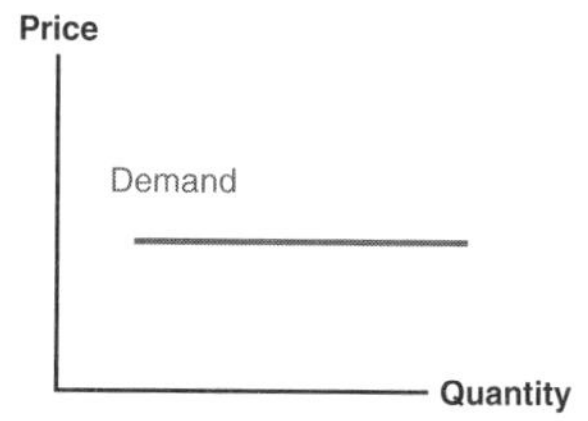

B. Monopolistic Competition market structures are quite common. Generally, there are a significant number of competitors in these markets, and products and services provided are similar. The competition can be tough, but reasonable (even strong) profits are available for firms in these kinds of markets. However, there is a constant pressure on these markets to slide toward Perfect Competition. Hence, competitors work hard to create differentiation (i.e., branding) on their products to keep the consumers' focus off of price. The Demand curve for a firm in this market is sloping, which indicates that firms can influence price. Nevertheless, demand tends to be elastic, so a firm that increases price can expect to lose revenue. Examples of Monopolistic Competition market structures include restaurants, hotels, and common retail products.

Market Structure	Number of Firms	Type of Product	Barriers to Entry	Firm's Influence on Price
Monopolistic Competition	Many	Trying to be "Unique"	Low	Moderate

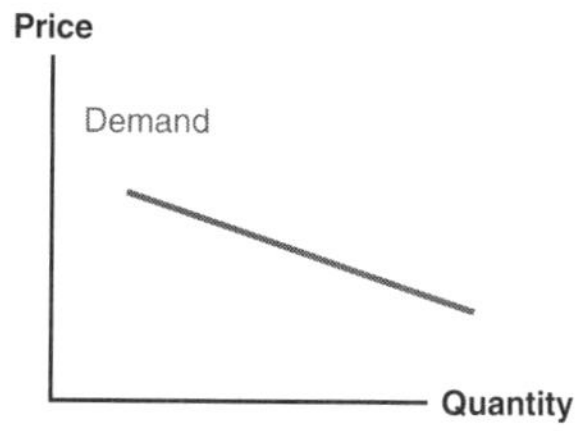

C. Oligopoly market structures are also common. There are few competitors in an oligopoly due to high barriers to entry, usually resulting from the significant capital investment required to compete in the market. Because the products or services in these kinds of markets are generally fairly similar, competition can be fierce, resulting in Demand curves that are "kinked" at the current price point for each firm. Below the current price point, demand is more inelastic. If the firm in the oligopoly reduces price, the other firms are forced to follow down on the price, resulting in little change in the demand quantity for each firm. Conversely, demand is more elastic above the current price point. If a firm tries to increase price, the other firms generally do not respond. As a result, the market reacts swiftly to the price change by the one firm, and moves demand to the other firms. Major airlines, cellular service providers, and movie studios are all examples of Oligopoly market structures.

Market Structure	Number of Firms	Type of Product	Barriers to Entry	Firm's Influence on Price
Oligopoly	Few	Somewhat Similar	High	Moderate to Substantial

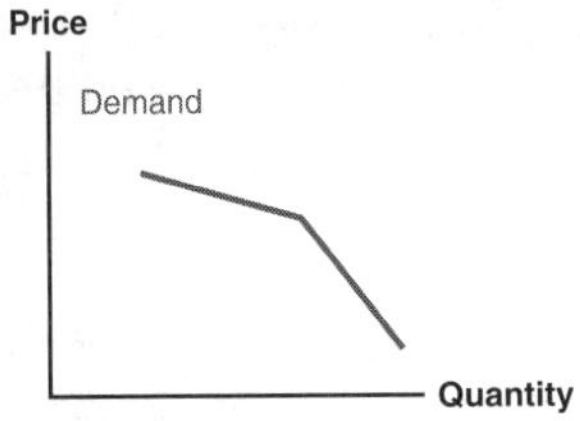

D. Monopoly market structures are easy to recognize due to the single competitor with a unique product or service in the market space. Monopolies exist because of extremely high barriers to entry, these barriers being the result of government mandates, patents, dominant technology, sole access to certain supplies, etc. The Demand curve will be quite inelastic as consumers have little choice other than to stop consuming the product or service. Hence, the monopolist can have a lot of influence on price, so much so that government oversight and regulation is often imposed to reduce or avoid price gouging. Examples of Monopoly market structures include public utilities, computer operating systems, and pharmaceutical companies holding patents on certain drugs.

Market Structure	Number of Firms	Type of Product	Barriers to Entry	Firm's Influence on Price
Monopoly	One	Unique	Very High	Substantial

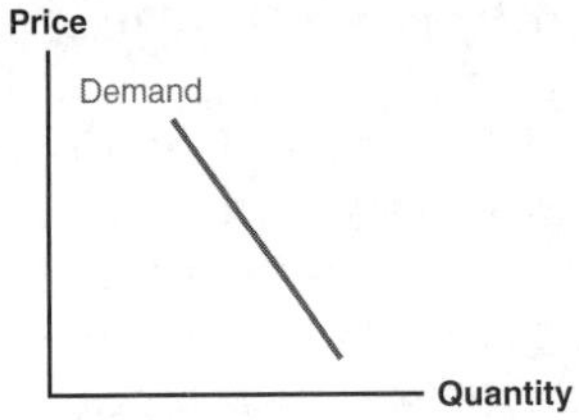

VI. Maximizing Profit

A. Marginal revenue for a firm is equal to the price of selling one more (i.e., the next) product or service. Similarly, marginal cost for a firm is the cost of providing that same product or service. These are important measures that firms must focus on in order to maximize profit.

B. Despite shifting price elasticities of demand across different types of market structures, firms can generally optimize profit by supplying products or services at the price point where marginal revenue is equal to marginal cost. Moving to a price point where marginal price is greater than marginal cost is certainly profitable on that product sold, but it also suggests that the firm can further increase overall profit by selling "the next product," even if the price must be lowered to do so. Hence, the "MR = MC Rule" is important to firms seeking to maximize profit.

Summary

Oversupply or shortages take place when the quantity of good and services supplied is not equal to the quantity of goods and services demanded. The classic microeconomic diagram demonstrates this relationship of price movement as supply and demand curves shift in the market. Working with competition-based pricing requires a clear understanding of how price will affect the quantity demanded. If demand is inelastic to price, then increasing price will increase revenue. Conversely, if demand is elastic to price, then increasing price will decrease revenue. The nature of demand (and, therefore, the approach organizations need to take when managing price) is different across the four different types of market structures: pure competition, monopolistic competition, oligopoly, and monopoly.

Customer-Based Pricing

After studying this lesson, you should be able to:

- Identify techniques used to set prices based on understanding customers' perceptions of value and competitors' technologies, products, and costs (2.C.3.g).
- Define value engineering (2.C.3.i).
- Define and distinguish between a value-added cost and a nonvalue-added cost (2.C.3.k).

In this lesson, you will learn about how organizations use different pricing tactics (economy, premium, penetration, and skimming) to optimize consumers' buying behavior. These pricing tactics assume the organization has a good understanding of the price elasticity of demand in the market for its product or service. Some understanding of consumer psychology is important in customer-based pricing methods. One crucial focus of customer-based pricing is a clear understanding of what customers care about or value in the product or service and what they are willing to pay for that particular value.

Note: Customer-based pricing is also referred to as value-based pricing.

I. Pricing Tactics

A. In general, cost-based pricing involves formulas, and competition-based pricing is centered on models. In contrast to these first two pricing methodologies, customer-based pricing is primarily focused on strategy and explores specific tactics to achieve a particular pricing strategy.

B. There are four basic customer-focused tactics for setting price.

1. Economy pricing is used to drive sales volume by setting price based on the lowest acceptable profit margins. However, if the price is determined strictly in comparison with cost, then this approach is not much different from cost-based pricing methods. To the extent that the economy pricing tactic identifies the "value" created by the product or service for the customer, and considers that value in establishing price, then this tactic is distinct from pure cost-based pricing methods. Economy pricing is based on an expectation that consumer demand is price elastic.

2. Premium pricing signals to the customer the unique or premium qualities of the product. Profit is focused on high profit margins with low sales volumes. Note that this approach largely depends on consumer demand that is relatively price inelastic.

3. Penetration pricing, similar to economy pricing, is focused on low price and low profit margins. The focus of this tactic is to establish consumer sales and a solid market share. Then the strategy is to either subsequently raise price (i.e., "bait and switch") or use sales on the low margin product to drive sales on complementary products or services with higher margins.

4. Price skimming, similar to premium pricing, sets a high price to capture significant profit margin. In contrast to premium pricing, the price skimming tactic is short term. The focus is on early adopters who are relatively price inelastic. As the market expands with more typical consumers who are more price elastic, then the price is lowered to a competition-sustaining level.

C. These four consumer-based pricing tactics can be represented relative to each other in a 2×2 matrix (shown below) that contrasts by price level across time horizon.

Pricing Tactics Matrix		Time Horizon	
		Short	Long
Price Level	High	Price Skimming	Premium Pricing
	Low	Penetration Pricing	Economy Pricing

D. An important characteristic of effective consumer-based pricing methods is understanding and effectively using the psychological effects of certain tactics to affect consumer behavior (i.e., choice). All pricing tactics have some basis in pricing psychology. One common psychological factor that works across the four tactics described above is an emphasis on the "left digit" versus the "right digit" of the price.

1. The cheap pricing psychology that takes place with economy pricing and penetration pricing tactics can be underscored with an emphasis on the left digit of the product price. To keep the left digit in the price from incrementing to the next whole number, prices are set using a "9" factor. This tactic includes prices on vehicles at economy or value prices (e.g., $18,999), prices on milk (e.g., $3.99 per gallon), and prices on gas ($\$3.23^{9/10}$). The left digit in front of the 9 is the "charm digit."

2. On the other hand, the premium pricing psychology is focused on the right digit. Both the premium pricing and price skimming tactics depend on consumer demand that is price inelastic. In fact, these consumers may demonstrate some level of pride in *not* paying a cheap price for the product, and are sensitive to the signal of cheapness when the price involves a "9" factor. Hence, these types of consumers prefer a "round digit" on the right side. For example, $90,000 for a luxury vehicle or $100 for a luxury bottle of wine.

II. Putting a Price on Value

A. It is fruitless to justify to your customers that prices must be increased in order to cover increasing costs. That argument is unconvincing to customers. Making the case for a price increase must be based on the *value* that the product or service provides to the customer. The customer then demonstrates the validity of that value by willingly paying an increased price. Hence, the focus on presenting price to customers must be based on putting a price on the value received by the customers.

B. Value can be defined by customers across a wide range of product or service characteristics. For example, customers may value quality, timeliness, convenience, fashion, safety, environment, etc.

C. The process of evaluating a price for differentiated value (that is, value that is provided over and above the next best alternative in the market) is a three-step process.

1. Identify the product or service characteristics that are different compared to the next best alternative for the customer.

2. Determine the price customers would be willing to pay for the *collective set* of differential product features provided by the product. This is often done using surveys or focus-group feedback.

3. Combine the acceptable price of the differential product features with the current price of the next best alternative. Note that the final market price may be higher or lower than this combined price depending on a pricing tactic being followed by the organization.

III. Value Engineering

A. It is important to understand that organizations generally create most of their product's value in the initial *design* of the product.

B. That being said, there is value established in the process used to produce the product, and in the process used to deliver and support the product. But product and delivery value is significantly limited or significantly enhanced by choices and investments made in the original design of the product.

C. Hence, investments made in the design of the product or service are largely how the organization *creates* value. Then that value is divided with the customer. That is, the price set by the organization effectively *captures* some value back to the organization, and shares some value with the customer.

Practice Question

A cosmetics company is launching a new skin cleanser product in the market, and needs to establish price as part of its product strategy. This new cleanser has several new features that the marketing department believes will interest, and perhaps even excite, customers. The production design for the cleanser is very efficient, and will result in significant cost reduction compared to the old skin cleanser product being replaced.

The company essentially has four different price tactics it can consider, and must choose one tactic as part of the product strategy. The four price tactics are economy, premium, penetration, and price skimming tactics. What are the basic objectives the company must consider with respect to each of the four price tactics?

Answer:

Economy price tactic: With economy pricing, the company is signaling a price to generate a lot of sales volume by customers who are price conscious with cosmetic products (i.e., the market has high price *elasticity* of demand). However, it is difficult with this tactic to signal the premium quality of the new product's features, and it will be very difficult to subsequently raise price to represent these new features.

Premium price tactic: With premium pricing, the company is signaling the high-quality or unique features of the cleanser product, and suggesting that the purchasing customer is in an elite class of cosmetic consumers. Of course, the product must actually demonstrate high quality, high fashion, high innovation, or whatever key features are motivating the customer to purchase the cleanser. This market has high price *inelasticity* of demand.

Penetration price tactic: With penetration pricing, the company is making an aggressive move to capture market share and establish brand and buying relationship with new customers. Penetration pricing may even involve selling below cost. Once the market is secured by the company, the next move is to either raise price or sell complementary cosmetic products or services in order to create profit. Of course, the risk is in the "second move." If price for the cleanser product can't be raised enough, or if enough complementary product cannot be sold, then the penetration price tactic can backfire and damage profits. This tactic assumes that demand is initially price elastic, but subsequently becomes more price inelastic.

Price skimming tactic: With price skimming, the general assumption is the market for the cleanser product has a short lifespan. Hence, price skimming sets the price as high as possible to capture as much profit as possible before customers stop buying the cleanser. This aggressive tactic is risky to the extent that high price dramatically accelerates the market's demise, perhaps so quickly that profits can't be realized. It all depends on how price elastic the demand is in this short-term market.

Summary

Consumer-based pricing methods are generally represented by four different price tactics. Economy pricing uses low prices to drive a lot of sales volume on lower profit margins. Conversely, premium pricing uses high prices to signal special or unique features, and depends on the higher profit margins to make up for lower sales volume. Penetration pricing uses aggressively low prices in order to initially establish a strong market, and then subsequently raises prices or introduces complementary products with higher profit margins. Price skimming assumes a short-term demand for the product and, therefore, sets a high price in order to harvest as much profit as possible before the market goes away. These four tactics make important assumptions about the price elasticity of demand in the market. These tactics are often based on understanding the psychology of the consumer being targeted for sales. When changing prices, it is important to understand that consumers are focused on the value received by the product. In the consumers' eyes, price is justified based on value. Establishing or changing price based on value is a three-step process. Strategy involving the creation of value in order to establish price in the marketplace is best done by focusing on the initial design of the product or service.

Pricing Strategy and the Product Life Cycle

After studying this lesson, you should be able to:

- Define product life cycle; identify and explain the four stages of the product life cycle; and explain why pricing decisions might differ over the life of a product (2.C.3.q).
- Evaluate and recommend pricing strategies under specific market conditions (2.C.3.r).

In this final lesson on pricing, we'll use the four-stage product life cycle (introduction, growth, maturity, and decline) to explore all three pricing methods (cost-based, competition-based, and customer-based) in a specific business setting. You learn in this lesson that pricing strategy evolves as the company and product matures, and that all three pricing methods can work together to guide an organization's pricing decisions over time.

I. The Product Life Cycle

A. Business tends to move in a life cycle. A life cycle can involve the life of a product, the life of a market, the life of a customer or customer group, or the life of a company. There are four basic stages in the product life cycle: introduction, growth, maturity, and decline. This lesson describes life cycle in terms of the life of a specific product or service, but the descriptions below would be very similar for a company, a market, a customer, or a customer group.

II. A Business Case

A. The product used in this lesson to demonstrate the product life cycle is "Life Wash," which is a high-end convenience service offering car wash, dog wash, and hair wash services at a one-stop location. We'll discuss pricing issues across all three pricing methods as we work through the Life Wash product life cycle.

B. The *Introduction Stage* for Life Wash, which can also be called the startup stage, is the time when design and launch investments are being made and production and delivery processes are working to become more efficient. Hence, costs are high.

1. In this product life cycle stage for Life Wash, a cost-based pricing method would result in a high price for Life Wash services. The competition-based analysis reveals that early clients have a lot of interest in the convenience and uniqueness of this service. Hence, demand is price inelastic, and a high price could be sustained in the market.

2. Hence, the company could choose to use a price skimming tactic to initially set prices high in order to help recover the initial high costs. Instead, the company chose to use a penetration pricing tactic to aggressively build the brand and establish the market share.

C. Using a penetration pricing tactic, Life Wash quickly moved into the *Growth Stage*. Costs are still somewhat high in this stage as the company works to become more efficient with its car wash, dog wash, and hair wash services.

1. Due to the choice to use penetration pricing, Life Wash was not profitable in the introductory stage. Price needs to adjust based on some measure of costs. The company is not publically owned; hence, it doesn't need to publicly report a gross margin based on cost of goods sold (COGS). Instead of using COGS-based pricing, the company would prefer to focus on full cost-based pricing.

2. Because significant competition hasn't evolved yet, demand is still somewhat price inelastic, which means the company is not pressured yet to reduce price to minimum profit margin targets.

3. In order to encourage customers to not focus on price, the company begins adding additional features to the Life Wash services in order to signal that this is a premium product. As a result, the company keeps the price at a premium, which is even higher than what is needed to achieve a target margin on full or variable costs. (Note: additional service features could include haircuts or nail trims for dogs, engine cleaning or paint scratch repair for cars, and highlights or styling for the owners.)

D. In the *Maturity Stage* for Life Wash, the operation is nearly at capacity and production costs are optimally efficient. All initial investment costs have been recovered. Hence, it would be safe for the company to base price on variable costs of production.

1. A competitive oligopoly market has emerged with three other competitors offering combined services that are similar to Life Wash. With more competition in the market, customers are becoming sensitive to price as they make choices about what organization gets their dog, car, and hair wash business. This means demand is becoming price elastic. However, it is important for the company not to initiate a price war by aggressively cutting price too much.
2. In order to avoid a price war, the company works to differentiate its services by offering more product features and doing more marketing in order to strengthen its Life Wash brand. And it focuses on a "round right digit" in its prices in order to maintain a premium price psychology in the market. For example, this means that instead of a left-digit oriented price with a "9" factor like $89.99 for its three combined services, the Life Wash company would instead use a right-digit-oriented price with a round number like $100.00 for its three combined services.

E. Eventually, Life Wash moves into the *Decline Stage* in the product life cycle. Demand for the Life Wash product begins dropping as more competitors enter the market and introduce alternative products, such as mobile dog, car, and hair wash services that come to the customer's home or business. As a result, there is excess production capacity building up at the Life Wash location.

1. This increase in the size and type of competition represents a shift from an oligopoly market to a monopolistic competition market. In this market, the price elasticity of demand is becoming very high.
2. With excess production capacity, the company is tempted to move to a full cost-based pricing model in order to cover the fixed costs of capacity. This may be the right choice, but there are actually three different price choices available to the company during the decline stage.
   - **a.** First, the company could *restart* its produce life cycle by physically moving to a new geographic market space. Alternatively, the company may be able to completely reinvent its product by reengineering its technology to provide a different service, such as industrial cleaning of heavy-duty machinery (e.g., delivery trucks, construction equipment, etc.).
   - **b.** Second, the company could *harvest* the current Life Wash product by maintaining a full cost-based or premium price, cutting costs aggressively, and capturing all remaining profit as its market quickly shrinks and closes out. This is a high margin/low sales volume approach.
   - **c.** Third, the company could more slowly *discontinue* the Life Wash product by using economy pricing to extend the market as long as possible in order to capture all remaining sales opportunities that may be available. This is a low margin/high sales volume approach.

Analysis Summary for Life Wash Pricing Strategy

Introduction Stage

- High investment costs and high production costs while inefficiencies are being worked out. Market competition is low, which makes demand inelastic to price.
- Penetration pricing tactic is used to build brand and market share.

Growth Stage

- Production costs are improving, but continue to be high.
- Competition is beginning, but demand is still relatively price inelastic.
- Premium pricing tactic is used to emphasize additional service features.

Maturity Stage

- Production costs arc leveled out and efficient as the facility is at full capacity.
- Competition is strong in an oligopoly market with three main competitors, which creates price elasticity in the market demand.
- Variable cost-based pricing is available to target a profit margin, but investments arc made in additional features and marketing campaigns to keep the market focused on premium features of the service.

Decline Stage

- Excess production capacity is emerging, resulting in cost inefficiencies.
- Competition is very strong and alternative services arc disrupting the market, leading to significant pricc elasticity of demand.
- Three choiccs arc now available at this stage: 1) Recreate the product to restart the life cycle, 2) Harvest the product with high close-out prices, or 3) Discontinue the product naturally with low close-out prices to extend the sales volume.

Summary

This lesson on pricing, which is essentially a business case, demonstrates many aspects of each of the three pricing methods for a particular product as it moves through the four stages of the product life cycle. Remember that the product life cycle is composed of the Introduction (or startup) stage, the Growth stage, the Maturity stage, and the Decline stage. Costs are higher in the first two stages and lower in the last two stages. Competition tends to be lower in the first two stages and higher in the last two stages. As the product moves into the Decline stage, the organization has some choices, including restarting the product life cycle with a new market or reengineered product, harvesting the product profits with high prices that accelerate the decline, or more slowly discontinuing product by cutting price to extend the product life as much as possible.

Section C Review Questions

aq.comp.bp.0010_1710

1. Which statement *best* characterizes the response to higher gold prices by a jewelry manufacturing company in the short run and long run, respectively?

   A. Use cheaper alternative metal in the short run. Increase prices in the long run.
   B. Use cheaper alternative metal in the short run. Decrease prices in the long run.
   C. Increase prices in the short run. Use cheaper alternative metal in the long run.
   D. Decrease prices in the short run. Use cheaper alternative metal in the long run.

aq.cost.bp.0005_0720

2. Almelo Manpower Inc. provides contracted bookkeeping services. Almelo has annual fixed costs of $100,000 and variable costs of $6 per hour. This year the company budgeted 50,000 hours of bookkeeping services. Almelo prices its services based on full cost and uses a cost-plus pricing approach. The company developed a billing price of $9 per hour. The company's markup level would be:

   A. 50.0%.
   B. 12.5%.
   C. 33.3%.
   D. 66.6%.

cont.mar.aq.0017_0820

3. The financial analyst for the company calculates that the breakeven point in revenue for a product is $250,000. The product sells for $25 per unit. Fixed costs are $100,000. What is the contribution margin per unit?

   A. $15.00
   B. $10.00
   C. $5.00
   D. $8.00

aq.risk.u.0008_0820

4. Justin Lake operates a kiosk in downtown Chicago, at which he sells one style of baseball hat. He buys the hats from a supplier for $13 and sells them for $18. Justin's current breakeven point is 15,000 hats per year. Based on a 30% income tax rate, Justin Lake is projecting an after-tax profit of $14,000. What is Justin's current margin of safety in sales revenue?

   A. $75,000
   B. $20,000
   C. $50,400
   D. $72,000

aq.marg.anal.pld.0003_0720

5. Manor Company plans to discontinue a department that currently provides a $24,000 contribution margin and has allocated overhead of $48,000, of which $21,000 cannot be eliminated. Manor's average income tax rate is 30%. The effect of this discontinuance on Manor's after-tax profit would be a(n):

   A. increase of $2,100.
   B. increase of $3,000.
   C. decrease of $24,000.
   D. decrease of $16,800.

aq.tar.pt.0009_0820

6. Carl's Corp is experiencing significant competition that is driving down price from $60 to $50 per unit. If the company chooses to match the new price in the market, the marketing team estimates that sales will rise from 700,000 to 800,000 units. Carl's Corp's current variable cost per unit is $45, and total fixed costs are $500,000. Suppose Carl's Corp would like to maintain a 25% target contribution margin on its sales revenue. To achieve this target, the company must lower its variable production costs by how much?

   A. $0.00 per unit
   B. $7.50 per unit
   C. $11.45 per unit
   D. $15.00 per unit

aq.mp.cvp.0009_0820

7. Simon's Wholesale Flowers produces two types of flower bouquets that it distributes to retail shops: simple bouquets and upgraded bouquets. Total fixed costs for the firm are $184,000. Variable costs and sales data for these bouquets are presented here.

	Simple Bouquets	**Upgraded Bouquets**
Selling price per unit	$24.00	$40.00
Variable cost per unit	$20.00	$32.00
Budgeted sales (units)	20,000	30,000

   How many bouquets will be required to reach the breakeven point?

   A. 10,615 simple bouquets and 17,692 upgraded bouquets
   B. 15,333 simple bouquets and 15,333 upgraded bouquets
   C. 10,952 simple bouquets and 17,524 upgraded bouquets
   D. 11,500 simple bouquets and 17,250 upgraded bouquets

aq.cost.be.0007_0820

8. Breakeven quantity is defined as the volume of output at which revenues are equal to:

   A. total costs.
   B. marginal costs.
   C. variable costs.
   D. fixed costs.

aq.cost.be.0006_0820

9. Given a unit selling price of $100, fixed costs of $3,000, variable costs per unit of $75, and a total quantity of 150 units actually sold, what is the breakeven point?

   A. 60 units
   B. 40 units
   C. 120 units
   D. 30 units

aq.cust.bp.0004_0720

10. A consumer products company prices one of its new products significantly higher than competitor products currently in the market. The higher price is based on customer focus studies indicating that customers in a certain income bracket are willing to pay more for the superior characteristics of the product. This pricing tactic is an example of:

   A. premium pricing.
   B. price gouging.
   C. penetration pricing.
   D. tiered pricing.

aq.risk.u.0002_0820

11. Arvin Tax Preparation Services has annual total budgeted revenues of $618,000, based on an average price of $206 per tax return prepared. The company's current fixed costs are $326,600 and variable costs average $64 per tax return.

Calculate Arvin's break-even point and margin of safety in units.

A. Breakeven point is 2,300 tax returns; margin of safety is 3,000 tax returns
B. Breakeven point is 2,300 tax returns; margin of safety is 700 tax returns
C. Breakeven point is 1,586 tax returns; margin of safety is 1,414 tax returns
D. Breakeven point is 1,586 tax returns; margin of safety is 3,000 tax returns

aq.sunk.opp.cap.0004_0720

12. The Lantern Corporation has 1,000 obsolete lanterns that are carried in inventory at a manufacturing cost of $20,000. If the lanterns are remachined for $5,000, they can be sold for $9,000. If the lanterns are scrapped, they can be sold for $1,000. What alternative is more desirable and what is the cash flow under that alternative?

A. Remachine; $24,000
B. Scrap; $21,000
C. Remachine; $4,000
D. Scrap; $1,000

aq.mp.cvp.0010_0820

13. Simon's Wholesale Flowers produces two types of flower bouquets that it distributes to retail shops: simple bouquets and upgraded bouquets. Total fixed costs for the firm are $184,000. Variable costs and sales data for these bouquets are presented here.

	Simple Bouquets	Upgraded Bouquets
Selling price per unit	$24.00	$40.00
Variable cost per unit	$20.00	$32.00
Budgeted sales (units)	20,000	30,000

If the product sales mix were to change to three upgraded bouquets sold for each simple bouquet sold, the breakeven volume for each of these products would be:

A. 11,500 simple bouquets and 17,250 upgraded bouquets.
B. 15,333 simple bouquets and 15,333 upgraded bouquets.
C. 27,600 simple bouquets and 9,200 upgraded bouquets.
D. 6,572 simple bouquets and 19,715 upgraded bouquets.

aq.cost.bp.0002_0720

14. The cost-plus target pricing approach is generally in what formula?

A. Unit cost ÷ Selling price = Markup percentage
B. Unit cost × (1 + Markup % on unit cost) = Targeted selling price
C. Variable cost + Fixed cost + Contribution margin = Targeted selling price
D. Cost base + Gross margin = Targeted selling price

aq.def.rel.costs.0007_0720

15. Maize Company incurs a cost of $35 per unit, of which $20 is variable, to make a product that normally sells for $58. A foreign wholesaler offers to buy 6,000 units at $30 each. Maize has the capacity to take on this order, but will incur additional costs of $4 per unit to imprint a logo and to pay for shipping. Compute the increase or decrease in net income that Maize will realize by accepting the special order.

A. $60,000
B. ($54,000)
C. ($30,000)
D. $36,000

Section D: Risk Management

Enterprise Risk

Types of Enterprise Risk

After studying this lesson, you should be able to:

- Identify and explain the different types of risk, including business risk, hazard risks, financial risks, operational risks, and strategic risks (2.D.1.a).
- Demonstrate an understanding of operational risk (2.D.1.b).
- Define legal risk, compliance risk, and political risk (2.D.1.c).
- Demonstrate an understanding of how volatility and time impact risk (2.D.1.d).
- Define the concept of capital adequacy; i.e., solvency, liquidity, reserves, sufficient capital, etc. (2.D.1.e).
- Demonstrate an understanding of the concept of residual risk and distinguish it from inherent risk (2.D.1.j).

Risk is a broad term commonly used when discussing business strategy and decision making. This lesson provides definitions for the various types of risk a firm might face.

I. Types of Risks

A. Organizations face a variety of risks. *Risk* is a term used generally to refer to uncertainty of an outcome. Three essential components of risk are: (1) the materialization of an event is not guaranteed, (2) the event will affect firm value, and (3) the effect of the event could be positive or negative.

B. *Volatility* refers to the unpredictability of an outcome. When an outcome is more volatile it increases the uncertainty of an event taking place and thereby is considered riskier. Risk is also affected by the *time horizon* in which an event is expected to take place. In general, the further away an event or outcome is, the more difficult it is to anticipate and it is therefore considered more risky.

C. While risk is a general concept, it can be broken down into numerous sub-concepts that help define and understand what the risk is. The following are a few of the most common types of risk:

1. *Business risk*—The possibility that an organization either will have a lower profit than expected or will experience a loss instead of a profit.
2. *Hazard risk*—The risk that the workplace environment or a natural disaster can disrupt the operations of an organization.
3. *Financial risk*—The risk that an organization's cash flow will not satisfy the shareholders' ability to recover the cash invested in the business, particularly when the organization carries debt.
4. *Operational risk*—The risk of loss for an organization occurring from inadequate systems, processes, or external events.
5. *Strategic risk*—The risk that a company's strategy will not be sufficient for the organization to achieve its objectives and maximize shareholder value.
6. *Legal risk*—The risk that litigation (either civil or criminal) can negatively affect the organization.
7. *Compliance risk*—The risk associated with the organization's ability to meet rules and regulations set forth by governmental agencies.

8. *Political risk*—The risk that political influence and decisions may impact the profitability and effectiveness of an organization
9. *Inherent risk*—Broad term for all the risk a firm faces without any controls applied to business activities or processes.
10. *Residual risk*—Broad term for the level of risk a firm faces after controls are applied and assumptions about their effectiveness are made.

II. Operational Risk

A. Operational risk in particular is difficult to define, but understanding the factors that affect operational risk can aid in knowing what it is.

1. The organization may not hire people with the skills or ethical background necessary to make the right decisions.
2. Internal control processes may not be properly documented or reviewed, or the organization's employees may not properly execute the procedures.
3. Product issues, such as supply chain risks or defective quality, can affect the organization's risk from operations.
4. External events, such as natural disasters, information technology hacking, or additional events outside of the organization, can also affect an organization's operational risk.
5. Other examples of operational risk:
   - **a.** Inadequate backup or redundancy in computer systems
   - **b.** Lack of segregation of duties, increasing the risk of employee fraud
   - **c.** Natural disasters, such as floods, earthquakes, and fires
   - **d.** Failure to comply with appropriate laws and regulations

III. Liquidity Risk

A. *Liquidity risk* is a type of financial risk that refers specifically to a firm's inability to meet its cash flow needs without affecting the daily operations or financial condition of the firm.

B. *Solvency* refers to the ability of a firm to meet its long-term financial obligations. A firm that is solvent is one that is able to pay its debt obligations.

C. Organizations can reduce liquidity risk in several ways including the following:

1. Securing lines of credit to access cash during times of cash shortages, such as inventory buildups before key selling seasons.
2. Ensuring appropriate internal cash reserves to fund operations in the event of cash shortages.
3. Reducing the reliance on short-term loans to fund cash requirements.

Summary
Firms face a variety of risks. Risk is affected by the volatility of an outcome and the time horizon an event is expected to take place. The most common types of risk are business risk, hazard risk, financial risk, operational risk, strategic risk, legal risk, compliance risk, political risk, inherent risk, residual risk, and liquidity risk.

Further Reading
Parrino, R., Kidwell, D., and Bates, T. (2017). *Fundamentals of Corporate Finance*, 4th Edition. Hoboken, NJ: John Wiley & Sons.

Risk Identification and Assessment: Enterprise Risk Management

After studying this lesson, you should be able to:

- Identify and explain the benefits of risk management (2.D.1.k).
- Identify and describe the key steps in the risk management process (2.D.1.l).
- Define enterprise risk management (ERM) and identify and describe key objectives, components, and benefits of an ERM program (2.D.1.t).
- Identify event identification techniques and provide examples of event identification within the context of an ERM approach (2.D.1.u).
- Explain how ERM practices are integrated with corporate governance, risk analytics, portfolio management, performance management, and internal control practices (2.D.1.v).
- Demonstrate an understanding of the COSO Enterprise Risk Management - Integrated Framework (2017) (2.D.1.y).

This lesson discusses risk management. The COSO ERM conceptual framework is reviewed along with risk-management techniques firms can use to manage their risk exposure.

I. Enterprise Risk Management

A. *Enterprise risk management* (ERM) concerns the identification and management of events and circumstances that can affect the ability of a firm to achieve its objectives. ERM is the process of a coordinated, organization-wide risk management system. It is not a department or a function, but rather a holistic approach to a firm's culture, capabilities, and practices. ERM emphasizes cooperation among departments to manage the organization's full range of risks as a whole instead of merely responding to each individual event on its own.

B. Following the high-profile business scandals and failures in the early 2000s, in 2004 the COSO (Committee of Sponsoring Organizations of the Treadway Commission) ERM model was developed to facilitate a broader understanding of an entity's overall strategies and goals and the threats to those strategies and goals. COSO issued an updated framework in 2017.

C. According to COSO ERM, the benefits of enterprise risk management include:

1. *Increasing the range of opportunities*—By considering all possibilities—both positive and negative aspects of risk—management can identify new opportunities and unique challenges associated with current opportunities.
2. *Identifying and managing risk entity-wide*—Every entity faces myriad risks that can affect many parts of the organization. Sometimes a risk can originate in one part of the entity but impact a different part. Consequently, management identifies and manages these entity-wide risks to sustain and improve performance.
3. *Increasing positive outcomes and advantage while reducing negative surprises*—Enterprise risk management allows entities to improve their ability to identify risks and establish appropriate responses, reducing surprises and related costs or losses, while profiting from advantageous developments.
4. *Reducing performance variability*—For some, the challenge is less with surprises and losses and more with variability in performance. Performing ahead of schedule or beyond expectations may cause as much concern as performing short of scheduling and expectations. Enterprise risk management allows organizations to anticipate the risks that would affect performance and enable them to put in place the actions needed to minimize disruption and maximize opportunity.

5. *Improving resource deployment*—Every risk could be considered a request for resources. Obtaining robust information on risk allows management, in the face of finite resources, to assess overall resource needs, prioritize resource deployment, and enhance resource allocation.

6. *Enhancing enterprise resilience*—An entity's medium- and long-term viability depends on its ability to anticipate and respond to change, not only to survive but also to evolve and thrive. This is, in part, enabled by effective enterprise risk management. It becomes increasingly important as the pace of change accelerates and business complexity increases.

D. COSO ERM Framework

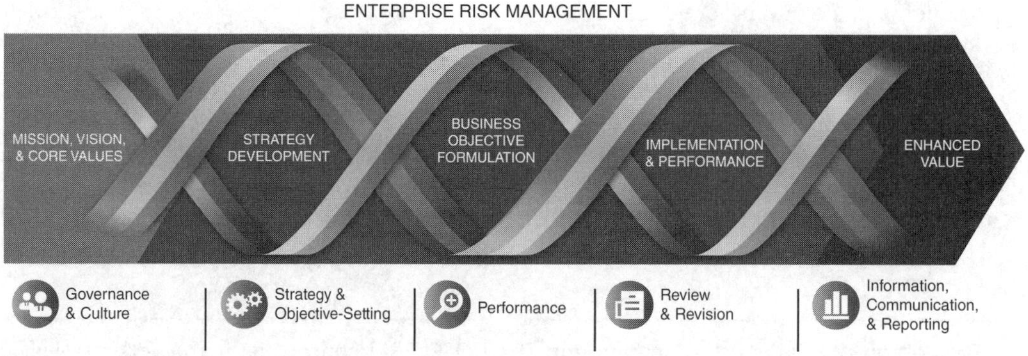

E. The COSO ERM framework has five interrelated components:

1. *Governance and Culture*—Governance sets the organization's tone, reinforcing the importance of, and establishing oversight responsibilities for, enterprise risk management. Culture pertains to ethical values, desired behaviors, and understanding of risk in the entity.

2. *Strategy and Objective-Setting*—Enterprise risk management, strategy, and objective-setting work together in the strategic-planning process. A risk appetite is established and aligned with strategy; business objectives put strategy into practice while serving as a basis for identifying, assessing, and responding to risk.

3. *Performance*—Risks that may impact the achievement of strategy and business objectives need to be identified and assessed. Risks are prioritized by severity in the context of risk appetite. The organization then selects risk responses and takes a portfolio view of the amount of risk it has assumed. The results of this process are reported to key risk stakeholders.

4. *Review and Revision*—By reviewing entity performance, an organization can consider how well the enterprise risk management components are functioning over time and in light of substantial changes, and what revisions are needed.

5. *Information, Communication, and Reporting*—Enterprise risk management requires a continual process of obtaining and sharing necessary information, from both internal and external sources, which flows up, down, and across the organization.

II. Risk Events

A. As part of an ERM development process, firms should identify specific events that may occur and present risk to the firm.

B. The risks facing an organization can be external or internal in nature.

1. *Examples of external risks*

   a. Natural disasters, particularly those common in the area of operations

   b. External computer hacking

   c. Technological change making current offerings obsolete

   d. Competitive pressure

   e. Relationships with key suppliers and/or customers
   f. Risk of political issues disrupting operations
2. *Examples of internal risks*
   a. Fraud and collusion by employees
   b. Management departures
   c. Employee morale
   d. Liquidity and solvency concerns

C. Firms can construct a portfolio of different activities, products, services, and strategies to mitigate the impact of a single event on the overall risk management program.

1. *Diversification within an organization can take many different forms.*
   a. A manufacturing company may offer repair services with products or serve customers in different industries to lessen the impact of lower sales in one line of business.
   b. A service organization may serve customers in different industries or offer different services to protect itself in the event of a slowdown in one particular area.
      i. Accounting firms may offer audit and tax services, which are needed in any economic climate, in addition to technology and consulting services, which may be more dependent on strong economic conditions.
      ii. A web design firm may also offer graphic design or logo design to lessen the impact of businesses not requiring web design services.
2. *Firms with strong portfolios of different activities and risk management tools can rely on the strength of their other areas to offset risks in riskier areas.*

Summary
The identification and management of events and circumstances that affect the ability of a firm to achieve its objectives is called enterprise risk management (ERM). The COSO ERM conceptual framework uses specific goals and components to help manage risk. As part of risk management, firms should also identify specific events that could present risk to the firm and construct a portfolio of ways to mitigate the impact of a single event.

Further Reading
Enterprise Risk Management: Integrating with Strategy and Performance. COSO. June 2017.

Risk Identification and Assessment: Risk Assessment Tools

After studying this lesson, you should be able to:

- Identify and explain qualitative risk assessment tools, including risk identification, risk ranking, and risk maps (2.D.1.q).
- Identify and explain quantitative risk assessment tools, including cash flow at risk, earnings at risk, earnings distributions, and earnings per share (EPS) distributions (2.D.1.r).
- Identify and explain Value at Risk (VaR) (calculations not required) (2.D.1.s).

This lesson discusses tools that firms can use to assess risk. Both qualitative and quantitative tools are discussed.

I. Qualitative Risk Assessment Methods

A. Qualitative risk assessment methods do not have specific numerical or financial data associated with the risk of loss, but organizations still can identify the risk of loss associated with these events.

B. *Risk ranking* requires the organization to assign a relative ranking to prioritize risks and assign resources to address the risks in order of importance.

C. *Risk maps* allow organizations to classify events into a variety of risk levels. An example risk map is provided below.

RISK MAP MODEL

Criticality of Achievement			
Level Impact	6 Yellow (Level III) *Close monitoring for increased impact and/or variability*	8 Red (Level IV) • *Segment Commitment* • *Reported to Segment Leadership* • *Close monitoring of risk action plan*	9 Red (Level V) • *Commitment* • *Reported to Audit Committee* • *Reported to Segment Leadership* • *Close monitoring of risk action plan*
Segment/Intersegment Level Impact	3 Green (Level II) *High-level monitoring for increased impact and/or variability*	5 Yellow (Level III) *Close monitoring for increased impact and/or variability*	7 Red (Level IV) • *Segment Commitment* • *Reported to Segment Leadership* • *Close monitoring of risk action plan*
Process/Business Level Impact	1 Green (Level I) *High-level monitoring for increased impact and/or variability*	2 Green (Level II) *High-level monitoring for increased impact and/or variability*	4 Yellow (Level III) *Close monitoring for increased impact and/or variability*
	Low *(Consistently within tolerable variance in key metric improvement or target)*	**Moderate** *(Sometimes within tolerable variance in key metric improvement or target)*	**High** *(Mostly outside of tolerable variance in key metric improvement or target)*

Actual/Potential Performance Variability Around Targets

Achievement of Objective/Execution of Process/Implementation of Change/Management of Risk

Source: Download the report here: https://www.imanet.org/insights-and-trends/risk-management/test?ssopc=1

II. Quantitative Risk Assessment Methods

A. Quantitative risk assessment methods assign specific metrics or financial measurement to risk events. Organizations can use several methods to assess quantitative risk.

1. *Earnings distributions* show the effect of risk management on reducing the volatility of earnings associated with an event.
2. *Earnings at risk* show how a particular event will cause earnings (or cash flow) to vary around an expected amount. (*Cash flow at risk* is a very similar method.)
3. *Sensitivity analysis* can show how events such as a change in interest rates or a delay in a product introduction can affect earnings or cash flow at risk.
4. Organizations with strong forecasting and financial analysis methods can use these at-risk models to quantify the effect of key financial metrics and design appropriate strategies and tactics to effectively manage risk.

B. A common risk measure is *Value at Risk (VaR)*. This measure indicates potential loss by a firm due to its trading activities. A firm may have hundreds if not thousands of trading positions. The potential for loss is accumulated across these positions at a particular confidence interval. This summary number is used by firms as a tracking measure over time to assess whether their risk position is increasing or decreasing. Calculations of VaR are not required on the CMA exam, but an understanding of its conceptual meaning is.

Summary

Many tools are available to help firms assess risk. Risk ranking and risk maps are qualitative methods that can help identify the risk of loss but do not have specific numerical or financial data associated with them. Organizations can also use several quantitative methods to help assign specific financial measurement to risk events.

Further Reading

Laycock, Mark. *Risk Management at the Top: A Guide to Risk and Its Governance in Financial Institutions*. Hoboken, NJ: John Wiley & Sons, 2014, pp. 41–42.

Use of Probabilities

After studying this lesson, you should be able to:

- Explain the use of probabilities in determining exposure to risk and calculate expected loss given a set of probabilities (2.D.1.f).
- Define the concepts of unexpected loss and maximum possible loss (extreme or catastrophic loss) (2.D.1.g).

This lesson discusses how probabilities are used for risk assessments. Probabilities allow for a quantitative assessment of risk outcomes, in particular, losses.

I. Probabilities

A. Firms can use probabilities to help identify, quantify, and assess the risks facing an organization. To assess risk, firms must determine what are possible outcomes and how likely it is for each outcome to occur. At times, it can be more difficult to estimate the likelihood of an outcome than to determine the possible outcomes.

B. Estimating the likelihood of an outcome is typically done with expert opinion and data. The estimation process can be subject to bias due to the subjectivity involved in judging the likelihood of an outcome.

C. Most risk assessments focus on the downside or negative consequences. One common technique is to assign probabilities to likelihood of an outcome to determine the *Expected Loss*, or the weighted-average probability of the amount of loss a firm could incur.

D. For example, consider the following table:

	Loss	**Probability**	**Weighted loss**
Loss Event 1	(100,000)	30%	(30,000)
Loss Event 2	(250,000)	60%	(150,000)
Loss Event 3	(1,000,000)	10%	(100,000)
Expected loss			**(280,000)**

The firm has determined that in the event of a loss, there are three possible outcomes. The firm has assigned to each event the probability it will occur along with the severity of the loss. To calculate the expected loss, the amount of each event is multiplied by its probability to determine the weighted loss amount. The weighted loss amounts are then summed to determine the expected loss. When the loss is actually incurred, the Unexpected Loss amount can be determined. Unexpected Loss is the difference between the actual loss and the expected loss. For example, if the firm actually lost $350,000 then the Unexpected Loss would be equal to $70,000 ($350,000 - $280,000).

E. Some caution should be used when evaluating an expected loss. It does provide useful information as a benchmark for what the firm could lose. However, the loss once realized could be significantly greater than the expected loss amount. Firms should prepare for the worst-case scenario while reasonably expecting losses to be less. Firms should be aware of the maximum possible loss (also referred to as an extreme or catastrophic loss) and prepare contingency plans in the event this takes place. While typically a low probability event, if the maximum possible loss does occur, it can be very damaging to a firm.

Summary

Probabilities help firms identify, quantify, and assess the risks they face. Experts are used to estimate the likelihood of a loss but the process is subject to bias due to the subjectivity involved. One common technique for assigning probabilities is to determine the expected loss.

Further Reading

Laycock, Mark. *Risk Management at the Top: A Guide to Risk and Its Governance in Financial Institutions*. Hoboken, NJ: John Wiley & Sons, 2014, pp. 41–42.

Risk Mitigation Strategies

After studying this lesson, you should be able to:

- Identify strategies for risk response (or treatment), including actions to avoid, retain, reduce (mitigate), transfer (share), and exploit (accept) risks (2.D.1.h).
- Define risk transfer (e.g., purchasing insurance, issuing debt) (2.D.1.i).
- Demonstrate a general understanding of the use of liability/hazard insurance to mitigate risk (detailed knowledge not required) (2.D.1.n).
- Evaluate scenarios and recommend risk mitigation strategies (2.D.1.w).

This lesson reviews how firms can reduce or limit their risk exposure. Tools available for risk mitigation are discussed.

I. Risk Mitigation

A. Firms can respond to risk in several ways. Common risk response strategies include the following: avoid, retain, reduce, transfer, or accept.

a. *Avoid the risk*—If a firm is not able to manage the risk through means such as insurance or operations, it can simply avoid the risk and not put itself in the situation to incur it. Avoiding a risk is the only strategy that can eliminate the risk of that activity.

b. *Retain the risk*—Firms can develop internal activities to manage risk. For example, a firm could retain a risk by maintaining a reserve fund to pay expenses in the event of decreased revenue or cash.

c. *Reduce (mitigate) the risk*—Firms can engage in actions that will reduce the risk associated with a particular action. Financial instruments such as hedges, swaps, and options can help firms mitigate risk exposure.

d. *Transfer the risk*—Firms can enter into agreements that transfer the risk to another party. This is similar to the concept of reducing risk. Insurance is an example of transferring risk. Insurance spreads the risk of a loss across a wide pool of different organizations that may experience a similar loss. Insurance is generally less expensive than a firm attempting to self-insure or maintain a reserve to protect against the risk of loss. Firms that choose this risk response generally identify the maximum, or catastrophic, loss amount associated with an insurable event and design an insurance strategy to mitigate all or most of this catastrophic amount.

e. *Accept the risk*—Firms can also do nothing and just accept the risk. In this case, the firm accepts the risk of loss and manages its operations around the possible loss.

Summary
Firms have a variety of ways that they can respond to risk. The most common strategies are to avoid or eliminate the risk, retain the risk by preparing for it, engage in actions to reduce the risk, transfer the risk to another party, or do nothing and just accept the risk.

Managing Risk

After studying this lesson, you should be able to:

- Identify and explain the benefits of risk management (2.D.1.k).
- Identify and describe the key steps in the risk management process (2.D.1.l).
- Explain how attitude toward risk might affect the management of risk (2.D.1.m).
- Identify methods of managing operational risk (2.D.1.o).
- Identify and explain financial risk management methods (2.D.1.p).
- Prepare a cost-benefit analysis and demonstrate an understanding of its uses in risk assessment and decision making (2.D.1.x).

This lesson reviews the steps in the risk management process. It discusses methods firms may employ to manage risk. The importance of the right risk attitude is also discussed.

I. Risk Management Cycle

A. The process of risk assessment is an iterative process. The key steps in a risk management process are the following:

1. Identify the risk.
2. Analyze the risk.
3. Evaluate the risk.
4. Manage the risk.
5. Monitor and review the risk.

II. Managing operational and financial risk

A. Firms must develop the appropriate processes, monitoring, and communications to reduce the risk of loss arising from operational risk factors. *Operational risk* is the risk of loss resulting from inadequate or failed internal processes, people, and systems, or from external events. Firms can manage operational risk through processes and policies such as the following:

1. Segregating key duties so employees are not able to misappropriate assets or create fictitious accounting entries to misstate financial records.
2. Ensuring key information systems and data are backed up, preferably through a remote backup process.
3. Training employees through education and training programs that can help firms comply with legal and regulatory issues. This education reduces the possibility of an employee unknowingly violating laws or regulations and causing financial loss.

B. Firms also have many methods of protecting against *financial risk* associated with business operations. Financial risk is a risk arising from financial issues such as exchange rates, interest rates, granting credit, borrowing money, and input prices. It also involves decisions concerning using debt and equity to fund activities, as well as the company's cost of capital. Foreign exchange risk is the risk that changes in exchange rates will cause the number of dollars received from a sale made in a foreign currency or the number of dollars needed to make a payment in a foreign currency fluctuate. Foreign exchange risk is part of financial risk.

1. Insurance allows organizations to pay a smaller amount of money in association with many other insured parties to protect against infrequent, but potentially expensive, losses.

2. Firms with exposure to currency or commodity risk can enter into various contracts to fix prices and reduce the risk associated with currency or commodity fluctuation.

3. Firms with inventory can purchase more inventory at low prices to protect against later potential prices increases. Firms that do so must have sufficient storage space and often incur higher storage and handling costs. They must also consider the probability of inventory spoilage or obsolescence when evaluating additional inventory purchases.

III. Risk Attitude

A. It is important to recognize that a firm's approach to risk management can be directly influenced by the board of directors' and management's attitude toward risk. In many industries typically considered high-risk industries, such as technology or energy, an attitude of accepting higher risk may allow the firm to seize opportunities that other firms would not undertake.

B. In other cases, excessive acceptance of risk may cause significant negative consequences. The 2001–2002 Enron collapse shows the impact of excessive risk attitudes in industries with high risk. Firms must find the appropriate balance between protecting against risk and exploiting risk. Firms not willing to accept enough risk may survive, but they may not achieve maximum success compared to other firms willing to accept greater risk.

C. It is critical for firms to understand the cost-benefit impact of risk management to avoid spending unnecessary resources. The benefit associated with a risk management action should always exceed the cost associated with executing the benefit. In a simple example, a firm should not spend $50,000 on a risk management action if it will generate only a $25,000 benefit.

D. The following table provides an example of how a firm might determine its risk response based on the degree of loss it faces and the likelihood of its occurrence.

	Frequency of occurrence		
Degree of loss	***Low***	***Medium***	***High***
High	Retain or mitigate	Avoid or mitigate	Avoid
Medium	Accept or retain	Mitigate or retain	Avoid or mitigate
Low	Acccpt	Acccpt or retain	Retain or mitigate

Summary

Key steps in a risk management process are identify the risk, analyze the risk, evaluate the risk, manage the risk, and monitor and review the risk. Firms should develop processes and policies to help manage operational risk. Methods can also be developed to protect against financial risk. Firms must find the appropriate balance between protecting against risk and exploiting risk.

Further Reading

Laycock, Mark. *Risk Management at the Top: A Guide to Risk and Its Governance in Financial Institutions*. Hoboken, NJ: John Wiley & Sons, 2014, pp. 65–74, 191–214.

Section D Review Questions

aq.risk.ms.0001_1710

1. Which of the following is **not** a common risk mitigation strategy?

   A. Avoid the risk
   B. Reduce the risk
   C. Transfer the risk
   D. Amplify the risk

aq.man.risk.0003_1710

2. An investor owns stock and is concerned that prices may fall in the future. Which strategy could help her hedge against adverse market conditions?

   A. Buy a call option.
   B. Buy an over-the-counter forward.
   C. Buy a put option.
   D. Buy a futures contract.

aq.risk.ms.0002_1710

3. Insurance is an example of which of the following risk mitigation strategies?

   A. Avoid the risk
   B. Retain the risk
   C. Accept the risk
   D. Transfer the risk

aq.ent.risk.m.0004_1710

4. Which of the following most accurately describes enterprise risk management (ERM)?

   A. ERM is affected primarily by upper management.
   B. ERM is not designed to provide any assurance to an entity's management or board of directors.
   C. ERM does not assist management in identifying and seizing opportunities.
   D. ERM is designed to identify potential events that may affect the entity.

aq.risk.ass.tools.0003_1710

5. Which of the following measures the effect of risk management on reducing the volatility of earnings associated with an event?

   A. Earnings distributions
   B. Earnings at risk
   C. Average earnings
   D. Median earnings

aq.risk.ass.tools.0005_1710

6. Value at Risk (VaR) is most commonly used as a:

   A. year-end measure of a firm's trading activities.
   B. tracking measure to assess a firm's risk position.
   C. benchmark for a firm's cash flows.
   D. benchmark for executives' compensation.

aq.man.risk.0001_1710

7. When evaluating financial risk, which ratios will be *most beneficial* to the analyst?

   A. Total debt and interest coverage ratios
   B. Gross profit margin and the operating profit margin
   C. Collection period and inventory turnover
   D. Current and quick ratios

aq.man.risk.0004_1710

8. Which of the following is the correct order of the risk management cycle?

   A. Identify the risk, evaluate the risk, manage the risk, analyze the risk, monitor the risk.
   B. Identify the risk, monitor the risk, analyze the risk, evaluate the risk, manage the risk.
   C. Analyze the risk, identify the risk, evaluate the risk, monitor the risk, manage the risk.
   D. Identify the risk, analyze the risk, evaluate the risk, manage the risk, monitor the risk.

aq.risk.ms.0003_1710

9. When a firm develops internal activities to manage risk, it is using which of the following risk mitigation strategies?

   A. Avoid the risk
   B. Retain the risk
   C. Accept the risk
   D. Transfer the risk

aq.u.prob.0005_1710

10. Based on risk assessment techniques and the use of probabilities, firms should be prepared for which of the following outcomes?

    A. Best-case scenario
    B. Most-likely scenario
    C. Expected-loss scenario
    D. Worst-case scenario

aq.types.ent.risk.0001_1710

11. When purchasing temporary investments, which of the following *best* describes the risk associated with the ability to sell the investment in a short time without significant price concessions?

    A. Liquidity risk
    B. Investment risk
    C. Interest rate risk
    D. Purchasing power risk

aq.types.ent.risk.0002_1710

12. Which of the following sources of uncertainties would be affected by the firm's debt versus equity decision?

    A. Liquidity risk
    B. Financial risk
    C. Country risk
    D. Business risk

aq.u.prob.0002_1710

13. Dough Distributors has decided to increase its daily muffin purchases by 100 boxes. A box of muffins costs $2 and sells for $3 through regular stores. Any boxes not sold through regular stores are sold through Dough's thrift store for $1. Dough assigns the following probabilities to selling additional boxes:

Additional Sales	Probability
60	.6
100	.4

What is the expected value of Dough's decision to buy 100 additional boxes of muffins?

A. $28
B. $12
C. $40
D. $52

aq.types.ent.risk.0005_1710

14. The uncertainty in return on assets due to the nature of a firm's operations is known as:

A. business risk.
B. tax efficiency.
C. financial leverage.
D. financial flexibility.

aq.u.prob.0004_1710

15. Your client wants your advice on which of two alternatives he should choose. One alternative is to sell an investment now for $10,000. Another alternative is to hold the investment for three days, after which he can sell it for a certain selling price based on the following probabilities:

Selling Price	Probability
$5,000	.4
$8,000	.2
$12,000	.3
$30,000	.1

Using probability theory, which of the following is the *most reasonable* statement? (Note: This solution does not provide for an analysis or evaluation of the individual's aversion to risk.)

A. Hold the investment three days because of the chance of getting $30,000 for it.
B. Hold the investment three days because the expected value of holding exceeds the current selling price.
C. Sell the investment now because the current selling price exceeds the expected value of holding.
D. Sell the investment now because there is a 60% chance that the selling price will fall in three days.

Section E: Investment Decisions

Topic 1. Capital Budgeting Process

Introducing the Capital Budgeting Process

After studying this lesson, you should be able to:

- Define capital budgeting and identify the steps or stages undertaken in developing and implementing a capital budget for a project (2.E.1.a).
- Identify and discuss qualitative considerations involved in the capital budgeting decision (2.E.1.m).
- Describe the role of the post-audit in the capital budgeting process (2.E.1.n).

Making good capital investments is crucial to organizations, and your ability to work successfully with capital investment analysis can be crucial to your career success. This first lesson will introduce you to the capital budgeting process. You'll learn how to define capital investments, and the different purposes for making capital investments. We'll talk about the uncertainty and risk involved in capital investment analysis and quickly describe the different sets of analysis tools available in this process (these tools will be fully explored in later lessons). Finally, we'll define the overall capital budgeting process as three distinct management steps.

I. Defining *Capital Investments*

A. Capital investments represent the core assets and resources for the organization. They include both tangible investments and intangible investments.

1. Tangible capital investments traditionally include investments in buildings, equipment, land, etc.

2. On the other hand, intangible capital investments can include investments in patents, trademarks, and goodwill.

B. One way to view capital investments is to think of the financial accounting concept *capitalized assets*. Investments that are capitalized and listed as long-term assets on the balance sheet meet the classic definition as a capital investment.

1. However, it is not a strict rule that a capital investment must meet the financial accounting guidelines necessary to report the investment as a long-term asset on the balance sheet.

2. For example, R&D (research and development) assets have different reporting rules across U.S. GAAP (generally accepting accounting principles) and IFRS (International Financial Reporting Standards). The result is that some R&D investments are listed on the balance sheet for IFRS but not for GAAP. Regardless of the reporting environment, R&D typically fits the definition of a capital investment and should be handled as a capital budgeting process.

C. The core definition of investment decisions that should be managed with capital budgeting tools is twofold.

1. Capital investments involve significant sums of money for the organization.

2. Capital investments have a long future horizon; that is, these investments are made for the long term.

II. Purposes for Making Capital Investments

A. There are three reasons or purposes for making significant investments in a business that stretch across long time horizons. Capital investments for *operational* purposes typically focus on either reducing operating costs or increasing revenue for the organization. Either or both of these improvements should directly increase operating profits.

B. Capital investments for *strategic* purposes are often concentrated on strengthening the organization's competitive position in its marketplace, which should eventually result in protecting or improving profits. These kinds of investments may be done to establish a barrier against possible competitors, to strengthen relationships with suppliers or customers, or to create and improve the brand image of the organization.

C. Capital investments for *regulatory* purposes are not likely to improve profits. Examples of these kinds of capital investments include large-scale spending on environmental protection equipment or testing, significant spending on HR (human resource) training to meet a legal requirement, and substantial investments in tools or technology to ensure safety of employees or customers. While not done to enhance profit, these investments allow the organization to continue to operate in its industry or market, and should be analyzed in a capital budgeting process to be as cost efficient as possible.

III. Uncertainty and Risk in Capital Investments

A. The biggest challenge with capital investments is the uncertainty involved in making these management decisions. Greater uncertainty means there is greater risk in the decision. This uncertainty results primarily from the fact that capital investment decisions are based on estimates about the future.

B. As the time frame for the capital investment increases, there is more uncertainty in the estimates of future costs, revenues, and other crucial characteristics of the investment. This means that as the time frame gets longer, risk in the decision is increasing.

C. Managing risk due to uncertainty in the capital investment can be done by increasing flexibility on certain characteristics in the investment.

1. The ability to accelerate or delay future payments involved in the capital investment can help the organization soften the impact of other unexpected events in its future that would otherwise create stress around these committed capital investment payments.
2. The ability to expand or reduce the size of the investment in the future provides the organization with opportunities to take advantage of changes in its economic strength.
3. The ability to extend or early exit the timeline of the investment commitment provides the organization with an ability to pull money out of the investment should it have crucial needs in other aspects of its business.

D. In short, flexibility in the capital investment can help counter the effects of uncertainty in the future, and this reduces risk for the organization. However, increasing flexibility in order to reduce risk is rarely free. The organization will need to either pay something extra or give up some potential profit in order to have more flexibility in the investment decision.

IV. Choice and Tradeoffs in Capital Budgeting

A. Capital budgeting involves making choices among several possible capital investments, and different investment options typically have a variety of variable characteristics that trade off against each other in the investment choice to be made.

B. Some investment choices may be more operationally efficient in terms of cost savings or direct revenue improvements. Other investment choices may be more strategically focused in terms of the impact on competitive position, a stakeholder relationship, or the organization's brand image. And some investment choices may provide a more effective or efficient solution to a regulatory requirement. Overall, organizations must often evaluate investment choices across a wide array of characteristics that trade off one against another in terms of operating efficiency, strategic focus, and regulatory compliance. Different capital budgeting tools can be brought to bear to help make assessments that support the final management decision.

V. Capital Budgeting Tools

A. There are a wide range of tools available to help with the capital investment decision. The first set of tools are financial analysis tools, which include net present value (NPV), internal rate of return (IRR), payback, and return on investment (ROI) tools.

B. The second set of tools are risk analysis tools, which include scenario analysis, sensitivity analysis, and Monte Carlo analysis.

C. The third set of tools, unlike financial analysis tools or risk analysis tools, are not computational. Qualitative analysis tools are typically models or *themes* that provide a meaningful way to consider non-quantitative characteristics of capital investment choices. These models include quality, cultural, strategic, brand, environmental, and ethical considerations.

D. Each of these sets of tools is individually considered in subsequent lessons in this section of the course. The diagram below is a visual display of these toolsets.

Tools to Help with the Capital Budgeting Choice

- **Financial analysis tools**
  - ☑ NPV ☑ Payback
  - ☑ IRR ☑ ROI
- **Risk analysis tools**
  - ☑ Scenario analysis
  - ☑ Sensitivity analysis
  - ☑ Monte Carlo analysis
- **Qualitative analysis "tools"**
  - ☑ Quality ☑ Brand
  - ☑ Culture ☑ Environment
  - ☑ Strategy ☑ Ethics

VI. The Capital Budgeting Process

A. The capital budgeting tools listed above tend to focus on only one of the three key steps in a capital budgeting process or system—Step 2. However, it is important to understand that capital budgeting is about more than choosing which capital investment to make. The entire capital budgeting process is depicted in the diagram below.

Big Picture → The Capital Budgeting Process

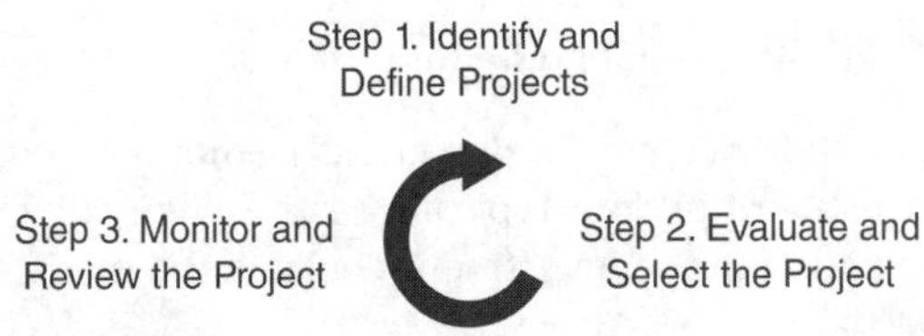

1. The first step in the capital budgeting process involves effectively assembling a set of viable investment projects or choices. Most organizations are very much limited in what capital investments they can afford to make. Hence, management needs to clearly identify and define each possible capital investment project in terms of its financial, risk, and qualitative dimensions.

2. The second step, which is typically the focus of capital investment decision making, is selecting the actual project or asset in which management determines to invest significant resources. These kinds of decisions are obviously crucial to the success of the organization's business. Hence, careful analysis takes place in this second step.

3. The third step begins once the investment is made. This is a long-term step in that it is a process of monitoring the investment and reviewing the assumptions and projections that

went into the decision analysis. This is essentially an audit of the investment decision, and it is used to evaluate the effectiveness of the first two capital budgeting steps.

B. Note in the diagram above that the capital budgeting process is depicted as a feedback loop. As monitoring and reviewing of previous capital investment decisions take place (Step 3 in the process), crucial feedback is provided to future work to successfully identify and define potential projects (Step 1), and successfully evaluate and select projects in which to invest (Step 2).

Practice Question

An e-commerce startup company is preparing to make its first significant capital investment in a new server system. Management has identified a number of possible systems in which the company might invest and needs to make a choice. Management obviously wants to make this decision carefully, and as much as possible improve the odds that the investment will be successful. What kinds of issues should the company consider in making this investment decision, and what does management need to understand about reducing risk in this decision?

Answer

There are three overall considerations that should explicitly be considered for this significant capital investment in a new server system.

The first consideration involves the operational effectiveness of each proposed server system. What are the future effects on costs and revenues for the e-commerce company related to each system?

The second consideration involves the strategic impact of each proposed server system. How does each system help the company protect and enlarge its competition position or its brand image? Do these systems help the e-commerce company improve stakeholder relationships with key suppliers or customer groups?

The third consideration involves regulatory issues, most likely involving security requirements with sensitive supplier and customer information. What are the regulatory requirements the e-commerce company must follow with respect to its server system, and how well does each investment alternative meet those regulatory demands?

The e-commerce company also needs to evaluate the uncertainty involved in projecting costs, revenues, competitive and branding impacts, regulatory performance, etc. for each potential server system investment. To the extent there is more or less uncertainty in the analysis of each proposed server system, there is more or less risk in that particular investment. This risk needs to be incorporated into the selection decision.

Summary

Capital investments involve significant amounts of money and commit the organization to long-term positions. Often, but not always, capital investments are reported as capital assets on the balance sheet. These investments should be evaluated based on three key sets of issues involving operational effectiveness, strategic impact, and regulatory compliance. Because these are long-term investments, there can be significant uncertainty in making estimates or projections involving these three sets of issues, and more uncertainty in a particular investment analysis means there is more risk in the investment. However, to the extent the organization can create flexibility in future commitments surrounding the investment, then risk can be reduced. Tools used to assess capital investments can be grouped into financial analysis tools, risk analysis tools, and qualitative analysis tools. Remember that the capital budgeting process is not only about making a good capital investment selection. Before making an investment, managers need to successfully develop a set of investment alternatives that are each clearly defined in terms of key characteristics. And after the investment is made, managers need to commit to ongoing monitoring of the investment decision in order to understand and improve the capital budgeting process for future investment decisions.

Cash Flows and Profits in the Capital Budgeting Process

After studying this lesson, you should be able to:

- Identify and calculate the relevant cash flows of a capital investment project on both a pretax and after-tax basis (2. E.1.b).
- Demonstrate an understanding of how income taxes affect cash flows (2.E.1.c).
- Distinguish between cash flows and accounting profits and discuss the relevance to capital budgeting of incremental cash flow, sunk cost, and opportunity cost (2.E.1.d).
- Explain the importance of changes in net working capital in capital budgeting (2.E.1.e).

Computing cash flows is absolutely critical to successful capital budgeting. In fact, this can be the most challenging part of capital investment analysis. NPV, IRR, and Payback analysis methods depend on accurate cash flow predictions. Cash flows are handled as three separate sets of computations: initial investment, operations, and disposal. It is important to point out, though, that the ROI analysis method uses profit flows rather than cash flows in assessing operations.

I. Computing Cash Flows

A. It is absolutely critical to accurately forecast and compute cash flows. Otherwise, the subsequent capital investment analysis will not be successful.

B. Computing cash flows is challenging and needs to be approached carefully with a clear distinction on cash flows across three separate stages of the capital investment: (1) the initial investment, (2) the ongoing operations using the investment, and (3) the final disposal of the investment.

C. The cash flow computations in each of the three stages of the capital investment will result in a *net* cash flow amount. Typically, cash is flowing both in and out of the organization at each stage. In addition, there is often an income tax effect that needs to be netted into the cash flow computations.

II. Cash Investment

A. The cash investment for the capital project is almost always a net outflow. Taxes are not paid on the acquisition cost of the new asset. However, if the new asset is replacing an old asset, there is often a tax effect on the cash received for the old asset.[1]

B. The after-tax cash received for the sale of an old asset being replaced by the new capital asset should be netted against the initial cash cost of the new asset.

C. To compute the after-tax cash received for an old asset being replaced in the capital investment, first determine the accounting book value of the old asset (original purchase price minus accumulated depreciation). Then compute the tax effect on the gain or loss on the old asset.

1. The gain or loss is determined by cash received minus the book value. If the transaction is a gain, then the tax cost is gain $\times$ tax rate. This cost is deducted from the cash received.
2. If the transaction is a loss, then a tax shield (tax savings) results from the sale of the old asset. The tax shield is loss $\times$ tax rate. This amount represents tax savings for the organization and is added to the cash received.[2]

D. Cash investment computations are demonstrated below in the Practice Question.

---

[1] Note that cash investments in this lesson do *not* assume like-kind exchange transactions for tax purposes.

[2] Note that tax losses in this lesson are assumed to be realizable in the current year (no carryback or carryforward to other tax years).

III. Operating Cash Flows

A. Capital investment analysis methods like NPV (net present value), IRR (internal rate of return), and Payback are based on cash flows from operations. It is important, therefore, to distinguish operating cash flows from operating profits. The ROI (return on investment) method uses operating profits in its analysis.

B. When computing operating cash flows, pay attention to cash expenses and non-cash expenses such as depreciation.[3] Depending on which approach you take to computing operating cash flows (an indirect approach versus a direct approach), the computation approach to non-cash expenses is different.

1. An indirect approach to computing operating cash flows is similar to the indirect method used in the statement of cash flows. Essentially, the approach is to add back all non-cash expenses (e.g., depreciation) to the after-tax profit.

$$\text{Indirect approach: After-Tax Profit} + \text{Non-Cash Expense}$$

2. A direct approach to computing operating cash flows is a two-step method of directly computing the after-tax amount of revenue and cash expenses, and then in the second step adding the tax shield that results from non-cash expenses.

$$\text{Direct approach: After-Tax Cash} + \text{Tax Shield}$$

C. Operating cash flow computations are demonstrated below in the Practice Question.

IV. Cash from Disposal

A. Forecasting and computing cash flows resulting from future disposal of the capital investment is similar to computing cash flows involved in the original investment. Typically, there is a cash inflow when the investment is discontinued and the asset is scrapped or sold. And there is often a tax effect on the cash flow that results.

B. Remember that any cash received from the disposal, unless it is exactly equal to the book value of the investment asset at that time, will have a tax effect. If the cash received is greater than the book value, it is a gain. The tax cost is gain $\times$ tax rate, and this cost is deducted from the cash received.

C. If the cash received is less than the book value, then the disposal is a loss. The tax shield (tax savings) is loss $\times$ tax rate. This amount is added to any cash received.

V. Working Capital Cash Flows

A. Capital asset investments are almost always used in some operating process for the organization. As part of supporting that process, the organization often needs to commit cash that is then unavailable for any other use until the end of the capital investment life.

B. The cash committed as working capital to support the investment's operating process is identified on the balance sheet as incremental current assets minus the incremental current liabilities. More specifically, the organization identifies increases in the following accounts necessary to support the capital investment, and uses the formula below to compute working capital:[4]

---

[3] Because depreciation expense creates tax savings, whenever possible cash flows used in capital budgeting should be based on tax-regulated depreciation methods. For example, the U.S. tax system of depreciation is currently based on MACRS (Modified Accelerated Cost Recovery System). Note that MACRS systems never use salvage values in the depreciation computation.

[4] If you're preparing for the CMA© exam, the ICMA formula sheet uses an abbreviation of this formula. It is: current assets – current liabilities.

	Cash
+	Accounts Receivable
+	Inventory
	Accounts Payable
	Working Capital

C. The increase in working capital due to the capital investment represents cash inflow that must be added to the initial capital investment.

D. When the capital investment is disposed of at the end of its operating life, the decrease in working capital that results represents a cash outflow that is added to the cash from disposal.

E. Working capital investments are not depreciated, nor do working capital cash flows have any effect on taxes. Hence, do not include working capital when computing tax costs or tax shield.

VI. Cash versus Profit for ROI Analysis

A. Remember that you are computing cash flows to subsequently perform capital budgeting with analysis methods like NPV (net present value), IRR (internal rate of return), and payback. But the ROI (return on investment) uses operating profits in its analysis, and operating cash flow is *not* the same as operating profit!

B. There are many versions of the ROI method, including ROA (return on assets), ROIC (return on invested capital), and ARR (accounting rate of return). Many of these "return" methods you may have studied in other sections of this course. The basic ROI formula is:

$$\frac{\text{Income}}{\text{Investment}}$$

C. "Income" in the numerator of the ROI formula above is represented by some version of Income or profit. Hence, you need to be sure that your computations clearly distinguish between operating cash flows and operating profits as you use different capital budgeting analysis methods. You can use the indirect approach described earlier in this lesson to distinguish between cash flows and profit.

After-Tax Profit + Non-Cash Expense = After-Tax Cash Flow

After-Tax Cash Flow − Non-Cash Expense = After-Tax Profit

D. It is worth noting that ROI analysis can be based on the initial income and investment, or on the average income and average investment book value over the life of the project.

Practice Question

The Circle-M Company is planning to make a $200,000 investment into a new piece of equipment to replace an old piece of equipment. The old equipment has $20,000 book value, and can be sold for $15,000. The new equipment will require Circle-M to increase working capital by $15,000 (which will be recovered at the end of this investment's life). The new equipment has a 10-year life and will generate annual revenue of $80,000 and out-of-pocket expense of $40,000. In addition, Circle-M will recognize depreciation expense using the straight-line depreciation method. Despite an expectation that the new equipment can be sold for approximately $30,000 at the end of its life, for tax purposes Circle-M can base depreciation on zero salvage value (i.e., can fully depreciate the asset to $0). Circle-M's average tax rate is 40%.

What is the net cash investment, the annual net operating cash flow, and the net cash on disposal for this new capital asset?

Continues...

Answer

Cash Investment		
New asset purchase	($200,000)	
Old asset sale	$15,000	
Old asset BV	(20,000)	
Loss	($5,000)	
Tax Shield	$2,000	= $5,000 × 40%
Cash from sale	$17,000	= $15,000 + 2,000
Working capital	($15,000)	
Net Cash Investment	**($198,000)**	= ($200,000) + $17,000 + ($15,000)

Operating Cash Flow		
Revenue (cash)	$80,000	
Expense (cash)	($40,000)	
Cash income	$40,000	
After-tax cash	$24,000	$40,000 × (1 – 40%)
Depreciation	$20,000	= $200,000 ÷ 10 years
Tax shield	$8,000	= $20,000 × 40%
Net Operating Cash Flow	**$32,000**	= $24,000 + $8,000

Cash from Disposal		
Cash received	$30,000	
Book value	$0	
Gain	$30,000	
Tax cost	$12,000	= $30,000 ÷ 40%
Working capital released	$15,000	
Net Cash from Disposal	**$33,000**	= $30,000 + ($12,000) + $15,000

Summary

Computing cash flows accurately is crucial to successful capital budgeting using NPV, IRR, and Payback analysis methods. These cash flows should be computed net of tax. The net cash investment includes not only the acquisition cost of the new asset, but the after-tax cash flow from disposal of any old investment being replaced. It also includes any necessary increase in working capital. Be sure to adjust the net operating cash flow to account for the tax shield from non-cash expenses such as depreciation. The net cash from disposal is adjusted for any tax effects and includes as well the release of any working capital that was necessary to support the capital investment. Remember that operating cash flow is not the same as operating profit. This is important because ROI analysis is based on profit, not cash.

Topic 2. Capital Investment Analysis Methods

NPV and IRR Computations

After studying this lesson, you should be able to:

- Discuss how the effects of inflation are reflected in capital budgeting analysis (2.E.1.f).
- Define hurdle rate (2.E.1.g).
- Demonstrate an understanding of the two main discounted cash flow (DCF) methods: net present value (NPV) and internal rate of return (IRR) (2.E.2.a).
- Calculate NPV and IRR (2.E.2.b).
- Demonstrate an understanding of the decision criteria used in NPV and IRR analyses to determine acceptable projects (2.E.2.c).

In the previous lesson we studied how to compute cash flows associated with a capital investment. In this lesson you'll learn about the time value of money and discounted cash flow analysis. Using your calculator, you'll compute NPV (net present value) and IRR (internal rate of return).

Note: All IRR and NPV solutions in this lesson are computed using a financial calculator. Due to rounding errors, solutions may be slightly different if present value tables are used.

I. The Time Value of Money

A. You likely understand already that time and interest rates are strongly connected. To state it concisely, interest rates are what make money equal across time. Put another way, using an interest rate can make one amount of money equal to a different amount of money at a different point in time. The key to establishing equality between two different amounts of money is identifying the right interest rate.

B. You personally experience the equalizing power of interest rates all the time. With the right interest rate, you are ambivalent between two different amounts of money at two different points in time. You can think of making a loan to experience the characteristics of an interest rate. When making a loan to another person, you are (or should be) concerned about three issues.

1. Since you likely prefer to have your money available right now to spend, you expect some type of compensation for delaying the use of your own money.
2. You're probably concerned about the risk that you may not get your money back at the end of the loan, and you want to be rewarded for taking on that risk. Further, as the risk gets higher, you need more reward.
3. Inflation in the economy causes prices to rise, which means that when you get your money back at the end of the loan, you can't purchase the same goods and services. Hence, you'll need the payback amount adjusted in order to maintain the same ability to consume goods and services.

C. These three factors, desire to consume now, risk of loss, and inflation effects, combine to form the interest rate you demand on the loan you make to another person. Similarly, you are (or should be!) considering these same factors on an investment you make in a business. When the three factors (desire, risk, inflation) are efficiently combined, you should be largely ambivalent between the money you loan today and the money paid back to you in the future.

D. The concept of time value of money teaches us that, with the correct interest rate, the money you loan today and the money paid back in the future is *really* the same money. We call these two different amounts of money (present value and future value) the *nominal* amounts. When adjusted for the correct interest rate, these two amounts are the same amount, and are the "real" value in terms of time value of money.

E. In capital budgeting, the interest rate concept is described using a variety of different terms, including discount rate, hurdle rate, required rate of return, and the weighted average cost of capital (WACC).

II. Working with Your Calculator

A. The time value of money is central to capital budgeting using analysis techniques such as NPV (net present value) and IRR (internal rate of return). Both of these techniques base the analysis on discounting future nominal cash flows to present value terms using the interest rate (i.e., discount rate) that correctly captures expectations regarding desire, risk, and inflation. This approach is known as discounted cash flow analysis.

B. Using a financial calculator, computer spreadsheet, or present value factor tables, you can do discounted cash flow analysis involved in NPV and IRR computations. In this lesson, we will do discounted cash flow computations using a financial calculator. Currently, the most common financial calculators in the accounting and finance profession are various editions of the Hewlett-Packard™ 10Bii+ and the Texas Instruments™ BA II Plus. The calculator instructions provided in this lesson will relate to these two types of calculators. It's important that you have access to specific guidelines for your calculator, available on the Internet or in the instructions that accompany your calculator.

C. Before beginning discount cash flow computations, it's critical that your calculator has the proper settings for this lesson. There are two settings you need to verify, and adjust if needed, on your calculator.

1. Be sure that your calculator is set to *end*-of-period payments (rather than beginning-of-period payments). End-of-period payments is typically the default setting of financial calculators. In these lessons, we assume ordinary annuity payment streams (versus annuity-due payment streams). Most calculators will constantly display a "BEG" on the screen if set to beginning-of-period payments.

2. Be sure that your calculator is set to 1 period per year (rather than 12 periods per year). The default setting for most calculators is 12 periods per year, so this is an important setting to verify and adjust if needed. In these lessons, we treat operating cash flows as taking place annually (which is a significant assumption). Any number of periods per year can be used in discounted cash flow analyses (quarterly, monthly, weekly, etc.), but be sure to adjust the discount rate to match the time period of the payment.

a. On Hewlett-Packard™ calculators, you can see the periods-per-year setting by pressing [Gold shift] key, then [C ALL] key.

b. On Texas Instruments™ calculators, press [2nd], then [P/Y]. If the display presents 12 or any other number than 1, you'll need to access instructions for your calculator to change the periods per year to 1.

D. Finally, it is highly recommended before beginning a discount cash flow analysis on your calculator that you clear the memory of all work from previous time value of money computations.

1. On Hewlett-Packard™ calculators, press [Gold shift] key, then [C ALL] key.

2. On Texas Instruments™ calculators, press [2nd] key, then [CLR TVM] key.

III. Net Present Value (NPV)

A. Remember when computing cash flows that there are three categories of cash flows: Initial cash investment, Operating cash flows, and Cash from final disposal. These cash flows happen at different points in time. Remember that we can't directly compare nominal amounts of money today with nominal amounts of money in the future. We must adjust these cash flows by an appropriate interest (i.e., discount) rate to put all the money amounts in "real" terms.

B. The NPV method is a straightforward approach to discounting future nominal cash flows back to the present period in order to be able to directly compare future flows to present costs. The figure below uses a timeline to demonstrate the nature of how discounted cash flows work in the NPV analysis method. This analysis assumes the following cash flows.

Net cash investment: $92,200

Net operating cash flows: $22,900 for five years

Net cash from disposal: $17,000 at end of five years

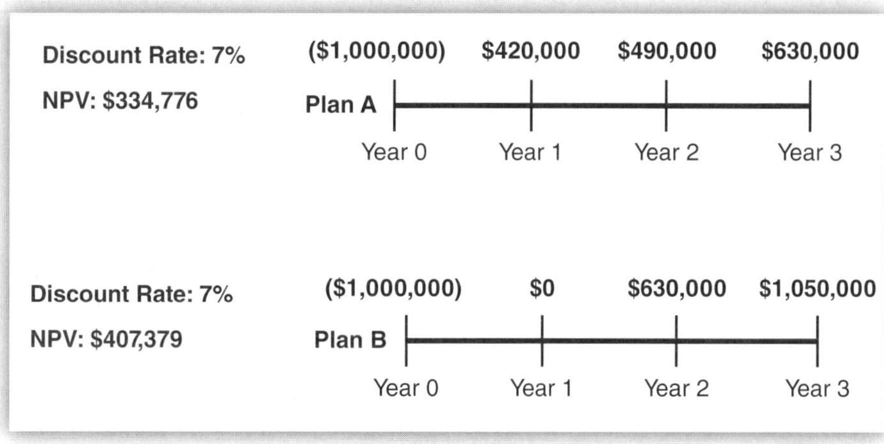

C. The discounted cash flow analysis figure above demonstrates an example of flows for a capital investment that takes place across a five-year time period. And it demonstrates discounting all of the future cash flows back to "Year 0," which is the current time period when the initial cash investment was made. The cash flow discounting takes place using an effective discount rate to bring back each nominal cash flow across its particular number of time periods to be comparable with the initial net cash investment. For example, the operating cash flow $22,900 in Year 2 was discounted back two time periods to Year 0, and both the operating cash flow of $22,900 and cash from disposal of $17,000 in Year 5 are discounted back five time periods to Year 0. We will assume in this NPV computation example that the effective discount rate for this analysis is 8% annual.

D. To compute the NPV, we must first discount all future cash flows to the present value. And then we compare the present value of these future cash flows to the net cash investment. If the present value of future cash in flows is less than the initial net cash investment outflow, then the capital investment NPV is less than zero (negative).

1. On Hewlett-Packard™ calculators, complete the following key strokes:

   [Gold shift], [C ALL] → to clear all memory

   5, [N] → to enter 5 years as the time period of the investment

   8, [I/YR] → to enter 8% as the annual discount rate

   22900, [PMT] → to enter $22,900 as the annual operating cash flow

   17000, [FV] → to enter $17,000 as the cash from disposal

   [PV] → simply pressing this key will compute the combined present value of all future cash flows

   Display: –103,003

2. On Texas Instruments™ calculators, complete the following key strokes:

   [2nd], [CLR TVM] → to clear memory of all time value of money computations

   5, [N] → to enter 5 years as the time period of the investment

   8, [I/Y] → to enter 8% as the annual discount rate

22900, [PMT] → to enter $22,900 as the annual operating cash flow

17000, [FV] → to enter $17,000 as the cash from disposal

[CPT], [PV] → to compute the combined present value of all future cash flows

Display: –103,003

E. The present value –$103,003 is negative because the calculator is indicating that a $103,003 current investment (outflow) is equal to all the future inflows (positive payments) that you entered in the computation, *assuming an 8% discount rate.*

F. Finally, computing the NPV (net present value) is done by comparing the present value of future cash flows $103,003 to the net cash investment $92,200. The difference is $10,803 (= 103,003 – 92,200).

1. It's important to note that this is a *positive* NPV because the present value of the future inflows is more than the current net cash investment.
2. Also note that this positive NPV indicates that the internal rate of return (IRR) for this capital investment is *more* than the discount rate used to compute this discounted cash flow analysis.

IV. Internal Rate of Return (IRR)

A. As noted above, a positive NPV indicates that the IRR is higher than the discount rate used to compute the NPV. On the other hand, a negative NPV would indicate the IRR is less than the discount rate used. This begs the question: What is the actual internal rate of return for the capital investment?

B. Keep your attention on the figure above that illustrates the timing and the discounting of future cash flows for our example. The calculator keystrokes to compute IRR are not much different from computing NPV. In order to compute IRR, the calculator will determine a discount rate that sets the combined value of all future cash flows *exactly equal* to the net cash investment.

1. On Hewlett-Packard™ calculators, complete the following key strokes:

   [Gold shift], [C ALL] → to clear all memory

   5, [N] → to enter 5 years as the time period of the investment

   –92200, [PV] → to enter the *negative* $92,200 net cash investment as an *outflow*

   22900, [PMT] → to enter $22,900 as the annual operating cash flow (inflows)

   17000, [FV] → to enter $17,000 as the cash from disposal (an inflow)

   [I/YR] → simply pressing this key will compute the IRR for this capital investment

   Display: 12.00

2. On Texas Instruments™ calculators, complete the following key strokes:

   [2nd], [CLR TVM] → to clear memory of all time value of money computations

   5, [N] → to enter 5 years as the time period of the investment

   –92200, [PV] → to enter the *negative* $92,200 net cash investment as an *outflow*

   22900, [PMT] → to enter $22,900 as the annual operating cash flow

   17000, [FV] → to enter $17,000 as the cash from disposal

   [CPT], [I/Y] → to compute the IRR for this capital investment

   Display: 12.00

C. The IRR for this example is 12.00% (more precisely, 11.998%). Be sure to remember the relationship between NPV and IRR. For this capital investment example, computing NPV with any discount rate less than 12.00% would result in a positive NPV. And computing NPV with a discount rate set higher than 12.00% would result in a negative NPV.

V. Going Forward

A. The example we've explored in this lesson assumes a constant operating cash flow; that is, all operating cash flows are the same amount each year. That's not typical of capital investments for most organizations. In the next lesson, we'll learn how to compute NPV and IRR with uneven operating cash flows.

B. Also bear in mind that capital investment decisions are not based solely on the financial performance of the capital investment. There are often a number of investment choices available, and some investment choices may have lower financial performance but have non-financial values (safety, brand, environment, etc.) that are important to the organization. NPV and IRR performance, while important, is certainly not the sole basis for making capital investment decisions.

Practice Question

The Circle-M Company is planning to make an investment into a new piece of equipment to replace an old piece of equipment. Circle-M's expected rate of return is 10% and the new equipment has a 10-year life. Below are the expected cash flows associated with this capital investment.

Net cash investment: $198,000

Net operating cash flows: $32,000 for ten years

Net cash from disposal: $33,000 at end of ten years

What is the NPV and IRR for this investment? Use a business calculator to compute these values.

Answer

NPV (Net Present Value):

On a Hewlett-Packard™ calculator (for example), complete the following key strokes:

Gold shift], [C ALL] → to clear all memory

10, [N] → to enter 10 years as the time period of the investment

10, [I/YR] → to enter 10% as the annual discount rate

32000, [PMT] → to enter $32,000 as the annual operating cash flow

33000, [FV] → to enter $33,000 as the cash from disposal

[PV] → simply pressing this key will compute the combined present value of all future cash flows

Display: –209,349 → $209,349 present value of future cash flows

$209,349 – $198,000 = $11,349 NPV

IRR (Internal Rate of Return):

On a Hewlett-Packard™ calculator (for example), complete the following key strokes:

[Gold shift], [C ALL] → to clear all memory

10, [N] → to enter 10 years as the time period of the investment

–198000, [PV] → to enter the *negative* $198,000 net cash investment as an *outflow*

32000, [PMT] → to enter $32,000 as the annual operating cash flow (inflows)

33000, [FV] → to enter $33,000 as the cash from disposal (an inflow)

[I/YR] → press this key to compute the IRR for this capital investment

Display: 11.23 → 11.23% IRR

Summary

Interest rates are based on three characteristics that are specific to organizations and investments: (1) the desire to have money available now rather than in the future, (2) the inherent risk that the investment will not pay back the initial amount, and (3) the expectation of rising prices over time (inflation). Interest rates and discount rates are effectively the same thing for purposes of computing NPV (net present value) and IRR (internal rate of return). Using discounted cash flow analysis, NPV determines the present value of all future cash flows and compares that amount to the initial net cash investment. IRR analysis is similar to NPV analysis, but instead of using a discount rate to determine and compare the present value of future flows to the initial investment, this method identifies this discount rate (which is the IRR) that forces the present value of future cash flows to be equal to the initial investment. Be sure to practice NPV and IRR computations on your own calculator.

Comparing NPV and IRR Methods with Uneven Cash Flows

After studying this lesson, you should be able to:

- Compare NPV and IRR focusing on the relative advantages and disadvantages of each method, particularly with respect to independent vs. mutually exclusive projects and the "multiple IRR problem" (2.E.2.d).
- Explain why NPV and IRR methods can produce conflicting rankings for capital projects if not applied properly (2.E.2.e).
- Identify assumptions of NPV and IRR (2.E.2.f).
- Evaluate and recommend project investments on the basis of DCF analysis (2.E.2.g).

Discounted cash flow analysis using NPV (net present value) and IRR (internal rate of return) methods is fairly simple when operating cash flows are constant from year to year. But operating cash flows in most capital budgeting projects will differ from year to year. This lesson will teach you how to do NPV and IRR with uneven cash flows. Also, NPV and IRR sometimes results in conflicting signals when choosing between different capital investments. This lesson will explore important advantages and disadvantages of each analysis method.

Note: All IRR and NPV solutions in this lesson are computed using a financial calculator. Due to rounding errors, solutions may be slightly different if present value tables are used.

I. Uneven Cash Flows and Your Calculator

A. Operating cash flows are often *not* at a constant level from period to period. Much more realistically, these cash flows will be at different levels across the life of the capital investment, which is more challenging to analyze in your calculator or spreadsheet (but not much more challenging).

B. The key to analyzing uneven cash flows in your calculator is to locate your cash flow key. On a Hewlett-Packard™ business calculator, it is the CF*j* key. On a Texas Instruments™ calculator, it is the CF key.

C. To use the cash flow key on your calculator, you need to enter all cash flows in sequential order, beginning with the initial cash investment. Be sure that cash *outflows* are indicated with a *negative* sign before you enter these flows into the cash flow key.

D. As an example, consider a decision to invest $1,000,000 in one of two different marketing campaigns: Plan A and Plan B. Plan A has the following set of cash flows, including the initial net cash investment of $1,000,000.

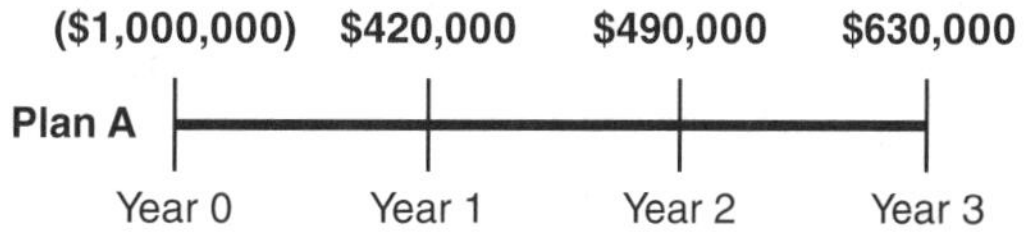

E. Note that the net cash investment outflow takes place at time period Year 0, with the three subsequent after-tax inflows projected in Years 1, 2, and 3. Assuming a discount rate (also known as a cost of capital rate) of 7%, compute the NPV and IRR as follows.

1. On various editions of the **Hewlett-Packard™ 10Bii**+, complete the following key strokes:

   [Gold shift], [C ALL] → to clear all memory

   7, [I/YR] → to enter 7% as the annual discount rate

   –1000000, [CF*j*] → to enter –$1,000,000 as the cash outflow at Period 0.

420000, [CF*j*] → to enter $420,000 as the first cash inflow at Period 1.

490000, [CF*j*] → to enter $490,000 as the second cash inflow at Period 2.

630000, [CF*j*] → to enter $630,000 as the third cash inflow at Period 3.

[Gold shift], [NPV] → to compute the net present value of all four cash flows.

Display: 334,776.00

To compute IRR, *do not* clear the memory.

[Gold shift], [IRR/YR] → to compute the internal rate of return for all four cash flows.

Display: 23.24

2. On various editions of the **Texas Instruments™ BA II Plus**, complete the following key strokes:

   [CF], [CLR TVM] → to enter cash flow worksheet.

   [2nd], [CLR Work] → to clear memory of all cash flow worksheet computations.

   –1000000, [ENTER] → to enter –$1,000,000 as the cash outflow at Period 0.

   [↓] → to move to the next line in the cash flow worksheet.

   420000, [ENTER] → to enter $420,000 as the first cash inflow at Period 1.

   [↓], [↓] → to leave F01 as 1 (since this cash flow only occurs once) and move to the next line in the cash flow worksheet.

   490000, [ENTER] → to enter $490,000 as the second cash inflow at Period 2.

   [↓], [↓] → to leave F02 as 1 (since this cash flow only occurs once) and move to the next line in the cash flow worksheet.

   630000, [ENTER] → to enter $630,000 as the third cash inflow at Period 3.

   [NPV] → to start the NPV calculation (the screen should show an "I")

   7, [ENTER] → to enter 7% as the annual discount rate.

   [↓], [CPT] → to compute the net present value of all four cash flows.

   Display: 334,776.00

   To compute IRR, *do not* clear the memory.

   [IRR], [CPT] → to compute the internal rate of return for all four cash flows.

   Display: 23.24

F. Based on these computations, Marketing Plan A provides an NPV of $334,776 and an IRR of 23.24%. Note that with a positive NPV, the IRR is expected to be higher than the discount rate of 7% used to compute the NPV.

G. Now practice computing NPV and IRR for Marketing Plan B, which has the following cash flows and also assumes a 7% discount rate (cost of capital). Be sure to clear your calculator memory before beginning this new analysis.

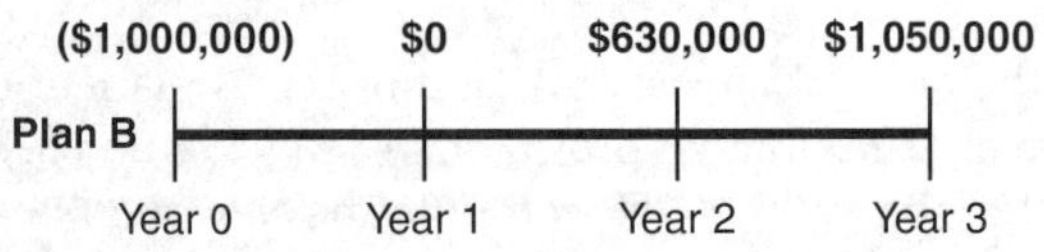

H. If you handle the calculator computations correctly, you will find that Marketing Plan B provides an NPV of $407,379 and an IRR of 22.07%.

II. Comparing NPV and IRR Analysis Methods

A. Note in the example above for Marketing Plans A and B that the NPV and IRR results are inconsistent. Specifically, the NPV computations indicate that Plan B is better than Plan A ($407,379 versus $334,776, respectively). On the other hand, the IRR computations indicate that Plan A is better than Plan B (23.25% versus 22.07%, respectively).

B. NPV and IRR analysis methods do not always provide consistent results when comparing and choosing investments in capital budgeting. Generally, when the two methods disagree on how to prioritize different investments, the most consistently correct comparison method is NPV. This is because the IRR method is based on an assumption that cash flows can be reinvested elsewhere in the organization at the same internal rate of return. This assumption is a major problem in IRR analysis when the internal rate of return of the capital investment is high (compared to the cost of capital) and cash flows vary substantially from period to period.

C. The NPV method has the following *advantages* compared to the IRR method:

1. NPV can adjust the discount rate for different periods of time, which provides more control in the analysis if different years have different expectations on risk or inflation.
2. NPV captures the total value (in money) added to the organization based on capital investment decisions, which provides better decision incentives to managers who may be worried about maintaining a high average IRR performance level.

D. The NPV method also has some *disadvantages* compared to the IRR method, including the following:

1. NPV results are difficult to evaluate in relative terms. That is, a positive NPV is good, but *how good* is a particular dollar amount of a positive NPV? It is clearer for most business professionals to describe the value of an investment in terms of a rate of return on the investment.
2. NPV results do not highlight important differences in cash invested when comparing different capital investment projects. It is hard to compare one NPV to another unless the initial net cash investments for both projects are the same.

E. In comparison, the IRR method has the following *advantages* compared to the NPV method:

1. IRR provides results that are relatively easier than NPV to describe in terms of "value" for the organization, i.e., using classic investment rates of return.
2. IRR results are better for comparing performance across different capital projects when initial net investment amounts are different across the projects.

F. To summarize the lists above, *disadvantages* of the IRR methods compared to the NPV method include the following:

1. IRR assumes that cash provided by the investment can be reinvested at the same IRR, which creates problems in the quality of the analysis at higher internal rates of return.
2. IRR results are also less reliable with big variations in cash flows, especially when cash flows vary between negative and positive values.

Practice Question

Marshall Company has purchased a technology patent for $600,000 that is expected to have a four-year life before the technology becomes obsolete. Marshall will amortize the patent cost using a straight-line method. In the third year of the patent's use, Marshall expects an overall cash loss due to halting business while updating and relocating the technology. Marshall's average income tax rate is 34%, and its cost of capital is 9%. Below are the computations for the expected after-tax cash flows on this investment. Be sure that you can reproduce these cash flow computations yourself.

Continues ...

	Operating Cash Flow	Operating After Tax	Tax Shield	Total After-Tax Cash Flow
Year 1	$250,000	$165,000	$51,000	$216,000
Year 2	$280,000	$184,800	$51,000	$235,800
Year 3	$(100,000)	$(66,000)	$51,000	$(15,000)
Year 4	$300,000	$198,000	$51,000	$249,000

What is the NPV and IRR for this patent investment? Use a business calculator to compute these values.

Answer

1. On various editions of the **Hewlett-Packard™ 10Bii+**, complete the following key strokes:

   [Gold shift], [C ALL] → to clear all memory

   9, [I/YR] → to enter 9% as the annual discount rate

   –600000, [CF*j*] → to enter –$600,000 as the cash outflow at Period 0.

   216000, [CF*j*] → to enter $216,000 as the first cash inflow at Period 1.

   235800, [CF*j*] → to enter $235,800 as the second cash inflow at Period 2.

   –15000, [CF*j*] → to enter –$15,000 as the third cash inflow at Period 3.

   249000, [CF*j*] → to enter $249,000 as the fourth cash inflow at Period 4.

   [Gold shift], [NPV] → to compute the net present value of all four cash flows.

   [**Display: –38,551.59**

   To compute IRR, *do not* clear the memory.

   [Gold shift], [IRR/YR] → to compute the internal rate of return for all five cash flows.

   Display: 5.87

2. On various editions of the **Texas Instruments™ BA II Plus**, complete the following key strokes:

   [CF], [CLR TVM] → to enter cash flow worksheet.

   [2nd], [CLR Work] → to clear memory of all cash flow worksheet computations.

   –600000, [ENTER] → to enter –$600,000 as the cash outflow at Period 0.

   [↓] → to move to the next line in the cash flow worksheet.

   216000, [ENTER] → to enter $216,000 as the first cash inflow at Period 1.

   [↓], [↓] → to leave F01 as 1 (since this cash flow only occurs once) and move to the next line in the cash flow worksheet.

   235,800, [ENTER] → to enter $235,800 as the second cash inflow at Period 2.

   [↓], [↓] → to leave F02 as 1 (since this cash flow only occurs once) and move to the next line in the cash flow worksheet.

   –15000, [ENTER] → to enter –$15,000 as the third cash inflow at Period 3.

   [↓], [↓] → to leave F03 as 1 (since this cash flow only occurs once) and move to the next line in the cash flow worksheet.

   249000, [ENTER] → to enter $249,000 as the fourth cash inflow at Period 4.

   [NPV] → to start the NPV calculation (the screen should show an "I")

   9, [ENTER] → to enter 9% as the annual discount rate.

Continues ...

[↓], [CPT] → to compute the net present value of all four cash flows.

Display: –38,551.59

To compute IRR, *do not* clear the memory.

[IRR], [CPT] → to compute the internal rate of return for all four cash flows.

Display: 5.87

Summary

Most capital budgeting projects do not involve consistently even levels of operating cash flows. Much more typically, operating cash flows levels differ across periods of time, which complicates the computational analysis. However, most business calculators can handle uneven cash flows without significant difficulty, but each cash flow needs to be individually entered into the calculator using either the CFj key (in most Hewlett-Packard™ business calculators) or the CF key (in most Texas Instruments™ business calculators). When working with uneven cash flows, differences can begin to appear in the usefulness of NPV analysis methods versus IRR analysis methods. These differences are most apparent when dealing with investments with significantly high IRR rates and with cash flows that vary significantly across the life of the investment. Generally, when NPV and IRR results conflict with respect to recommending one investment or another investment, the best approach is to use the NPV results.

The Payback Method

After studying this lesson, you should be able to:

- Demonstrate an understanding of the payback and discounted payback methods (2.E.2.h).
- Identify the advantages and disadvantages of the payback and discounted payback methods (2.E.2.i).
- Calculate payback periods and discounted payback periods (2.E.2.j).

This lesson introduces the Payback method, which differs significantly from NPV and IRR methods. Payback helps assess the financial risk involved in the capital investment by measuring the time involved before the net cash investment is recovered (paid back). Conversely, NPV and IRR methods focus more on assessing the financial performance of the capital investment.

I. The Payback "Signal"

A. The Payback method is not really an analysis on the financial *performance* for a capital investment. Payback is much more focused on the financial *risk* for a capital investment.

B. By measuring the amount of time it takes for the original net cash investment to be recovered (i.e., paid back), the Payback method provides important information on the *exposure* and *flexibility* characteristics of the investment.

1. The longer it takes for the net cash investment to be recovered, the more exposed the organization is to economic and operating events that can negatively affect the capital project. Reducing exposure (by reducing the Payback period) effectively reduces the risk of harmful future events affecting the organization's investment.

2. The longer it takes for the net cash investment to be recovered, the less flexibility the organization has to use its resources to explore and invest in other opportunities. Increasing flexibility (by reducing the Payback period) effectively reduces the risk of missing out on desirable future events in which the organization may want to invest.

C. In summary, the Payback method is a *signal* on the financial risk of a capital investment. In contrast, by reporting on the net present value of earnings and on the rate of return, NPV and IRR (respectively) provide important signals on the financial performance of a capital investment. Both types of perspectives are important in capital budgeting decisions.

II. Payback Method—Even Cash Flows

A. The basic Payback concept is a simple formula:

$$\frac{\text{Investment}}{\text{Cash Flow}}$$

B. For example, if net cash investment is \$1,500,00 and \$400,000 is the annual net operating cash flow, then Payback would be:

$$\frac{\$1{,}500{,}000}{\$400{,}000} = 3.75$$

C. The Payback measure of 3.75 represents 3.75 periods of time before the investment is recovered. Since these are annual cash flows, then Payback in this example is 3.75 years. However, be sure to understand that the number of periods the Payback represents is based on the length of time of an operating cash flow. For example, if the \$400,000 represents monthly cash flows, then the Payback would be 3.75 months (i.e., approximately 3 months and 3 weeks).

D. The Payback solution can be represented visually on a timeline. For the example above, the timeline solution looks like this:

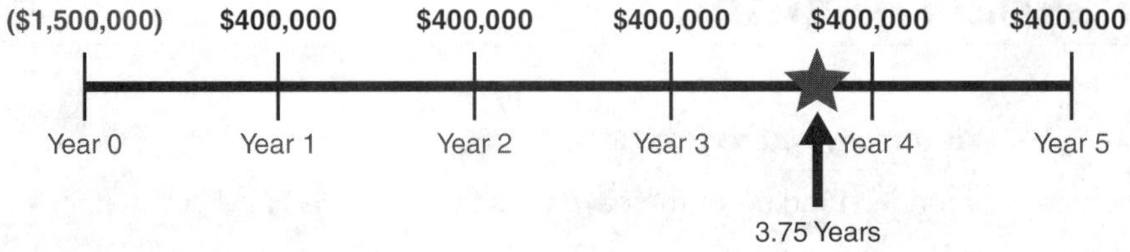

E. Note the Payback method assumes that cash flows take place evenly throughout the operating period, rather than at the end of the period. In the example above, the 3.75 solution indicates that the investment is fully recovered by October 1 of the third year. This can be true only if operating cash flows take place at least by the end of each month. Remember an assumption in previous lessons using NPV and IRR methods was that cash flow takes place at the *end* of each period (e.g., each year). Be sure to pay attention to when cash flows actually take place in the exam problem or in your organization, and adjust your capital budgeting analysis accordingly.

III. Payback Method—Uneven Cash Flows

A. Most operating processes do not produce constant levels of net cash flows each period of time. Realistically, most operating cash flows are uneven from period to period, and this complicates the Payback computation approach.

B. With uneven operating cash flows, a simple single-step math solution is not available. Instead, the cash flow in each operating time period needs to be individually evaluated to determine if and when the net cash investment is recovered.

C. For example, consider a situation similar to our Payback example above (which also results in total future cash flows of $2,000,000). Note, though, that in this case the cash flows are uneven as represented in the timeline below:

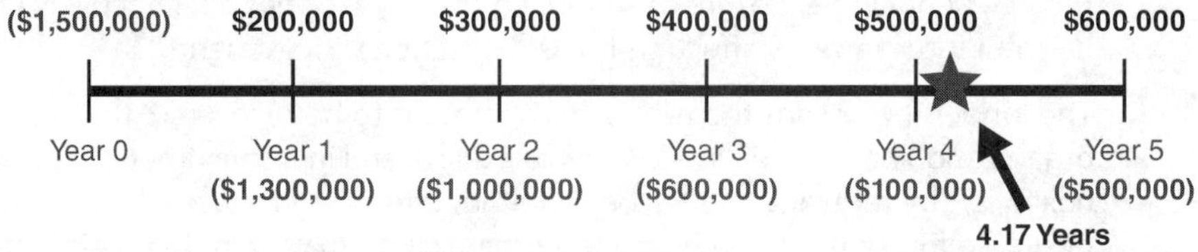

D. Note in the timeline above that the Payback solution is 4.17 years. The solution approach is a year-by-year analysis. For example, the operating cash flow in Year 1 is $200,000. By the end of Year 1, the net cash investment has been paid down to $1,300,000 (= $1,500,000 – $200,000), which is also represented in the timeline above. Similarly, by the end of Year 2, the investment has been paid down to $1,000,000 (= $1,300,000 – $300,000).

1. By the end of Year 4, there is only $100,000 remaining to be paid back on the original investment. Assuming operating cash is flowing throughout the year, then we can compare the remaining cash to be recovered at the end of Year 4 to the total cash flow in Year 5, and estimate that the payback takes place approximately 0.17 into Year 5 (0.17 = $100,000 ÷ $600,000), resulting in a Payback solution of 4.17 years.

2. Typically, organizations don't try to specify the payback as precisely as 4.17 years. More likely, the organization might round off the payback to a number like 4.2, which places the payback event sometime in the month of March in Year 5.

IV. Payback Method—Discounted Cash Flows[1]

A. Look again at the timeline in our last Payback example and notice that by the end of the investment's life, there remains $500,000 cash flow above and beyond the original investment. The key question is, does this $500,000 represent the long-term profit of the investment? Remember what you know about the time-value of money. Spending $1,500,000 and then

[1] Discounted payback solutions in this lesson are computed using a financial calculator. Due to rounding errors, solutions may be slightly different if present value tables are used.

waiting nearly five years before seeing positive overall cash flow does not feel like a $500,000 profit on the investment! Due to the time value of money, the future cash flows are not directly comparable to the original investment. These cash flows need to be discounted back to present value before making the comparison.

B. Return back to the first Payback example with even cash flows of $400,000 each year. Note that the excess cash after the Payback at 3.75 years is also $500,000. Using your business calculator, you can discount back to present value each of the future cash flows before using those discounted cash flows to compute the Payback solution. Using the example above with uneven cash flows, and assuming a discount rate of 8%, compute the present value of each cash flow as follows:

1. On various editions of the **Hewlett-Packard™ 10Bii+**, complete the following key strokes:

   [Gold shift], [C ALL] → to clear all memory

   8, [I/YR] → to enter 8% as the annual discount rate

   1, [N] → to enter Period 1 (Year 1) in the analysis.

   400000, [FV] → to enter $400,000 as the future cash inflow at end of Period 1.

   [PV] → returns the present value of this future cash flow.

   Display: –370,370 → this is the present value of the $400,000 cash flow in Year 1

   Do not clear the memory!

   2, [N] → to enter Year 2 in the analysis (note that the FV is still $400,000).

   [PV] → returns the present value of this future cash flow.

   Display: –342,936 → this is the present value of the $400,000 cash flow in Year 2

   3, [N] → to enter Year 3 in the analysis.

   [PV] → returns the present value of this future cash flow.

   Display: –317,533 → this is the present value of the $400,000 cash flow in Year 3

   4, [N] → to enter Year 4 in the analysis.

   [PV] → returns the present value of this future cash flow.

   Display: –294,012 → this is the present value of the $400,000 cash flow in Year 4

   5, [N] → to enter Year 5 in the analysis.

   [PV] → returns the present value of this future cash flow.

   Display: –272,233 → this is the present value of the $400,000 cash flow in Year 5

2. On various editions of the **Texas Instruments™ BA II Plus**, the keystroke sequence is similar.

   Remember [2nd], [CLR TVM] to clear memory of all time value of money computations.

   Remember [CPT], [PV] to compute the present value of each future cash flow.

C. The result of discounting each of the future even cash flows is to create an uneven cash flow analysis when performing the Discounted Payback computation. The timeline below demonstrates the solution. Each of the nominal operating cash flows ($400,000 annual) are represented with the individual discounted cash flow amount right below.

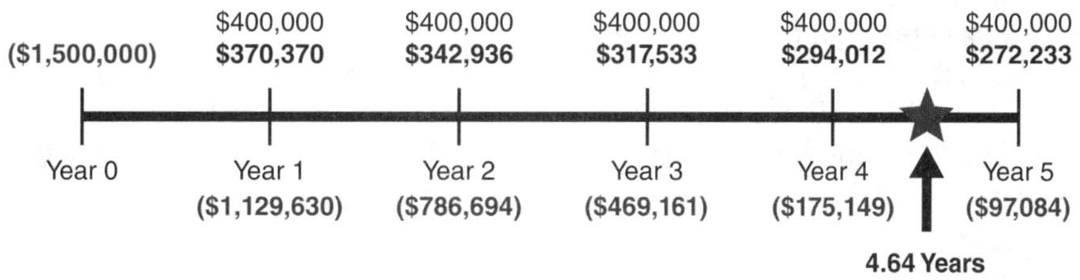

D. Note at the end of Year 1 there remains $1,129,630 "real" dollars to be paid back on the original investment (= $1,500,000 – $370,370), and this computation continues forward year-by-year. Year 4 ends with $175,149 remaining in real (present value) dollars to be paid back on the investment, and a $272,233 present value cash flow in Year 5. The ratio of these two numbers ($175,149 ÷ $272,233) is 0.64, which means that the Discounted Payback is 4.64 years. In other words, the original investment is fully recovered in *real* dollars approximately sometime in the month of August in Year 5.

E. Note that the excess real (present value) cash after the Payback at 4.64 years is $97,084. This actually represents the net present value after the investment is paid back. In other words, this is the NPV you would compute on your calculator based on comparing the $1,500,000 initial investment to five years of $400,000 cash flows at an 8% discount rate. Try it on your calculator! As you can see, the Discounted Payback method is now providing insight similar to the NPV method regarding the *financial performance* of the investment.

1. In this regard, the Payback method is now shifting the focus of the analysis from assessing the risk of returning nominal dollars to focus on assessing the performance of the investment in terms of real dollars.
2. Sometimes the Discounted Payback method is referred to as an "improved" method because it incorporates the time value of money. That being said, NPV and IRR methods are more efficient and more effective in analyzing discounted cash flows, and are the recommended approach for assessing financial performance. Hence, in practice the Payback method is usually based on nominal dollars and is viewed as a reasonably effective way to assess the exposure and flexibility (i.e., risk) of the nominal cash represented in the original investment.

V. Advantages and Disadvantages of the Payback Method

A. Remember that the Payback method, when it is based on nominal (undiscounted) cash flows, is primarily focused on financial *risk* analysis. By comparison, more traditional discounted cash analysis methods like NPV and IRR are focused on financial *performance* analysis.

B. The traditional (i.e., undiscounted cash flow) Payback method has the following *advantages* compared to the discounted cash flow methods like NPV and IRR:

1. Payback addresses a common, and often crucial, issue in business investment, which is the "time to money" issue. In other words, how long does it take to return the original investment? This is often an important focus in capital budgeting analysis.
2. As described in the beginning of this lesson, by knowing the "time to money" (i.e., the time needed to recover the investment), managers are able to consider the *exposure* of the investment to negative events in the future. Managers are also able to consider the *flexibility* of the investment to have money available in the future to consider other investment opportunities.

C. The traditional Payback method has the following *disadvantages* compared to the NPV and IRR methods:

1. The Payback method does not distinguish money today from money tomorrow. In other words, it does not consider the time value of money. We've demonstrated, however, that this concern can be addressed based on the needs of managers.
2. More importantly, the Payback method pays no attention to "value" created past the Payback point. In other words, once the investment hits the Payback point, any additional cash flow is not factored into the analysis. For example, consider our original Payback example with five years of even operating cash flows at $400,000. The Payback was 3.75 years. What if the investment actually had six, seven, or even more years of operating cash flows? That added value in the investment doesn't change the Payback solution, as demonstrated below. This is a significant limitation of this capital budgeting method.

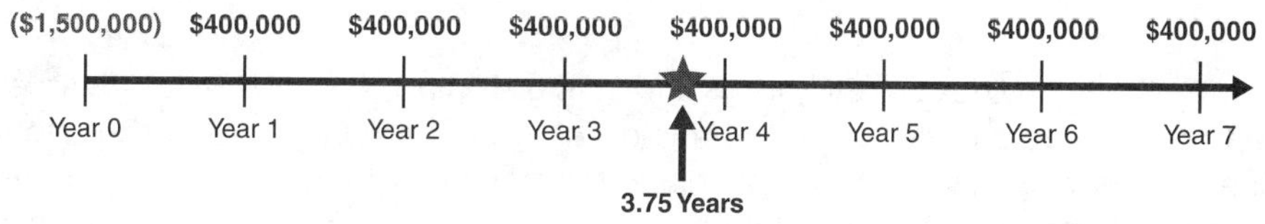

Practice Question

Cole, Inc. is considering an $800,000 investment with a three-year life and expects the following annual operating cash flows:

Year 1: $325,000

Year 2: $375,000

Year 3: $400,000

Cole's cost of capital is 12%.

What is the traditional Payback on this investment? What is the Discounted Payback on this investment?

Answer

Traditional Payback

Year 1: $800,000 – $325,000 = $475,000 remaining to be recovered

Year 2: $475,000 – $375,000 = $100,000 remaining to be recovered

Year 3: $100,000 ÷ $400,000 = 0.25 years

Traditional Payback = 2.25 years

Discounted Payback

For example, on a **Hewlett-Packard™** business calculator, complete the following key strokes:

[Gold shift], [C ALL] → to clear all memory

12, [I/YR] → to enter 12% as the annual discount rate

1, [N] → to enter Period 1 (Year 1) in the analysis.

325000, [FV] → to enter $325,000 as the future cash inflow at end of Period 1.

[PV] → returns the present value of **Year 1 cash flow 290,179** (rounded).

2, [N] → to enter Year 2 in the analysis

375000, [FV] → to enter $375,000 as the future cash inflow at end of Period 2.

[PV] → returns the present value of **Year 2 cash flow 298,948** (rounded).

3, [N] → to enter Year 3 in the analysis.

400000, [FV] → to enter $400,000 as the future cash inflow at end of Period 3.

[PV] → returns the present value of **Year 3 cash flow 284,712** (rounded).

Year 1: $800,000 – $290,179 = $509,821 remaining to be recovered

Year 2: $509,821 – $298,948 = $210,873 remaining to be recovered

Year 3: $210,873 ÷ $284,712 = 0.74 years

Discounted Payback = 2.74 years

Summary

The Payback method provides an analysis of underlying risk in the capital investment, especially with respect to exposure and flexibility in terms of recovering the initial net cash investment. By dividing annual operating cash flows into the net investment, the Payback method returns a measure that represents the periods of time required to recover the investment. However, a straightforward ratio of investment to operating cash only works with constant levels of operating cash flows. When cash flows are uneven, then the cash from each operating period needs to be individually factored against the initial investment, and periods of time summed until the Payback point is reached. One disadvantage of the Payback method is that future cash flows are not discounted (i.e., brought back to present value) before assessing the Payback point. This issue can be addressed by individually discounting each future cash flow before factoring the cash flow against the initial investment. The results of the Discounted Payback method are similar to the NPV (net present value method), although the Discounted Payback method is somewhat cumbersome compared to the NPV method.

Risk Analysis and Qualitative Issues in Capital Budgeting

After studying this lesson, you should be able to:

- Identify alternative approaches to dealing with risk in capital budgeting (2.E.1.h).
- Distinguish among sensitivity analysis, scenario analysis, and Monte Carlo simulation as risk analysis techniques (2.E.1.i).
- Explain why a rate specifically adjusted for risk should be used when project cash flows are more or less risky than is normal for a firm (2.E.1.j).
- Explain how the value of a capital investment is increased if consideration is given to the possibility of adding on, speeding up, slowing up, or discontinuing early (2.E.1.k).
- Demonstrate an understanding of real options, including the options to abandon, delay, expand, and scale back (calculations not required) (2.E.1.l).
- Identify and discuss qualitative considerations involved in the capital budgeting decision (2.E.1.m)

This last lesson on managing investment decisions explores three different risk analysis tools: scenario analysis, sensitivity analysis, and Monte Carlo simulation. These three tools are very helpful to understanding, measuring, and managing uncertainty in the investment decision. Finally, with a good understanding of a number of financial analysis and risk analysis tools available to use in making capital investment decisions, we'll conclude by focusing on crucial qualitative issues in capital investment decision making.

Note: All IRR and NPV solutions in this lesson are computed using a financial calculator. Due to rounding errors, solutions may be slightly different if present value tables are used.

I. Uncertainty and Risk in Capital Budgeting

A. Risk in capital budgeting is a matter of having the analysis turn out to be wrong. NPV, IRR, and Payback measures are based on forecasts of cash flows in a capital investment analysis. These forecasts (i.e., predictions) are less than certain. Rarely can any cash forecast in the capital budgeting process be measured with high confidence *and* high precision.

B. In fact, when forecasting cash flows, confidence and precision move in opposite directions. That is, as the demand for more precision in the estimate increases, confidence in being correct diminishes. This is a common law of statistics. Note that confidence can be measured in terms of the probability of being correct.

C. Capital budgeting measures are often based on very precise cash forecasts, which results in very precise measures of expected financial performance. Consider the following capital investment analyses on two investment plans based on projected cash flows.

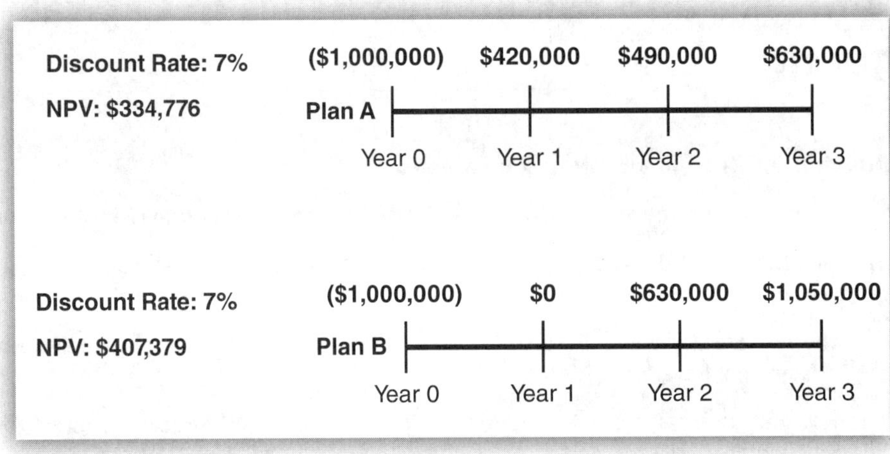

What is the probability a post-investment audit at the end of the Plan A investment life will demonstrate that the NPV turned out to be exactly $334,776? For this precise NPV to result, each of the estimated cash flows in Years 1 through 3 will have to turn out to be exactly as predicted, and that is not at all likely.

D. Forecasting cash flows is risky work, and the further out in the future the cash flows are predicted, the less likely the cash flow will actually result with any degree of precision. Consider both Plan A and Plan B in the analyses above. Which plan is most dependent on cash flows further out in the future? Plan B, which has the higher NPV, is very much dependent on a large operating cash flow far out in Year 3. Hence, Plan B has more risk (that is, uncertainty) in the forecast than Plan A.

E. One way to address the difference in risk between these two investments is to adjust the discount rate. Remember that discount rates (i.e., interest rates) are a function of desire, risk, and inflation. The discount rate should be higher for investments with higher risk. Since Plan B risk is higher than Plan A risk, the discount rate to evaluate Plan B should be increased. Let's assume that a more appropriate discount rate for Plan B is 10%. The capital investment analysis would then indicate that Plan B's NPV is $309,542. This result dramatically changes how the budgeted performance of Plan B compares to Plan A.

II. Scenario Analysis

A. Adjusting discount rates to better represent the inherent risk on one capital investment versus another is one way to handle uncertainty in the capital budgeting process. Another approach is to use scenario analysis.

B. The basic approach with scenario analysis is to include best-case and worst-case forecasts in the capital budgeting process and then estimate the probability of these alternative results. Subsequently, all scenarios are combined to establish the "Expected Value" of the capital investment using the following formula:

$$\sum(EV)$$

where EV is Expected Value $=$ Result $\times$ Probability

C. Returning to the capital budgeting example above involving Plan A and Plan B, we can compute the Expected Value of NPV of each capital investment.

1. For example, the crucial challenge for Plan B is the forecast of $1,050,000 in Year 3. Let's assume that the analyst team putting together the operating cash flow forecasts on Plan B estimates that the probability of achieving operating cash flow reasonably close to $1,050,000 in Year 3 is 50:50. In other words, there's a 50% chance that the Year 3 operating cash flow will be approximately $1,050,000.

2. Further analysis determines that there's a 20% probability that the Year 3 cash flow will be approximately \$1,400,000 and there's a 30% probability the cash flow will be approximately \$350,000. Essentially, three scenarios for Plan B have been identified. Note that all probabilities in this scenario analysis must add up to 100% (= 50% + 20% + 30%).

3. Now compute the NPV for each Plan B scenario (remember to use a 10% discount rate), and bear in mind the probability of each NPV result.

   Scenario 1 (\$1,050,000 cash flow): \$309,542 → 50% probability

   Scenario 2 (\$1,400,000 cash flow): \$572,502 → 20% probability

   Scenario 3 (\$350,000 cash flow): –\$216,379 → 30% probability

4. Finally, using the Expected Value formula, we can compute an overall expected NPV that combines the probability of each scenario.

\$309,542 × 50% = \$154,771
\$572,502 × 20% = \$114,500
–\$216,379 × 30% = –\$64,914
Expected Value = \$204,357

D. Using scenario analysis, we are able to measure and incorporate uncertainty regarding *outcomes* of capital budgeting methods.

III. Sensitivity Analysis

A. Scenario analysis focuses on uncertainty in the outcomes of capital budgeting methods. In contrast, sensitivity analysis is focused on uncertainty in the *inputs* for capital budgeting methods.

B. The basic approach for sensitivity analysis is to identify the input estimate that is most likely to cause the capital investment results to be unacceptable. Once this weak link in the investment is identified, then management can focus attention and resources on assessing and managing that particular issue in the investment.

C. Sensitivity analysis follows two basic steps.

1. For each input in the analysis, identify the point where the input generates an unacceptable investment outcome.

2. Identify the probability of the unacceptable event for each input.

D. For example, let's consider a capital investment analysis of purchasing a patent for \$6,000,000 with a 10-year life and annual after-tax cash flows of \$900,000. The company's cost of capital is 7%. The investment has an NPV of \$321,223 (be sure to calculate this NPV yourself to confirm). Management wants to perform a sensitivity analysis to identify the most likely factor (i.e., input) for the patent investment that would result in a negative NPV.

E. There are three key factors involved in this patent investment's NPV performance: the life of the patent, the annual operating cash flow from the patent, and the company's cost of capital rate. Each of these factors was evaluated to identify the point at which the factor would result in a negative NPV on the investment, and the probability of the factor actually reaching that point was identified. The results are as follows:

Factor	Point Resulting in Negative NPV	Probability[1]
Life of Patent	Less than 9.3 Years	10%
Operating Cash Flow	Less than \$855,000	50%
Cost of Capital	More than 8%	20%

[1]These are probabilities for independent events. Hence, they do not add up to 100%.

F. The sensitivity analysis indicates that the investment factor (or input) most likely to result in an unacceptable investment performance is the annual operating cash flow. Hence, management will invest attention and resources to better forecast, and subsequently better manage, the investment's operating cash flow performance.

IV. Monte Carlo Simulations

A. Scenario analysis is focused on estimating the probability of a certain set of possible results (e.g., original analysis scenario, best-case scenario, worst-case scenario). However, in a complex investment with a long-term life, there are usually too many possible results to individually evaluate each one.

B. Sensitivity analysis is about identifying the investment input factor that is most likely (i.e., has the most risk) to lead to an unacceptable result in the financial performance of the investment. However, as you can see in the example above for sensitivity analysis, there were three uncertain factors in the patent investment (life, cash flow, and cost of capital), and all three are "moving targets." The interaction of these fluctuating inputs will actually lead to many possible financial results in the investment.

C. Monte Carlo simulation uses fairly complex computer analyses to represent the probability of each input factor for the capital investment, and then runs random numbers into the probability distribution of each factor across a thousand or more iterations (i.e., repetitions). The financial result of each iteration is captured and plotted, and statistics are used to evaluate the average and variance of the total set of results. Rather than a single number for NPV or IRR, the final outcome of a Monte Carlo simulation is an analysis of possible results for the investment that gives management the ability to estimate the probability of being within a certain range of the desired financial performance target (remember that the probabilty estimate goes down when the range of acceptable performance results gets tighter, and vice-versa).

V. Real Options in Capital Budgeting

A. Remember that risk in capital budgeting represents the potential for the analysis to turn out to be wrong. Real options in an investment can limit a financial loss when the performance begins moving in the wrong direction. Without any options in an investment, once the decision is made to go forward with the investment, the organization is completely exposed to all events that then result in undesirable outcomes.

B. Essentially, an investment has real options when the organization has choices available in the investment to limit its losses. Real options can also provide management with the opportunity to take advantage of future positive events that improve investment outcomes. In short, real options are inherent characteristics in the actual capital asset that give management flexibility to take action in the future as changing events affect the performance of the asset.

C. Examples of real options include the flexibility in an investment to subsequently expand or reduce the size of the operation, extend the life or exit early from the investment, and change the supply input or customer output focus of the operation.

D. Putting a financial value on real options is challenging. Generally, the value is captured by comparing the expected NPV of an investment with and without the real option(s). Investments without real options usually have lower NPV. The value of the NPV forgone when entering into an investment without options is effectively the value of the real option.

VI. Qualitative Analysis

A. The lessons we have studied in this section on investment decisions have largely centered on quantitative tools used for financial analysis and risk analysis. These are rigorous and valuable management tools, but qualitative analysis in capital budgeting is usually how the final capital investment decision is made.

B. Qualitative analysis requires a cross-functional view of the investment, and involves professional input from many disciplines across the organization, including finance, marketing, operations, HR (human resources), safety, environment, ethics, brand management, etc.

C. It's important to understand that financial analysis and risk analysis is the work done to *prepare* for the decision meeting where the qualitative analysis takes place and where the final decision is usually made. It is critical the organizations establish clear procedures that guides managers as they carefully and thoughtfully consider all qualitative issues relevant to the particular capital budgeting process. The qualitative process is essentially the organization's strategy for making capital investment decisions that are core to the success of its business.

D. The best strategic choice for capital investment is not always the investment with the highest projected financial performance and the lowest project risk exposure. Do not underestimate the importance of qualitative analysis in capital investment decisions.

Practice Question

Stratton Associates has performed an NPV analysis on a possible $5,100,000 investment in a fleet of delivery trucks. The size and strategic value of the investment is crucial to the success of Stratton Associates. Management wants to incorporate an analysis of risk given the uncertainty involved in the investment. To prepare for the risk analysis, the following data have been gathered.

Possible NPV scenarios and the likelihood of each scenario's outcome:

Scenario 1: –$400,000 NPV; 20% likelihood

Scenario 2: $840,000 NPV; 30% likelihood

Scenario 3: $1,300,000 40% NPV; likelihood

Scenario 4: $2,100,000 10% NPV; likelihood

Key input factors for this investment, and the level at which each input results in a negative NPV, are as follows:

Expected life of the fleet: 7 years → Less than 5 years will result in a negative NPV.

Annual operating cash: $1,250,000 → Less than $1,000,000 will result in a negative NPV.

Salvage value on disposal: $900,000 → Even a zero amount will still result in a positive NPV.

Stratton's cost of capital is 11%.

What is the expected value of the NPV for this investment?

What does the management at Stratton Associates need to consider with respect to investment sensitivity to the key input factors?

Answer:

Scenario Analysis

Scenario 1: –$400,000 × 20% = –$80,000

Scenario 2: $840,000 × 30% = $252,000

Scenario 3: $1,300,000 × 40% = $520,000

Scenario 4: $2,100,000 × 10% = <u>$210,000</u>

Total Expected Value of NPV = $902,000

Sensitivity Analysis

The management team at Stratton Associates needs to consider the likelihood (i.e., probability) of the fleet investment lasting less than 5 years, and the probability of annual operating cash flows being less than $1,000,000. For whichever of these input factors has the highest probability, management should invest additional analysis and management effort to reduce the investment's sensitivity to that risk. Stratton Associates could also use Monte Carlo simulation to assess the combined effect of the probable range of all input factors, including the salvage value, to build a more complete view of all possible NPV performance outcomes.

Summary

Incorporating uncertainty and probability of future cash flows is fundamental to the analysis of risk in a capital investment. One way to measure and accommodate for uncertainty is using scenario analysis, which is to establish multiple possible outcomes or scenarios and then estimate the probability of each outcome. The overall expected outcome on the investment is measured by multiplying each possible outcome by its probability and then adding up all results (this approach is sometimes referred to as a weighted averaging method). In contrast to an outcome focus in scenario analysis, sensitivity analysis focuses on evaluating each input factor for the investment analysis and determining the probability of each factor generating an unacceptable investment result. The factor with the highest probability of leading to unacceptable results is the "weak link" factor creating the most sensitivity in the investment's potential success. Monte Carlo simulation is a sophisticated computer analysis method that incorporates uncertainties and probability distributions for all inputs and uses random number inputs to map the range of possible financial results. Real options in investments are opportunities to flexibly adjust the investment going forward in order to accommodate for changing conditions. Rigorous risk analysis is important to the capital budgeting process, as is effective use of well-established financial analysis methods such as NPV and Payback. But financial analysis and risk analysis are often subordinate to crucial qualitative factors involved in each investment opportunity. The qualitative issues are often the focus of the final strategic choice for the organization.

Section E Review Questions

aq.payback.discount.0002_0720

1. Fitzgerald Company is planning to acquire a $250,000 machine that will provide increased efficiencies, thereby reducing annual pretax operating costs by $80,000. The machine will be depreciated by the straight-line method over a five-year life with no salvage value at the end of five years. Assuming a 40% income tax rate, the machine's payback period is:

   A. 3.68 years.
   B. 5.21 years.
   C. 2.50 years.
   D. 3.13 years.

aq.intro.cbp.0008_0720

2. The capital budgeting decision process addresses:

   A. how a firm's day-to-day financial matters should be managed.
   B. which productive assets a firm should purchase.
   C. how a firm should finance its assets.
   D. All of these answers are correct.

aq.cash.flows.0007_0720

3. Which of the following costs does **not** impact taxes in a capital budgeting context?

   A. Loss on the disposal of an existing machine, which is being replaced as part of the capital investment proposal
   B. An increase in the revenues resulting from the capital investment
   C. Depreciation expense recorded for the capital investment during its useful life
   D. The release of net working capital at the end of the capital investment's useful life

aq.cash.flows.0009_0720

4. Premier Steel, Inc. is considering the purchase of a new machine for $100,000 that will have a useful life of three years. The firm's cost of capital is 11% and the tax rate is 40%. This machine is expected to be sold for its salvage value of $20,000 at the end of three years. The machine will require an ongoing working capital commitment of $2,500 in spare parts inventory. In addition to the purchase price, Premier estimates that it will incur the following additional costs related to the machine purchase: $8,000 for shipping and $4,000 for installation.

   Expected sales are as follows: Year 1 = $90,000; Year 2 = $97,500; Year 3 = $105,000. Estimated operating expenses are Year 1 = $25,000; Year 2 = $27,000; Year 3 = $29,000. The investment in working capital will be liquidated at termination of the project at the end of Year 3. MACRS rates: Year 1 = 33%, Year 2 = 45%, Year 3 = 15%, Year 4 = 7%.

   Using MACRS to compute depreciation expense, what is the after-tax operating cash flow in Year 1?

   A. $53,784
   B. $16,824
   C. $51,144
   D. $51,200

aq.npv.irr.ucf.0005_0720

5. As the director of capital budgeting for Denver Corporation, an analyst is evaluating two mutually exclusive projects with the net cash flows shown here.

	Project X	Project Z
0	–$100,000	–$100,000
1	$50,000	$10,000
2	$40,000	$30,000
3	$30,000	$40,000
4	$10,000	$60,000

If Denver's cost of capital is 15%, which project should be chosen?

***Solutions are computed using a financial calculator. Due to rounding errors, the solution may be slightly different if present value tables are used.*

A. Project X should be chosen since it has a better internal rate of return (IRR).
B. Project X should be chosen since it has a better net present value (NPV).
C. Neither project should be chosen.
D. Project Z should be chosen since it has the higher IRR.

aq.cash.flows.0004_0720

6. Alexander Manufacturing is planning to purchase a machine costing $185,000 to replace fully depreciated production equipment. For the duration of the new machine's useful life, management estimates needing to commit working capital of $6,000. Management also anticipates that investing in this machine will increase annual net after-tax cash flows by $105,000. The new equipment will be depreciated by the straight-line method over a five-year life with a salvage value of $25,000. Owen expects to receive $2,200 through the sale of the old equipment, which was purchased six years ago for $137,000. Which of the amounts detailed in the problem represent a sunk cost?

   A. $6,000
   B. $25,000
   C. $105,000
   D. $137,000

aq.npv.irr.0001_0720

7. The discount rate (hurdle rate of return) must be determined in advance in order to use the:

   A. payback period method.
   B. time-adjusted rate of return method.
   C. net present value method.
   D. internal rate of return method.

aq.cash.flows.0002_0720

8. A bank is considering building a branch on a piece of property it already owns. Which of the following cash flows should **not** be considered in the capital budgeting analysis?

   A. Money spent when the property was originally purchased to determine whether there are any environmental issues regarding the property
   B. Cash the firm will forgo from the sale of the property if the company decides to build
   C. Cash flows resulting from several hundred new customers who will switch from local competitors to the new branch if the bank makes the investment
   D. Shipping and installation charges the bank must spend to get equipment in the new branch

aq.payback.discount.0001_0720

9. When evaluating capital budgeting analysis techniques, the payback method emphasizes:

   A. profitability.
   B. cost of capital.
   C. net income.
   D. liquidity.

aq.cash.flows.0003 0720

10. Owen Eyewear is planning to purchase a $520,000 machine to improve the quality and lead time of its eyewear production. Management estimates that this investment will result in an increase in annual cash revenues of $380,000 with related cash operating costs of $32,000. The machine will be depreciated by the straight-line method over a five-year life. Assume a 30% income tax rate and a 12% hurdle rate. What is the amount of the depreciation tax shield for Year 1?

    A. $104,000
    B. $31,200
    C. $27,857
    D. $0

aq.npv.irr.0004_0720

11. Michael Company is considering the purchase of new computer equipment to improve its production scheduling. This new equipment would cost $300,000 with working capital of $14,000 to be committed for the life of the asset. Management estimates that the equipment will improve after-tax cash flows (which already include the tax shield from depreciation) by $96,500 per year. The equipment will have an estimated useful life of four years with no residual (salvage) value. Michael Company has a minimum required return for similar investments of 10%.Â Assume that the asset will be placed in service at the beginning of the fiscal year. Calculate the net present value for this investment opportunity.

    ***Solutions are computed using a financial calculator. Due to rounding errors, the solution may be slightly different if present value tables are used.*

    A. ($8,108)
    B. $1,454
    C. $5,892
    D. $15,454

aq.npv.irr.ucf.0008_0720

12. Salem Ltd. is considering the purchase of a new machine that has a purchase price of $1,200,000. Management estimates that the machine will result in a net after-tax cash inflow of $341,976 per year. The machine will have an estimated useful life of five years and a residual (salvage) value of $50,000. Salem has a minimum required return for similar investments of 14%.Â When using this 14% hurdle rate, the NPV for the project was calculated as –$0.27. What does this net present value imply about the internal rate of return?

    ***Solutions are computed using a financial calculator. Due to rounding errors, the solution may be slightly different if present value tables are used.*

    A. IRR is definitely less than 14%.
    B. IRR is almost exactly equal to 14%.
    C. IRR is definitely greater than 14%.
    D. No implications can be made about IRR from an NPV calculation.

aq.cash.flows.0008_0720

13. Quad Company is considering buying new equipment costing $450,000 to update its tailgating business. Management anticipates that the machine will produce cash sales of $265,000 each year over the next five years. Annual cash expenses are projected as $70,000. Quad plans to use straight-line depreciation with a residual (salvage) value of $15,000. Quad's combined income tax rate is 30%. Determine the annual after-tax cash flow for the investment.

    A. $75,600
    B. $136,500
    C. $162,600
    D. $223,500

aq.payback.discount.0005_0720

14. Which of the following is a limitation inherent in the payback method?

    A. It is difficult to compute and understand.
    B. It encourages investment in long-term projects to the detriment of considering short-term opportunities.
    C. It does not consider the risk of a project.
    D. It fails to consider the cash flows over a project's entire useful life.

aq.cash.flows.0005_1710

15. Mangione Company is selling an existing machine that is being replaced with new equipment. The existing machine originally cost $50,000, with an estimated useful life of four years and a salvage value of $500 when it was initially placed in service four years ago.

    Mangione, in seeking to dispose of the existing machine, has found a scrapyard that is offering $700. Assume an effective tax rate of 30%. What is the after-tax cash effect related to the sale of the existing machine?

    A. ($60)
    B. $140
    C. $200
    D. $640

Section F: Professional Ethics

Topic 1. Business Ethics

Moral Philosophies and Ethical Decision Making

After studying this lesson, you should be able to:

- Define business ethics (2.F.1.a).
- Analyze the concepts of morality and virtue (2.F.1.b).
- Define moral philosophy (2.F.1.c).
- Demonstrate an understanding of the following moral philosophies and concepts used in making business decisions: teleology, utilitarianism, deontology, relativism, virtue ethics, and justice (2.F.1.d).
- Define the concepts of fairness, integrity, due diligence, and fiduciary responsibility, and how they impact ethical decision making (2.F.1.e).

This first lesson in business ethics takes a very philosophical approach to establishing a number of alternative models that can help business professionals and organizations think carefully about morality and virtue in making ethical decisions.

I. Can Ethics Be Learned?

- **A.** Most individuals consider themselves to be ethical. And most individuals in fact value ethics and expect themselves to act ethically.
- **B.** However, nearly everyone can strengthen their understanding of, and their discipline to, act ethically in various situations. Too often accounting and finance professionals find themselves caught by surprise in a situation that turns out to be very much a matter of ethics.
- **C.** It's difficult to make wise ethical choices when we're not sure exactly what is the ethical problem in the situation. Hence, accounting and finance professionals can always improve their ability to be ethical in two specific ways.
  1. Recognizing and anticipating *when* ethics will be challenged in a particular situation.
  2. Recognizing and describing exactly *how* ethics are being challenged in a particular situation.
- **D.** *Bottom line:* Everyone can be informed and more conscientious about ethics. The *practice* of ethics is a learned skill.

II. Business Ethics

- **A.** Business ethics relate to both organizations and individuals, and can be described generally as the social responsibility and responsiveness of a firm and a business professional.
- **B.** At the firm level, business ethics is the expressed mission, standards, and culture of behavior that sets the ethical tone of the organization and provides direction to individual managers in their work and decision making.
- **C.** At the individual level, business ethics is a set of principles and personal commitments that guides the professional in the scope of their job when a conflict of values is presented.

III. Morality and Virtue

- **A.** Morality and virtue are not the same concept. It is possible for an individual to make a decision or choice that is morally correct and yet not be a virtuous person.

B. Moral principles focus on our actions. We "apply" these principles in order to make decisions. However, this approach to ethics can be described as following a set of rules or principles in order to answer the question, "What should I do?"

C. Virtue is defined by our attitudes and character traits. A virtue-based approach to ethics (described as virtue ethics) answers the question, "What kind of person should I be?"

D. Virtues are habits that are developed intentionally through learning and practice. A person who has developed virtues will be naturally inclined to act in ways that are consistent with moral principles.

IV. Moral Philosophy

A. Moral philosophy is the branch of philosophy that contemplates what is right and wrong with respect to action and character. It explores the nature of morality, examines how people should live their lives in relation to others, and evaluates specific moral issues or questions in society. There are a number of key moral philosophies that are very briefly described below.

B. Teleology. *Telos* is a Greek word meaning "end" or "goal." Teleological ethics is concerned with how choices will affect a particular desired moral outcome. What is the "end" or "purpose" of an accountant (teleologically speaking)? To gain and protect the public trust? To serve the shareholders' interest? Answering these questions about results then determines whether the act (or choice) is good or bad.

C. Deontology. *Deont* is a Greek word meaning "to bind" or "duty." Principle-based behavior and choice is at the core of deontology. Rather than focusing on good character or desirable consequences, deontology ethics requires individuals to identify and commit to imperatives that they believe should form a universal law that everyone in the world should be following. Framed as a question, the deontological ethicist will ask themself, "Is this action something everyone should always do, no matter the cost?" If the answer is yes, then it is right; if no, it is wrong.

D. Virtue ethics. The philosophy of virtue ethics is related somewhat to deontology. Focusing first on character and then on action is at the core of this moral philosophy. Virtue ethics really stresses the fact that character, whether good or bad, defines a person. Having good character means that person is driven to behave in virtuous ways in situations that call for a virtuous response. When facing an ethical decision, ask the question, "How would a virtuous person act in this situation?"

E. Utilitarianism. Utilitarian ethics is related somewhat to teleology. In its most basic form, utilitarianism argues that if you can increase the overall happiness of the world in some way, then you should. In contrast to virtue ethics, results are given all the ethical emphasis in utilitarian ethics. Following principles and developing the appropriate character aren't nearly as important. The key question with utilitarianism is, "Which choice will result in the most good for the most people?"

F. Relativism. There are two distinct forms of moral relativism. The first is individual relativism, which holds that individual people create their own moral standards. The second is cultural relativism, which maintains that morality is grounded in the approval of one's own society. Hence, rather than an absolute or universal approach to ethics, relativism recognizes moral values that change throughout time and throughout the world.

G. Justice. The equitable distribution of benefits and costs is the focus of justice. The underlying moral philosophy of justice can be approached from two fundamentally different perspectives. The Platonic concept of justice is that each individual case is determined by individual rights, regardless of what happens in other cases. The Aristotelian concept is based on the idea that results are interrelated; that is, justice should be comparable or consistent with results in other cases.

V. Ethical Decision Making

A. Ethics are based on moral philosophies. As business professionals better understand key moral philosophies, their ethical decisions will be more informed and intentional. Remember, though, that decision *making* is a *process*, not an outcome. There are some fundamental qualities of good ethical decision making that should be considered and applied. These qualities are briefly described below.

B. Fairness. Decision making involving ethical consequences should be a transparent process that emphasizes empathy for others and consideration for their needs and expectations. This approach to ethical decision making is *sustainable* in the sense that other stakeholders will understand and support the process in the future.

C. Integrity. The quality of integrity in decision making means the process is always consistent with, and accountable to, the individual's moral philosophy or the organization's code of ethics. An inconsistent process is fragmented, which is the opposite of the quality of wholeness or completeness (the root meaning of the word *integrity*).

D. Due diligence. After gathering all of the relevant facts involved in an ethical decision, important aspects of due diligence include a clear understanding of the organization's mission, values, and long-term goals. In addition, due diligence requires compliance with all legal requirements, consideration of stakeholders involved, and a conscious reflection on one's own moral philosophy that is used to make ethical decisions.

E. Fiduciary responsibility. As key agents of the organization, finance professionals have a fiduciary responsibility to their managers and to the owners or shareholders of the company. Fiduciary responsibility includes handling all company resources as your own, prioritizing the interests of the company over personal interests, protecting the company against unnecessary risks, pursuing opportunities for the company as they present themselves, acting with speed when necessary, and being responsive on important requests made by managers or owners.

Practice Question

A small company is struggling to comply with the covenants (requirements) of its bank loan. Specifically, there are two financial ratios based on the company's income statement and balance sheet that are lower than allowed by the bank. The owner and her accountant believe the company's business and business model are sound. However, if the bank calls in the loan, the business will collapse and the company will have to declare bankruptcy, putting its 28 employees and their families in significant financial stress. The accountant has met with the bank's loan officer to explain the actual condition of the business and request that the loan covenants be adjusted to keep the loan out of default. The loan officer agrees that the two financial ratios are probably not good indicators of the actual risk of the loan but is unable to adjust the loan covenants due to bank policy. The accountant is informed that if the company can't correct its financial condition to get the ratios back into compliance, the loan will be in default and the company likely forced into foreclosure.

The owner agrees with the accountant that nothing can be done with the company's business to bring its financial reporting into compliance with the loan covenants. The owner strongly urges the accountant to make whatever adjustments are necessary in the company's accounting system to push the financial ratios into compliance.

How might the accountant use each of the following moral philosophies to evaluate the ethical decision he must now make?

a. Teleology

b. Deontology

c. Utilitarianism

d. Virtue ethics

Answer

a. A moral philosophy based on teleology would have the accountant determine what is his end goal or objective in the decision. Protecting the employees from financial harm is potentially an important objective, but is it ultimately the long-term goal for the accountant or for the company? Once this end goal is clearly established, then the accountant can determine whether the decision to be made about the financial ratios is in line with that goal.

Continues ...

b. If the accountant aligns his ethical decision making with deontology, he needs to focus on what core principle is at stake in the decision. He might consider what he'd want another accountant to do in this position if he were instead the president or a shareholder of the bank. He might consider how all accountants throughout the profession should handle this situation, and what it would mean to the profession of accounting. He needs to identify the core principle at stake in this decision, consider it to be a universal law of accounting behavior, and then make a decision in line with that principle.

c. A utilitarian approach to this decision might be as straightforward as a numbers-based decision. How many people are helped, and by how much, if he falsifies some accounting numbers to get the ratios back into compliance? On the other side of the decision, how many people are helped if he maintains the integrity of the accounting system? He should be careful to consider this analysis from both a short-term and long-term view of the results.

d. If the accountant is committed to the practice of virtue ethics, then he needs to consider how this decision reflects on his own character, and more importantly, how this decision will *affect* his character. He should be careful to define what virtue means in this kind of a situation and reflect on how an absolutely virtuous professional would act. Aligning his choice with that kind of behavior should then guide his decision.

Summary

Choices about business or professional ethics take place at both the individual level and the organizational level. A clear moral philosophy can provide useful context in which to take action and make decisions. There are a number of important moral philosophies that have evolved over centuries of consideration and debate. Basing decisions on the ultimate end goal or purpose of the decision maker essentially describes the philosophy of teleology. In contrast, deontology does not consider outcomes but core principles at stake in the decision. Ethical decisions based on utilitarianism will prioritize choices that create the most good for the most people or that minimize harm for the most people. Virtue ethics, in contrast to the external view of preceding philosophies, focuses on the internal character of the decision maker and demands that decisions should be based on good character and on strengthening good character. Relativism advocates and allows for subjective moral values that are specific, and sometimes unique, to an individual or society. The moral philosophy of justice helps clarify decisions involving the distribution of benefits and costs in society. Remember that the decision-making *process* should be characterized by fairness, integrity, due diligence, and fiduciary responsibility.

Topic 2. Ethical Considerations for Management Accounting and Financial Management Professionals

Principles and Standards of Professional Ethics

After studying this lesson, you should be able to:

- Identify and describe the four overarching ethical principles and the four standards (2.F.2.a).
- Evaluate a given business situation for its ethical implications (2.F.2.b).
- Identify and describe relevant standards that may have been violated in a given business situation and explain why the specific standards are applicable (2.F.2.c).

The IMA (Institute of Management Accountants) provides very specific guidance on principles and standards of professional ethics. We'll study and apply the specifics of *IMA Statement of Ethical Professional Practice* in this lesson.

I. Keep It Personal

A. In addition to improving our ethical skills, we need to also stay energized about our personal commitment to ethics. Many professionals find that when presented with difficult decisions that challenge ethics at a very personal level, the personal commitment needed to make the hard decision can be energized by asking oneself the following question: Would the person you most love and admire be proud to watch the decision you're about to make?

B. Evidence of your commitment to ethics is tied very closely to your "personal brand." Organizations spend significant resources to guard and strengthen their brand in the marketplace. As a business professional, you have a personal brand. A single decision, for good or bad, can have an incredible and long-lasting impact on your personal brand.

C. Remember that "Perception = Reality." Not only do you need to make ethically based decisions, but the ethics in your decisions must to be clear to others around you. Like it or not, the perception that others have of you as an ethically-based professional matters very much, despite any argument you might want to make that your ethics are not being perceived correctly. Hence, be sure that the ethics in your decisions and actions are clear for others to see.

II. *IMA Statement of Ethical Professional Practice*—Principles

A. The IMA (Institute of Management Accountants) has an important brand, and continually invests significant resources to strengthen that brand across the world. An important element of the IMA brand is represented in explicit principles and standards of professional ethics as described in the *IMA Statement of Ethical Professional Practice.*[1]

B. IMA members are expected to fully comply with the *IMA Statement of Ethical Professional Practice.* The IMA Statement distinguishes between two separate but related views on professional ethics:

1. Overarching *principles* that express ethical *values*, and
2. Specific *standards* that guide ethical *conduct.*

C. The IMA Statement lists four overarching ethical principles to guide member conduct. These principles with specific descriptions follow below.

[1] This statement is available on the IMA website.

1. *Honesty*. IMA members should be honest and truthful in their professional communication and in their professional analysis and work.
2. *Fairness*. IMA members should be fair and balanced, without favoritism, in their professional work and decisions involving other colleagues and stakeholders.
3. *Objectivity*. IMA members' analysis and decision making should be reasoned, thorough, and dispassionate.
4. *Responsibility*. IMA members are responsible to comply with and uphold the standards of Competence, Confidentiality, Integrity, and Credibility.

D. Note that the last IMA guiding principle, Responsibility, is the bridge to the IMA's standards of ethical conduct.

III. *IMA Statement of Ethical Professional Practice*—Standards

A. After listing the four overarching principles, the IMA Statement then describes four specific standards of ethical conduct. These standards are crucial as failure to comply may result in disciplinary action by the IMA. Each of these standards is detailed across several specific aspects of the standard.

B. The first IMA standard of conduct is *Competence*. IMA members with ethical competence will demonstrate the following specific characteristics.

1. Maintain an appropriate level of professional leadership and expertise by enhancing knowledge and skills.
2. Perform professional duties in accordance with relevant laws, regulations, and technical standards.
3. Provide decision support information and recommendations that are accurate, clear, concise, and timely. Recognize and help manage risk.

C. The second IMA standard of conduct is *Confidentiality*. IMA members who take an ethical approach to confidentiality will engage in the following processes.

1. Keep information confidential except when disclosure is authorized or legally required.
2. Inform all relevant parties regarding appropriate use of confidential information. Monitor to ensure compliance.
3. Refrain from using confidential information for unethical or illegal advantage.

D. The third IMA standard of conduct is *Integrity*. IMA members who have integrity in their conduct are committed to the following professional practices.

1. Mitigate actual conflicts of interest. Regularly communicate with business associates to avoid apparent conflicts of interest. Advise all parties of any potential conflicts of interest.
2. Refrain from engaging in any conduct that would prejudice carrying out duties ethically.
3. Abstain from engaging in or supporting any activity that might discredit the profession.
4. Contribute to a positive ethical culture and place integrity of the profession above personal interests.

E. The fourth and final IMA standard of conduct is *Credibility*. IMA members who are credible in their conduct will be observed to do the following actions.

1. Communicate information fairly and objectively.
2. Provide all relevant information that could reasonably be expected to influence an intended user's understanding of the reports, analyses, or recommendations.

3. Report any delays or deficiencies in information, timeliness, processing, or internal controls in conformance with organization policy and/or applicable law.

4. Communicate professional limitations or other constraints that would preclude responsible judgment or successful performance of an activity.

F. A careful study of the specifics involved in each IMA standard of professional ethics, and a candid assessment of one's personal practice with respect to these standards, will help finance and accounting professionals better assess specific situations to directly recognize and successfully respond to ethical conflicts.

Practice Question

You have recently been hired as an accountant for the largest residential construction company in the state. Your primary responsibility is to track costs for each home being constructed. Tracking the costs for direct materials and direct labor is relatively straightforward. Accounting for manufacturing overhead costs, on the other hand, presents a challenge. The company's current practice is to allocate overhead costs on the basis of direct labor hours. As a result, larger houses that require more labor construction time are allocated a larger share of the overhead. While larger homes do tend to require more management and engineering design support, this is not always true. Hence, you've been working on an activity-based costing system to improve the overhead cost assignment process.

Your company was recently selected by the state to build a number of low-income housing complexes. The state has agreed to an arrangement whereby it will pay costs plus a 10% profit margin. Construction of these low-income housing units will be relatively simple. These smaller buildings are based on a straightforward design used consistently for each house. Compared to the average house the company builds for the open market, these government project houses will require substantially less management and engineering support.

At a meeting following the granting of the construction contract by the state, the production supervisor proposes the following idea:

> Since the state has agreed to pay our costs plus 10%, the higher the costs on the project, the more money we make. What we need to do is funnel as much overhead cost as we reasonably can to this low-income housing project. Now I don't want anyone to think I am proposing something unethical. I am not saying that we should charge the state for fictitious costs. I'm simply proposing that we allocate overhead cost on a per-house basis with each house, regardless of size, being allocated the same amount of overhead.

As the cost accountant for the company, it is clear to you (and you believe it is clear to everyone else) that allocating overhead costs as a constant amount per house instead of per direct labor hour will shift a substantial amount of overhead in the organization from the company's core-product homes that are priced competitively in the open market to the government-project homes that are priced based on cost. This approach would be a significant misrepresentation of how overhead costs are actually created in the organization. If this cost assignment proposal goes forward, you will be the one expected to design and deploy the new system. You can see that most in attendance at the meeting are being persuaded by the production supervisor's idea.

The *IMA Statement of Ethical Professional Practice* provides very specific aspects of ethical conduct for each of its four standards of behavior. Carefully consider those aspects in light of this scenario, and indicate for each aspect if it applies to the scenario. More specifically, your determination can be one of three levels: (1) *Clearly* applies, (2) *Maybe* applies, and (3) *Does Not* apply.

Continues ...

Answer:

(Note that this is a subjective analysis. Be sure that you understand your response in comparison to the suggested solution below.)

A. Competence

Not 1. Maintain an appropriate level of professional leadership and expertise by enhancing knowledge and skills.

Maybe 2. Perform professional duties in accordance with relevant laws, regulations, and technical standards.

Clearly 3. Provide decision support information and recommendations that are accurate, clear, concise, and timely. Recognize and help manage risk.

B. Confidentiality

Not 1. Keep information confidential except when disclosure is authorized or legally required.

Not 2. Inform all relevant parties regarding appropriate use of confidential information. Monitor to ensure compliance.

Maybe 3. Refrain from using confidential information for unethical or illegal advantage.

C. Integrity

Maybe 1. Mitigate actual confilicts of interest. Regularly communicate with business associates to avoid apparent conflicts of interest. Advise all parties of any potential conflicts of interest.

Clearly 2. Refrain from engaging in any conduct that would prejudice carrying out duties ethically.

Clearly 3. Abstain from engaging in or supporting any activity that might discredit the profession.

Clearly 4. Contribute to a positive ethical culture and place integrity of the profession above personal interests.

D. Credibility

Clearly 1. Communicate information fairly and objectively.

Clearly 2. Provide all relevant information that could resonably be expected to influence an intended user's understanding of the reports, analyses, or recommendations.

Maybe 3. Report any delays or deficiencies in information, timeliness, processing, or internal controls in conformance with organization policy and/or applicable law.

Not 4. Communicate professional limitations or other constraints that would preclude responsible judgment or successful performance of an activity.

Summary

It is crucial that we teach, learn, and improve our ability to specifically recognize and successfully address a variety of ethical challenges and conflicts in business. The *IMA Statement of Ethical Professional Practice* provides valuable guidance on principles and standards of ethics that can help IMA members better practice their ethical values as business professionals. IMA principles describe the specific values that should describe IMA members who are committed to be ethical professionals. These four principles are Honesty, Fairness, Objectivity, and Responsibility. The IMA Statement then goes on to specifically describe four standards that should guide the ethical conduct of IMA members. These standards are Competence, Confidentially, Integrity, and Credibility. Each of these standards has very specific aspects that should be understood and thoughtfully considered in addressing all business processes, analyses, and decisions.

Controlling Fraud and Resolving Ethical Issues

After studying this lesson, you should be able to:

- Recommend a course of action for management accountants to take when confronted with an ethical dilemma in the business environment (2.F.2.d).
- Evaluate and propose resolutions for ethical issues such as fraudulent reporting, or improper manipulation of forecasts, analyses, results, and budgets (2.F.2.e).
- Identify the three components of the Fraud Triangle (2.F.2.f).
- Use the Fraud Triangle model to explain how a management accounting and financial management professional can identify and manage the risk of fraud (2.F.2.g).

The best way to control fraud is to anticipate it by watching for the three conditions that motivate fraudulent behavior. In this lesson, we'll study the Fraud Triangle, which outlines these conditions. We'll also learn about how to resolve ethical dilemmas using guidance from the *IMA Statement of Ethical Professional Practice*.

I. The Fraud Triangle

A. *Fraud* is formally defined as "wrongful or criminal deception intended to result in financial or personal gain." Accounting and finance professionals, particularly those who belong to the IMA (Institute of Management Accountants), are expected to understand, watch for, and control fraud.

B. The best way to anticipate and control fraud is to know the warning signs. The Fraud Triangle is a research-based and well-tested model for recognizing conditions that create incentives for fraud. There are, in fact, three conditions that create increasing motivation for individuals and organizations to engage in fraud. These three conditions are: Financial Pressure, Opportunity, and Rationalization.

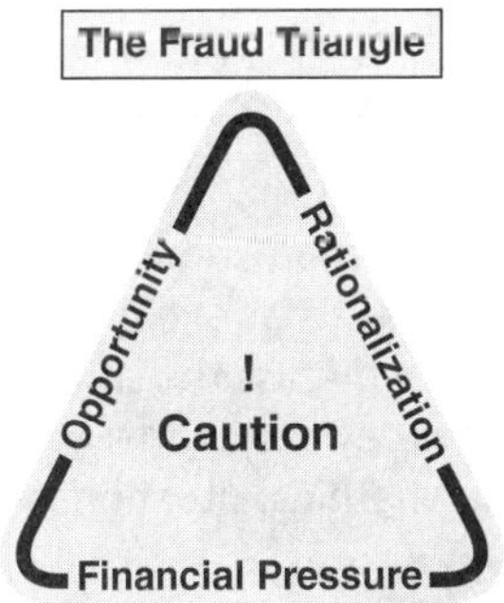

1. There is no particular order of sequence for these conditions. Each condition is independent of the others; that is, one condition doesn't necessary lead to another condition.
2. It isn't necessary for all three, or even one, of these conditions to be present in order for fraud to occur. But as each condition comes into a situation, risk increases and you should pay increasingly close attention to the potential for fraud.
3. In addition to watching others based on motivation represented in the Fraud Triangle, it is even more crucial to watch yourself as any of these three conditions begins to appear in your own circumstances.

C. *Financial Pressure* for fraud can be either negative or positive. Negative Financial Pressure is taking place when an individual or group is in a bad financial situation (e.g., heavy debt) that does not appear to be resolvable using a legal route that isn't somehow painful or humiliating. Positive Financial Pressure is taking place when an individual or group is facing a great financial opportunity that doesn't appear to be accessible using a legal route available to the individual or group.

D. *Opportunity* for fraud is represented by a situation that makes it easier to engage in fraud. Generally, these situations involve a lack of strong internal controls in the organization. Opportunity for fraud is also present when an individual or group has an extraordinary ability or is in an extraordinary position to successfully engage in a fraudulent process.

E. *Rationalization* for fraud is essentially about "telling a story." Fraudsters generally need to rationalize the fraud with their own internal moral compass. In order to do this, often the individual or group will see themselves as a "victim" of the organization that will be defrauded. Alternatively (or perhaps, in addition), the individual or group will strengthen the Rationalization based on external factors such as the need to help someone else, such as family or friends; or based on the perceived bad behavior of a fellow employee or supervisor, which somehow creates a favorable comparison.

II. Resolving Ethical Issues

A. When confronted with an ethical dilemma, it is important to be rational and thoughtful. Stress and fear can lead to reactive decisions that further complicate or worsen the situation. The *IMA Statement of Ethical Professional Practice* provides guidance to help its members resolve ethical situations.

B. The first counsel provided by the IMA Statement is to not ignore an ethical situation. As the accounting or finance professional in the organization, and particularly as an IMA member, you need to take action when you encounter an ethical situation or dilemma. It is tempting to ignore the situation, but lack of action almost always leads to a worsening situation, and may implicate you since you likely have a professional expectation to deal with these kinds of situations.

C. However, before taking any action, it is important to thoughtfully consider all risks involved by your choices. Consider the possibility of retaliation by individuals or groups in your organization. Be wise. There are paths likely available in the situation that would be personally risky for you and may be unwise to pursue. Nevertheless, it may be that the right decision will put you at some professional risk. Be sure, though, that you've carefully explored all possible paths before taking action.

D. To help you fully consider your choices in responding to the situation, your first focus should be your own organization's policies and procedures with respect to ethical practice. Hopefully, your organization has policy and guidance in place that you can reference. If not, or if you believe the policy is irrelevant or even inappropriate, then you can and should consider other resources for guidance.

E. Often, your first line of discussion should be your own supervisor. Be very careful about communicating with individuals above or outside of your line of authority. There are conditions when it would be unwise to discuss the situation with your own supervisor, but those conditions almost always involve clear evidence that your supervisor is involved in perpetuating or consciously allowing the unethical situation, and any discussion with your supervisor would have undesirable results.

F. If discussion with your immediate supervisor can't resolve the situation, you should escalate the discussion to the next management level in your organization, but only to the next level. If needed, continue to proceed to the next higher level, including eventually contacting the board of directors or owners.

G. The IMA provides an anonymous ethics helpline for its members. After a preliminary discussion of the problem to determine the kind of ethics issue being reported, a member of IMA's Committee on Ethics will telephone the caller, if desired, to help that professional understand and apply the provisions of the *IMA Statement of Ethical Professional Practice*. Confidentiality is maintained at all times. The IMA cannot provide a specific resolution but will discuss how the issue relates to the provisions of the IMA Statement.

1. The Helpline number for callers in the United States and Canada is (800) 245-1383.
2. Individuals outside of the U.S. and Canada may have to dial another toll-free access code first before dialing the Ethics Helpline.

H. Do *not* hesitate employing your own attorney in ethical situations where the best path of resolution is not clear to you. Too often professionals are reluctant to invest in good legal counsel. Remember that when the dilemma involves ethics, your professional career and personal brand on are the line. Good legal counsel is often an important investment.

I. Finally, once all other avenues for resolution have been exhausted, consider resigning from your organization and making clear to the proper management *within your organization* the reason for your departure. It is important to note that the IMA Statement at no time recommends disclosure of the ethical situation to outside groups, such as the news media or social media. Remember that confidentially is a key standard of professional ethics for IMA members.

Practice Question

The previous lesson described a scenario wherein you were recently hired as the cost accountant for a large residential construction company. The company has been selected by the state government to build low-income housing in a contract that bases price on cost plus a 10% profit margin. At a management meeting you are attending, the senior production supervisor has proposed a cost allocation system to shift an inappropriate (i.e., unethical) amount of overhead costs from its normal open-market housing projects to this government housing project. The supervisor notes that the company is not creating "fictional costs" on the government contract—simply changing the overall allocation system to adjust the assignment of costs. You can see that most in attendance at the meeting are being persuaded by the production supervisor's idea.

Using the Fraud Triangle, what are the motivations for those at the management meeting to support this proposal?

Using guidance in the *IMA Statement of Ethical Professional Practice*, what pathway might you follow to resolve this situation?

Answer:

The Fraud Triangle identifies three types of motivation to engage in fraud: Financial Pressure, Opportunity, and Rationalization. With respect to Financial Pressure, this is likely a big contract for the company with significant profit opportunity at stake. Further, the company may be experiencing low overall profits, which puts pressure on management to artificially elevate price on the government housing project. With respect to Opportunity, the company effectively now has two business lines—one with competitive price pressure (the open-market projects) and one with no competitive pressure (the government housing contract). To the extent the state audit on the contract is less than adequate, there is opportunity to shift overhead costs within the organization. Finally, with respect to Rationalization, the production supervisor is clearly "telling a story" with respect to his position that the costs being assigned to the project are real costs that exist in the company, and that no "fictional costs" are being created.

As you leave the management meeting, you clearly have an ethical dilemma. Being the new member of the team as the recently hired cost accountant puts extra pressure on you to resolve this situation appropriately. Guidance from the *IMA Statement of Ethical Professional Practice* first directs that you must take action, despite any temptation you have to not engage yourself. First, be sure to access and review any company policy or procedure as guidance on how leadership in the organization expects employees to conduct themselves with respect to ethics. Then meet with your supervisor to discuss the situation and the company policy (if there is one). If this meeting isn't advisable or doesn't resolve the situation, then escalate to the next management level. Likely, at some point in these discussions, you'll encounter resistance or perhaps even duplicity. If possible, skip that management level and proceed to the next level.

As you engage in these internal discussions, do not hesitate to access guidance and consultation from the IMA Ethics Helpline, *and* even from your own attorney.

Finally, if a resolution cannot be found that allows you to be comfortable with your personal values *and* to be in compliance with the IMA standards of ethical behavior, you should consider resigning your position in the company.

Summary
One of the best ways to control and prevent fraud is the ability to recognize conditions that motivate individuals and groups to commit fraud. The well-known Fraud Triangle describes three conditions that create motivation to commit fraud. The three conditions are Financial Pressure, Opportunity, and Rationalization. The IMA's *Statement of Ethical Professional Practice* provides very useful guidance to help you deal with ethical dilemmas or situations as they arise. That guidance can be listed as a series of steps as follows:

1. Take action.
2. Evaluate personal risks to yourself.
3. Follow your organization's policies.
4. Discuss with your immediate supervisor.
5. If your supervisor is involved, go to the next management level.
6. Use the IMA's Ethics Helpline to receive anonymous guidance.
7. Consult your own attorney.
8. If needed, resign from your organization.

Topic 3. Ethical Considerations for the Organization

Ethics in an International Environment

After studying this lesson, you should be able to:

- Discuss corporate responsibility for ethical conduct (2.F.3.r)
- Identify the purpose of anti-bribery laws, such as the U.S. Foreign Corrupt Practices Act and the U.K. Bribery Act (2.F.3.p)
- Define facilitating payments and why these payments create both ethical and legal issues (2.F.3.q)
- Discuss the issues organizations face in applying their values and ethical standards internationally (2.F.3.a)
- Demonstrate an understanding of the differences between ethical and legal behavior (2.F.3.o)
- Define and demonstrate an understanding of the major issues of sustainability and social responsibility (2.F.3.s)
- Identify and define the four levels of social responsibility; economic, legal, ethical, and philanthropic (2.F.3.t)
- Identify and define the three conceptual spheres of sustainability: economic, environmental, and social (2.F.3.u)

The first step to establishing an ethical organization is compliance with the law. Two legal acts that pertain to legal requirements of ethical practice are the U.S. Foreign Corrupt Practices Act of 1977 (FCPA) and the U.K. Bribery Act 2010. But ethics goes beyond compliance with law. Carroll's CSR Pyramid and the triple bottom line of profits, planet and people are useful tools for organizations to use to guide their corporate responsibility and sustainability.

I. The U.S. Foreign Corrupt Practices Act of 1977 (FCPA)

  A. In the mid-1970s hundreds of U.S. Companies were making "questionable" payments to foreign government officials. Generally, these payments were described as a "commission" or a "facilitating payment" paid to a local government officer, and were considered to be necessary in order to transact business in that country.

  B. The U.S. Foreign Corrupt Practices Act, or FCPA, was established in 1977 to define and enforce against bribery of foreign officials. Essentially, FCPA forbids any "American" to pay bribes to a foreign government or representative to obtain contracts or secure business.

  C. Note that the FCPA does not deal with the illegality of bribes or facilitation payments to U.S. government officials. Generally, each state establishes legal definitions and penalties for bribery that doesn't involve foreign officials.

  D. The "nationality principle" of FCPA defines that this law applies to both companies and individuals, whether or not the company or individual is physically present in the U.S. Specifically, FCPA jurisdiction includes:

    1. Any U.S. business or any foreign corporation that has a class of securities registered in the U.S.

    2. Any individual who is a citizen, national, or resident of the United States

    3. Any foreign businesses and persons who make a corrupt payment while physically present in the U.S.

E. FCPA governs payments to foreign officials, candidates, and parties. FCPA also applies to any other payment if part of the bribe ultimately ends up with a foreign official, candidate, or party.

F. FCPA also includes mandates related to accounting transparency and internal controls within organizations to guard against bribery of foreign officials.

G. Finally, the size of the payment does not matter in terms of whether the payment is considered to be a bribe for FCPA purposes. The issue is the *intent* of the bribery rather than the amount. Further, FCPA applies not only to monetary payments, but also to disbursements or gifts of any value.

II. The U.K. Bribery Act 2010

A. The U.K. Bribery Act, established in 2010, applies to businesses and individuals in the United Kingdom. The Bribery Act is broader in scope than the FCPA and imposes more severe penalties. Important differences between the FCPA and the Bribery Act are listed below.

1. The FCPA is focused on bribes offered to foreign officials, but the Bribery Act expands the focus to bribes paid to *any person or organization*.
2. While the FCPA makes it illegal to pay bribes to produce improper business behavior, the Bribery Act also makes it illegal to *accept* bribes.
3. The FCPA requires companies to establish internal controls that guard against bribery of foreign officials. However, these internal control mandates are focused on accounting systems and procedures. The Bribery Act expands the control focus *beyond accounting systems* to include a much wider array of organizational procedures, policies, and processes.
4. The FCPA limits its jurisdiction over bribery activities of foreign companies to only those listed on U.S stock exchanges. In contrast, the Bribery Act expands its scope to include *any foreign organization* that is established or conducts some part of its business in the U.K.
5. Payments that expedite or secure the performance of a routine (non-discriminating) government action are permissible under the FCPA, but the Bribery Act forbids facilitating payments *even for routine outcomes* that are typically (eventually) available without the need for a bribe.
6. Penalties under the FCPA can be as high as five years' imprisonment and $250,000 in fines for individuals, or fines for organizations up to $2 million. On the other hand, under the Bribery Act prison terms can be as high as ten years, and fines are unlimited for both individuals and organizations.

B. Note that neither the Bribery Act nor the FCPA makes illegal the act of genuine hospitality. This means, for example, that business expenditures to provide tickets to sporting events, to take clients to dinner, or to pay suitable travel expenses are appropriate so long as the costs are reasonable and balanced.

C. Finally, note that these two laws are focused strictly on facilitation payments. They do not extend to other legal and ethical issues in the conduct of business such as fraud, theft, money laundering, unfair competition, misleading financial reporting, etc.

Practice Question

You've been recently hired as the controller for a company which, over the last three years, has been developing a new business segment in a small but strategically crucial foreign country. Establishing good relations with that country's Office of Foreign Trade has been particularly central to the success of launching the new business segment. In the last visit to that country, you accompanied the CEO and several other executive officers, including the CFO. On the plane ride over, the CEO described the gift he was bringing to the Minister of Foreign Trade. The gift is significant in terms of its value, so much so that you commented with surprise. The CEO responded he had been advised on the last trip that the size (i.e., value) of the gift was important to this Minister, who expected the gift exchange to demonstrate the seriousness of the company's commitment to the county and its economy. As the discussion continued, the CFO expressed her hope that the CEO's gift would be

Continues ...

adequate as she believed that the Minister would either smooth over some regulatory demands or delay enhanced regulatory compliance processes based on how the gift was received.

What concerns do you have in this situation with respect to the U.S Foreign Corrupt Practices Act?

Answer

Neither the CEO nor CFO indicate any ethical concerns in this situation, which suggests inadequate commitment to a code of ethics in this company. In the case of this substantial gift, and the expectation that it will help facilitate business in the foreign country, there is potentially a serious breach of compliance with the FCPA. These senior officers do not seem to be considering certain FCPA requirements that specifically restrict against providing gifts to foreign officers with the expectation or hope that delivery of the gift (regardless of monetary value) will secure or improve business prospects or processes beyond what might be expected normally.

III. Social Responsibility

A. It can be challenging for an organization to conduct business in countries where cultural "norms" of behavior are different than the organization's home nation. This challenge is increasingly prevalent as advances in technology and travel bring together different norms. Hence, ethical challenges are part of the complexity of risks that exists when conducting business across international lines.

B. The risk of unethical decisions by employees or organizations is not solely about illegal actions. Being in compliance with laws such as the U.S. FCPA or the U.K Bribery Act does not mean that the organization is ethical. It is certainly possible and, unfortunately, too often the case that some organizations are in compliance with the law while making unethical decisions and engaging in disreputable actions.

C. Corporate ethics requires a larger view of stewardship than legal compliance. Many would argue that companies should place the pursuit of profits within a larger framework of social responsibility. One popular framework of social responsibility is Carroll's CSR (corporate social responsibility) Pyramid.

D. Carroll's CSR Pyramid is a four-fold view of social responsibility. This pyramid is depicted below. Note that It Is established on a foundation of economic success; that is, companies must be profitable in order to successfully pursue other social responsibilities.

Source: Carroll, A.B. (1991). "The pyramid of corporate social responsibility: Toward the moral management of organizational stakeholders," *Business Horizons*, 34(4): 39–48.

E. Organizations that institute a financially viable business model need to ensure their business practice complies with all laws and regulations in their marketplace. This means that companies are responsible to be both legal and profitable. Hence, legal responsibility forms the second tier of the CSR Pyramid.

F. The third tier of responsibility is ethics. Organizations must extend themselves beyond profits and compliance with the law to consider their ethical responsibilities to their employees, suppliers, customers, etc.

G. Once the organization has established economic, legal, and ethical responsibility, Carroll's CSR Pyramid finally directs attention to the responsibility to be philanthropic. This fourth responsibility is based on a compelling view that organizations have both an opportunity and an obligation to give back to society. How the organization approaches its philanthropy is a discretionary choice.

IV. Business Sustainability

A. Business sustainability is often defined as managing the organization's performance in terms of a triple bottom line. In other words, sustainability is a process by which companies manage their *financial*, *social*, and *environmental* risks, obligations, and opportunities. These three impacts are sometimes referred to as profit, people, and planet.

The Triple Bottom Line

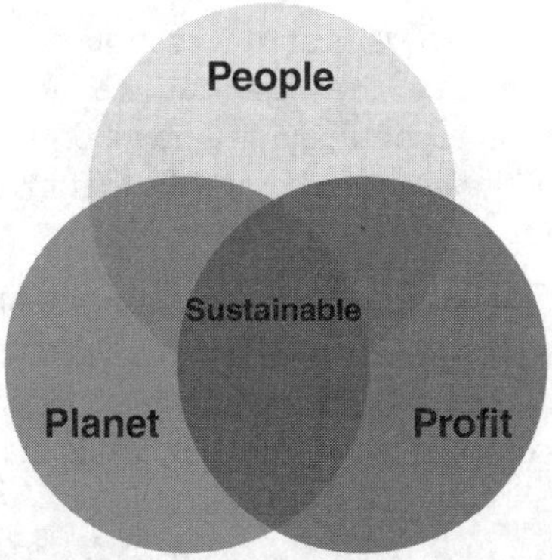

B. Business sustainability represents resiliency over time. Companies that are committed to healthy economic, social, and ecological results are better positioned to survive shocks in their environment.

C. Specifically, the triple bottom line involves managing important economic issues such as growth, innovation, and productivity; social issues involving poverty, health and wellness, and human rights; and environmental issues that include climate change, land use, and pollution. This threefold approach to business provides a framework for organizations to manage themselves ethically no matter where in the world they might operate.

Practice Question

Your software design company is working with an automotive manufacturer to develop and release a new line of cars with self-driving capability. The success of this project is essential to both the design company and the manufacturer. Developing the necessary technology is a complicated process with substantial business risk in terms of serious cost overruns or significant delays in the release schedule. There is considerable pressure on management to do whatever is necessary to deliver the software designs needed by the manufacturer. How can Carroll's Corporate Social Responsibility Pyramid be used to guide decision making in this situation?

Answer

The pressure to perform in this environment creates serious ethical risk for the software design company. Carroll's CSR Pyramid emphasizes the importance of responsibly managing the organization's economic viability in compliance with all applicable laws. With a clear understanding of both its economic and legal commitments, the organization is positioned to then consider its ethical and philanthropic responsibilities. Ethical issues the company should consider include how decisions being made impact its business partner, its employees, and its suppliers. Assuming the project is successful, leading to a profitable result for both partners, the opportunity to make a philanthropic contribution within its community is a responsibility that the software design company should finally deliberate and then take action.

Summary

Compliance with the law is essential and is the first step toward establishing an ethics-based organization. To this end, two particularly crucial laws affecting organizations and professionals that operate across international lines are the U.S. Foreign Corrupt Practices Act of 1977 (FCPA) and the U.K Bribery Act 2010. The FCPA makes it illegal for companies and individuals to pay any type of bribe to a foreign government or official in order to secure a business need or advantage. The Bribery Act expands the responsibility to include paying or receiving bribes to facilitate business processes with any individual or organization. Business ethics extends significantly beyond the legality of facilitation payments. Organizations operating anywhere in the world should be committed to corporate responsibility and sustainability practices. Carroll's CSR Pyramid emphasizes a four-fold commitment to economic, legal, ethical, and philanthropic responsibilities. Business sustainability (resiliency) can be established using a triple bottom line structure involving performance related to profits, planet, and people.

Ethics and the Organization

After studying this lesson, you should be able to:

- Apply relevant provisions of IMA's Statement on Management Accounting, "Values and Ethics: From Inception to Practice," to a business situation (2.F.3.h).
- Demonstrate an understanding of the ways ethical values benefit an organization (2.F.3.e).
- Demonstrate an understanding of the importance of a code of conduct and how it contributes to an organization's ethical culture (2.F.3.d).
- Demonstrate an understanding of the role of "leadership by example" or "tone at the top" in determining an organization's ethical environment (2.F.3.i).
- Analyze the impact of groupthink on ethical behavior (2.F.3.f).
- Discuss how diversity of thought can lead to good ethical decisions (2.F.3.g).
- Define ethical leadership and identify and explain the traits of ethical leaders (2.F.3.j).

Building an ethically grounded organization is serious strategic work for management. The IMA's Statement on Management Accounting (SMA), "Values and Ethics: From Inception to Practice," provides guidance that effectively forms an eight-step process to design and implement an organization-wide system of ethical conduct. We'll study the first five steps of that process in this lesson. Be sure to note in this lesson the discussion on the ethical challenges of groupthink.

I. Enterprise Risk Management

A. Enterprise Risk Management (ERM) is the process of planning, organizing, leading, and controlling the activities of an organization in order to minimize the effects of risk. A key characteristic of effective ERM is the alignment of employee behavior with an ethical code of conduct.

B. Individual behavior is a vital aspect of managing enterprise risk. There are many stories of how the decisions or actions of a single employee either destroyed the reputation and viability of an organization, or firmly established the organization as a sustainable and contributing member of its business community.

C. The challenge of managing ethical decisions and actions of individuals increases as the organization expands in size. When the organization is small, the owner or key executive is clearly in sight of everyone. Within that line of sight, the owner or key executive is better able to plan, organize, lead, and control everyone in the organization to align their work with desired values and principles.

D. As the organization increases in size, employees will be more disconnected from the values and principles that define the strategy of the owner or key executives. Significant risk exists in that vacuum of leadership in the day-to-day work of employees—risk that unethical decisions will be made.

II. An Ethics Culture

A. Too often organizations have a clear mission and statement of values; that is, "clear" in the sense that expectations have been written and published in the organization. But just as ethics is more than being legal, ethics is also more than a statement of words. An ethically-based organization is established on a strong culture and clear, actionable principles that guide everyone's conduct.

B. Culture and principles are crucial. Large organizations working with fast-paced processes in increasingly competitive economies don't have the ability to institute an increasingly larger list of specific rules to guide every possible action or decision by their employees. Organizations need to design a system for ethical conduct that is based on principles and standards and is guided and supported by leaders who are committed and capable to the demands of professional ethics.

III. A Framework for Creating a System of Ethical Conduct

A. Establishing a principle-based code of conduct that provides clear guidance and aligns employee decisions and behavior with the mission and values of the organization is central to successful risk management. An effective system of ethical conduct is also core to a successful internal control system.

B. Building a system of ethical conduct across the whole organization requires a significant investment of resources and management focus. In one of its Statements on Management Accountant (SMA), *Values and Ethics: From Inception to Practice*, the IMA lays out a framework for creating such a system. This framework is illustrated below.

A Framework for Creating a System of Ethical Conduct

Source: "Values and Ethics: From Inception to Practice," *IMA Statement of Management Accounting* (Montvale, NJ, Institute of Management Accountants, 2014).

C. With the clear support of top leadership, the organization forms a cross-functional team to design and implement a system of ethical conduct across the organization. Beginning with Step 1, the team evaluates the current understanding of, commitment to, and practice of professional ethics in the organization. With Step 2, the team, working with top leadership, determines clear objectives of professional ethics for the organization. Step 1 and Step 2 are basically an "audit" that effectively forms a *gap analysis* with respect to current practice of professional ethics.

D. With that gap analysis in hand, the team is able to proceed forward to the next steps in the framework. Step 3 and Step 4 above connect with the *IMA Statement of Ethical Professional Practice* that we studied earlier. Remember that the IMA Statement distinguishes between two separate but related views on individual professional ethics:

1. Overarching *principles* that express ethical *values*, and
2. Specific *standards* that guide ethical *conduct.*

E. Principles describe the *values* of the organization and essentially determine what the organization is expected to *be* or become. These principles are used to establish actionable standards. Standards describe the *conduct* of the organization, and essentially determine what the organization is expected to *do* in every decision setting.

F. With the gap analysis completed in Steps 1 and 2, and clearly defined principles and standards established in Steps 3 and 4, the next step is working with the leadership of the organization.

IV. Ethics and Leadership

A. In Step 5 of the Framework, the design and implementation team works to institute the necessary training and incentives to ensure that top managers understand and are committed to the organization's newly defined principles and standards of professional ethics.

B. The phrase "tone at the top" describes a clear signal and consistent example of ethical practice by the organization's leadership. If the company's mission statement describes an expectation of ethical practice, but the leaders' "tone" is inconsistent with that mission statement, there will be problems with professional ethics throughout the organization.

C. Employees believe what they see rather than what they are told in the company "pep talk," and that belief will inform their decisions. Employees consider the top management team as ultimately responsible for the firm's moral authority, and should be held to a higher standard. Hence, senior managers must avoid creating the perception that they are "above the rules."

V. Groupthink

A. When a group of well-intentioned people is making irrational or unethical decisions, there is likely strong pressure in that group to be unified. This condition is described as groupthink. It results from the natural inclination to conform by avoiding dissent.

B. Groupthink processes include downplaying risk in the decision, ignoring data that are inconsistent with the decision, and inventing new arguments to support the decision.

C. In a groupthink situation, group members feel pressure to agree with the consensus of the group and refrain from expressing personal doubts and judgments. In order to be unified with the group, individuals may ignore their own moral beliefs.

D. Watch for these symptoms of groupthink in your own organization: belief in the collective power or morality of the group, stereotyping or casting out individuals, pressuring or ignoring dissenters, and group-censoring of individuals or self-censoring by individuals.

E. One very effective tool to counterbalance the natural inclination to groupthink is establishing the role of a devil's advocate in the group. The job of the devil's advocate is to point out a different or larger "reality," identify risks and potential pitfalls, and provide alternative decisions or actions. In addition, the group can periodically evaluate the morality or rationality of its decisions by assigning everyone the task of critically evaluating decisions being made.

F. Diversity of thought is important to avoid unethical groupthink. Note that diversity of thought will often interrupt the harmony in the organization. It is important to understand that conflict can actually be a good thing for organizations. Conflict that represents diversity of thought provides "space" for individuals to present their concerns and engage their own ethical values and philosophies.

VI. Characteristics of Ethical Leaders

A. Ethical leaders must first lead by example. Without a clear view of her or his own moral commitments, the leader is going to struggle to demonstrate good professional ethics, and that failure will be seen by others in the organization.

B. Ethical leaders are careful to not push their own view across the organization. They need to be mindful of the power of their position. Strong leaders can create a groupthink condition throughout the organization unless they encourage feedback, even criticism, on decisions being made.

C. As shown in the Framework for Creating a System of Ethical Conduct, leadership is the foundation of a system of ethical conduct in the organization. Once key executives are trained and committed to the organization's principles and standards of ethics, then the detailed work can begin to train, control, and evaluate the system of professional ethics throughout the organization. This work forms Steps 6, 7, and 8 in the framework above, and will be the focus of the next lesson

Practice Question

Rosenbloom, Inc. is a fast-growing residential landscaping company with operations throughout the southern U.S. After an over-pricing incident at one of its offices became a bit of a scandal in the local press, the Rosenbloom executive team determined to launch a stronger and more explicit system of ethical conduct throughout the company. A cross-functional team was established to design and deliver the new system. This team is composed of the executive vice-president of Human Relations (HR), the assistant controller, the social media manager, operations supervisors from two different local offices, and crewmembers from two other local offices.

According to the IMA Statement on Management Accounting *Values and Ethics: From Inception to Practice*, what are the initial steps for this team to accomplish before it begins rolling out a new system of ethical conduct throughout the company?

Answer

The first effort for the team should be a gap analysis of the company. This involves two steps. First, the team needs to evaluate the current state of understanding and practice of professional ethics across the organization. This can be done by conducting interviews, reviewing current training, evaluating all incidents involving ethics, etc. Next, the team needs to work with the Rosenbloom executive leadership team to determine the company goals for professional ethics across the organization. Comparing current and desired practices forms the gap analysis.

With that gap analysis in hand, the next step for the team is to work with the executive leaders to identify core principles and values for Rosenbloom. With a clear grasp of core principles, the team then moves forward to design clear standards of ethical conduct that employees should be able to confidently reference in day-to-day operations throughout Rosenbloom.

The final step before the team can begin rolling out the new system of ethical conduct throughout the company is to work carefully with the executive leadership and other key managers to ensure that these leaders understand and are thoroughly committed to the new system. If the "tone at the top" is not obviously aligned with the new system of ethical conduct, the message will be subsequently lost on employees, and Rosenbloom will continue to be at risk of unethical events.

Summary

Establishing a system of ethical conduct is crucial to ERM (Enterprise Risk Management) in the organization. The act of a single employee can make or break the organization. As the firm becomes larger and the competitive environment more complex, employees naturally become more and more disconnected from the core values of the owners and key executive unless a significant investment is made to establish an ethical culture and clear principles to guide decisions and actions. The IMA Statement on Management Accounting laid out in this lesson describes an eight-step framework for creating a system of ethical conduct throughout the organization. Steps 1 and 2 in the framework are a gap analysis of the current state of ethics in the organization, and where the organization needs to be. In Steps 3 and 4 the organization develops a statement of values (or principles) and a code of conduct to provide actionable guidance to all employees. Ethical leaders (Step 5) are foundational to a system of ethical conduct. By encouraging feedback, even dissent, ethical leaders can work to reduce the risk of groupthink in the executive team. With ethical leadership in place, the rollout process of establishing ethics throughout the organization can move forward (as is discussed in the next lesson).

Ethics and HR Management

After studying this lesson, you should be able to:

- Demonstrate an understanding of the relationship between ethics and internal controls (2.F.3.b).
- Define corporate culture and demonstrate an understanding of the role corporate culture plays in ethical decision making (2.F.3.c).
- Explain the importance of an organization's core values and how they promote ethical behavior and ethical decision making (2.F.3.l).
- Explain the importance of human capital to an organization in creating a climate where "doing the right thing" is expected (e.g., hiring the right people, providing them with training, and practicing consistent values-based leadership) (2.F.3.k).
- Discuss the importance of employee training to maintaining an ethical organizational culture (2.F.3.m).
- Explain the importance of a whistleblowing framework to maintain an ethical organizational culture (2.F.3.n).

In this final lesson, we conclude working with the IMA's Statement on Management Accounting (SMA), "Values and Ethics: From Inception to Practice," which provides guidance to design and implement an organization-wide system of ethical conduct. We studied the first five steps of that process in the previous lesson. Now we'll conclude on the last three steps in the process, the result of which should be a strong ethical culture in the organization. In particular, we'll discuss the details of what it means to have a *whistleblower* framework in the organization.

I. Human Capital

A. Most organizations make significant investments in capital assets, such as land, buildings, machinery, patents, and trademarks. These investments are carefully considered before being made, and subsequently carefully managed and evaluated to be sure that the investment pays off in terms of cash or income flows. Most organizations, though, spend considerably more resources on human capital, which includes the health, knowledge, motivation, skills, *and ethics* of its employees. Given the size and the potential of human capital versus traditional capital assets, most organizations are committed to making smart investments in, and effectively managing, their human capital for long-term value and sustainability. This work is both crucial and strategic to the organization.

B. Remember that everyone can improve their professional ethics, particularly with respect to being more conscious and aware of *specific* ethical issues and how they relate to different business decisions and activities. Hence, organizations can establish *specific* expectations and make *specific* investments to strengthen the ethical practice of their employees, which is a crucial aspect of the human capital in the organization.

C. If you are familiar with the traditional Balanced Scorecard framework, you'll remember that at the foundation of this strategic management model is the "Learning & Growth Performance" perspective (see below). Learning and growth is not entirely about employees. This perspective includes the development of systems and structure in the organization as well. If establishing better professional ethics in the organization is a strategic imperative, then building a clear and effective system of ethical conduct by employees falls squarely in this perspective.

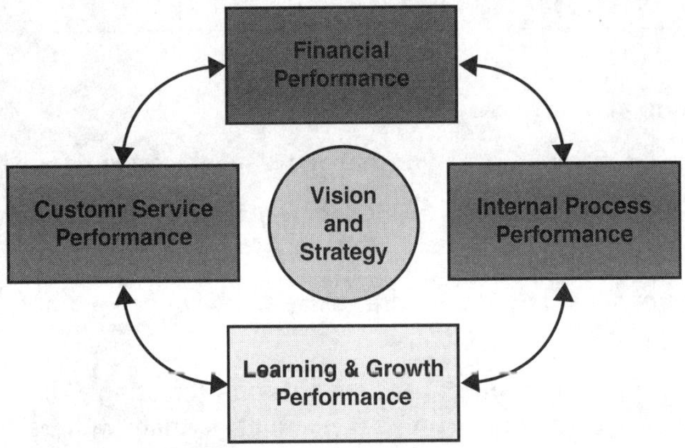

II. Operational Development

A. In the previous lesson, we studied the first five steps of an eight-step framework for building a system of ethical conduct as described in the IMA's *Statement on Management Accounting (SMA), Values and Ethics: From Inception to Practice*. The last three steps of this framework are depicted below. Each of these steps involves significant and detailed work.

B. Step 6—Operational Development of Ethical Practice—is perhaps the most detailed and intensive work in the process of establishing strong professional ethics across the entire organization. There are essentially three aspects to this work. The first aspect involves investments in the three core HR processes to institute a focus on professional ethics. The three core HR processes are:

1. Carefully *hiring* employees who are personally committed to professional ethics
2. Deploying solid *training* in professional ethics
3. Establishing effective *incentives* to practice professional ethics

C. The second aspect of Step 6 is a careful review and, as necessary, a reengineering of the core operational processes in the organization to ensure that these processes are anchored on ethical practices. For most organizations, there are three core operational processes as follows:

1. *Research and development* (R&D) processes
2. *Production* processes
3. *Post-sale* service processes

D. Once the organization's internal processes (i.e., HR process and operational process) are grounded in professional ethics, the third and final aspect of implementing Step 6 is to turn attention to partnering with external suppliers to ensure that the supply-chain process has a clear ethical orientation. This work may include reviewing and restructuring some supply-chain relationships.

III. Monitoring and Measuring

A. Step 7—Monitor Ethical Behavior and Measure Results—is primarily about establishing an internal control system around ethical behavior in the organization. The *IMA SMA on Values and Ethics* recommends three well-known business processes as highly effective methods for strengthening internal controls on ethical processes. Remember, "You can't manage what you don't measure."

B. *Business process reengineering* (BPR) involves periodically returning back to the original design phase of the company's ethics system to completely evaluate every aspect to determine how the system can be better built, and then rebuilding and redeploying the system.

C. *Total Quality Management* (TQM) is fundamentally a teams-based approach to create a high-quality ethics system with zero tolerance for error. TQM is about moving the responsibility for high-quality ethics from a few individuals to ownership by the whole organization.

D. *Continual process improvement* (CPI) is a mindset of constantly evolving the organization's system for ethical conduct not only in response to the ever-expanding demands of business and competition, but also anticipating those demands by continuously investing in improved ethical practices.

IV. Feedback and Improving

A. Step 8—Gather Feedback and Make Improvements—is used to establish a feedback loop environment in the organization, both for *individual employees* and for the *organization* as a whole.

B. There are various methods organizations can employ to provide feedback for employees in support of continuous improvement in professional ethics. These methods include annual reviews that include feedback on ethical performance. Rather than be scheduled "as needed," refresher training events on professional ethics should take place regularly. And awards, recognitions, and other celebration events can be used to reinforce and exemplify excellent ethical performance.

C. The organization itself needs to evolve its own feedback and learning system. One obvious approach is to invest in survey systems of employees, clients, suppliers, and other stakeholders. If designed well, these surveys can capture candid and helpful feedback to help map the organization's progress toward an ethical culture that contributes significantly to both a successful enterprise risk management program and a sustainable company strategy. An ethical culture is the culminating objective of a management campaign to build and deploy a system of organization-wide ethical conduct, as illustrated once again in the framework below.

A Framework for Creating a System of Ethical Conduct

V. A Whistleblower Framework

A. We'll conclude this lesson by describing a particularly powerful method for feedback and improvement in support of the organization's commitment to ethics. This method is a whistleblower framework. This formidable management tool effectively gives everyone in the organization the right and responsibility to say, "Stop! This isn't right. We need to address this situation." There are six very specific facets of a successful whistleblower framework in an organization.

1. Everyone needs to be *trained* in what whistleblowing means and how it will specifically work in the organization.
2. Everyone needs to feel safe in a whistleblowing framework. Hence, there needs to be clear and effective *protection systems* established to encourage everyone to take action when needed.
3. *Anonymous helplines* are then set up to capture whistleblower reports.
4. There are differences between *concerns and grievances*, and those differences should be described in the training process. But employees should be encouraged to report both concerns and grievances, and let the whistleblowing process distinguish between the two.
5. An *independent analysis* is set up to distinguish between concerns to be considered and serious grievances that must be addressed. Those designated to provide these analyses must be independent and empowered to move forward appropriate concerns and grievances directly to those responsible to address the report.
6. When the grievance is serious enough, the reporting system in the independent analysis must be able to provide *direct feedback to directors and owners.*

B. Establishing a successful whistleblower framework is a serious investment in the practice of professional ethics. If done well, the result should be a significant reduction of the potential for ethical failure, which is a major contribution to enterprise risk management in the organization.

Practice Question

Continuing from the previous lesson, Rosenbloom, Inc., a fast-growing residential landscaping company with operations throughout the southern United States, is working through the design and delivery of a new system of ethical conduct across its entire organization. At this point, it has completed a gap analysis of ethical practice, defined its values and standards for ethical practice, and thoroughly trained and committed its executive leadership team to ethical practice.

According to the IMA Statement on Management Accounting, "Values and Ethics: From Inception to Practice," what are the remaining steps for Rosenbloom's cross-functional implementation team to accomplish as they roll out a new system of ethical conduct throughout the company?

Answer:

With the vision and mission of ethics effectively defined for Rosenbloom, and its executive team fully trained and committed, the implementation team is ready to begin the detailed and challenging work of operationally developing the company's ethical practice. This is the next step in the IMA framework for creating a system of ethical practice. Operational development of ethical practice is threefold. First, HR processes for hiring, training, and incentivizing need to be carefully anchored to the organization's values and standards. Second, processes throughout the organization's core operations involving R&D, production, and service-after-sale need to be evaluated and, as needed, redesigned to assure adherence to the organization's values and standards for ethical practice. Finally, the organization needs to consider how to strengthen partnerships with key suppliers with respect to its values and standards.

Once the operational development of ethical practice is complete, the next step for the implementation team is to monitor ethical behavior and measure results. A number of classic management models can be used in this effort to capture performance measures and track progress.

Continues ...

These models include BPR (business process reengineering), TQM (total quality management), and CPI (continual process improvement).

Finally, the implementation team should understand that the work of establishing a system of ethical conduct is never complete. The organization must make investments to gather feedback and make improvements in the future. A feedback loop (i.e., learning system) should be built to provide improvement data both to individual employees and to the organization as a whole. Regular feedback reviews, refresher training, and celebration events are great investments in individual employee improvement. Regular company-wide surveys and a whistleblower framework are valuable mechanisms to help the organization improve and control its overall structure for professional ethics.

Summary

This lesson concludes our discussion of the IMA Statement on Management Accounting, "Values and Ethics: From Inception to Practice." In the previous lesson, we described the first five steps in a framework for creating a system of ethical conduct throughout the organization. In this lesson, we laid out the final three steps of the eight-step framework. Step 6 is a significant multilayered effort to develop ethical practice throughout the entire operation of the organization, and involves work with HR management, core operating processes, and partner suppliers. Step 7 describes the process of establishing the internal control system for ethical practice. Measurement is a key aspect of Step 7. Step 8 involves creating a learning organization using feedback that operates both at the level of each employee and for the organization as a whole. One very powerful feedback method is the establishment of a whistleblower framework across the organization.

Section F Review Questions

aq.ei.fraud.0003_0720

1. According to the *IMA Statement of Ethical Professional Practice*, which of the following responses is an appropriate step in the process of resolving an ethical conflict or dilemma?

   A. Contacting a newspaper reporter to report the situation
   B. Avoiding conflict by reducing involvement in the situation
   C. Engaging an attorney to receive counsel on the situation
   D. Communicating concerns about the situation with outside investors

aq.org.eth.law.0003_0720

2. While doing business overseas, the CEO of a U.S. car manufacturer delivers a gift of an expensive luxury car after successfully negotiating a contract to expand operations into that country. Does this potentially violate the FCPA?

   A. This does not violate the FCPA since negotiations for the overseas expansion had already concluded.
   B. Such an action does violate the FCPA since there can be no social interactions during the negotiation of an overseas business deal by a U.S. corporation.
   C. This action violates the FCPA since the giving and accepting of such a gift could be a nonmonetary bribe, and therefore potentially a violation of the FCPA.
   D. Giving this gift is not in violation of the FCPA because even though the company is headquartered in the United States, the action takes place overseas.

aq.moral.phil.008_1907

3. If the decision-making process is always consistent with and accountable to the individual's moral philosophy or the organization's code of ethics, it is said to have what?

   A. Relativism
   B. Justice
   C. Integrity
   D. Fairness

aq.moral.phil.010_0720

4. All of the following are fiduciary responsibilities that finance professionals have to their managers and to the owners or shareholders of the company **except**:

   A. Being responsive on important requests made by managers or owners
   B. Pursuing opportunities for the company as they present themselves
   C. Handling all company resources as your own
   D. Prioritizing personal interests over the interests of the company

aq.ei.fraud.0002_0720

5. Connect the three situations below with the relevant condition from the Fraud Triangle.

   Situation 1: The assistant controller is having problems paying her mortgage.

   Situation 2: The sales team is frustrated about the new sales commission policy.

   Situation 3: There isn't enough staff to have more than one person work with cash receipts and recording.

   A. Situation 1 is an Opportunity condition; Situation 2 is a Rationalization condition; and Situation 3 is a Financial Pressure condition.
   B. Situation 1 is a Financial Pressure condition; Situation 2 is a Rationalization condition; and Situation 3 is an Opportunity condition.

C. Situation 1 is a Rationalization condition; Situation 2 is a Financial Pressure condition; and Situation 3 is an Opportunity condition.
D. Situation 1 is a Financial Pressure condition; Situation 2 is an Opportunity condition; and Situation 3 is a Rationalization condition.

aq.eth.hr.0010_0720

6. Which statement best describes the benefits of establishing a whistle-blower hotline for an organization working to maintain an ethical culture and organization?

A. By establishing a whistle-blower hotline, management can afford to replace ethics training and internal controls since the ethics hotline provides a system for reporting unethical behavior.
B. A whistle-blower hotline that has employees report their names when they call is beneficial because it ensures management is aware of ongoing ethics issues.
C. Setting up a whistle-blower hotline provides a means by which employees can report potential ethics issues and demonstrates strong management commitment to an ethical culture and values.
D. Since only senior level management team members have to comply with most of the mandates or protocols included in a code of ethics, the impact of such a hotline is limited.

aq.ps.prof.ethics.0006_0720

7. Scott Bestor is an accountant for Westfield Company. Early this year, Scott made a highly favorable projection of sales and profits over the next three years for Westfield's hot-selling computer PLEX. As a result of the projections Scott presented to senior management, the company decided to expand production in this area. This decision led to dislocations of some plant personnel who were reassigned to one of the company's newer plants in another state. However, no one was fired, and in fact the company expanded its workforce slightly. Unfortunately, Scott rechecked his projection computations a few months later and found that he had made an error that would have reduced his projections substantially. Luckily, sales of PLEX have exceeded projections so far, and management is satisfied with its decision. Scott, however, is not sure what to do. Should he confess his honest mistake and jeopardize his possible promotion? He suspects that no one will catch the error because PLEX sales have exceeded his original and corrected projections, and it appears that profits will materialize close to his original projections.

If Scott says nothing about the error, which of the following standards of conduct as outlined in the *IMA Statement of Ethical Professional Practice* is most clearly being compromised?

A. Credibility
B. Confidentiality
C. Integrity
D. Fairness

aq.eth.org.0001_0720

8. Based on the IMA's Statement of Management Accounting *Value and Ethics: From Inception to Practice*, what is an ethical challenge that an organization faces as it increases in size and scope?

A. Increases in sales put a strain on the supply chain that may result in shipment delays and stock-out incidents.
B. As organizations expand and grow in size, there are usually not any issues related to ethics that occur. Instead, expansion and growth issues are primarily related to supply chain challenges.
C. As a company grows, a key challenge is that ethical behaviors and codes of conduct must move from an informal "lead by example" model to a more formal and standardized framework.
D. There are usually no significant ethical issues at growing organizations as long as the CEO or founder can maintain a hands-on approach with hiring and training initiatives.

aq.eth.org.0003_0720

9. Which of the following is a way in which an organization can benefit from implementing and publicizing a code of conduct?

   A. Since stock prices always go up when an organization publicly embraces an ethical code of conduct, there is a clear financial benefit to adopting ethics.
   B. As the stock prices of an organization almost universally go down when ethics failures are publicized about an organization, there is always a positive and immediate economic benefit for ethics.
   C. Adopting ethics procedures and policies will improve both the quality of employees attracted to the organization, and develop a culture where ethical behavior is rewarded as a matter of course.
   D. By adopting a code of ethical behavior, establishing ethics training, and reinforcing ethical norms at the organization, the management team will never be held liable for unethical behavior conducted at the firm.

aq.ps.prof.ethics.0005_1710

10. The president of your company has a reputation for using the company jet for personal trips, and for extending business trips in order to vacation with his family in exotic locations. This use of company resources frustrates many of the employees. Your good friend has a social media channel that she uses to promote corporate responsibility issues, and would love for you to provide some "real life" stories for her website. She assures you that she can adjust any information you give her to keep the report anonymous.

    Assuming you talk with your friend about what is happening in your company with respect to the president, which of the following standards of conduct as outlined in the *IMA Statement of Ethical Professional Practice* are you violating?

    A. Competence
    B. Confidentiality
    C. Integrity
    D. Credibility

aq.moral.phil.007_1907

11. "The equitable distribution of benefits and costs" describes which moral philosophy?

    A. Virtue ethics
    B. Justice
    C. Teleology
    D. Relativism

aq.moral.phil.005_1907

12. "Identifying and committing to imperatives that should form a universal law that everyone in the world should be following" describes which moral philosophy?

    A. Utilitarianism
    B. Justice
    C. Deontology
    D. Relativism

aq.org.eth.law.0002_0720

13. Which definition best describes the fundamental purpose of the Foreign Corrupt Practices Act?

    A. The FCPA focuses on reducing regulation to help ensure U.S. corporations succeed while doing business in overseas markets.
    B. As a regulatory body, the FCPA overseas enforcement of antifraud initiatives undertaken by U.S. corporations.
    C. The FCPA regulates the activities of foreign entities that are headquartered overseas, but are doing business in the United States.
    D. The FCPA regulates behaviors with regard to bribery efforts of foreign officials by U.S. citizens and firms.

aq.moral.phil.004_0720

14. Which of the following is the definition of *teleology*?

    A. Focusing first on character and then on action is at the core of this moral philosophy, stressing the fact that character, whether good or bad, defines a person.
    B. A moral philosophy that argues if you can increase the overall happiness of the world in some way, then you should. Results are given all the ethical emphasis.
    C. Rather than focusing on good character or desirable consequences, this moral philosophy requires individuals to identify and commit to imperatives that they believe should form a universal law that everyone in the world should be following.
    D. A moral philosophy that is concerned with how choices will affect a particular desired moral outcome. Answering a few questions about the "end" or "purpose" of something can then determine whether the act (or choice) is good or bad.

aq.eth.org.001_0720

15. What impact does groupthink have on ethical behavior?

    A. In a groupthink situation, group members will disagree with the consensus of the group and express personal doubts and judgments.
    B. When a group of well-intentioned people is making irrational or unethical decisions, there is likely strong pressure in that group to be unified.
    C. In a groupthink situation, group members will brainstorm ideas on how the group can make the most ethical decisions.
    D. Groupthink has no effect on ethical behavior.

Review Questions and Answers

Section A: Financial Statement Analysis

aq.sales.revenues.0004_1710

1. Diamond, Inc. (Diamond) has a 5-year construction contract to build a canal for $600,000. The estimate of total costs is $400,000. Year 1 and Year 2 incurred costs are, respectively, $100,000 and $20,000. If the ultimate payment is assured, the cost estimate is reliable, and Diamond uses an input method of costs expended to recognize revenue, which of the following realized profits would Diamond report for Year 1 and Year 2, respectively?

   A. $0; $0
   B. $40,000; $40,000
   C. $50,000; $60,000
   D. $50,000; $10,000

   Answer: D

   Because Diamond is using an input method of costs expended to recognize revenue, some revenue will be recognized.

Contract price	$600,000
Total cost estimate	(400,000)
Total profit estimate	$200,000

Year 1 Degree of completion: (Costs to date) ÷ (Estimated total costs). $100,000 ÷ $400,000 = 25%
Profit: (Degree of completion) × (Expected total profit). 25% × $200,000 = $50,000
Profit realized in Year 1: (Profit to date) – (Previously recognized profit). $50,000 – $0 = $50,000
Year 2 Degree of completion: (Costs to date) ÷ (Estimated total costs). $120,000 ÷ $400,000 = 30%
Profit: (Degree of completion) × (Expected total profit). 30% × $200,000 = $60,000 Profit realized in Year 2: (Profit to date) – (Previously recognized profit). $60,000 – $50,000 = $10,000

aq.liquid.ratios.0006_1904

2. Cash that normally would have been used to pay the firm's accounts payable is used instead to pay off some of the firm's long-term debt. This will cause the firm's:

   A. current ratio to rise.
   B. payables turnover to rise.
   C. quick ratio to fall.
   D. cash conversion cycle to lengthen.

   Answer: C

   The quick ratio = (cash + marketable securities + receivables) ÷ current liabilities, thus if cash is reduced the numerator will decrease as will the ratio.

aq.horiz.financial.0001_1710

3. In which scenario would a horizontal analysis be the best choice?

   A. A bank wishes to compare progress among different companies.
   B. A company wishes to market its growth to potential stockholders.
   C. A vendor wishes to evaluate financial statement data in a given year.
   D. An investor wishes to evaluate financial statement data by expressing each item in a financial statement as a percentage of a base amount.

   Answer: B

   Horizontal analysis involves analyzing trends in financial statements. This type of information is useful for assessing growth potential. Therefore, this is the correct answer.

aq.solvency.rat.0004_1710

4. The following data pertain to Ruhl Corp.'s operations for the year ended December 31, Year 1:

Operating income	$800,000
Interest expense	100,000
Income before income tax	700,000
Income tax expense	210,000
Net income	$490,000

The times interest earned ratio is:

A. 8.0 to 1.
B. 7.0 to 1.
C. 2.1 to 1.
D. 4.9 to 1.

Answer: A

Times interest earned = Net income before interest and taxes ÷ Interest expense
= $800,000 ÷ $100,000 = 8 or 8 to 1

aq.common.size.0001_1710

5. Which of the following would **not** be included on a balance sheet?

A. Prepaid rent
B. Retained earnings
C. Cost of goods sold
D. Accumulated depreciation

Answer: C

Cost of goods sold are expenses incurred to manufacture a product—therefore, they are classified as an income statement account.

aq.cost.sales.0005_1710

6. Given the following information about a firm, what are the gross and operating profit margins, respectively?

- Net Sales = $1,000
- Cost of Goods Sold = $600
- Operating Expenses = $200
- Interest Expenses = $50
- Tax Rate = 34%

A. 20%; 15%
B. 40%; 20%
C. 40%; 10%
D. 20%; 10%

Answer: B

Gross Profit Margin = ($1,000 Net Sales – $600 COGS) ÷ $1,000 Net Sales = $400 ÷ $1,000 = 0.4

Operating Profit Margin = ($1,000 Net Sales – $600 COGS – $200 Operating Expenses) ÷ $1,000 Net Sales = $200 ÷ $1000 = 0.2

aq.inflation.fin.0003_1710

7. If the consumer price index is 135 and was 122 a year ago, the rate of inflation was:

   A. 9.6%.
   B. −9.6%.
   C. 10.7%.
   D. −10.7%.

   Answer: C

   The formula to calculate inflation is (Year 2 – Year 1) ÷ Year 1. (135 – 122) ÷ 122 = 10.7%.

aq.profit.market.0003_1710

8. Which ratio must be calculated using an amount external to a company's financial statements?

   A. Current ratio
   B. Times interest earned
   C. Price-earnings ratio
   D. Inventory turnover

   Answer: C

   The price-earnings ratio is defined as Market Price ÷ Earnings per Share. The market price of a share of stock is not found on any financial statement. Therefore, this is the correct answer.

aq.eff.ratios.0003_1710

9. Early in 20x7, Rivers Company switched to a JIT (just-in-time) inventory system. Financial information for the two most recent years are listed here.

	20x6	**20x7**
Net sales revenue	$2,000,000	$1,800,000
Cost of goods sold	800,000	788,000
Beginning inventory	200,000	130,000
Ending inventory	130,000	30,000

   How many times did inventory turnover increase by as a result of the switch to the JIT system?

   A. 2.1 times
   B. 5.1 times
   C. 20.1 times
   D. 3.8 times

   Answer: B

   Inventory turnover is correctly calculated as Cost of Goods Sold ÷ Average Inventory. In 20x6, it was 4.8 times {$800,000 ÷ [($200,000 + $130,000) ÷ 2]} and in 20x7 it was 9.9 times {$788,000 ÷ [($130,000 + $30,000) ÷ 2]}. This is an increase of 5.1 times.

aq.eff.ratios.0008_1710

10. The cash conversion cycle is the:

    A. length of time it takes to sell inventory.
    B. length of time it takes the firm to pay the credit extended to it for purchases.
    C. sum of the time it takes to sell inventory and the time it takes to collect accounts receivable.
    D. sum of the time it takes to sell inventory and collect on accounts receivable, less the time it takes to pay for credit purchases.

Answer: D

Cash conversion cycle = (Average receivables collection period) + (Average inventory processing period) – (Payables payment period)

aq.profit.eps.0006_1710

11. All else being equal, which of the following will help decrease a company's total debt-to-equity ratio?

A. Buying Treasury stock
B. Paying cash dividends to stockholders
C. Converting long-term debt to short-term debt
D. Lowering the dividend payout ratio

Answer: D

Lowering the dividend payout ratio will increase retained earnings, thus increasing stockholders' equity and decreasing the debt-to-equity ratio.

aq.profit.vertical.0006_1710

12. Four home decor stores have net income and average total assets as shown here.

	Net Income	**Average Total Assets**
Store 1	$186,000	$2,250,000
Store 2	$342,000	$4,700,000
Store 3	$4,900,000	$58,000,000
Store 4	$2,300,000	$29,500,000

Which store has the *lowest* return on assets?

A. Store 2
B. Store 1
C. Store 3
D. Store 4

Answer: A

Return on assets is defined as Net Income ÷ Average Total Assets. Store 2 has an ROA of 7.28% ($342,000 ÷ $4.7 million). This is the lowest of the four stores. Therefore, this is the correct answer.

aq.book.vs.market.0002_1710

13. The following data pertains to a machine owned by Showman Corporation:

- Historical cost: $35,000
- Accumulated depreciation: $30,000
- Showman uses straight-line depreciation
- 7 years is the useful life of the machine
- No estimated salvage value was used

The machine is being sold to another company for $4,000. What amount needs to be recognized as a gain/loss to Showman Company?

A. Loss of $5,000
B. Loss of $1,000
C. $0
D. Gain of $4,000

Answer: B

Showman Company should recognize a loss of $1,000 at the time of the disposal: $35,000 original cost – $30,000 accumulated depreciation to date = $5,000 carrying value, $4,000 proceeds – $5,000 book value = ($1,000) loss on the disposition of the machine.

aq.forex.fluctuations.0003_1710

14. On November 15, Year 1, Celt, Inc., a U.S. company, ordered merchandise FOB shipping point from a German company for 200,000 Euros. The merchandise was shipped and invoiced to Celt on December 10, Year 1. Celt paid the invoice on January 10, Year 2. The spot rates for Euros on the respective dates are as shown here.

November 15, Year 1	$0.4955
December 10, Year 1	$0.4875
December 31, Year 1	$0.4675
January 10, Year 2	$0.4475

In Celt's December 31, Year 1, income statement, the foreign exchange gain is:

A. $9,600.
B. $4,000.
C. $8,000.
D. $1,600.

Answer: B

Celt Inc. obtained title of the merchandise and became accountable for the liability collected in a foreign currency on December 10, Year 1. A gain/loss will result if the exchange rate on the settlement date is different from the rate existing on the transaction date. A gain/loss must be recognized at any intervening balance sheet date, if necessary. At the end of the year, the liability is translated at the December 31, Year 1 rate in order to accurately calculate the current cost of the liability at year end. When compared to the translated amount as of the shipping date, a foreign exchange gain of $4,000 is calculated.

Amount recorded in accounts payable by Celt, Inc.	
Dec. 10, Year 1, recorded on date of invoice (200,000 × $0.4875)	$97,500
Balance due Dec. 31, Year 1 (200,000 × $0.4675)	93,500
Gain reported 12/31/Year 1	$4,000

aq.op.lev.0010_1710

15. Which of the following is *likely* to encourage a firm to increase the amount of debt in its capital structure?

A. The firm's assets become less liquid.
B. The corporate tax rate increases.
C. The firm's earnings become more volatile.
D. The personal tax rate increases.

Answer: B

An increase in the corporate tax rate will increase the tax benefit of debt financing to the corporation because interest expense is deductible in calculating taxable income.

Section B: Corporate Finance

aq.acc.rm.0003_1710

1. The accounts receivable turnover ratio is a measure of:

   A. the number of times a customer made a purchase on account.
   B. the number of times the firm's inventory was replaced.
   C. the amount of credit sales within a reporting period.
   D. the number of times a company cycles its accounts receivable.

   Answer: D

   The accounts receivable turnover ratio is a measure of the number of times a company cycles its accounts receivable.

aq.bonds.0007_1710

2. For a bond issue which sells for less than its par value, the market rate of interest is:

   A. dependent on the rate stated on the bond.
   B. higher than the rate stated on the bond.
   C. equal to the rate stated on the bond.
   D. less than the rate stated on the bond.

   Answer: B

   A bond issued at a discount reflects that the market rate is greater than the contract rate.

aq.val.de.0004_1710

3. If a firm pays a constant dividend of $10 and the required rate of return or discount rate is equal to 10%, what is the price of the stock using the zero-growth dividend model?

   A. $1
   B. $10
   C. $50
   D. $100

   Answer: D

   The zero-growth dividend model is represented by the following equation:
   P0 = Constant Dividend ÷ Discount Rate and is calculated as $10 ÷ 10% = $100

aq.coc.0009_1710

4. When calculating the weighted-average cost of capital (WACC), an adjustment is made for taxes because:

   A. equity is risky.
   B. the interest on debt is tax deductible.
   C. preferred stock is used.
   D. equity earns higher return than debt.

   Answer: B

   Interest expense is deductible for corporate taxes.

aq.fff.er.0002_1710

5. Which type of foreign exchange system allows for governments to intervene and influence exchange rates?

   A. Managed floating exchange rate
   B. Flexible exchange rate
   C. Floating exchange rate
   D. Fixed exchange rate

   Answer: A

   A managed floating exchange rate system combines features of the fixed and floating exchange rate systems. In such a system, governments can intervene in markets when required, but market forces generally dictate foreign currency exchange rates.

aq.fff.er.0004_1710

6. Consider two countries: Country A and Country B. If Country A's currency is more valuable than Country B's, how will country A's imports from Country B be affected?

   A. Imports will increase.
   B. Imports will decrease.
   C. Imports will not be affected.
   D. Not enough information is given.

   Answer: A

   A country with a more valuable currency will benefit more from importing from other countries.

aq.cap.ass.0004_1710

7. Consider the information below. Using the capital asset pricing model, what is the firm's cost of equity (round to 2 decimals)?

   Risk-free rate of return = 0.05

   Market rate of return = 0.12

   Firm's beta = 1.2

   A. 13%
   B. 19%
   C. 8%
   D. 11%

   Answer: A

   Remember that the CAPM equation is $Ke = Rf + \beta(Rm - Rf)$, where Ke = Investment's required rate of return or Cost of equity capital, Rf = Risk-free rate, and Rm = Market rate of return. The CAPM is determined from this information as $0.05 + 1.2\ (0.12 - 0.05) = 13\%$.

aq.cap.ass.0003_1710

8. The capital asset pricing model (CAPM) is used to determine the cost of what?

   A. Cost of capital
   B. Cost of debt
   C. Cost of equity
   D. Cost of leasing

   Answer: C

   The CAPM is used to determine the cost of equity.

aq.mark.e.0002_1710

9. Which form of market efficiency is described below?

   Security prices reflect all public information but not all private information. For example, investors who have private information could acquire such information through analysis of the firm or discussions with a firm's customers. This form is a reasonable representation of how most large stock markets function.

   A. Strong-form efficiency
   B. Semistrong-form efficiency
   C. Weak-form efficiency
   D. Semiweak-form efficiency

   Answer: B

   This is the correct description of semistrong-form efficiency.

aq.val.de.0003_0720

10. Schmidt, Inc. issues a $10 million bond with a 6% coupon rate, 4-year maturity, and annual interest payments when market interest rates are 7%. Time value of money factors are listed below.

   PV of $1 @ 7% for 4 years = 0.7629

   PV ordinary annuity @ 7% for 4 years = 3.38721*

   Solutions are computed using present value tables. Due to rounding errors, the solution may be slightly different if a calculator is used.

   What is the initial carrying value of the bonds?

   A. $9,661,326
   B. $9,400,000
   C. $10,000,000
   D. $10,338,721

   Answer: A

   The present value of a 4-year annuity of $600,000 plus a 4-year lump sum of $10 million, all valued at a discount rate of 7%, equals $9,661,326. The present value (PV) would be $600,000 × 3.38721, or $2,032,326. (The 3.38721 PV factor is the 7%, 4-period factor.) The PV of a single sum of the $10,000,000 would be $10,000,000 × 0.76290, or $7,629,000. (The 0.76290 PV factor is the 7%, 4-period factor.) The sum of $2,032,326 and $7,629,000 is $9,661,326.*

   Solutions are computed using present value tables. Due to rounding errors, the solution may be slightly different if a calculator is used.

aq.fin.it.0004_1710

11. Which of the following financial tools involves an exporter sending goods to an importer before the good has been sold to a customer?

   A. Letters of credit
   B. Countertrading
   C. Consignment
   D. Sight drafts

   Answer: C

   Consignment takes place when an exporter sends goods to be sold to an importer. The importer will pay the exporter once the goods are sold.

aq.mark.sm.0005_1710

12. Which of the following is best described as unsecured (without collateral), short-term borrowing by very large, creditworthy firms?

    A. Commercial paper
    B. Eurodollars
    C. Repurchase agreements
    D. Bankers' acceptances

    Answer: A

    Commercial paper is unsecured, short-term borrowing by very large, creditworthy firms.

aq.restruc.c.0003_1710

13. Which of the following types of business divestitures would a firm use in order to most effectively monitor the performance of a strategic business unit?

    A. Spin-off
    B. Equity carve-out
    C. Split-up
    D. Tracking stock

    Answer: D

    Tracking stocks are ownership shares that are issued by a parent company to monitor the performance of one t SBU.

aq.eval.bc.0004_1710

14. When using the discounted cash flow method to evaluate a business combination, what is the appropriate assumption about longevity of the target firm?

    A. Three to five years
    B. Product's projected useful life
    C. Industry average firm life
    D. Indefinite life

    Answer: D

    Firms are considered to have an indefinite life.

aq.term.struc.0005_1710

15. The real rate of interest is:

    A. the nominal interest rate plus expected inflation.
    B. the risk-free rate plus expected inflation.
    C. the nominal interest rate minus expected inflation.
    D. the nominal interest rate plus the risk-free rate.

    Answer: C

    The real rate of interest is the base interest rate in the economy. It is calculated as the nominal interest rate minus expected inflation.

Section C: Decision Analysis

aq.comp.bp.0010_1710

1. Which statement *best* characterizes the response to higher gold prices by a jewelry manufacturing company in the short run and long run, respectively?

   A. Use cheaper alternative metal in the short run. Increase prices in the long run.
   B. Use cheaper alternative metal in the short run. Decrease prices in the long run.
   C. Increase prices in the short run. Use cheaper alternative metal in the long run.
   D. Decrease prices in the short run. Use cheaper alternative metal in the long run.

   Answer: C

   The short-run response is an adjustment of prices, and the long-run response is a change in production methodology.

aq.cost.bp.0005_0720

2. Almelo Manpower Inc. provides contracted bookkeeping services. Almelo has annual fixed costs of \$100,000 and variable costs of \$6 per hour. This year the company budgeted 50,000 hours of bookkeeping services. Almelo prices its services based on full cost and uses a cost-plus pricing approach. The company developed a billing price of \$9 per hour. The company's markup level would be:

   A. 50.0%.
   B. 12.5%.
   C. 33.3%.
   D. 66.6%.

   Answer: B

   The full cost per unit at 50,000 hours is calculated as follows:

   Unit cost at 50,000 hours = (Fixed costs ÷ Number of hours) + Variable cost per hour

   Unit cost at 50,000 hours = (\$100,000 ÷ 50,000) + \$6 = \$2 + \$6 = \$8 per hour

   Using the cost markup formula: Targeted Price = Cost × (1 + Markup%)

   Given the price of \$9, the markup level on cost = (Price – Cost) ÷ Cost

   Markup level on cost = (\$9 – \$8) ÷ \$8 = 1/8 = 12.5%

   Alternatively, using the markup target price formula,

   \$9 = \$8 × (1 + Markup%)

   \$9 = \$8 + \$8(Markup%)

   \$9 – \$8 = \$8(Markup%)

   \$1 = \$8(Markup%)

   \$1 ÷ \$8 = Markup% = 12.5%

cont.mar.aq.0017_0820

3. The financial analyst for the company calculates that the breakeven point in revenue for a product is \$250,000. The product sells for \$25 per unit. Fixed costs are \$100,000. What is the contribution margin per unit?

   A. \$15.00
   B. \$10.00
   C. \$5.00
   D. \$8.00

Answer: B

At the operating breakeven point, operating income is zero. Thus, total revenues and total costs are equal.

Breakeven formula: Revenues – Variable costs – Fixed costs = Operating income

Inserting known values into the formula: \$250,000 – Variable costs – \$100,000 = \$0

Total variable costs = \$250,000 – \$100,000 = Variable costs = \$150,000

Volume sold = Revenues ÷ Unit selling price = \$250,000 ÷ \$25 = 10,000 units

Unit variable costs = Total variable costs ÷ units = \$150,000 ÷ 10,000 = \$15.00

Contribution margin = Price per unit – Variable cost per unit = \$25.00 – \$15.00 = \$10.00

aq.risk.u.0008_0820

4. Justin Lake operates a kiosk in downtown Chicago, at which he sells one style of baseball hat. He buys the hats from a supplier for \$13 and sells them for \$18. Justin's current breakeven point is 15,000 hats per year. Based on a 30% income tax rate, Justin Lake is projecting an after-tax profit of \$14,000. What is Justin's current margin of safety in sales revenue?

   A. \$75,000
   B. \$20,000
   C. \$50,400
   D. \$72,000

Answer: D

First, determine total fixed costs by solving the C-V-P equation at the breakeven point.

Price(Volume) – Variable cost per hat(Volume) – Total fixed costs = Profit

\$18(15,000) – \$13(15,000) – Total fixed costs = \$0

\$270,000 – \$195,000 = \$75,000

Next, determine projected sales revenue based on after-tax profit of \$14,000

Pretax profit = After-tax profit ÷ (1–Tax rate) = \$14,000 ÷ (1–0.3) = \$20,000

\$18(Volume) – \$13(Volume) – \$75,000 = \$20,000

\$5(Volume) = \$75,000 + \$20,000

Projected sales volume = \$95,000 ÷ \$5 = 19,000 hats

Margin of safety = Current sales – Breakeven sales = 19,000 hats – 15,000 hats = 4,000 hats

Margin of safety in sales revenue = 4,000 hats × \$18 = \$72,000

aq.marg.anal.pld.0003_0720

5. Manor Company plans to discontinue a department that currently provides a \$24,000 contribution margin and has allocated overhead of \$48,000, of which \$21,000 cannot be eliminated. Manor's average income tax rate is 30%. The effect of this discontinuance on Manor's after-tax profit would be a(n):

   A. increase of \$2,100.
   B. increase of \$3,000.
   C. decrease of \$24,000.
   D. decrease of \$16,800.

Answer: A

Allocated overhead	$48,000
Less: Unavoidable overhead	(21,000)
Fixed overhead cost savings	$27,000
Less decrease in contribution margin	(24,000)
Increase in pretax income	$3,000
Income tax expense (30%)	(900)
Increase in after-tax income	$2,100

aq.tar.pt.0009_0820

6. Carl's Corp is experiencing significant competition that is driving down price from $60 to $50 per unit. If the company chooses to match the new price in the market, the marketing team estimates that sales will rise from 700,000 to 800,000 units. Carl's Corp's current variable cost per unit is $45, and total fixed costs are $500,000. Suppose Carl's Corp would like to maintain a 25% target contribution margin on its sales revenue. To achieve this target, the company must lower its variable production costs by how much?

A. $0.00 per unit
B. $7.50 per unit
C. $11.45 per unit
D. $15.00 per unit

Answer: B

Total revenue at new sales price and new sales volume = $50 × 800,000 units = $40,000,000

Target contribution margin at 25% on sales = $40,000,000 × 25% = $10,000,000

Target contribution margin = (Sales price × volume) – (Variable cost × Volume) = $10,000,000

Target contribution margin = ($50 × 800,000 units) – (Variable cost × 800,000 units) = $10,000,000

($50 × 800,000 units) – $10,000,000 = (Variable cost × 800,000 units)

$30,000,000 = Variable cost × 800,000 units

$30,000,000 ÷ 800,000 units = Variable cost = $37.50 per unit

$45.00 original variable cost – $37.50 target variable cost = $7.50 decrease in variable cost per unit

aq.mp.cvp.0009_0820

7. Simon's Wholesale Flowers produces two types of flower bouquets that it distributes to retail shops: simple bouquets and upgraded bouquets. Total fixed costs for the firm are $184,000. Variable costs and sales data for these bouquets are presented here.

	Simple Bouquets	**Upgraded Bouquets**
Selling price per unit	$24.00	$40.00
Variable cost per unit	$20.00	$32.00
Budgeted sales (units)	20,000	30,000

How many bouquets will be required to reach the breakeven point?

A. 10,615 simple bouquets and 17,692 upgraded bouquets
B. 15,333 simple bouquets and 15,333 upgraded bouquets
C. 10,952 simple bouquets and 17,524 upgraded bouquets
D. 11,500 simple bouquets and 17,250 upgraded bouquets

Answer: D

The sales mix (units) = 2:3

Sales mix basket:

Sales price = 2 × \$24 + 3 × \$40 = \$168

Variable cost = 2 × \$20 + 3 × \$32 = \$136

C-V-P solution:

\$168(Baskets) – \$136(Baskets) – \$184,000 = \$0

\$32(Baskets) = \$184,000

Breakeven units (baskets) = 5,750 baskets

Multiply baskets by sales mix:

Simple bouquets: 5,750 baskets × 2 bouquets = 11,500 simple bouquets

Upgraded bouquets: 5,750 baskets × 3 bouquets = 17,250 upgraded bouquets

aq.cost.be.0007_0820

8. Breakeven quantity is defined as the volume of output at which revenues are equal to:

   A. total costs.
   B. marginal costs.
   C. variable costs.
   D. fixed costs.

Answer: A

Breakeven quantity is defined as the volume of output at which revenues are equal to total costs. Therefore, profits equal zero.

aq.cost.be.0006_0820

9. Given a unit selling price of \$100, fixed costs of \$3,000, variable costs per unit of \$75, and a total quantity of 150 units actually sold, what is the breakeven point?

   A. 60 units
   B. 40 units
   C. 120 units
   D. 30 units

Answer: C

The formula and calculations for determining breakeven using the equation method follows:

(Sales price × Volume) – (Variable cost per unit × Volume) – Total fixed costs = Profit

(\$100 × Volume) – (\$75 × Volume) – \$3,000 = \$0

(\$100 – \$75) × Volume – \$3,000 = \$0

\$25 × Volume = \$3,000

Breakeven volume = \$3,000 ÷ \$25 = 120 units

aq.cust.bp.0004_0720

10. A consumer products company prices one of its new products significantly higher than competitor products currently in the market. The higher price is based on customer focus studies indicating that customers in a certain income bracket are willing to pay more for the superior characteristics of the product. This pricing tactic is an example of:

A. premium pricing.
B. price gouging.
C. penetration pricing.
D. tiered pricing.

Answer: A

This is an example of premium pricing, which is a customer-focused pricing tactic.

aq.risk.u.0002_0820

11. Arvin Tax Preparation Services has annual total budgeted revenues of $618,000, based on an average price of $206 per tax return prepared. The company's current fixed costs are $326,600 and variable costs average $64 per tax return.

Calculate Arvin's break-even point and margin of safety in units.

A. Break-even point is 2,300 tax returns; margin of safety is 3,000 tax returns
B. Break-even point is 2,300 tax returns; margin of safety is 700 tax returns
C. Break-even point is 1,586 tax returns; margin of safety is 1,414 tax returns
D. Break-even point is 1,586 tax returns; margin of safety is 3,000 tax returns

Answer: B

Using the C-V-P formula, Arvin's break-even point is found by solving:

$206(Volume) – $64(Volume) – $326,600 = $0

$142(Volume) = $326,600

Break-even volume = $326,600 ÷ $142 = 2,300 tax returns

Current sales volume = $618,000 ÷ $206 = 3,000 tax returns

Margin of safety = 3,000 tax returns – 2,300 tax returns = 700 tax returns

aq.sunk.opp.cap.0004_0720

12. The Lantern Corporation has 1,000 obsolete lanterns that are carried in inventory at a manufacturing cost of $20,000. If the lanterns are remachined for $5,000, they can be sold for $9,000. If the lanterns are scrapped, they can be sold for $1,000. What alternative is more desirable and what is the cash flow under that alternative?

A. Remachine; $24,000
B. Scrap; $21,000
C. Remachine; $4,000
D. Scrap; $1,000

Answer: C

	Remachine	**Scrap**
Proceeds	$9,000	$1,000
Additional cost	$5,000	$0
Net proceeds	$4,000	$1,000

The inventory carrying value of $20,000 is not relevant to the decision since under either alternative the $20,000 is a sunk cost.

aq.mp.cvp.0010_0820

13. Simon's Wholesale Flowers produces two types of flower bouquets that it distributes to retail shops: simple bouquets and upgraded bouquets. Total fixed costs for the firm are $184,000. Variable costs and sales data for these bouquets are presented here.

	Simple Bouquets	Upgraded Bouquets
Selling price per unit	$24.00	$40.00
Variable cost per unit	$20.00	$32.00
Budgeted sales (units)	20,000	30,000

If the product sales mix were to change to three upgraded bouquets sold for each simple bouquet sold, the breakeven volume for each of these products would be:

A. 11,500 simple bouquets and 17,250 upgraded bouquets.
B. 15,333 simple bouquets and 15,333 upgraded bouquets.
C. 27,600 simple bouquets and 9,200 upgraded bouquets.
D. 6,572 simple bouquets and 19,715 upgraded bouquets.

Answer: D

The sales mix (units) = 1:3

Sales mix basket:

Sales price = 1 × $24 + 3 × $40 = $144

Variable cost = 1 × $20 + 3 × $32 = $116

C-V-P solution:

$144(Baskets) – $116(Baskets) – $184,000 = $0

$28(Baskets) = $184,000

Breakeven units (baskets) = 6,571.4 baskets

Multiply baskets by sales mix:

Simple bouquets: 6,571.4 baskets × 1 bouquet = 6,571.4 simple bouquets

Upgraded bouquets: 6,571.4 baskets × 3 bouquets = 19,714.3 upgraded bouquets

Rounded up to 6,572 simple bouquets and 19,715 upgraded bouquets

aq.cost.bp.0002_0720

14. The cost-plus target pricing approach is generally in what formula?

A. Unit cost ÷ Selling price = Markup percentage
B. Unit cost × (1 + Markup % on unit cost) = Targeted selling price
C. Variable cost + Fixed cost + Contribution margin = Targeted selling price
D. Cost base + Gross margin = Targeted selling price

Answer: B

Cost-plus pricing involves setting the target price of a product so as to earn an established markup percentage on sales, and is based on this formula. Note that one must first determine the critical markup percentage before using the cost-plus target pricing formula.

aq.def.rel.costs.0007_0720

15. Maize Company incurs a cost of $35 per unit, of which $20 is variable, to make a product that normally sells for $58. A foreign wholesaler offers to buy 6,000 units at $30 each. Maize has the capacity to take on this order, but will incur additional costs of $4 per unit to imprint a logo and to pay for shipping. Compute the increase or decrease in net income that Maize will realize by accepting the special order.

A. $60,000
B. ($54,000)
C. ($30,000)
D. $36,000

Answer: D

	Accept the Order
Special Order Revenues	$180,000
Special Order Costs	(144,000)*
Increase in Net Income	$36,000

*(6,000 × $20) + (6,000 × $4)

Given the results of the above analysis, Maize Company should accept the special order.

Section D: Risk Management

aq.risk.ms.0001_1710

1. Which of the following is **not** a common risk mitigation strategy?

   A. Avoid the risk
   B. Reduce the risk
   C. Transfer the risk
   D. Amplify the risk

   Answer: D

   Amplifying the risk would increase risk exposure, not reduce it.

aq.man.risk.0003_1710

2. An investor owns stock and is concerned that prices may fall in the future. Which strategy could help her hedge against adverse market conditions?

   A. Buy a call option.
   B. Buy an over-the-counter forward.
   C. Buy a put option.
   D. Buy a futures contract.

   Answer: C

   Buying a put option will help the investor hedge against adverse market conditions by having the option to sell the stock at a set price.

aq.risk.ms.0002_1710

3. Insurance is an example of which of the following risk mitigation strategies?

   A. Avoid the risk
   B. Retain the risk
   C. Accept the risk
   D. Transfer the risk

   Answer: D

   Insurance is an example of transferring risk. Insurance spreads the risk of a loss across a wide pool of different organizations that may experience a similar loss.

aq.ent.risk.m.0004_1710

4. Which of the following most accurately describes enterprise risk management (ERM)?

   A. ERM is affected primarily by upper management.
   B. ERM is not designed to provide any assurance to an entity's management or board of directors.
   C. ERM does not assist management in identifying and seizing opportunities.
   D. ERM is designed to identify potential events that may affect the entity.

   Answer: D

   ERM enhances management's ability to identify and take advantage of business opportunities due to enhanced and timely information availability.
   ERM is designed to identify potential events that may affect the entity, to manage risk to be within the risk appetite, and to provide assurance regarding the achievement of objectives.

aq.risk.ass.tools.0003_1710

5. Which of the following measures the effect of risk management on reducing the volatility of earnings associated with an event?

   A. Earnings distributions
   B. Earnings at risk
   C. Average earnings
   D. Median earnings

   Answer: A

   Earnings distributions show the effect of risk management on reducing the volatility of earnings associated with an event.

aq.risk.ass.tools.0005_1710

6. *Value at Risk (VaR)* is most commonly used as a:

   A. year-end measure of a firm's trading activities.
   B. tracking measure to assess a firm's risk position.
   C. benchmark for a firm's cash flows.
   D. benchmark for executives' compensation.

   Answer: B

   VaR indicates potential loss by a firm due to its trading activities. A firm may have hundreds, if not thousands, of trading positions. The potential for loss is accumulated across these positions at a particular confidence interval. This summary number is used by firms as a tracking measure over time to assess whether their risk position is increasing or decreasing.

aq.man.risk.0001_1710

7. When evaluating financial risk, which ratios will be *most beneficial* to the analyst?

   A. Total debt and interest coverage ratios
   B. Gross profit margin and the operating profit margin
   C. Collection period and inventory turnover
   D. Current and quick ratios

   Answer: A

   The total debt and interest coverage ratios are most beneficial for analyzing financial risk. The total debt ratio indicates the amount of leverage the firm is employing and the interest coverage ratio compares the firm's ability to meet interest payments by the amount of those payments.

aq.man.risk.0004_1710

8. Which of the following is the correct order of the risk management cycle?

   A. Identify the risk, evaluate the risk, manage the risk, analyze the risk, monitor the risk.
   B. Identify the risk, monitor the risk, analyze the risk, evaluate the risk, manage the risk.
   C. Analyze the risk, identify the risk, evaluate the risk, monitor the risk, manage the risk.
   D. Identify the risk, analyze the risk, evaluate the risk, manage the risk, monitor the risk.

   Answer: D

   This is the correct order of the risk management cycle.

aq.risk.ms.0003_1710

9. When a firm develops internal activities to manage risk, it is using which of the following risk mitigation strategies?

   A. Avoid the risk
   B. Retain the risk
   C. Accept the risk
   D. Transfer the risk

   Answer: B

   Retaining the risk involves a firm developing internal activities to manage risk. For example, a firm could retain a risk by maintaining a reserve fund to pay expenses in the event of decreased revenue or cash.

aq.u.prob.0005_1710

10. Based on risk assessment techniques and the use of probabilities, firms should be prepared for which of the following outcomes?

    A. Best-case scenario
    B. Most-likely scenario
    C. Expected-loss scenario
    D. Worst-case scenario

    Answer: D

    Firms should prepare for the worst-case scenario while reasonably expecting losses to be less.

aq.types.ent.risk.0001_1710

11. When purchasing temporary investments, which of the following *best* describes the risk associated with the ability to sell the investment in a short time without significant price concessions?

    A. Liquidity risk
    B. Investment risk
    C. Interest rate risk
    D. Purchasing power risk

    Answer: A

    Liquidity risk relates to the risk of selling an investment in a short time without significant price concessions.

aq.types.ent.risk.0002_1710

12. Which of the following sources of uncertainties would be affected by the firm's debt versus equity decision?

    A. Liquidity risk
    B. Financial risk
    C. Country risk
    D. Business risk

    Answer: B

    The firm's financial risk is the uncertainty introduced through the method by which the firm finances its investments, which includes the debt versus equity decision.

aq.u.prob.0002_1710

13. Dough Distributors has decided to increase its daily muffin purchases by 100 boxes. A box of muffins costs \$2 and sells for \$3 through regular stores. Any boxes not sold through regular stores are sold through Dough's thrift store for \$1. Dough assigns the following probabilities to selling additional boxes:

Additional Sales	Probability
60	.6
100	.4

What is the expected value of Dough's decision to buy 100 additional boxes of muffins?

A. $28
B. $12
C. $40
D. $52

Answer: D

Additional sales 60 boxes		
60 boxes × ($3 selling price – $2 cost)	$60	
40 boxes × ($1 selling price – $2 cost)	$(40)	
Profit	$20	
Probability	×.6	
Expected Value		$12
Additional sales 100 boxes		
100 boxes × ($3 selling price – $2 cost)	$100	
0 boxes × ($1 selling price – $2 cost)	$0	
Profit	$100	
Probability	×.4	
Expected Value		$40
Expected Profit (Value) of Decision		$52

aq.types.ent.risk.0005_1710

14. The uncertainty in return on assets due to the nature of a firm's operations is known as:

A. business risk.
B. tax efficiency.
C. financial leverage.
D. financial flexibility.

Answer: A

Business risk is a function of the firm's revenue and expenses, resulting in operating income, or earnings before interest and taxes (EBIT). The main factors affecting business risk are demand variability, sales price variability, input price variability, ability to adjust output prices, and operating leverage. Tax efficiency is tied to mutual fund investing, while both financial leverage and financial flexibility require the existence of debt.

aq.u.prob.0004_1710

15. Your client wants your advice on which of two alternatives he should choose. One alternative is to sell an investment now for $10,000. Another alternative is to hold the investment for three days, after which he can sell it for a certain selling price based on the following probabilities:

Selling Price	Probability
$5,000	.4
$8,000	.2
$12,000	.3
$30,000	.1

Using probability theory, which of the following is the *most reasonable* statement? (Note: This solution does not provide for an analysis or evaluation of the individual's aversion to risk.)

A. Hold the investment three days because of the chance of getting $30,000 for it.
B. Hold the investment three days because the expected value of holding exceeds the current selling price.
C. Sell the investment now because the current selling price exceeds the expected value of holding.
D. Sell the investment now because there is a 60% chance that the selling price will fall in three days.

Answer: B

Computation of expected selling price is as follows:

Selling Price ×	Probability of Selling Price	= Expected Value
$5,000	.4	$2,000
$8,000	.2	$1,600
$12,000	.3	$3,600
$30,000	.1	$3,000
Expected Selling Price		$10,200

Section E: Investment Decisions

aq.payback.discount.0002_0720

1. Fitzgerald Company is planning to acquire a $250,000 machine that will provide increased efficiencies, thereby reducing annual pretax operating costs by $80,000. The machine will be depreciated by the straight-line method over a five-year life with no salvage value at the end of five years. Assuming a 40% income tax rate, the machine's payback period is:

   A. 3.68 years.
   B. 5.21 years.
   C. 2.50 years.
   D. 3.13 years.

   Answer: A

   The payback period is computed by dividing the initial cost by the annual net after-tax cash inflows (assuming equal inflows each year).
   The inflows consist of two items, the first of which is the $80,000 in operating cost savings. If the tax rate is 40%, the company keeps 60% of the $80,000 after tax, which is $48,000.
   The second inflow is the depreciation tax shield. The company will deduct depreciation expense of $50,000 per year. At a 40% tax rate, this will save the company 40% of $50,000, which is $20,000.
   Thus, the total after-tax cash inflow per year is $48,000 + $20,000, or $68,000.
   Finally, the payback period is $250,000 ÷ $68,000 savings per year, or 3.68 years.

aq.intro.cbp.0008_0720

2. The capital budgeting decision process addresses:

   A. how a firm's day-to-day financial matters should be managed.
   B. which productive assets a firm should purchase.
   C. how a firm should finance its assets.
   D. All of these answers are correct.

   Answer: B

   The capital budgeting process is a process utilized by organizations to select between long-term investment opportunities.

aq.cash.flows.0007_0720

3. Which of the following costs does **not** impact taxes in a capital budgeting context?

   A. Loss on the disposal of an existing machine, which is being replaced as part of the capital investment proposal
   B. An increase in the revenues resulting from the capital investment
   C. Depreciation expense recorded for the capital investment during its useful life
   D. The release of net working capital at the end of the capital investment's useful life

   Answer: D

   The release of working capital does not result in an income or expense effect that is subject to taxes. Note, however, that the release of working capital does impact cash flows and the calculation of net present value.

aq.cash.flows.0009_0720

4. Premier Steel, Inc. is considering the purchase of a new machine for $100,000 that will have a useful life of three years. The firm's cost of capital is 11% and the tax rate is 40%. This machine is expected to be sold for its salvage value of $20,000 at the end of three years. The machine will require an ongoing working capital commitment of $2,500 in spare parts inventory. In addition to the purchase price, Premier

estimates that it will incur the following additional costs related to the machine purchase: $8,000 for shipping and $4,000 for installation.

Expected sales are as follows: Year 1 = $90,000; Year 2 = $97,500; Year 3 = $105,000. Estimated operating expenses are Year 1 = $25,000; Year 2 = $27,000; Year 3 = $29,000. The investment in working capital will be liquidated at termination of the project at the end of Year 3. MACRS rates: Year 1 = 33%, Year 2 = 45%, Year 3 = 15%, Year 4 = 7%.

Using MACRS to compute depreciation expense, what is the after-tax operating cash flow in Year 1?

A. $53,784
B. $16,824
C. $51,144
D. $51,200

Answer: A

The calculation is as follows:

The cash operating income for Year 1 = Sales – Operating costs = $90,000 – $25,000 = $65,000.

Depreciation for Year 1 = Cost of asset × MACRS Year 1 rate = ($100,000 + $8,000 + $4,000) × 33% = $36,960 (note that with MACRS, the salvage value is not considered in the depreciation calculation).

After-tax operating income = ($90,000 – $25,000 – $36,960) × (1 – 40%) = $16,824.

After-tax operating cash flows = $16,824 + $36,960 = $53,784.

aq.npv.irr.ucf.0005_0720

5. As the director of capital budgeting for Denver Corporation, an analyst is evaluating two mutually exclusive projects with the net cash flows shown here.

	Project X	Project Z
0	–$100,000	–$100,000
1	$50,000	$10,000
2	$40,000	$30,000
3	$30,000	$40,000
4	$10,000	$60,000

If Denver's cost of capital is 15%, which project should be chosen?*

**Solutions are computed using a financial calculator. Due to rounding errors, the solution may be slightly different if present value tables are used.*

A. Project X should be chosen since it has a better internal rate of return (IRR).
B. Project X should be chosen since it has a better net present value (NPV).
C. Neither project should be chosen.
D. Project Z should be chosen since it has the higher IRR.

Answer: C

See the calculation for Project X:

Calculator steps: Clear All

Enter 15 in the I/YR key

Enter –100,000 in the CF*j* key

Enter 50,000 in the CF*j* key

Enter 40,000 in the CF*j* key

Enter 30,000 in the CF*j* key

Enter 10,000 in the CF*j* key

Compute NPV → −832.97 is the exact NPV solution

Compute IRR/YR → 14.48 is the exact IRR solution

See the calculation for Project Z:

Calculator steps: Clear All

Enter 15 in the I/YR key

Enter −100,000 in the CF*j* key

Enter 10,000 in the CF*j* key

Enter 30,000 in the CF*j* key

Enter 40,000 in the CF*j* key

Enter 60,000 in the CF*j* key

Compute NPV → −8,014.19 is the exact NPV solution

Compute IRR/YR → 11.79 is the exact IRR solution

Reject both projects because neither has a positive NPV.

aq.cash.flows.0004_0720

6. Alexander Manufacturing is planning to purchase a machine costing $185,000 to replace fully depreciated production equipment. For the duration of the new machine's useful life, management estimates needing to commit working capital of $6,000. Management also anticipates that investing in this machine will increase annual net after-tax cash flows by $105,000. The new equipment will be depreciated by the straight-line method over a five-year life with a salvage value of $25,000. Owen expects to receive $2,200 through the sale of the old equipment, which was purchased six years ago for $137,000. Which of the amounts detailed in the problem represent a sunk cost?

   A. $6,000
   B. $25,000
   C. $105,000
   D. $137,000

   Answer: D

   The $137,000 represents the purchase price of the old equipment, which is a sunk cost (any cost that was incurred in the past). To be relevant, a cost must occur in the future and change between decision alternatives. Given that a cost incurred in the past cannot be changed, the original cost of the old equipment is a sunk cost and as a result, is not relevant.

aq.npv.irr.0001_0720

7. The discount rate (hurdle rate of return) must be determined in advance in order to use the:

   A. payback period method.
   B. time-adjusted rate of return method.
   C. net present value method.
   D. internal rate of return method.

   Answer: C

   The net present value method discounts future cash flow benefits using the cost of capital as the discount rate.

aq.cash.flows.0002_0720

8. A bank is considering building a branch on a piece of property it already owns. Which of the following cash flows should **not** be considered in the capital budgeting analysis?

A. Money spent when the property was originally purchased to determine whether there are any environmental issues regarding the property
B. Cash the firm will forgo from the sale of the property if the company decides to build
C. Cash flows resulting from several hundred new customers who will switch from local competitors to the new branch if the bank makes the investment
D. Shipping and installation charges the bank must spend to get equipment in the new branch

Answer: A

Money previously spent on an environmental analysis is a sunk cost and should not be considered in the analysis. The cash received in the event the property is sold is an opportunity cost and should be considered. The transferred customers result in cash flows that are externalities/cannibalization for the bank and must be considered. Finally, the shipping and installation charges are added to the investment basis and are counted.

aq.payback.discount.0001_0720

9. When evaluating capital budgeting analysis techniques, the payback method emphasizes:

A. profitability.
B. cost of capital.
C. net income.
D. liquidity.

Answer: D

The payback period emphasizes liquidity. The project with the shortest period required to recover capital invested is preferred.

aq.cash.flows.0003_0720

10. Owen Eyewear is planning to purchase a \$520,000 machine to improve the quality and lead time of its eyewear production. Management estimates that this investment will result in an increase in annual cash revenues of \$380,000 with related cash operating costs of \$32,000. The machine will be depreciated by the straight-line method over a five-year life. Assume a 30% income tax rate and a 12% hurdle rate. What is the amount of the depreciation tax shield for Year 1?

A. \$104,000
B. \$31,200
C. \$27,857
D. \$0

Answer: B

Depreciation expense is not a cash flow. However, since it is tax deductible, depreciation expense reduces the cash outflows for the tax liability. Thus, the cash flow impact of depreciation is through the reduction of the tax liability. The calculation is: Year 1 Depreciation = Machine Cost ÷ the Machine's Useful Life = \$520,000 ÷ 5 years = \$104,000. Depreciation Tax Shield = (Year 1 Depreciation × Tax Rate) = \$104,000 × 30% = \$31,200.

aq.npv.irr.0004_0720

11. Michael Company is considering the purchase of new computer equipment to improve its production scheduling. This new equipment would cost \$300,000 with working capital of \$14,000 to be committed for the life of the asset. Management estimates that the equipment will improve after-tax cash flows (which already include the tax shield from depreciation) by \$96,500 per year. The equipment will have an estimated useful life of four years with no residual (salvage) value. Michael Company has a minimum required return for similar investments of 10%. Assume that the asset will be placed in service at the beginning of the fiscal year. Calculate the net present value for this investment opportunity.*

**Solutions are computed using a financial calculator. Due to rounding errors, the solution may be slightly different if present value tables are used.*

A. ($8,108)
B. $1,454
C. $5,892
D. $15,454

Answer: B

The NPV for the investment opportunity:

Calculator steps: Clear All

Enter 4 in the N key

Enter 10 in the I/YR key

Enter 96,500 in the PMT key

Enter 14,000 in the FV key

Compute PV → –315,454* is the present value solution.

Net present value = $315, 454 – ($300,000 + $14,000) = $1,454

*The present value is negative because the calculator is indicating that $315,454 current investment (outflow) is equal to all the future inflows (positive payments), assuming a 10% discount rate.

aq.npv.irr.ucf.0008_0720

12. Salem Ltd. is considering the purchase of a new machine that has a purchase price of $1,200,000. Management estimates that the machine will result in a net after-tax cash inflow of $341,976 per year. The machine will have an estimated useful life of five years and a residual (salvage) value of $50,000. Salem has a minimum required return for similar investments of 14%. When using this 14% hurdle rate, the NPV for the project was calculated as –$0.27. What does this net present value imply about the internal rate of return?*

**Solutions are computed using a financial calculator. Due to rounding errors, the solution may be slightly different if present value tables are used.*

A. IRR is definitely less than 14%.
B. IRR is almost exactly equal to 14%.
C. IRR is definitely greater than 14%.
D. No implications can be made about IRR from an NPV calculation.

Answer: B

When NPV is equal to zero, the discount rate used in the calculation is equal to the internal rate of return. In this case, the NPV of –$0.27 is essentially zero. Thus, the IRR is essentially equal to the discount rate of 14%. To be precise, the IRR is 13.99999%.

aq.cash.flows.0008_0720

13. Quad Company is considering buying new equipment costing $450,000 to update its tailgating business. Management anticipates that the machine will produce cash sales of $265,000 each year over the next five years. Annual cash expenses are projected as $70,000. Quad plans to use straight-line depreciation with a residual (salvage) value of $15,000. Quad's combined income tax rate is 30%. Determine the annual after-tax cash flow for the investment.

A. $75,600
B. $136,500
C. $162,600
D. $223,500

Answer: C

After-tax cash flow can be calculated as follows:

Annual depreciation = (Machine cost – Salvage value) ÷ Estimated useful life = ($450,000 – $15,000) ÷ 5 = $87,000.

Taxable operating income = Increase in sales – Cash operating expenses – Depreciation = ($265,000 – $70,000 – $87,000) = $108,000.

Tax liability = ($108,000 × 30%) = $32,400.

After-tax income = ($108,000 – $32,400) = $75,600.

After-tax cash flows = After-tax income + Annual depreciation = $75,600 + $87,000 = $162,600.

Alternatively, after-tax cash flow can be calculated as follows:

After-tax operating cash flow = Increase in sales – Cash operating expenses = $265,000 – $70,000 = $195,000. $195,000 × (1 – 30%) = $136,500.

Depreciation tax shield = $87,000 × 30% = $26,100.

After-tax cash flows = After-tax operating cash flow + Depreciation tax shield = $136,500 + $26,100 = $162,600.

aq.payback.discount.0005_0720

14. Which of the following is a limitation inherent in the payback method?

A. It is difficult to compute and understand.
B. It encourages investment in long-term projects to the detriment of considering short-term opportunities.
C. It does not consider the risk of a project.
D. It fails to consider the cash flows over a project's entire useful life.

Answer: D

The payback method determines the length of time it takes to return the initial investment. Once that payback point is reached, further cash flows are ignored.

aq.cash.flows.0005_1710

15. Mangione Company is selling an existing machine that is being replaced with new equipment. The existing machine originally cost $50,000, with an estimated useful life of four years and a salvage value of $500 when it was initially placed in service four years ago.

Mangione, in seeking to dispose of the existing machine, has found a scrapyard that is offering $700. Assume an effective tax rate of 30%. What is the after-tax cash effect related to the sale of the existing machine?

A. ($60)
B. $140
C. $200
D. $640

Answer: D

This solution includes both the cash inflow from the sale of the existing asset, as well as the tax effect of the gain.

Gain on Sale = Sales Price ($700) – Net Book Value ($500) = $200.

Tax effect of the gain = $200 gain times the 30% tax rate = $60 increase in income taxes.

Thus, the net after-tax cash flow = cash sales price of $700 less the increase in income taxes of $60 = $640.

Section F: Professional Ethics

aq.ei.fraud.0003_0720

1. According to the *IMA Statement of Ethical Professional Practice*, which of the following responses is an appropriate step in the process of resolving an ethical conflict or dilemma?

   A. Contacting a newspaper reporter to report the situation
   B. Avoiding conflict by reducing involvement in the situation
   C. Engaging an attorney to receive counsel on the situation
   D. Communicating concerns about the situation with outside investors

   Answer: C

   This is an appropriate step in the process of resolving an ethical conflict or dilemma. The *IMA Statement of Ethical Professional Practice* advises professionals to *not* hesitate employing an attorney in ethical situations where the best path of resolution is not clear. Too often professionals will hesitate to invest in good legal counsel.

aq.org.eth.law.0003_0720

2. While doing business overseas, the CEO of a U.S. car manufacturer delivers a gift of an expensive luxury car after successfully negotiating a contract to expand operations into that country. Does this potentially violate the FCPA?

   A. This does not violate the FCPA since negotiations for the overseas expansion had already concluded.
   B. Such an action does violate the FCPA since there can be no social interactions during the negotiation of an overseas business deal by a U.S. corporation.
   C. This action violates the FCPA since the giving and accepting of such a gift could be a nonmonetary bribe, and therefore potentially a violation of the FCPA.
   D. Giving this gift is not in violation of the FCPA because even though the company is headquartered in the United States, the action takes place overseas.

   Answer: C

   A key clause of the FCPA is that the provisions of the Act apply to monetary and nonmonetary gifts and potential bribes. These gifts are sometimes called a "commission" or a "facilitating payment." Giving such a gift exposes the firm to potential violation of the FCPA.

aq.moral.phil.008_1907

3. If the decision-making process is always consistent with and accountable to the individual's moral philosophy or the organization's code of ethics, it is said to have what?

   A. Relativism
   B. Justice
   C. Integrity
   D. Fairness

   Answer: C

   The quality of integrity in decision making means the process is always consistent with and accountable to the individual's moral philosophy or the organization's code of ethics. An inconsistent process is fragmented, which is the opposite of the quality of wholeness or completeness (the root meaning of the word *integrity*).

aq.moral.phil.010_0720

4. All of the following are fiduciary responsibilities that finance professionals have to their managers and to the owners or shareholders of the company **except**:

   A. Being responsive on important requests made by managers or owners
   B. Pursuing opportunities for the company as they present themselves
   C. Handling all company resources as your own
   D. Prioritizing personal interests over the interests of the company

   Answer: D

   Prioritizing personal interests is not a fiduciary responsibility. As key agents of the organization, finance professionals have a fiduciary responsibility to their managers and to the owners or shareholders of the company. Fiduciary responsibility includes handling all company resources as your own, prioritizing the interests of the company over personal interests, protecting the company against unnecessary risks, pursuing opportunities for the company as they present themselves, acting with speed when necessary, and being responsive on important requests made by managers or owners.

aq.ei.fraud.0002_0720

5. Connect the three situations below with the relevant condition from the Fraud Triangle.

   Situation 1: The assistant controller is having problems paying her mortgage.

   Situation 2: The sales team is frustrated about the new sales commission policy.

   Situation 3: There isn't enough staff to have more than one person work with cash receipts and recording.

   A. Situation 1 is an Opportunity condition; Situation 2 is a Rationalization condition; and Situation 3 is a Financial Pressure condition.
   B. Situation 1 is a Financial Pressure condition; Situation 2 is a Rationalization condition; and Situation 3 is an Opportunity condition.
   C. Situation 1 is a Rationalization condition; Situation 2 is a Financial Pressure condition; and Situation 3 is an Opportunity condition.
   D. Situation 1 is a Financial Pressure condition; Situation 2 is an Opportunity condition; and Situation 3 is a Rationalization condition.

   Answer: B

   The assistant controller having problems paying her mortgage is an example of an individual in a bad financial situation that does not appear to be resolvable using a legal route, which is a financial pressure condition. The sales team is frustrated about the new sales commission policy is an example of finding reasons that make it okay to commit fraud, which is a rationalization condition. Not enough staff to have more than one person work with cash receipts and recording is an example of a situation that makes it easier to engage in fraud, which is an opportunity condition.

aq.eth.hr.0010_0720

6. Which statement best describes the benefits of establishing a whistle-blower hotline for an organization working to maintain an ethical culture and organization?

   A. By establishing a whistle-blower hotline, management can afford to replace ethics training and internal controls since the ethics hotline provides a system for reporting unethical behavior.
   B. A whistle-blower hotline that has employees report their names when they call is beneficial because it ensures management is aware of ongoing ethics issues.
   C. Setting up a whistle-blower hotline provides a means by which employees can report potential ethics issues and demonstrates strong management commitment to an ethical culture and values.
   D. Since only senior level management team members have to comply with most of the mandates or protocols included in a code of ethics, the impact of such a hotline is limited.

   Answer: C

   This is an excellent summary of the benefits of establishing an ethics hotline at an organization, which underscores management commitment to establishing an ethical culture.

aq.ps.prof.ethics.0006_0720

7. Scott Bestor is an accountant for Westfield Company. Early this year, Scott made a highly favorable projection of sales and profits over the next three years for Westfield's hot-selling computer PLEX. As a result of the projections Scott presented to senior management, the company decided to expand production in this area. This decision led to dislocations of some plant personnel who were reassigned to one of the company's newer plants in another state. However, no one was fired, and in fact the company expanded its workforce slightly. Unfortunately, Scott rechecked his projection computations a few months later and found that he had made an error that would have reduced his projections substantially. Luckily, sales of PLEX have exceeded projections so far, and management is satisfied with its decision. Scott, however, is not sure what to do. Should he confess his honest mistake and jeopardize his possible promotion? He suspects that no one will catch the error because PLEX sales have exceeded his original and corrected projections, and it appears that profits will materialize close to his original projections.

   If Scott says nothing about the error, which of the following standards of conduct as outlined in the *IMA Statement of Ethical Professional Practice* is most clearly being compromised?

   A. Credibility
   B. Confidentiality
   C. Integrity
   D. Fairness

   Answer: A

   This violates two characteristics related to Credibility; specifically, of (1) providing all relevant information that could reasonably be expected to influence an intended user's understanding of the reports, analyses, or recommendations and (2) communicate professional limitations or other constraints that would preclude responsible judgment or successful performance of an activity, both of which are found in the standards of conduct as outlined in the *IMA Statement of Ethical Professional Practice.*

aq.eth.org.0001_0720

8. Based on the IMA's Statement of Management Accounting *Value and Ethics: From Inception to Practice*, what is an ethical challenge that an organization faces as it increases in size and scope?

   A. Increases in sales put a strain on the supply chain that may result in shipment delays and stock-out incidents.
   B. As organizations expand and grow in size, there are usually not any issues related to ethics that occur. Instead, expansion and growth issues are primarily related to supply chain challenges.
   C. As a company grows, a key challenge is that ethical behaviors and codes of conduct must move from an informal "lead by example" model to a more formal and standardized framework.
   D. There are usually no significant ethical issues at growing organizations as long as the CEO or founder can maintain a hands-on approach with hiring and training initiatives.

   Answer: C

   This ethical challenge is a key hurdle that smaller businesses must overcome as they increase in scale and scope.

aq.eth.org.0003_0720

9. Which of the following is a way in which an organization can benefit from implementing and publicizing a code of conduct?

   A. Since stock prices always go up when an organization publicly embraces an ethical code of conduct, there is a clear financial benefit to adopting ethics.
   B. As the stock prices of an organization almost universally go down when ethics failures are publicized about an organization, there is always a positive and immediate economic benefit for ethics.

C. Adopting ethics procedures and policies will improve both the quality of employees attracted to the organization, and develop a culture where ethical behavior is rewarded as a matter of course.
D. By adopting a code of ethical behavior, establishing ethics training, and reinforcing ethical norms at the organization, the management team will never be held liable for unethical behavior conducted at the firm.

Answer: C

An organization that embraces and develops ethics will tend to attract ethical employees, and will reinforce ethical behavior throughout the firm and employee members.

aq.ps.prof.ethics.0005_1710

10. The president of your company has a reputation for using the company jet for personal trips, and for extending business trips in order to vacation with his family in exotic locations. This use of company resources frustrates many of the employees. Your good friend has a social media channel that she uses to promote corporate responsibility issues, and would love for you to provide some "real life" stories for her website. She assures you that she can adjust any information you give her to keep the report anonymous.

Assuming you talk with your friend about what is happening in your company with respect to the president, which of the following standards of conduct as outlined in the *IMA Statement of Ethical Professional Practice* are you violating?

A. Competence
B. Confidentiality
C. Integrity
D. Credibility

Answer: B

This violates the characteristic related to Confidentiality of keeping information confidential except when disclosure is authorized or legally required, found in the standards of conduct as outlined in the *IMA Statement of Ethical Professional Practice.*

aq.moral.phil.007_1907

11. "The equitable distribution of benefits and costs" describes which moral philosophy?

A. Virtue ethics
B. Justice
C. Teleology
D. Relativism

Answer: B

The equitable distribution of benefits and costs is the focus of justice. The underlying moral philosophy of justice can be approached from two fundamentally different perspectives. The Platonic concept of justice is that each individual or individual case is determined by individual rights, regardless of what happens in other cases. The Aristotelian concept is based on the idea that results are interrelated; that is, justice should be comparable or consistent with results in other cases.

aq.moral.phil.005_1907

12. "Identifying and committing to imperatives that should form a universal law that everyone in the world should be following" describes which moral philosophy?

   A. Utilitarianism
   B. Justice
   C. Deontology
   D. Relativism

   Answer: C

   This answer is correct. *Deont* is a Greek word meaning "to bind" or "duty." Principle-based behavior and choice is at the core of deontology. Rather than focusing on good character or desirable consequences, deontology ethics requires individuals to identify and commit to imperatives that they believe should form a universal law that everyone in the world should be following. Framed as a question, the deontological ethicist will ask herself, "Is this action something everyone should always do, no matter the cost?" If the answer is yes, then it is right; if no, it is wrong.

aq.org.eth.law.0002_0720

13. Which definition best describes the fundamental purpose of the Foreign Corrupt Practices Act?

   A. The FCPA focuses on reducing regulation to help ensure U.S. corporations succeed while doing business in overseas markets.
   B. As a regulatory body, the FCPA overseas enforcement of antifraud initiatives undertaken by U.S. corporations.
   C. The FCPA regulates the activities of foreign entities that are headquartered overseas, but are doing business in the United States.
   D. The FCPA regulates behaviors with regard to bribery efforts of foreign officials by U.S. citizens and firms.

   Answer: D

   This is the best definition of the FCPA, and includes a broad overview of what this regulation attempts to control with respect to U.S. individuals and firms doing business outside of the United States.

aq.moral.phil.004_0720

14. Which of the following is the definition of *teleology*?

   A. Focusing first on character and then on action is at the core of this moral philosophy, stressing the fact that character, whether good or bad, defines a person.
   B. A moral philosophy that argues if you can increase the overall happiness of the world in some way, then you should. Results are given all the ethical emphasis.
   C. Rather than focusing on good character or desirable consequences, this moral philosophy requires individuals to identify and commit to imperatives that they believe should form a universal law that everyone in the world should be following.
   D. A moral philosophy that is concerned with how choices will affect a particular desired moral outcome. Answering a few questions about the "end" or "purpose" of something can then determine whether the act (or choice) is good or bad.

   Answer: D

   Telos is a Greek word meaning "end" or "goal." Teleological ethics is concerned with how choices will affect a particular desired moral outcome. What is the "end" or "purpose" of an accountant (teleologically speaking)? To gain and protect the public trust? To serve the shareholders' interest? Answering these questions about results then determines whether the act (or choice) is good or bad.

aq.eth.org.001_0720

15. What impact does groupthink have on ethical behavior?

   A. In a groupthink situation, group members will disagree with the consensus of the group and express personal doubts and judgments.
   B. When a group of well-intentioned people is making irrational or unethical decisions, there is likely strong pressure in that group to be unified.
   C. In a groupthink situation, group members will brainstorm ideas on how the group can make the most ethical decisions.
   D. Groupthink has no effect on ethical behavior.

Answer: B

When a group of well-intentioned people is making irrational or unethical decisions, there is likely strong pressure in that group to be unified. This condition is described as groupthink. It results from the natural inclination to conform by avoiding dissent.

Appendixes

Content Specification Outlines

CMA® (Certified Management Accountant) Examinations

The Content Specification Outlines presented below represent the body of knowledge that will be covered on the CMA examinations. The outlines may be changed in the future when new subject matter becomes part of the common body of knowledge.

Candidates for the CMA designation are required to take and pass Parts 1 and 2.

Candidates are responsible for being informed about the most recent developments in the areas covered in the outlines. This includes understanding public pronouncements issued by accounting organizations as well as being up-to-date on recent developments reported in current accounting, financial, and business periodicals.

The Content Specification Outlines serve several purposes. The outlines are intended to:

- Establish the foundation from which each examination will be developed.
- Provide a basis for consistent coverage on each examination.
- Communicate to interested parties more detail as to the content of each examination part.
- Assist candidates in their preparation for each examination.
- Provide information to those who offer courses designed to aid candidates in preparing for the examinations.

Important additional information about the Content Specification Outlines and the examinations is listed below.

1. The coverage percentage given for each major topic within each examination part represents the relative weight given to that topic in an examination part. The number of questions presented in each major topic area approximates this percentage.
2. Each examination will sample from the subject areas contained within each major topic area to meet the relative weight specifications. No relative weights have been assigned to the subject areas within each major topic. No inference should be made from the order in which the subject areas are listed or from the number of subject areas as to the relative weight or importance of any of the subjects.
3. Each major topic within each examination part has been assigned a coverage level designating the depth and breadth of topic coverage, ranging from an introductory knowledge of a subject area (Level A) to a thorough understanding of and ability to apply the essentials of a subject area (Level C). Detailed explanations of the coverage levels and the skills expected of candidates are presented below.
4. The topics for Parts 1 and 2 have been selected to minimize the overlapping of subject areas among the examination parts. The topics within an examination part and the subject areas within the topics may be combined in individual questions.
5. With regard to U.S. federal income taxation issues, candidates will be expected to understand the impact of income taxes when reporting and analyzing financial results. In addition, the tax code provisions that impact decisions (e.g., depreciation, interest, etc.) will be tested.

6. Candidates for the CMA designation are assumed to have knowledge of the following: preparation of financial statements, business economics, time value of money concepts, statistics, and probability.

7. Parts 1 and 2 are four-hour exams and each contains 100 multiple-choice questions and two essay questions. Candidates will have three hours to complete the multiple-choice questions and one hour to complete the essay section. A small number of the multiple-choice questions on each exam are being validated for future use and will not count in the final score.

8. For the essay questions, both written and quantitative responses will be required. Candidates will be expected to present written answers that are responsive to the question asked, presented in a logical manner, and demonstrate an appropriate understanding of the subject matter.

In order to more clearly define the topical knowledge required by a candidate, varying levels of coverage for the treatment of major topics of the Content Specification Outlines have been identified and defined. The cognitive skills that a successful candidate should possess and that should be tested on the examinations can be defined as follows:

Knowledge: Ability to remember previously learned material such as specific facts, criteria, techniques, principles, and procedures (i.e., identify, define, list).

Comprehension: Ability to grasp and interpret the meaning of material (i.e., classify, explain, distinguish between).

Application: Ability to use learned material in new and concrete situations (i.e., demonstrate, predict, solve, modify, relate).

Analysis: Ability to break down material into its component parts so that its organizational structure can be understood; ability to recognize causal relationships, discriminate between behaviors, and identify elements that are relevant to the validation of a judgment (i.e., differentiate, estimate, order).

Synthesis: Ability to put parts together to form a new whole or proposed set of operations; ability to relate ideas and formulate hypotheses (i.e., combine, formulate, revise).

Evaluation: Ability to judge the value of material for a given purpose on the basis of consistency, logical accuracy, and comparison to standards; ability to appraise judgments involved in the selection of a course of action (i.e., criticize, justify, conclude).

The three levels of coverage can be defined as follows:

Level A: Requiring the skill levels of knowledge and comprehension.

Level B: Requiring the skill levels of knowledge, comprehension, application, and analysis.

Level C: Requiring all six skill levels of knowledge, comprehension, application, analysis, synthesis, and evaluation.

The levels of coverage as they apply to each of the major topics of the Content Specification Outlines are shown on the following pages with each topic listing. The levels represent the manner in which topic areas are to be treated and represent ceilings, i.e., a topic area designated as Level C may contain requirements at the "A," "B," or "C" level, but a topic designated as Level B will not contain requirements at the "C" level.

CMA Content Specification Overview

Part 1 - Financial Planning, Performance, and Analytics *(4 hours – 100 questions and 2 essay questions)*		
External Financial Reporting Decisions	15%	Level C
Planning, Budgeting, and Forecasting	20%	Level C
Performance Management	20%	Level C
Cost Management	15%	Level C
Internal Controls	15%	Level C
Technology and Analytics	15%	Level C

Part 2 - Strategic Financial Management *(4 hours – 100 questions and 2 essay questions)*		
Financial Statement Analysis	20%	Level C
Corporate Finance	20%	Level C
Decision Analysis	25%	Level C
Risk Management	10%	Level C
Investment Decisions	10%	Level C
Professional Ethics	15%	Level C

Part 2 - Strategic Financial Management

A. Financial Statement Analysis (20% - Levels A, B, and C)

1. *Basic financial statement analysis*

a. Common size financial statements

b. Common base year financial statements

2. *Financial ratios*

a. Liquidity

b. Leverage

c. Activity

d. Profitability

e. Market

3. *Profitability analysis*

a. Income measurement analysis

b. Revenue analysis

c. Cost of sales analysis

d. Expense analysis

e. Variation analysis

4. Special issues

a. Impact of foreign operations

b. Effects of changing prices and inflation

c. Impact of changes in accounting treatment

d. Accounting and economic concepts of value and income

e. Earnings quality

B. Corporate Finance (20% - Levels A, B, and C)

1. *Risk and return*

a. Calculating return

b. Types of risk

c. Relationship between risk and return

2. *Long-term financial management*

a. Term structure of interest rates

b. Types of financial instruments

c. Cost of capital

d. Valuation of financial instruments

3. *Raising capital*

a. Financial markets and regulation
b. Market efficiency
c. Financial institutions
d. Initial and secondary public offerings
e. Dividend policy and share repurchases
f. Lease financing

4. *Working capital management*

a. Working capital terminology
b. Cash management
c. Marketable securities management
d. Accounts receivable management
e. Inventory management
f. Types of short-term credit
g. Short-term credit management

5. *Corporate restructuring*

a. Mergers and acquisitions
b. Other forms of restructuring

6. *International finance*

a. Fixed, flexible, and floating exchange rates
b. Managing transaction exposure
c. Financing international trade

C. Decision Analysis (25% - Levels A, B, and C)

1. *Cost/volume/profit analysis*

a. Breakeven analysis
b. Profit performance and alternative operating levels
c. Analysis of multiple products

2. *Marginal analysis*

a. Sunk costs, opportunity costs, and other related concepts
b. Marginal costs and marginal revenue
c. Special orders and pricing
d. Make vs. buy
e. Sell or process further
f. Add or drop a segment
g. Capacity considerations

3. *Pricing*

a. Pricing methodologies
b. Target costing
c. Elasticity of demand
d. Product life-cycle considerations
e. Market structure considerations

D. Risk Management (10% - Levels A, B, and C)

1. *Enterprise risk*

a. Types of risk
b. Risk identification and assessment
c. Risk mitigation strategies
d. Managing risk

E. Investment Decisions (10% - Levels A, B, and C)

1. *Capital budgeting process*

a. Stages of capital budgeting
b. Incremental cash flows
c. Income tax considerations
d. Evaluating uncertainty

2. *Capital investment analysis methods*

a. Net present value
b. Internal rate of return
c. Payback
d. Comparison of investment analysis methods

F. Professional Ethics (15% - Levels A, B, and C)

1. *Business ethic*

a. Moral philosophies and values
b. Ethical decision making

2. *Ethical considerations for management accounting and financial management professionals*

a. IMA's Statement of Ethical Professional Practice
b. Fraud triangle
c. Evaluation and resolution of ethical issues

3. *Ethical considerations for the organization*

a. Organizational factors and ethical culture

b. IMA's Statement on Management Accounting, "Values and Ethics: From Inception to Practice"

c. Ethical leadership

d. Legal compliance

e. Responsibility for ethical conduct

f. Sustainability and social responsibility

Learning Outcome Statements

Part 2 – Strategic Financial Management

Section A. Financial Statement Analysis (20% - Levels A, B, and C)

Part 2 – Section A.1. Basic financial statement analysis

The candidate should be able to:

a. for the balance sheet and income statement, prepare and analyze common-size financial statements; i.e., calculate percentage of assets and sales, respectively; also called vertical analysis

b. for the balance sheet and income statement, prepare a comparative financial statement horizontal analysis; i.e., calculate trend year over year for every item on the financial statement compared to a base year

c. calculate the growth rate of individual line items on the balance sheet and income statement

Part 2 – Section A.2. Financial ratios

The candidate should be able to:

Liquidity

a. calculate and interpret the current ratio, the quick (acid-test) ratio, the cash ratio, the cash flow ratio, and the net working capital ratio

b. explain how changes in one or more of the elements of current assets, current liabilities, and/or unit sales can change the liquidity ratios and calculate that impact

c. demonstrate an understanding of the liquidity of current liabilities

Leverage

d. define solvency

e. define operating leverage and financial leverage

f. calculate degree of operating leverage and degree of financial leverage

g. demonstrate an understanding of the effect on the capital structure and solvency of a company with a change in the composition of debt vs. equity by calculating leverage ratios

h. calculate and interpret the financial leverage ratio, and determine the effect of a given change in capital structure on this ratio

i. calculate and interpret the following ratios: debt-to-equity, long-term debt-to-equity, and debt-to- total assets

j. define, calculate, and interpret the following ratios: fixed charge coverage (earnings to fixed charges), interest coverage (times interest earned), and cash flow to fixed charges

k. discuss how capital structure decisions affect the risk profile of a firm

Activity

l. calculate and interpret accounts receivable turnover, inventory turnover, and accounts payable turnover

m. calculate and interpret days sales outstanding in receivables, days sales in inventory, and days purchases in accounts payable

n. define and calculate the operating cycle and the cash cycle of a firm

o. calculate and interpret total assets turnover and fixed asset turnover

Profitability

p. calculate and interpret gross profit margin percentage, operating profit margin percentage, net profit margin percentage, and earnings before interest, taxes, depreciation, and amortization (EBITDA) margin percentage

q. calculate and interpret return on assets (ROA) and return on equity (ROE)

Market

r. calculate and interpret the market/book ratio and the price/earnings ratio

s. calculate and interpret book value per share

t. identify and explain the limitations of book value per share

u. calculate and interpret basic and diluted earnings per share

v. calculate and interpret earnings yield, dividend yield, dividend payout ratio, and shareholder return

General

w. identify the limitations of ratio analysis

x. demonstrate a familiarity with the sources of financial information about public companies and industry ratio averages

y. evaluate the financial strength and performance of an entity based on multiple ratios

Part 2 – Section A.3. Profitability analysis

The candidate should be able to:

a. demonstrate an understanding of the factors that contribute to inconsistent definitions of "equity," "assets," and "return" when using ROA and ROE

b. determine the effect on return on total assets of a change in one or more elements of the financial statements

c. identify factors to be considered in measuring income, including estimates, accounting methods, disclosure incentives, and the different needs of users

d. explain the importance of the source, stability, and trend of sales and revenue

e. demonstrate an understanding of the relationship between revenue and receivables and revenue and inventory

f. determine and analyze the effect on revenue of changes in revenue recognition and measurement methods

g. analyze cost of sales by calculating and interpreting the gross profit margin

h. distinguish between gross profit margin, operating profit margin, and net profit margin and analyze the effects of changes in the components of each

i. define and perform a variation analysis (percentage change over time)

j. calculate and interpret sustainable equity growth

Part 2 – Section A.4. Special issues

The candidate should be able to:

a. demonstrate an understanding of the impact of foreign exchange fluctuations
   i. identify and explain issues in the accounting for foreign operations (e.g., historical vs. current rate and the treatment of translation gains and losses)
   ii. define functional currency
   iii. calculate the financial ratio impact of a change in exchange rates
   iv. discuss the possible impact on management and investor behavior of volatility in reported earnings
b. demonstrate an understanding of the impact of inflation on financial ratios and the reliability of financial ratios
c. describe how to adjust financial statements for changes in accounting treatments (principles, estimates, and errors) and how these adjustments impact financial ratios
d. distinguish between book value and market value; and distinguish between accounting profit and economic profit
e. identify the determinants and indicators of earnings quality, and explain why they are important

Section B. Corporate Finance (20% - Levels A, B, and C)

Part 2 – Section B.1. Risk and return

The candidate should be able to:

a. calculate rates of return
b. identify and demonstrate an understanding of systematic (market) risk and unsystematic (company) risk
c. identify and demonstrate an understanding of credit risk, foreign exchange risk, interest rate risk, market risk, industry risk, and political risk
d. demonstrate an understanding of the relationship between risk and return
e. distinguish between individual security risk and portfolio risk
f. demonstrate an understanding of diversification
g. define beta and explain how a change in beta impacts a security's price
h. demonstrate an understanding of the Capital Asset Pricing Model (CAPM) and calculate the expected risk-adjusted returns using CAPM

Part 2 – Section B.2 Long-term financial management

The candidate should be able to:

a. describe the term structure of interest rates, and explain why it changes over time
b. define and identify the characteristics of common stock and preferred stock
c. identify and describe the basic features of a bond such as maturity, par value, coupon rate, provisions for redeeming, conversion provisions, covenants, options granted to the issuer or investor, indentures, and restrictions
d. identify and evaluate debt issuance or refinancing strategies

e. value bonds, common stock, and preferred stock using discounted cash flow methods
f. demonstrate an understanding of duration as a measure of bond interest rate sensitivity
g. explain how income taxes impact financing decisions
h. define and demonstrate an understanding of derivatives and their uses
i. identify and describe the basic features of futures and forwards
j. distinguish a long position from a short position
k. define options and distinguish between a call and a put by identifying the characteristics of each
l. define strike price (exercise price), option premium, and intrinsic value
m. demonstrate an understanding of the interrelationship of the variables that comprise the value of an option; e.g., relationship between exercise price and strike price, and value of a call
n. define interest rate and foreign currency swaps
o. define and identify characteristics of other sources of long-term financing, such as leases, convertible securities, and warrants
p. demonstrate an understanding of the relationship among inflation, interest rates, and the prices of financial instruments
q. define the cost of capital and demonstrate an understanding of its applications in capital structure decisions
r. determine the weighted average cost of capital and the cost of its individual components
s. calculate the marginal cost of capital
t. explain the importance of using marginal cost as opposed to historical cost
u. demonstrate an understanding of the use of the cost of capital in capital investment decisions
v. demonstrate an understanding of how income taxes impact capital structure and capital investment decisions
w. use the constant growth dividend discount model to value stock and demonstrate an understanding of the two-stage dividend discount model
x. demonstrate an understanding of relative or comparable valuation methods, such as price/earnings (P/E) ratios, market/book ratios, and price/sales ratios

Part 2 – Section B.3. Raising capital

The candidate should be able to:

a. identify the characteristics of the different types of financial markets and exchanges
b. demonstrate an understanding of the concept of market efficiency, including the strong form, semi-strong form, and weak form of market efficiency
c. describe the role of the credit rating agencies
d. demonstrate an understanding of the roles of investment banks, including underwriting, advice, and trading
e. define initial public offerings (IPOs)
f. define subsequent/secondary offerings
g. describe lease financing, explain its benefits and disadvantages, and calculate the net advantage to leasing using discounted cash flow concepts

h. define the different types of dividends, including cash dividends, stock dividends, and stock splits

i. identify and discuss the factors that influence the dividend policy of a firm

j. demonstrate an understanding of the dividend payment process for both common and preferred stock

k. define share repurchase and explain why a firm would repurchase its stock

l. define insider trading and explain why it is illegal

Part 2 – Section B.4. Working capital management

The candidate should be able to:

Working capital

a. define working capital and identify its components

b. calculate net working capital

c. explain the benefit of short-term financial forecasts in the management of working capital

Cash

d. identify and describe factors influencing the levels of cash

e. identify and explain the three motives for holding cash

f. prepare forecasts of future cash flows

g. identify methods of speeding up cash collections

h. calculate the net benefit of a lockbox system

i. define concentration banking

j. demonstrate an understanding of compensating balances

k. identify methods of slowing down disbursements

l. demonstrate an understanding of disbursement float and overdraft systems

Marketable securities

m. identify and describe reasons for holding marketable securities

n. define the different types of marketable securities, including money market instruments, T-bills, treasury notes, treasury bonds, repurchase agreements, federal agency securities, bankers' acceptances, commercial paper, negotiable CDs, Eurodollar CDs, and other marketable securities

o. evaluate the trade-offs among the variables in marketable security selections, including safety, marketability/liquidity, yield, maturity, and taxability

p. demonstrate an understanding of the risk and return trade-off

Accounts receivable

q. identify the factors influencing the level of receivables

r. demonstrate an understanding of the impact of changes in credit terms or collection policies on accounts receivable, working capital, and sales volume

s. define default risk

t. identify and explain the factors involved in determining an optimal credit policy

Inventory

u. define lead time and safety stock; identify reasons for carrying inventory and the factors influencing its level

v. identify and calculate the costs related to inventory, including carrying costs, ordering costs, and shortage (stockout) costs

w. explain how a just-in-time (JIT) inventory management system helps manage inventory

x. identify the interaction between high inventory turnover and high gross margin (calculation not required)

y. demonstrate an understanding of economic order quantity (EOQ) and how a change in one variable would affect the EOQ (calculation not required)

Short-term credit and working capital cost management

z. demonstrate an understanding of how risk affects a firm's approach to its current asset financing policy (aggressive, conservative, etc.)

aa. identify and describe the different types of short-term credit, including trade credit, short-term bank loans, commercial paper, lines of credit, and bankers' acceptances

bb. estimate the annual cost and effective annual interest rate of not taking a cash discount

cc. calculate the effective annual interest rate of a bank loan with a compensating balance requirement and/or a commitment fee

dd. demonstrate an understanding of factoring accounts receivable and calculate the cost of factoring

ee. explain the maturity matching or hedging approach to financing

ff. demonstrate an understanding of the factors involved in managing the costs of working capital

General

gg. recommend a strategy for managing current assets that would fulfill a given objective

Part 2 – Section B.5. Corporate restructuring

The candidate should be able to:

a. demonstrate an understanding of the following:

   i. mergers and acquisitions, including horizontal, vertical, and conglomerate

   ii. leveraged buyouts

b. identify defenses against takeovers (e.g., golden parachute, leveraged recapitalization, poison pill (shareholders' rights plan), staggered board of directors, fair price, voting rights plan, white knight)

c. identify and describe divestiture concepts such as spin-offs, split-ups, equity carve-outs, and tracking stock

d. evaluate key factors in a company's financial situation and determine if a restructuring would be beneficial to the shareholders

e. identify possible synergies in targeted mergers and acquisitions

f. value a business, a business segment, and a business combination using discounted cash flow method

g. evaluate a proposed business combination and make a recommendation based on both quantitative and qualitative considerations

Part 2 – Section B.6. International finance

The candidate should be able to:

a. demonstrate an understanding of foreign currencies and how foreign currency affects the prices of goods and services

b. identify the variables that affect exchange rates

c. calculate whether a currency has depreciated or appreciated against another currency over time, and evaluate the impact of the change

d. demonstrate how currency futures, currency swaps, and currency options can be used to manage exchange rate risk

e. calculate the net profit/loss of cross-border transactions, and evaluate the impact of this net profit/loss

f. recommend methods of managing exchange rate risk and calculate the net profit/loss of your strategy

g. identify and explain the benefits of international diversification

h. identify and explain common trade financing methods, including cross-border factoring, letters of credit, banker's acceptances, forfaiting, and countertrade

Section C. Decision Analysis (25% - Levels A, B, and C)

Part 2 – Section C.1. Cost/volume/profit analysis

The candidate should be able to:

a. demonstrate an understanding of how cost/volume/profit (CVP) analysis (breakeven analysis) is used to examine the behavior of total revenues, total costs, and operating income as changes occur in output levels, selling prices, variable costs per unit, or fixed costs

b. calculate operating income at different operating levels

c. differentiate between costs that are fixed and costs that are variable with respect to levels of output

d. explain why the classification of fixed vs. variable costs is affected by the time frame being considered

e. calculate contribution margin per unit and total contribution margin

f. calculate the breakeven point in units and dollar sales to achieve targeted operating income or targeted net income

g. demonstrate an understanding of how changes in unit sales mix affect operating income in multiple-product situations

h. calculate multiple-product breakeven points given percentage share of sales and explain why there is no unique breakeven point in multiple-product situations

i. define, calculate, and interpret the margin of safety and the margin of safety ratio

j. explain how sensitivity analysis can be used in CVP analysis when there is uncertainty about sales

k. analyze and recommend a course of action using CVP analysis

l. demonstrate an understanding of the impact of income taxes on CVP analysis

Part 2 – Section C.2. Marginal analysis

The candidate should be able to:

a. identify and define relevant costs (incremental, marginal, or differential costs), sunk costs, avoidable costs, explicit and implicit costs, split-off point, joint production costs, separable processing costs, and relevant revenues

b. explain why sunk costs are not relevant in the decision-making process

c. demonstrate an understanding of and calculate opportunity costs

d. calculate relevant costs given a numerical scenario

e. define and calculate marginal cost and marginal revenue

f. identify and calculate total cost, average fixed cost, average variable cost, and average total cost

g. demonstrate proficiency in the use of marginal analysis for decisions such as (i) introducing a new product or changing output levels of existing products; (ii) accepting or rejecting special orders; (iii) making or buying a product or service; (iv) selling a product or performing additional processes and selling a more value-added product; and (v) adding or dropping a segment

h. calculate the effect on operating income of a decision to accept or reject a special order when there is idle capacity and the order has no long-run implications

i. identify and describe qualitative factors in make-or-buy decisions, such as product quality and dependability of suppliers

j. calculate the effect on operating income of a make-or-buy decision

k. calculate the effects on operating income of a decision to sell or process further or to drop or add a segment

l. identify the effects of changes in capacity on production decisions

m. demonstrate an understanding of the impact of income taxes on marginal analysis

n. recommend a course of action using marginal analysis

Part 2 – Section C.3. Pricing

The candidate should be able to:

a. identify different pricing methodologies, including market comparables, cost-based, and value-based approaches

b. differentiate between a cost-based approach (cost-plus pricing, mark-up pricing) and a market-based approach to setting prices

c. calculate selling price using a cost-based approach

d. demonstrate an understanding of how the pricing of a product or service is affected by the demand for and supply of the product or service, as well as the market structure within which it operates

e. demonstrate an understanding of the impact of cartels on pricing

f. demonstrate an understanding of the short-run equilibrium price for the firm in (i) pure competition; (ii) monopolistic competition; (iii) oligopoly; and (iv) monopoly using the concepts of marginal revenue and marginal cost

g. identify techniques used to set prices based on understanding customers' perceptions of value and competitors' technologies, products, and costs

h. define and demonstrate an understanding of target pricing and target costing and identify the main steps in developing target prices and target costs

i. define value engineering

j. calculate the target operating income per unit and target cost per unit

k. define and distinguish between a value-added cost and a nonvalue-added cost

l. define the pricing technique of cost plus target rate of return

m. calculate the price elasticity of demand using the midpoint formula

n. define and explain elastic and inelastic demand

o. estimate total revenue given changes in prices and demand as well as elasticity

p. discuss how pricing decisions can differ in the short run and in the long run

q. define product life cycle; identify and explain the four stages of the product life cycle; and explain why pricing decisions might differ over the life of a product

r. evaluate and recommend pricing strategies under specific market conditions

Section D. Risk Management (10% - Levels A, B, and C)

Part 2 – Section D.1. Enterprise risk

The candidate should be able to:

a. identify and explain the different types of risk, including business risk, hazard risks, financial risks, operational risks, and strategic risks

b. demonstrate an understanding of operational risk

c. define legal risk, compliance risk, and political risk

d. demonstrate an understanding of how volatility and time impact risk

e. define the concept of capital adequacy; i.e., solvency, liquidity, reserves, sufficient capital, etc.

f. explain the use of probabilities in determining exposure to risk and calculate expected loss given a set of probabilities

g. define the concepts of unexpected loss and maximum possible loss (extreme or catastrophic loss)

h. identify strategies for risk response (or treatment), including actions to avoid, retain, reduce (mitigate), transfer (share), and exploit (accept) risks

i. define risk transfer (e.g., purchasing insurance, issuing debt)

j. demonstrate an understanding of the concept of residual risk and distinguish it from inherent risk

k. identify and explain the benefits of risk management

l. identify and describe the key steps in the risk management process

m. explain how attitude toward risk might affect the management of risk

n. demonstrate a general understanding of the use of liability/hazard insurance to mitigate risk (detailed knowledge not required)

o. identify methods of managing operational risk

p. identify and explain financial risk management methods

q. identify and explain qualitative risk assessment tools including risk identification, risk ranking, and risk maps

r. identify and explain quantitative risk assessment tools including cash flow at risk, earnings at risk, earnings distributions, and earnings per share (EPS) distributions

s. identify and explain Value at Risk (VaR) (calculations not required)

t. define enterprise risk management (ERM) and identify and describe key objectives, components, and benefits of an ERM program

u. identify event identification techniques and provide examples of event identification within the context of an ERM approach

v. explain how ERM practices are integrated with corporate governance, risk analytics, portfolio management, performance management, and internal control practices

w. evaluate scenarios and recommend risk mitigation strategies

x. prepare a cost-benefit analysis and demonstrate an understanding of its uses in risk assessment and decision making

y. demonstrate an understanding of the COSO Enterprise Risk Management - Integrated Framework (2017)

Section E. Investment Decisions (10% - Levels A, B, and C)

Part 2 – Section E.1. Capital budgeting process

The candidate should be able to:

a. define capital budgeting and identify the steps or stages undertaken in developing and implementing a capital budget for a project

b. identify and calculate the relevant cash flows of a capital investment project on both a pretax and after-tax basis

c. demonstrate an understanding of how income taxes affect cash flows

d. distinguish between cash flows and accounting profits and discuss the relevance to capital budgeting of incremental cash flow, sunk cost, and opportunity cost

e. explain the importance of changes in net working capital in capital budgeting

f. discuss how the effects of inflation are reflected in capital budgeting analysis

g. define hurdle rate

h. identify alternative approaches to dealing with risk in capital budgeting

i. distinguish among sensitivity analysis, scenario analysis, and Monte Carlo simulation as risk analysis techniques

j. explain why a rate specifically adjusted for risk should be used when project cash flows are more or less risky than is normal for a firm

k. explain how the value of a capital investment is increased if consideration is given to the possibility of adding on, speeding up, slowing up, or discontinuing early

l. demonstrate an understanding of real options, including the options to abandon, delay, expand, and scale back (calculations not required)

m. identify and discuss qualitative considerations involved in the capital budgeting decision

n. describe the role of the post-audit in the capital budgeting process

Part 2 – Section E.2. Capital investment analysis methods

The candidate should be able to:

a. demonstrate an understanding of the two main discounted cash flow (DCF) methods, net present value (NPV) and internal rate of return (IRR)

b. calculate NPV and IRR

c. demonstrate an understanding of the decision criteria used in NPV and IRR analyses to determine acceptable projects

d. compare NPV and IRR focusing on the relative advantages and disadvantages of each method, particularly with respect to independent vs. mutually exclusive projects and the "multiple IRR problem"

e. explain why NPV and IRR methods can produce conflicting rankings for capital projects if not applied properly

f. identify assumptions of NPV and IRR

g. evaluate and recommend project investments on the basis of DCF analysis

h. demonstrate an understanding of the payback and discounted payback methods

i. identify the advantages and disadvantages of the payback and discounted payback methods

j. calculate payback periods and discounted payback periods

Section F. Professional Ethics (15% - Levels A, B, and C)

Ethics may be tested in conjunction with any topic area.

Part 2 – Section F.1. Business ethics

The candidate should be able to:

a. define business ethics

b. analyze the concepts of morality and virtue

c. define moral philosophy

d. demonstrate an understanding of the following moral philosophies and concepts used in making business decisions: teleology, utilitarianism, deontology, relativism, virtue ethics, and justice

e. define the concepts of fairness, integrity, due diligence, and fiduciary responsibility, and how they impact ethical decision making

Part 2 – Section F.2. Ethical considerations for management accounting and financial management professionals

Using the standards outlined in IMA's Statement of Ethical Professional Practice, the candidate should be able to:

a. identify and describe the four overarching ethical principles and the four standards
b. evaluate a given business situation for its ethical implications
c. identify and describe relevant standards that may have been violated in a given business situation and explain why the specific standards are applicable
d. recommend a course of action for management accountants to take when confronted with an ethical dilemma in the business environment
e. evaluate and propose resolutions for ethical issues such as fraudulent reporting, or improper manipulation of forecasts, analyses, results, and budgets

Using the fraud triangle model, the candidate should be able to:

f. identify the three components of the triangle
g. use the model to explain how a management accounting and financial management professional can identify and manage the risk of fraud

Part 2 – Section F.3. Ethical considerations for the organization

The candidate should be able to:

a. discuss the issues organizations face in applying their values and ethical standards internationally
b. demonstrate an understanding of the relationship between ethics and internal controls
c. define corporate culture and demonstrate an understanding of the role corporate culture plays in ethical decision making
d. demonstrate an understanding of the importance of a code of conduct and how it contributes to an organization's ethical culture
e. demonstrate an understanding of the ways ethical values benefit an organization
f. analyze the impact of groupthink on ethical behavior
g. discuss how diversity of thought can lead to good ethical decisions
h. apply relevant provisions of IMA's Statement on Management Accounting, "Values and Ethics: From Inception to Practice," to a business situation
i. demonstrate an understanding of the role of "leadership by example" or "tone at the top" in determining an organization's ethical environment
j. define ethical leadership and identify and explain the traits of ethical leaders
k. explain the importance of human capital to an organization in creating a climate where "doing the right thing" is expected (e.g., hiring the right people, providing them with training, and practicing consistent values-based leadership)
l. explain the importance of an organization's core values and how they promote ethical behavior and ethical decision making
m. discuss the importance of employee training to maintaining an ethical organizational culture
n. explain the importance of a whistleblowing framework to maintain an ethical organizational culture
o. demonstrate an understanding of the differences between ethical and legal behavior

p. identify the purpose of anti-bribery laws, such as the U.S. Foreign Corrupt Practices Act and the U.K. Bribery Act

q. define facilitating payments and why these payments create both ethical and legal issues

r. discuss corporate responsibility for ethical conduct

s. define and demonstrate an understanding of the major issues of sustainability and social responsibility

t. identify and define the four levels of social responsibility: economic, legal, ethical, and philanthropic

u. identify and define the three conceptual spheres of sustainability: economic, environmental, and social

Time-Value of Money Tables

Present Value of $1

n	1%	2%	3%	4%	5%	6%	8%	10%	12%
1	0.99010	0.98039	0.97087	0.96154	0.95238	0.94340	0.92593	0.90909	0.89286
2	0.98030	0.96117	0.94260	0.92456	0.90703	0.89000	0.85734	0.82645	0.79719
3	0.97059	0.94232	0.91514	0.88900	0.86384	0.83962	0.79383	0.75131	0.71178
4	0.96098	0.92385	0.88849	0.85480	0.82270	0.79209	0.73503	0.68301	0.63552
5	0.95147	0.90573	0.86261	0.82193	0.78353	0.74726	0.68058	0.62092	0.56743
6	0.94205	0.88797	0.83748	0.79031	0.74622	0.70496	0.63017	0.56447	0.50663
7	0.93272	0.87056	0.81309	0.75992	0.71068	0.66506	0.58349	0.51316	0.45235
8	0.92348	0.85349	0.78941	0.73069	0.67684	0.62741	0.54027	0.46651	0.40388
9	0.91434	0.83676	0.76642	0.70259	0.64461	0.59190	0.50025	0.42410	0.36061
10	0.90529	0.82035	0.74409	0.67556	0.61391	0.55839	0.46319	0.38554	0.32197
11	0.89632	0.80426	0.72242	0.64958	0.58468	0.52679	0.42888	0.35049	0.28748
12	0.88745	0.78849	0.70138	0.62460	0.55684	0.49697	0.39711	0.31863	0.25668
13	0.87866	0.77303	0.68095	0.60057	0.53032	0.46884	0.36770	0.28966	0.22917
14	0.86996	0.75788	0.66112	0.57748	0.50507	0.44230	0.34046	0.26333	0.20462
15	0.86135	0.74301	0.64186	0.55526	0.48102	0.41727	0.31524	0.23939	0.18270
16	0.85282	0.72845	0.62317	0.53391	0.45811	0.39365	0.29189	0.21763	0.16312
17	0.84438	0.71416	0.60502	0.51337	0.43630	0.37136	0.27027	0.19784	0.14564
18	0.83602	0.70016	0.58739	0.49363	0.41552	0.35034	0.25025	0.17986	0.13004
19	0.82774	0.68643	0.57029	0.47464	0.39573	0.33051	0.23171	0.16351	0.11611
20	0.81954	0.67297	0.5537	0.45639	0.37689	0.31180	0.21455	0.14864	0.10367

Present Value of Ordinary Annuity

n	1%	2%	3%	4%	5%	6%	8%	10%	12%
1	0.99010	0.98039	0.97087	0.96154	0.95238	0.94340	0.92593	0.90909	0.89286
2	1.97040	1.94156	1.91347	1.88609	1.85941	1.83339	1.78326	1.73554	1.69005
3	2.94099	2.88388	2.82861	2.77509	2.72325	2.67301	2.50771	2.48685	2.40183
4	3.90197	3.80773	3.71710	3.62990	3.546595	3.46511	3.31213	3.16987	3.03735
5	4.85343	4.71346	4.57971	4.45182	4.32948	4.21236	3.99271	3.79079	3.60478
6	5.79548	5.60143	5.41719	5.24214	5.07569	4.91732	4.62288	4.35526	4.11141
7	6.72819	6.47199	6.23028	6.00205	5.78637	5.58238	5.20637	4.86842	4.56376
8	7.65168	7.32548	7.01969	6.73274	6.46321	6.20979	5.74664	5.33493	4.96764
9	8.56602	8.16224	7.78611	7.43533	7.10782	6.80169	6.24689	5.75902	5.32825
10	9.47130	8.98259	8.53020	8.11090	7.72173	7.36009	6.71008	6.14457	5.65022
11	10.36763	9.78685	9.25262	8.76048	8.30641	7.88687	7.13896	6.49506	5.93770
12	11.25508	10.57534	9.95400	9.38507	8.86325	8.38384	7.53608	6.81369	6.19437
13	12.13374	11.34837	10.63496	9.98565	9.39357	8.85268	7.90378	7.10336	6.42355
14	13.00370	12.10625	11.29607	10.56312	9.89864	9.29498	8.24424	7.36669	6.62817
15	13.86505	12.84926	11.93794	11.11839	10.37966	9.71225	8.55948	7.60608	6.81086
16	14.71787	13.57771	12.56110	11.65230	10.83777	10.10590	8.85137	7.82371	6.97399
17	15.56225	14.29187	13.16612	12.16567	11.27407	10.47726	9.12164	8.02155	7.11963
18	16.39827	14.99203	13.75351	12.65930	11.68959	10.82760	9.37189	8.20141	7.24967
19	17.22601	15.67846	14.32380	13.13394	12.08532	11.15812	9.60360	8.36492	7.36578
20	18.04555	16.35143	14.87747	13.59033	12.46221	11.46992	9.81815	8.51356	7.46944

Present Value of Annuity Due

n	1%	2%	3%	4%	5%	6%	8%	10%	12%
1	1.00000	1.00000	1.00000	1.00000	1.00000	1.00000	1.00000	1.00000	1.00000
2	1.99010	1.98039	1.97087	1.96154	1.95238	1.94340	1.92593	1.90909	1.89286
3	2.97040	2.94156	2.91347	2.88609	2.85941	2.83339	2.78326	2.73554	2.69005
4	3.94099	3.88388	3.82861	3.77509	3.72325	3.67301	3.57710	3.48685	3.40183
5	4.90197	4.80773	4.71710	4.62990	4.54595	4.46511	4.31321	4.16987	4.03735
6	5.85343	5.71346	5.57971	5.45182	5.32948	5.21236	4.99271	4.79079	4.60478
7	6.79548	6.60143	6.41719	6.24214	6.07569	5.91732	5.62288	5.35526	5.11141
8	7.72819	7.47199	7.23028	7.00205	6.78637	6.58238	6.20637	5.86842	5.56376
9	8.65168	8.32548	8.01969	7.73274	7.46321	7.20979	6.74664	6.33493	5.96764
10	9.56602	9.16224	8.78611	8.43533	8.10782	7.80169	7.24689	6.75902	6.32825
11	10.47130	9.98259	9.53020	9.11090	8.72173	8.36009	7.71008	7.14457	6.65022
12	11.36763	10.78685	10.25262	9.76048	9.30641	8.88687	8.13896	7.49506	6.93770
13	12.25508	11.57534	10.95400	10.38507	9.86325	9.38384	8.53608	7.81369	7.19437
14	13.13374	12.34837	11.63496	10.98565	10.39357	9.85268	8.90378	8.10336	7.42355
15	14.00370	13.10625	12.29607	11.56312	10.89864	10.29498	9.24424	8.36669	7.62817
16	14.86505	13.84926	12.93794	12.11839	11.37966	10.71225	9.55948	8.60608	7.81086
17	15.71787	14.57771	13.56110	12.65230	11.83777	11.10590	9.85137	8.82371	7.97399
18	16.56225	15.29187	14.16612	13.16567	12.27407	11.47726	10.12164	9.02155	8.11963
19	17.39827	15.99203	14.75351	13.65930	12.68959	11.82760	10.37189	9.20141	8.24967
20	18.22601	16.67846	15.32380	14.13394	13.08532	12.15812	10.60360	9.36492	8.36578

Future Value of $1

period	1%	2%	3%	4%	5%	6%	8%	10%	12%
1	1.01000	1.02000	1.03000	1.04000	1.05000	1.06000	1.08000	1.10000	1.12000
2	1.02010	1.0400	1.06090	1.08160	1.10250	1.12360	1.16640	1.21000	1.24550
3	1.03030	1.06121	1.09273	1.12486	1.15763	1.19102	1.25971	1.33100	1.40493
4	1.04060	1.08243	1.12551	1.16986	1.21551	1.26248	1.36049	1.46410	1.57352
5	1.05101	1.10408	1.15927	1.21665	1.27628	1.33823	1.46933	1.61051	1.76234
6	1.06152	1.12616	1.19405	1.26532	1.34010	1.41852	1.58687	1.77156	1.97382
7	1.07214	1.14869	1.22987	1.31593	1.40710	1.50363	1.71382	1.94872	2.21068
8	1.08286	1.17166	1.26677	1.36857	1.47746	1.59385	1.85093	2.14359	2.47596
9	1.09369	1.19509	1.30477	1.42331	1.55133	1.68948	1.99900	2.35795	2.77308
10	1.10462	1.21899	1.34392	1.48024	1.62889	1.79085	2.15892	2.59374	3.10585
11	1.11567	1.24337	1.38423	1.53945	1.71034	1.89830	2.33164	2.85312	3.47855
12	1.12683	1.26824	1.42576	1.60103	1.79586	2.01220	2.51817	3.13843	3.89598
13	1.13809	1.29361	1.46853	1.66507	1.88565	2.13293	2.71962	3.45227	4.36349
14	1.14947	1.31948	1.51259	1.73168	1.97993	2.26090	2.93719	3.79750	4.88711
15	1.16097	1.34587	1.55797	1.80094	2.07893	2.39656	3.17217	4.17725	5.47357
16	1.17258	1.37279	1.60471	1.87298	2.18287	2.54035	3.42594	4.59497	6.13039
17	1.18430	1.40024	1.65285	1.94790	2.29202	2.69277	3.70002	5.05447	6.86604
18	1.19615	1.42825	1.70243	2.02582	2.40662	2.95434	3.99602	5.55992	7.68997
19	1.20811	1.45681	1.75351	2.10685	2.52695	3.02560	4.31570	6.11591	8.61276
20	1.22019	1.48595	1.80611	2.19112	2.65330	3.20714	4.66096	6.72750	9.64629

Future Value of Ordinary Annuity

n	1%	2%	3%	4%	5%	6%	8%	10%	12%
1	1.00000	1.00000	1.00000	1.00000	1.00000	1.00000	1.00000	1.00000	1.00000
2	2.01000	2.02000	2.03000	2.04000	2.05000	2.06000	2.08000	2.10000	2.12000
3	3.03010	3.06040	3.09090	3.12160	3.15250	3.18360	3.24640	3.31000	3.37440
4	4.06040	4.12161	4.18363	4.24646	4.31013	4.37462	4.50611	4.64100	4.77933
5	5.10101	5.20404	5.30914	5.41632	5.52563	5.63709	5.86660	6.10510	6.35285
6	6.15202	6.30812	6.46841	6.63298	6.80191	6.97532	7.33593	7.71561	8.11519
7	7.21354	7.43428	7.66246	7.89829	8.14201	8.39384	8.92280	9.48717	10.08901
8	8.28567	8.58297	8.89234	9.21423	9.54911	9.89747	10.63663	11.43589	12.29969
9	9.36853	9.75463	10.15911	10.58280	11.02656	11.49132	12.48756	13.57948	14.77566
10	10.46221	10.94972	11.46388	12.00611	12.57789	13.18079	14.48656	15.93742	17.54874
11	11.56683	12.16872	12.80780	13.48635	14.20679	14.97164	16.64549	18.53117	20.65458
12	12.68250	13.41209	14.19203	15.02581	15.91713	16.86994	18.97713	21.38428	24.13313
13	13.80933	14.68033	15.61779	16.62684	17.71298	18.88214	21.49530	24.52271	28.02911
14	14.94742	15.97394	17.08632	18.29191	19.59863	21.01507	24.21492	27.97496	32.39260
15	16.09690	17.29342	18.59891	20.02359	21.57856	23.27597	27.15211	31.77248	37.27971
16	17.25786	18.63929	20.15688	21.82453	23.65749	25.67253	30.32429	35.94973	42.75328
17	18.43044	20.01207	21.76159	23.69751	25.84037	28.21288	33.75023	40.54470	48.88367
18	19.61475	21.41231	23.41444	25.64541	28.13238	30.90565	37.45024	45.59917	55.74971
19	20.81090	22.84056	25.11687	27.67123	30.53900	33.75999	41.44626	51.15909	63.43968
20	22.01900	24.29737	26.87037	29.77808	33.06595	36.78559	45.76196	57.27500	72.05244

Essay Tips

I. Writing CMA Essay Questions

A. Overview of CMA Exam Essay Questions

1. Each part of the CMA exam will have two essay questions to let you demonstrate a deep understanding of the subject matter tested.
2. The essay questions follow the 100 multiple-choice questions portion.
3. Exam takers have a maximum time of four hours to complete the entire exam.
    - **a.** 3 hours of multiple-choice questions (approximately 75% of the exam).
    - **b.** 1 hour of essay questions or 30 minutes each (approximately 25% of the exam).
4. At least 50% on multiple-choice questions must be earned in order to advance to essays and once advanced to essays, candidates cannot return to the multiple-choice portion.
5. Expect 3–6 questions for each essay scenario.
6. There is no spreadsheet application for computational problems on the exam.
    - **a.** Candidates will be expected to write supporting work in the essay word-processing application.
    - **b.** Candidates can use pencils and scratch paper provided at the test site to develop computations before writing them in the word-processing application.

B. How to Prepare an Essay Question Response

1. Each question should take 30 minutes of time.
2. Quickly scroll through both scenarios and determine which one is easier to answer.
3. Also scroll through each question within the scenario to determine how much time you will need for each question.
4. Answer the easier or more familiar question first.
    - **a.** This helps ensure not spending excessive time on the harder question, leaving little time for the easier question.
    - **b.** This gives candidates confidence to answer the more challenging question.
5. Follow these guidelines for budgeting time to complete an essay question in 30 minutes:
    - **a.** Spend the first 2 to 5 minutes reading the question and creating an outline.
        1. Read the entire question to ensure understanding of all requirements.
        2. The outline will allow you to collect your thoughts and structure a framework for answering the question.
        3. If time is short, type your outline as your answer to secure at least partial credit on the essay question.
    - **b.** Spend the next 20 to 25 minutes answering the question.
        1. Use the action verbs in the question to determine how to answer the question.
            - **a.** If the question asks you to compare and contrast two approaches, then list the benefits and costs of each approach and describe how one approach differs from another.
            - **b.** If the question asks to define a term, provide a definition of the term and demonstrate that you understand how to apply the definition.
        2. Rephrase the question's key words and phrases to make it easier for the grader.

3. Use bullet points to organize your answers. Show sufficient detail to allow the grader to understand your knowledge of the subject matter.

4. Write one to two sentences at the start of the question to introduce the topic and one to two sentences at the end of the topic to summarize key points.

c. Spend the final 3 to 5 minutes proofreading your answer.

1. Ensure your answer has addressed the key action words in the questions.

2. Review the organization, structure, and clarity of your answers.

3. Review basic grammar and writing skills.

4. Compare your answer to your initial outline to ensure you have addressed the points you wanted to cover.

6. Monitor your time. Do not spend too much time on one question.

7. Be brief and to the point; it is okay to use bullet points.

8. Do not leave a question blank.

a. If you do not have the time to write a full answer, at least use your outline of the main points to demonstrate your understanding of the topic.

9. The goal of the exam grader is to give you points, not take them away.

a. Essay grading rubrics (grade sheets) provide more possible answers than what is necessary to obtain maximum points.

b. Include as much detail as possible to add more points to your score.

c. You cannot score higher than the maximum number of points for the question. (e.g., If the question is 15 points and you provide enough detail for 18 points, you will only score 15 points).

II. CMA Exam Review Course Essay Questions

A. Practice essay questions are available as part of the test bank. Select "Question Type: Essay" when taking a quiz through the test bank to access these questions.

B. The practice essay questions are original questions and are not released ICMA questions.

CMA Exam Ratio Definitions

Abbreviations

EBIT = Earnings before interest and taxes

EBITDA = Earnings before interest, taxes, depreciation and amortization

EBT = Earnings before taxes

EPS = Earnings per share

ROA = Return on assets

ROE = Return on equity

Part 1: Financial Reporting, Planning, Performance, and Control

Section C Performance Management

Section C.3 Performance measures

e*. ROI = Income of business unit / Assets of business unit

g. Residual Income (RI) = Income of business unit – (Assets of business unit × required rate of return

Note: "Income" means operating income unless otherwise noted.

* *Letter references refer to subtopics in Learning Outcome Statements.*

Part 2: Financial Decision Making

Section A Financial Statement Analysis

Section A.1 Basic Financial Statement Analysis

a. Common size statement = line items on income statement and statement of cash flows presented as a percent of sales; line items on balance sheet presented as a percent of total assets

b. Common base year statements = (new line item amount / base year line item amount) × 100

c. Annual growth rate of line items = (new line item amount / old line item amount) – 1

Section A.2 Financial Ratios

Unless otherwise indicated, end of year data is used for balance sheet items; full year data is used for income statement and statement of cash flow items.

Liquidity

a(1). Current ratio = current assets / current liabilities

a(2). Quick ratio or acid test ratio = (cash + marketable securities + accounts receivable) / current liabilities

a(3). Cash ratio = (cash + marketable securities) / current liabilities

a(4). Cash flow ratio = operating cash flow / current liabilities

a(5). Net working capital ratio = net working capital / total assets

Leverage

f(1). Degree of financial leverage = % change in net income / % change in EBIT, or

= EBIT / EBT

f(2). Degree of operating leverage = % change in EBIT / % change in sales, or = contribution margin / EBIT

h. Financial leverage ratio = assets / equity

i(1). Debt to equity ratio = total debt / equity

I(2). Long-term debt to equity ratio = (total debt – current liabilities) / equity

I(3). Debt to total assets ratio = total debt / total assets

j(1). Fixed charge coverage = earnings before fixed charges and taxes / fixed charges

Fixed charges include interest, required principal repayment, and leases

j(2). Interest coverage (times interest earned) = EBIT / interest expense

j(3). Cash flow to fixed charges = (cash from operations + fixed charges + tax payments) / fixed charges.

Note: cash from operations is after-tax.

Activity

l(1). Accounts receivable turnover = credit sales / average gross accounts receivables

l(2). Inventory turnover = cost of goods sold / average inventory

l(3). Accounts payable turnover = credit purchases / average accounts payable

m(1). Days sales in receivables = average accounts receivable / (credit sales / 365), or = 365 / accounts receivable turnover

m(2). Days sales in inventory = average inventory / (cost of sales / 365), or = 365 / inventory turnover

m(3). Days purchases in payables = average payables / (purchase / 365), or =365 / payables turnover

n(1). Operating cycle = days sales in receivables + days sales in inventory

n(2). Cash cycle = Operating cycle – days purchases in payables

o(1). Total asset turnover = sales / average total assets

o(2). Fixed asset turnover = sales / average net plant, property and equipment

Profitability

p(1). Gross profit margin percentage = gross profit / sales

p(2). Operating profit margin percentage = operating income / sales

p(3). Net profit margin percentage = net income / sales

p(4). EBITDA margin = EBITDA / sales

q(1). ROA = net income / average total assets

q(2). ROE = net income / average equity

Market

r(1). Market-to-book ratio = current stock price / book value per share

r(2). Price earnings ratio = market price per share / EPS

s. Book value per share = (total stockholders' equity − preferred equity) / number of common shares outstanding

u(1). Basic EPS = (net income − preferred dividends) / weighted average common shares outstanding

(Number of shares outstanding is weighted by the number of months shares are outstanding)

u(2). Diluted EPS = (net income − preferred dividends) / diluted weighted average common shares outstanding

(Diluted EPS adjusts common shares by adding shares that may be issued for convertible securities and options)

v(1). Earnings yield = EPS / current market price per common share

v(2). Dividend yield = annual dividends per share / market price per share

v(3). Dividend payout ratio = common dividend / earnings available to common shareholders

v(4). Shareholder return = (ending stock price − beginning stock price + annual dividends per share) / beginning stock price

Section A.3 Profitability Analysis

a(1). ROA = Net profit margin × total asset turnover; (net income / sales) × (sales / average total assets) = net income / average total assets

b(2). ROE = ROA × financial leverage; (net income / average total assets) × (average total assets / average equity) = net income / average equity

g(1). Operating profit margin percentage = operating income / sales

g(2). Net profit margin percentage = net income / sales

j. Sustainable growth rate = (1− dividend payout ratio) × ROE

Section B Corporate Finance

Section B.4 Working capital management

b. Net working capital = current assets − current liabilities

Section C Decision Analysis

Section C.1 Cost/volume/profit analysis

f(1). Breakeven point in units = fixed costs / unit contribution margin

f(2). Breakeven point in dollars = fixed costs / (unit contribution margin / selling price)

i(1). Margin of safety = planned sales − breakeven sales

i(2). Margin of safety ratio = margin of safety / planned sales

Section C.3 Pricing

n. Elasticity is calculated using the midpoint formula. For price elasticity of demand

E = [change in quantity / (average of quantities)] / [change in price / (average of prices)]

Index

D